THE AMERICAN EXPERIENCE: FICTION

THE AMERICAN EXPERIENCE: FICTION

Marjorie Wescott Barrows

Formerly, General Editor
Macmillan Literary Heritage

H. Lincoln Foster

Housatonic Valley Regional High School
Falls River, Connecticut

Frank E. Ross

Professor of English
Eastern Michigan University
Ypsilanti, Michigan

Eva Marie Van Houten

Formerly, Head of English Department
Mumford High School
Detroit, Michigan

Clarence W. Wachner

Formerly, Divisional Director
Language Education Department
Detroit Public Schools

A revision of *The Early Years of American Literature, The Changing Years of American Literature,* and *Contemporary American Prose,* previously published by Macmillan Publishing Co., Inc.

MACMILLAN PUBLISHING COMPANY
NEW YORK

COLLIER MACMILLAN PUBLISHERS
LONDON

ACKNOWLEDGMENTS

For permission to reprint copyright material in this volume, grateful acknowledgment is made to the following:

Delacorte Press: For "Tomorrow and Tomorrow and Tomorrow," copyright 1954 by Kurt Vonnegut, Jr. Originally published in *Galaxy* as "The Big Trip Up Yonder." From *Welcome to the Monkey House* by Kurt Vonnegut, Jr., a Seymour Lawrence Book/Delacorte Press. Used with permission of the publisher.

Doubleday & Co., Inc.: For "The Trouble," copyright 1944 by J. F. Powers from the book, *Prince of Darkness and Other Stories* by J. F. Powers. Reprinted by permission of Doubleday & Co., Inc. For "The Cop and the Anthem" by O. Henry. From *The Four Million* by O. Henry. Reprinted by permission of the publishers.

Farrar, Straus & Giroux, Inc.: For "A Summer's Reading" by Bernard Malamud. Reprinted with permission of Farrar, Straus & Giroux, Inc. from *The Magic Barrel* by Bernard Malamud. Copyright © 1956 by Bernard Malamud. First published in *The New Yorker*.

Harcourt, Brace & World, Inc.: For "A Worn Path" copyright, 1941, by Eudora Welty. Reprinted from her volume *A Curtain of Green and Other Stories* by permission of Harcourt, Brace & World, Inc. For "Rope" copyright, 1930, 1958, by Katherine Anne Porter. Reprinted from her volume *Flowering Judas and Other Stories* by permission of Harcourt, Brace & World, Inc.

Harper & Row, Publishers: For "Buck Fanshaw's Funeral" (pp. 42-53) from *Roughing It*, Volume II by Mark Twain. Reprinted by permission of Harper & Row, Publishers.

Houghton Mifflin Co.: For "A White Heron" from *The Best Short Stories of Sarah Orne Jewett*. For "The Boom in the *Calaveras Clarion*" from *Bret Harte's Works*. Both reprinted by permission of Houghton Mifflin Co.

Cover design by Leo and Diane Dillon

Macmillan Publishing Company
866 Third Avenue, New York, New York 10022
Collier Macmillan Canada, Inc.
Printed in the United States of America
ISBN 0-02-194090-8
9 8 7 6

Contents

vii

Introduction

The end of the American Revolution did not mark a clean break between America and England. English influences on the newly formed country lingered on for many years. America's literature was hardly distinguishable from the literature of England until the nineteenth century, when a distinctly different type of American literature evolved. In contrast to the primarily religious writings of the seventeenth century and the primarily political writings of the eighteenth century, the writings of the ninetenth century showed the development of fiction as a major literary genre in American literature.

In the earliest works of fiction, writers such as Irving, Cooper, Poe, and Hawthorne emphasized individualism, emotionalism, nature, and the supernatural. Romanticism was the dominant strain. However, the best literature of a nation is a reflection of the characteristics of the life and people of that nation and as the harsh realities of westward expansion, civil war, and industrialism began to alter the American way of life, American fiction took on a tougher, more realistic aspect. In the latter part of the nineteenth century, writers such as Bret Harte and Mark Twain introduced the vigorous language and broad humor of the frontier in stories which more accurately portrayed the American character. Such realistic depictions of peculiarly American themes remained the dominant characteristic of American literature into the twentieth century. Modern American fiction has remained largely realistic, but the experimentations and explorations of such writers as Henry James, Ernest Hemingway, and William Faulkner in psychology, symbolism, and literary technique have kept the genre dynamic and open to further development.

In the first section of this volume, you will meet three of the most outstanding authors of the twentieth century—Ernest Hemingway,

John Steinbeck, and William Faulkner. Each of these writers has received both the highest national award—the Pulitzer Prize—and the highest international award—the Nobel Prize for Literature. Few writers in this century have equaled their achievements or success within the genre of fiction. Though they wrote in the period from the 1930's through the 1960's, their work still influences much of the fiction being written at the present time.

Having introduced you to writing that marks a high point in the development of American fiction to date, this book then explores the rich heritage that gave rise to modern American fiction. A selection of some of the most significant authors and themes in each period of literary development are offered for you to explore and enjoy. The final two sections of the book examine recent achievements and experiments in fiction by some of today's leading writers who are carrying on the tradition of Steinbeck, Hemingway, and Faulkner.

Many of the writers included in this anthology are best known for their achievements in the novel form. However, most of them have also written in the short story form with equal success. Wherever possible, each writer is represented by one of his successful short stories, because this form is better suited to what is a rather brief anthology. Only in those few cases where an author is known solely as a novelist has an excerpt from one of his longer works been included.

THREE DISTINGUISHED MODERNS

Though the twentieth century has produced a number of significant writers of American fiction, few have reached the distinction of Ernest Hemingway, John Steinbeck, and William Faulkner. Each has an impressive list of works to his credit, and each has been awarded the Nobel Prize for Literature in recognition of his achievement. However much readers may disagree about the relative merits of their particular works, these men are regarded in America and in Europe as three of the most influential figures in contemporary fiction.

All three writers became prominent during the years immediately preceding and following the depression of 1929, and continued their literary careers into the 1960's. In their lifetime, they knew the feeling of alienation that World War I produced in the so-called "lost generation" of the 1920's. They experienced prosperity and depression. They saw totalitarianism rise in Europe out of economic despair to threaten man's progress toward a civilized and humane life. They came through World War II with a mature and sensitive awareness of the human condition at mid-century. In 1950, William Faulkner stated the modern dilemma in his Nobel Prize acceptance speech: "There is only one question: When will I be blown up?" He then went on to affirm his faith in mankind, an affirmation welcomed everywhere by men of good will:

> I believe that man will not merely endure: he will prevail. He is immortal, not because he alone among creatures has an inexhaustible voice but because he has a soul, a spirit capable of compassion and sacrifice and endurance.

In 1921 a symposium of scholars, engaged in an impressive research project called *Civilization in the United States,* concluded that, for the artist-intellectual, "life in America is not worth living." In the middle twenties ERNEST HEMINGWAY, self-exiled to Europe as a member of the "lost generation," was the literary representative of this "romantic disillusion" and "set the favorite pose for the period."[1] He gained this reputation because of what he wrote and also because of the prose style he developed. His style has been widely imitated in modern literature, especially by the so-called "hard-boiled" school of writers. A fellow writer described it this way:

> Hemingway's words strike you, each one, as if they were pebbles fetched fresh from a brook. They live and shine, each in its place. So one of his pages has the effect of a brookbottom into which you look down through the flowing water. The words form a tesselation,[2] each in order before the other.[3]

Hemingway's spare, muscular style was ideal for his stories of initiation into the cruelty of life, a cruelty that each individual must learn to endure with courage. This theme appeared in his earliest stories of hunting and fishing in the Michigan woods. It was reinforced by the dangerous ex-

[1] Edmund Wilson, *The Wound and the Bow: Seven Studies in Literature* (Boston: Houghton Mifflin Company, 1941), p. 221.

[2] *tesselation:* mosaic

[3] Ford Madox Ford, quoted by Charles Poore, "Foreword," *The Hemingway Reader* (New York: Charles Scribner's Sons, 1953), p. xiv.

periences with bull-fighting, big-game hunting, and war that always fascinated Hemingway. He made the drama of a moment—sometimes of a lifetime—hinge on "some principle of courage, of honor, of pity—that is, some principle of sportsmanship in its largest sense."[4]

Hemingway was a disciplined and self-critical writer, but he did not always please his readers or the critics. To some his range of subjects and his view of life seemed unfortunately narrow, and he was occasionally charged with being a prisoner of his own style. At his best, however, he was incomparable in reflecting the modern temper. He probably exerted a more profound influence on contemporary literature, for better or for worse, than any other American writer.

Of JOHN STEINBECK, one critic has said: "The two basic impulses of the 30's, toward escape and toward social consciousness, found their sharpest expression in the writing of John Steinbeck, whose work represents more faithfully than any of his contemporaries the temperament of the angry decade."[5]

Although some of Steinbeck's writing might be described as escapist, the work that brought him distinction was *The Grapes of Wrath*, an immensely popular novel about the uprooted farmers who migrated from the Dust Bowl of Oklahoma to the overcrowded valleys of southern California. It was far superior to the many novels that depicted with literal but unconvincing realism the unhappy lives of the depression poor. This so-called "proletarian literature," created in a mood of social protest, was usually inept and soon forgotten. However, Steinbeck's novel not only told a memorable story well, it also asserted with power the dignity of the individual and the endurance of the "little people" of America, who would go on even under the most crushing circumstances. The novel won for Steinbeck the Pulitzer Prize in 1939.

Not only in method but also in style, WILLIAM FAULKNER seemed the opposite of Hemingway. Faulkner's words tumbled over each other in great rhetorical floods. Though

---

[4]Wilson, *op. cit.*, p. 220.
[5]Leo Gurko, *The Angry Decade* (New York: Dodd, Mead and Company, 1947), p. 201.

sometimes difficult to follow, his style conjured up rich images, bitter memories, and high emotions in an effect quite different from Hemingway's understatement. Faulkner's total literary output was also uneven—he frankly turned out some sensational potboilers[6]—but his stature as an artist was firmly established by the time of his death. He was recognized as not only the most brilliant writer in the modern literary renaissance of the South, but also a rare creative genius who might possibly be the greatest American writer of the first half of the twentieth century.

[6] *potboilers:* works of art or literature, often inferior produced only to make money

Ernest Hemingway

In several short stories, as well as in his novel *A Farewell to Arms*, Ernest Hemingway wrote about a young American serving in the Italian army during World War I. Hemingway himself had fought in the Italian infantry, and had been wounded in battle two weeks before his nineteenth birthday. The following story about a young soldier is Hemingway's unique way of expressing a theme that has been present throughout American fiction: man's sense of being painfully isolated and apart from the world around him. This theme surprisingly links Hemingway with writers very different from himself—most notably, Nathaniel Hawthorne.

In Another Country

In the fall the war was always there, but we did not go to it any more. It was cold in the fall in Milan and the dark came very early. Then the electric lights came on, and it was pleasant along the streets looking in the windows. There was much game hanging outside the shops, and the snow powdered in the fur of the foxes and the wind blew their tails. The deer hung stiff and heavy and empty, and small birds blew in the wind and the wind turned their feathers. It was a cold fall and the wind came down from the mountains.

We were all at the hospital every afternoon, and there were different ways of walking across the town through the dusk to the hospital. Two of the ways were alongside canals, but they were long. Always, though, you crossed a bridge across a canal to enter the hospital. There was a choice of three bridges. On one of them a woman sold roasted chestnuts. It was warm, standing in front of her charcoal fire, and the chestnuts were warm afterward in your pocket. The hospital was very old and very beautiful, and you entered through a gate

7

and walked across a courtyard and out a gate on the other side. There were usually funerals starting from the courtyard. Beyond the old hospital were the new brick pavilions, and there we met every afternoon and were all very polite and interested in what was the matter, and sat in the machines that were to make so much difference.

The doctor came up to the machine where I was sitting and said: "What did you like best to do before the war? Did you practice a sport?"

I said: "Yes, football."

"Good," he said. "You will be able to play football again better than ever."

My knee did not bend and the leg dropped straight from the knee to the ankle without a calf, and the machine was to bend the knee and make it move as in riding a tricycle. But it did not bend yet, and instead the machine lurched when it came to the bending part. The doctor said: "That will all pass. You are a fortunate young man. You will play football again like a champion."

In the next machine was a major who had a little hand like a baby's. He winked at me when the doctor examined his hand, which was between two leather straps that bounced up and down and flapped the stiff fingers, and said: "And will I too play football, captain-doctor?" He had been a very great fencer, and before the war the greatest fencer in Italy.

The doctor went to his office in the back room and brought a photograph which showed a hand that had been withered almost as small as the major's, before it had taken a machine course, and after was a little larger. The major held the photograph with his good hand and looked at it very carefully. "A wound?" he asked.

"An industrial accident," the doctor said.

"Very interesting, very interesting," the major said, and handed it back to the doctor.

"You have confidence?"

"No," said the major.

There were three boys who came each day who were about the same age I was. They were all three from Milan, and one of them was to be a lawyer, and one was to be a painter, and one had intended to be a soldier, and after we were finished with the machines, sometimes we walked back together to the Café Cova, which was next door to the Scala.¹ We walked the short way through the communist quarter because we were four together. The people hated us because we were officers, and from a wine shop some one called out, "A basso gli ufficiali!"² as we passed. Another boy who walked with us sometimes and made us five wore a black silk handkerchief across his face because he had no nose then and his face was to be rebuilt. He had gone out to the front from the military academy and had been wounded within an hour after he had gone into the front line for the first time. They rebuilt his face, but he came from a very old family and they could never get the nose exactly right. He went to South America and worked in a bank. But this was a long time ago, and then we did not any of us know how it was going to be afterward. We only knew then that there was always the war, but that we were not going to it any more.

We all had the same medals, except the boy with the black silk bandage across his face, and he had not been at the front long enough to get any medals. The tall boy with a very pale face who was to be a lawyer had been a lieutenant of Arditi³ and had three medals of the sort we each had only one of. He had lived a very long time with death and was a little detached. We were all a little detached, and there was nothing that held us together except that we met every afternoon at the hospital. Although, as we walked to the Cova through the tough part of town, walking in the dark, with light and singing coming out of the wine shops, and sometimes having to walk into the street when the men and women would crowd together on the sidewalk so that we would have had to jostle them to get by, we felt held together by there being something that happened that they, the people who disliked us, did not understand.

We ourselves all understood the Cova, where it was rich and warm and not too brightly lighted, and noisy and smoky at

¹*La Scala:* famous opera house in Milan
²*A basso gli ufficiali:* "down with the officers" (Italian)
³*Arditi:* Italian infantry storm troops

certain hours, and there were always girls at the tables and the illustrated papers on a rack on the wall. The girls at the Cova were very patriotic, and I found that the most patriotic people in Italy were the café girls—and I believe they are still patriotic.

The boys at first were very polite about my medals and asked me what I had done to get them. I showed them the papers, which were written in very beautiful language and full of *fratellanza* and *abnegazione*,[4] but which really said, with the adjectives removed, that I had been given the medals because I was an American. After that their manner changed a little toward me, although I was their friend against outsiders. I was a friend, but I was never really one of them after they had read the citations, because it had been different with them and they had done very different things to get their medals. I had been wounded, it was true; but we all knew that being wounded, after all, was really an accident. I was never ashamed of the ribbons, though, and sometimes, after the cocktail hour, I would imagine myself having done all the things they had done to get their medals; but walking home at night through the empty streets with the cold wind and all the shops closed, trying to keep near the street lights, I knew that I would never have done such things, and I was very much afraid to die, and often lay in bed at night by myself, afraid to die and wondering how I would be when I went back to the front again.

The three with the medals were like hunting hawks; and I was not a hawk, although I might seem a hawk to those who had never hunted; they, the three, knew better and so we drifted apart. But I stayed good friends with the boy who had been wounded his first day at the front, because he would never know now how he would have turned out; so he could never be accepted either, and I liked him because I thought perhaps he would not have turned out to be a hawk either.

The major, who had been the great fencer, did not believe in bravery, and spent much time while we sat in the machines correcting my grammar. He had complimented me on how I

---

[4] *fratellanza and abnegazione:* brotherhood and self-denial (Italian)

spoke Italian, and we talked together very easily. One day I had said that Italian seemed such an easy language to me that I could not take a great interest in it; everything was so easy to say. "Ah, yes," the major said. "Why, then, do you not take up the use of grammar?" So we took up the use of grammar, and soon Italian was such a difficult language that I was afraid to talk to him until I had the grammar straight in my mind.

The major came very regularly to the hospital. I do not think he ever missed a day, although I am sure he did not believe in the machines. There was a time when none of us believed in the machines, and one day the major said it was all nonsense. The machines were new then and it was we who were to prove them. It was an idiotic idea, he said, "a theory, like another." I had not learned my grammar, and he said I was a stupid impossible disgrace, and he was a fool to have bothered with me. He was a small man and he sat straight up in his chair with his right hand thrust into the machine and looked straight ahead at the wall while the straps thumped up and down with his fingers in them.

"What will you do when the war is over if it is over?" he asked me. "Speak grammatically!"

"I will go to the States."

"Are you married?"

"No, but I hope to be."

"The more of a fool you are," he said. He seemed very angry. "A man must not marry."

"Why, Signor Maggiore?"[5]

"Don't call me 'Signor Maggiore.'"

"Why must not a man marry?"

"He cannot marry. He cannot marry," he said angrily. "If he is to lose everything, he should not place himself in a position to lose that. He should not place himself in a position to lose. He should find things he cannot lose."

He spoke very angrily and bitterly, and looked straight ahead while he talked.

"But why should he necessarily lose it?"

[5] *Signor Maggiore:* Sir Major

"He'll lose it," the major said. He was looking at the wall. Then he looked down at the machine and jerked his little hand out from between the straps and slapped it hard against his thigh. "He'll lose it," he almost shouted. "Don't argue with me!" Then he called to the attendant who ran the machines. "Come and turn this damned thing off."

He went back into the other room for the light treatment and the massage. Then I heard him ask the doctor if he might use his telephone and he shut the door. When he came back into the room, I was sitting in another machine. He was wearing his cape and had his cap on, and he came directly toward my machine and put his arm on my shoulder.

"I am so sorry," he said, and patted me on the shoulder with his good hand. "I would not be rude. My wife has just died. You must forgive me."

"Oh——" I said, feeling sick for him. "I am *so* sorry."

He stood there biting his lower lip. "It is very difficult," he said. "I cannot resign myself."

He looked straight past me and out through the window. Then he began to cry. "I am utterly unable to resign myself," he said, and choked. And then crying, his head up looking at nothing, carrying himself straight and soldierly, with tears on both his cheeks and biting his lips, he walked past the machines and out the door.

The doctor told me that the major's wife, who was very young and whom he had not married until he was definitely invalided out of the war, had died of pneumonia. She had been sick only a few days. No one expected her to die. The major did not come to the hospital for three days. Then he came at the usual hour, wearing a black band on the sleeve of his uniform. When he came back, there were large framed photographs around the wall, of all sorts of wounds before and after they had been cured by the machines. In front of the machine the major used were three photographs of hands like his that were completely restored. I do not know where the doctor got them. I always understood we were the first to use the machines. The photographs did not make much difference to the major because he only looked out of the window.

FOR DISCUSSION

1. Even from a first reading of the opening paragraph of this story
   you were probably aware of the strong, straightforward description it provided of the setting. But there were also subtleties of
   style in this paragraph which heightened the effect Hemingway
   wished to produce, even though you might not have been
   conscious of them at the time.
   a. For example, the first sentence implies something more than
      the strangeness of an American in an alien land. "In the fall
      the war was always there, but we did not go to it anymore."
      The sentence suggests that the narrator and his fellow patients
      were "in another country" in the sense of being behind the
      battle lines, out of combat. They were no longer functioning
      as soldiers even though "the war was always there."
   b. "Then the electric lights came on, and it was pleasant along
      the streets looking in the windows." According to this sen-
      tence, from what other "country," besides the war, have the
      wounded soldiers been excluded?
2. What does the game hanging outside the shops suggest?
3. Notice in the first paragraph the repetition of these words: *fall,
   cold, wind.* What idea or feeling do these words help to reinforce?
4. One critic has observed of Hemingway's style: "The simplicity
   is there—but few things are more complex than Hemingway's
   simplicity." Examine Hemingway's style, noticing particularly
   his use of adjectives and adverbs, the kind of sentence structure
   dominant in his writing, and the nature of the dialogue. Point
   out what you have discovered.
5. Hemingway once wrote, "If a writer of prose knows enough
   about what he is writing about he may omit things that he knows
   and the reader, if the writer is writing truly enough, will have a
   feeling of those things as strongly as though the writer had
   stated them." Discuss the information about the young American
   that Hemingway omits from this story but that another writer
   would probably have included. What impressions, not explicitly
   stated but suggested almost by omission, have you formed of
   this young American? Trace the sources of these impressions
   in the story.
6. What is the effect of the apparently unfeeling description of the
   soldier with the black silk handkerchief across his face? What is
   ironic about his having no medals? Why do he and the young
   American both feel like outsiders?

7. Explain what you think Hemingway means when he writes of the tall boy who wants to be a lawyer: "He had lived a very long time with death and was a little detached."
8. An important part of the story is the young American's experience with the Italian major. The major's apparent attitudes toward the machines, grammar, and marriage are all clearly stated. What are they?
9. Why don't these attitudes tell you the most important truth about the man? What new dimension is added to his personality for you when you learn of his wife's death?
10. Whatever inferences the American draws from the major's despair are left unspoken. What conclusions do you think he reached? What would yours have been?

FOR COMPOSITION

1. Using the approach suggested by the first five questions "for discussion," analyze the last paragraph of the story. Pay close attention to both the technique and the content.
2. Imagine a situation of some seriousness, such as a marriage proposal, an election to high office, an automobile accident, or a bank robbery. Write a page of dialogue between two characters, using the same kind of understatement and restraint that Hemingway used in his dialogue.

John Steinbeck

John Steinbeck has often taken the plight of the downtrodden and the outcast as a basic theme of his fiction, picturing man as the unfortunate victim of his physical nature and his environment. In "Flight," however, he goes beyond this theme to a more universal one that has attracted many American writers. Sometimes, as in Hemingway's "The Killers," the story is about a young man's first encounter with evil. Sometimes, as in William Faulkner's "The Bear," it is about a boy's new awareness of his heritage as a man. Here, Steinbeck tells of a restless youth's eagerness to become an adult, and of his grim initiation into manhood as he suddenly finds himself in a life-and-death struggle with the law.

Flight

About fifteen miles below Monterey, on the wild coast, the Torres family had their farm, a few sloping acres above a cliff that dropped to the brown reefs and to the hissing white waters of the ocean. Behind the farm the stone mountains stood up against the sky. The farm buildings huddled like little clinging aphids[1] on the mountain skirts, crouched low to the ground as though the wind might blow them into the sea. The little shack, the rattling, rotting barn were gray-bitten with sea salt, beaten by the damp wind until they had taken on the color of the granite hills. Two horses, a red cow and a red calf, half a dozen pigs, and a flock of lean, multicolored chickens stocked the place. A little corn was raised on the sterile slope, and it grew short and thick under the wind, and all the cobs formed on the landward sides of the stalks. Mama Torres, a lean, dry woman with ancient eyes, had ruled the farm for ten years, ever since her husband tripped

[1] *aphids:* insects that live on plants by sucking their juice

15

over a stone in the field one day and fell full length on a rattlesnake. When one is bitten on the chest, there is not much that can be done.

Mama Torres had three children, two undersized black ones of twelve and fourteen, Emilio and Rosy, whom Mama kept fishing on the rocks below the farm when the sea was kind and when the truant officer was in some distant part of Monterey County. And there was Pepé, the tall, smiling son of nineteen, a gentle, affectionate boy, but very lazy. Pepé had a tall head, pointed at the top, and from its peak coarse black hair grew down like a thatch all around. Over his smiling little eyes, Mama cut a straight bang so he could see. Pepé had sharp Indian cheekbones and an eagle nose, but his mouth was as sweet and shapely as a girl's mouth, and his chin was fragile and chiseled. He was loose and gangling, all legs and feet and wrists, and he was very lazy. Mama thought him fine and brave, but she never told him so. She said, "Some lazy cow must have got into thy father's family, else how could I have a son like thee." And she said, "When I carried thee, a sneaking lazy coyote came out of the brush and looked at me one day. That must have made thee so."

Pepé smiled sheepishly and stabbed at the ground with his knife to keep the blade sharp and free from rust. It was his inheritance, that knife, his father's knife. The long heavy blade folded back into the black handle. There was a button on the handle. When Pepé pressed the button, the blade leaped out ready for use. The knife was with Pepé always, for it had been his father's knife.

One sunny morning when the sea below the cliff was glinting and blue and the white surf creamed on the reef, when even the stone mountains looked kindly, Mama Torres called out the door of the shack, "Pepé, I have a labor for thee."

There was no answer. Mama listened. From behind the barn she heard a burst of laughter. She lifted her full long skirt and walked in the direction of the noise.

Pepé was sitting on the ground with his back against a box. His white teeth glistened. On either side of him stood the two black ones, tense and expectant. Fifteen feet away a redwood post was set in the ground. Pepé's right hand lay limply in his lap, and in the palm the big black knife rested. The blade was closed back into the handle. Pepé looked smiling at the sky.

Suddenly Emilio cried, "Ya!"

Pepé's wrist flicked like the head of a snake. The blade seemed to fly open in mid-air, and with a thump the point dug into the redwood post, and the black handle quivered. The three burst into excited laughter. Rosy ran to the post and pulled out the knife and brought it back to Pepé. He closed the blade and settled the knife carefully in his listless palm again. He grinned self-consciously at the sky.

"Ya!"

The heavy knife lanced out and sunk into the post again. Mama moved forward like a ship and scattered the play.

"All day you do foolish things with the knife, like a toy baby," she stormed. "Get up on thy huge feet that eat up shoes. Get up!" She took him by one loose shoulder and hoisted at him. Pepé grinned sheepishly and came half-heartedly to his feet. "Look!" Mama cried. "Big lazy, you must catch the horse and put on him thy father's saddle. You must ride to Monterey. The medicine bottle is empty. There is no salt. Go thou now, Peanut! Catch the horse."

A revolution took place in the relaxed figure of Pepé. "To Monterey, me? Alone? *Si*, Mama."

She scowled at him. "Do you think, big sheep, that you will buy candy. No, I will give you only enough for the medicine and the salt."

Pepé smiled. "Mama, you will put the hatband on the hat?"

She relented then. "Yes, Pepé. You may wear the hatband."

His voice grew insinuating. "And the green handkerchief, Mama?"

"Yes, if you go quickly and return with no trouble, the silk green handkerchief will go. If you make sure to take off the handkerchief when you eat so no spot may fall on it."

"*Si*, Mama. I will be careful. I am a man."

"Thou? A man? Thou art a peanut."

He went into the rickety barn and brought out a rope, and he walked agilely enough up the hill to catch the horse.

When he was ready and mounted before the door, mounted

on his father's saddle that was so old that the oaken frame showed through torn leather in many places, then Mama brought out the round black hat with the tooled leather band, and she reached up and knotted the green silk handkerchief about his neck. Pepé's blue denim coat was much darker than his jeans, for it had been washed much less often.

Mama handed up the big medicine bottle and the silver coins. "That for the medicine," she said, "and that for the salt. That for a candle to burn for papa. That for *dulces*[2] for the little ones. Our friend Mrs. Rodriguez will give you dinner and maybe a bed for the night. When you go to the church, say only ten paternosters and only twenty-five Ave Marias. Oh! I know, big coyote. You would sit there flapping your mouth over Aves all day while you looked at the candles and the holy pictures. That is not good devotion to stare at the pretty things."

The black hat, covering the high pointed head and black thatched hair of Pepé, gave him dignity and age. He sat the rangy horse well. Mama thought how handsome he was, dark and lean and tall. "I would not send thee now alone, thou little one, except for the medicine," she said softly. "It is not good to have no medicine, for who knows when the toothache will come, or the sadness of the stomach. These things are."

"*Adios*, Mama," Pepé cried. "I will come back soon. You may send me often alone. I am a man."

"Thou art a foolish chicken."

He straightened his shoulders, flipped the reins against the horse's shoulder, and rode away. He turned once and saw that they still watched him, Emilio and Rosy and Mama. Pepé grinned with pride and gladness and lifted the tough buckskin horse to a trot.

When he had dropped out of sight over a little dip in the road, Mama turned to the black ones, but she spoke to herself. "He is nearly a man now," she said. "It will be a nice thing to have a man in the house again." Her eyes sharpened on the children. "Go to the rocks now. The tide is going out. There will be abalones[3] to be found." She put the

[2] *dulces*: sweets
[3] *abalones*: clam-like shellfish

iron hooks into their hands and saw them down the steep trail to the reefs. She brought the smooth stone metate[4] to the doorway and sat grinding her corn to flour and looking occasionally at the road over which Pepé had gone. The noonday came and then the afternoon, when the little ones beat the abalones on a rock to make them tender and Mama patted the *tortillas*[5] to make them thin. They ate their dinner as the red sun was plunging down toward the ocean. They sat on the doorsteps and watched a big white moon come over the mountaintops.

Mama said, "He is now at the house of our friend Mrs. Rodriguez. She will give him nice things to eat and maybe a present."

Emilio said, "Someday I, too, will ride to Monterey for medicine. Did Pepé come to be a man today?"

Mama said wisely, "A boy gets to be a man when a man is needed. Remember this thing. I have known boys forty years old because there was no need for a man."

Soon afterward they retired, Mama in her big oak bed on one side of the room, Emilio and Rosy in their boxes full of straw and sheepskins on the other side of the room.

The moon went over the sky, and the surf roared on the rocks. The roosters crowed the first call. The surf subsided to a whispering surge against the reef. The moon dropped toward the sea. The roosters crowed again.

The moon was near down to the water when Pepé rode on a winded horse to his home flat. His dog bounced out and circled the horse, yelping with pleasure. Pepé slid off the saddle to the ground. The weathered little shack was silver in the moonlight, and the square shadow of it was black to the north and east. Against the east the piling mountains were misty with light; their tops melted into the sky.

Pepé walked wearily up the three steps and into the house. It was dark inside. There was a rustle in the corner.

Mama cried out from her bed. "Who comes? Pepé, is it thou?"

"*Si*, Mama."

"Did you get the medicine?"

---

[4] *metate:* grindstone

[5] *tortillas:* flat unleavened corn cakes used in Mexico as the equivalent of bread

"*Si*, Mama."

"Well, go to sleep then. I thought you would be sleeping at the house of Mrs. Rodriguez." Pepé stood silently in the dark room. "Why do you stand there, Pepé? Did you drink wine?" "*Si*, Mama."

"Well, go to bed then and sleep out the wine." His voice was tired and patient, but very firm. "Light the candle, Mama. I must go away into the mountains."

"What is this, Pepé? You are crazy." Mama struck a sulfur match and held the little blue burr until the flame spread up the stick. She set light to the candle on the floor beside her bed. "Now, Pepé, what is this you say?" She looked anxiously into his face.

He was changed. The fragile quality seemed to have gone from his chin. His mouth was less full than it had been, the lines of the lips were straighter, but in his eyes the greatest change had taken place. There was no laughter in them any more, nor any bashfulness. They were sharp and bright and purposeful.

He told her in a tired monotone, told her everything just as it had happened. A few people came into the kitchen of Mrs. Rodriguez. There was wine to drink. Pepé drank wine. The little quarrel—the man started toward Pepé and then the knife—it went almost by itself. It flew, it darted before Pepé knew it. As he talked, Mama's face grew stern, and it seemed to grow more lean. Pepé finished. "I am a man now, Mama. The man said names to me I could not allow."

Mama nodded. "Yes, thou art a man, my poor little Pepé. Thou art a man. I have seen it coming on thee. I have watched you throwing the knife into the post, and I have been afraid." For a moment her face had softened, but now it grew stern again. "Come! We must get you ready. Go. Awaken Emilio and Rosy. Go quickly."

Pepé stepped over to the corner where his brother and sister slept among the sheepskins. He leaned down and shook them gently. "Come, Rosy! Come, Emilio! The Mama says you must arise."

The little black ones sat up and rubbed their eyes in the

candlelight. Mama was out of bed now, her long black skirt over her nightgown. "Emilio," she cried. "Go up and catch the other horse for Pepé. Quickly, now! Quickly." Emilio put his legs in his overalls and stumbled sleepily out the door.

"You heard no one behind you on the road?" Mama demanded.

"No, Mama. I listened carefully. No one was on the road." Mama darted like a bird about the room. From a nail on the wall she took a canvas water bag and threw it on the floor. She stripped a blanket from her bed and rolled it into a tight tube and tied the ends with string. From a box beside the stove she lifted a flour sack half full of black stringy jerky.[6] "Your father's black coat, Pepé. Here, put it on."

Pepé stood in the middle of the floor watching her activity. She reached behind the door and brought out the rifle, a long 38-56, worn shiny the whole length of the barrel. Pepé took it from her and held it in the crook of his elbow. Mama brought a little leather bag and counted the cartridges into his hand. "Only ten left," she warned. "You must not waste them."

Emilio put his head in the door. "'*Qui 'st 'l caballo,*[7] Mama."

"Put on the saddle from the other horse. Tie on the blanket. Here, tie the jerky to the saddle horn."

Still Pepé stood silently watching his mother's frantic activity. His chin looked hard, and his sweet mouth was drawn and thin. His little eyes followed Mama about the room almost suspiciously.

Rosy asked softly, "Where goes Pepé?"

Mama's eyes were fierce. "Pepé goes on a journey. Pepé is a man now. He has a man's thing to do."

Pepé straightened his shoulders. His mouth changed until he looked very much like Mama.

At last the preparation was finished. The loaded horse stood outside the door. The water bag dripped a line of moisture down the bay shoulder.

[6] *jerky:* cured or dried meat often carried by hunters
[7] '*Qui 'st 'l caballo:* Here is the horse. (Spanish)

The moonlight was being thinned by the dawn, and the big white moon was near down to the sea. The family stood by the shack. Mama confronted Pepé. "Look, my son! Do not stop until it is dark again. Do not sleep even though you are tired. Take care of the horse in order that he may not stop of weariness. Remember to be careful with the bullets—there are only ten. Do not fill thy stomach with jerky or it will make thee sick. Eat a little jerky and fill thy stomach with grass. When thou comest to the high mountains, if thou seest any of the dark watching men, go not near to them nor try to speak to them. And forget not thy prayers." She put her lean hands on Pepé's shoulders, stood on her toes and kissed him formally on both cheeks, and Pepé kissed her on both cheeks. Then he went to Emilio and Rosy and kissed both of their cheeks.

Pepé turned back to Mama. He seemed to look for a little softness, a little weakness in her. His eyes were searching, but Mama's face remained fierce. "Go now," she said. "Do not wait to be caught like a chicken."

Pepé pulled himself into the saddle. "I am a man," he said.

It was the first dawn when he rode up the hill toward the little canyon which let a trail into the mountains. Moonlight and daylight fought with each other, and the two warring qualities made it difficult to see. Before Pepé had gone a hundred yards, the outlines of his figure were misty; and long before he entered the canyon, he had become a gray, indefinite shadow.

Mama stood stiffly in front of her doorstep, and on either side of her stood Emilio and Rosy. They cast furtive glances at Mama now and then.

When the gray shape of Pepé melted into the hillside and disappeared, Mama relaxed. She began the high, whining keen[8] of the death wail. "Our beautiful—our brave," she cried. "Our protector, our son is gone." Emilio and Rosy moaned beside her. "Our beautiful—our brave, he is gone." It was the formal wail. It rose to a high piercing whine and subsided to a moan. Mama raised it three times, and then she turned and went into the house and shut the door.

Emilio and Rosy stood wondering in the dawn. They heard

[8] *keen:* dirge, lamentation

Mama whimpering in the house. They went out to sit on the cliff above the ocean. They touched shoulders. "When did Pepé come to be a man?" Emilio asked.

"Last night," said Rosy. "Last night in Monterey." The ocean clouds turned red with the sun that was behind the mountains.

"We will have no breakfast," said Emilio. "Mama will not want to cook." Rosy did not answer him. "Where is Pepé gone?" he asked.

Rosy looked around at him. She drew her knowledge from the quiet air. "He has gone on a journey. He will never come back."

"Is he dead? Do you think he is dead?"

Rosy looked back at the ocean again. A little steamer, drawing a line of smoke, sat on the edge of the horizon. "He is not dead," Rosy explained. "Not yet."

Pepé rested the big rifle across the saddle in front of him. He let the horse walk up the hill, and he didn't look back. The stony slope took on a coat of short brush so that Pepé found the entrance to a trail and entered it.

When he came to the canyon opening, he swung once in his saddle and looked back, but the houses were swallowed in the misty light. Pepé jerked forward again. The high shoulder of the canyon closed in on him. His horse stretched out its neck and sighed and settled to the trail.

It was a well-worn path, dark, soft, leaf-mold earth strewn with broken pieces of sandstone. The trail rounded the shoulder of the canyon and dropped steeply into the bed of the stream. In the shallows the water ran smoothly, glinting in the first morning sun. Small round stones on the bottom were as brown as rust with sun moss. In the sand along the edges of the stream, the tall, rich wild mint grew, while in the water itself the cress, old and tough, had gone to heavy seed.

The path went into the stream and emerged on the other side. The horse sloshed into the water and stopped. Pepé dropped his bridle and let the beast drink of the running water.

Soon the canyon sides became steep, and the first giant sentinel redwoods guarded the trail, great, round red trunks bearing foliage as green and lacy as ferns. Once Pepé was among the trees, the sun was lost. A perfumed and purple light lay in the pale green of the underbrush. Gooseberry bushes and blackberries and tall ferns lined the stream, and overhead the branches of the redwoods met and cut off the sky.

Pepé drank from the water bag, and he reached into the flour sack and brought out a black string of jerky. His white teeth gnawed at the string until the tough meat parted. He chewed slowly and drank occasionally from the water bag. His little eyes were slumberous and tired, but the muscles of his face were hard-set. The earth of the trail was black now. It gave up a hollow sound under the walking hoofbeats.

The stream fell more sharply. Little waterfalls splashed on the stones. Five-fingered ferns hung over the water and dripped spray from their finger tips. Pepé rode half over his saddle, dangling one leg loosely. He picked a bay leaf from a tree beside the way and put it into his mouth for a moment to flavor the dry jerky. He held the gun loosely across the pommel.

Suddenly he squared in his saddle, swung the horse from the trail and kicked it hurriedly up behind a big redwood tree. He pulled up the reins tight against the bit to keep the horse from whinnying. His face was intent, and his nostrils quivered a little.

A hollow pounding came down the trail, and a horseman rode by, a fat man with red cheeks and a white stubble beard. His horse put down his head and blubbered at the trail when it came to the place where Pepé had turned off. "Hold up!" said the man, and he pulled up his horse's head.

When the last sound of the hoofs died away, Pepé came back into the trail again. He did not relax in the saddle any more. He lifted the big rifle and swung the lever to throw a shell into the chamber, and then he let down the hammer to half cock.

The trail grew very steep. Now the redwood trees were smaller and their tops were dead, bitten dead where the wind reached them. The horse plodded on; the sun went slowly overhead and started down toward the afternoon.

Where the stream came out of a side canyon, the trail left

it. Pepé dismounted and watered his horse and filled up his water bag. As soon as the trail had parted from the stream, the trees were gone and only the thick brittle sage and manzanita and chaparral[9] edged the trail. And the soft black earth was gone, too, leaving only the light-tan broken rock for the trail bed. Lizards scampered away into the brush as the horse rattled over the little stones.

Pepé turned in his saddle and looked back. He was in the open now: he could be seen from a distance. As he ascended the trail, the country grew more rough and terrible and dry. The way wound about the bases of great square rocks. Little gray rabbits skittered in the brush. A bird made a monotonous high creaking. Eastward the bare rock mountaintops were pale and powder-dry under the dropping sun. The horse plodded up and up the trail toward a little V in the ridge which was the pass.

Pepé looked suspiciously back every minute or so, and his eyes sought the tops of the ridges ahead. Once, on a white barren spur, he saw a black figure for a moment; but he looked quickly away, for it was one of the dark watchers. No one knew who the watchers were, nor where they lived, but it was better to ignore them and never to show interest in them. They did not bother one who stayed on the trail and minded his own business.

The air was parched and full of light dust blown by the breeze from the eroding mountains. Pepé drank sparingly from his bag and corked it tightly and hung it on the horn again. The trail moved up the dry shale hillside, avoiding rocks, dropping under clefts, climbing in and out of old water scars. When he arrived at the little pass, he stopped and looked back for a long time. No dark watchers were to be seen now. The trail behind was empty. Only the high tops of the redwoods indicated where the stream flowed.

Pepé rode on through the pass. His little eyes were nearly closed with weariness, but his face was stern, relentless, and manly. The high mountain wind coasted sighing through the pass and whistled on the edges of the big blocks of broken

---

[9] *sage and manzanita and chaparral:* desert shrubs found in the West

granite. In the air, a red-tailed hawk sailed over close to the
ridge and screamed angrily. Pepé went slowly through the
broken jagged pass and looked down on the other side.

The trail dropped quickly, staggering among broken rock.
At the bottom of the slope, there was a dark crease, thick with
brush, and on the other side of the crease a little flat, in which
a grove of oak trees grew. A scar of green grass cut across the
flat. And behind the flat another mountain rose, desolate with
dead rocks and starving little black bushes. Pepé drank from
the bag again, for the air was so dry that it encrusted his
nostrils and burned his lips. He put the horse down the trail.
The hoofs slipped and struggled on the steep way, starting
little stones that rolled off into the brush. The sun was gone
behind the westward mountain now, but still it glowed brilliantly on the oaks and on the grassy flat. The rocks and the
hillsides still sent up waves of the heat they had gathered
from the day's sun.

Pepé looked up to the top of the next dry withered ridge.
He saw a dark form against the sky, a man's figure standing on
top of a rock, and he glanced away quickly not to appear
curious. When a moment later he looked up again, the figure
was gone.

Downward the trail was quickly covered. Sometimes the
horse floundered for footing, sometimes set his feet and slid
a little way. They came at last to the bottom where the dark
chaparral was higher than Pepé's head. He held up his rifle
on one side and his arm on the other to shield his face from
the sharp brittle fingers of the brush.

Up and out of the crease he rode, and up a little cliff. The
grassy flat was before him, and the round comfortable oaks.
For a moment he studied the trail down which he had come,
but there was no movement and no sound from it. Finally he
rode out over the flat, to the green streak, and at the upper
end of the damp he found a little spring welling out of the
earth and dropping into a dug basin before it seeped out
over the flat.

Pepé filled his bag first, and then he let the thirsty horse
drink out of the pool. He led the horse to the clump of oaks,
and in the middle of the grove, fairly protected from sight on

all sides, he took off the saddle and the bridle and laid them on the ground. The horse stretched his jaws sideways and yawned. Pepé knotted the lead rope about the horse's neck and tied him to a sapling among the oaks, where he could graze in a fairly large circle.

When the horse was gnawing hungrily at the dry grass, Pepé went to the saddle and took a black string of jerky from the sack and strolled to an oak tree on the edge of the grove, from under which he could watch the trail. He sat down in the crisp, dry oak leaves and automatically felt for his big black knife to cut the jerky, but he had no knife. He leaned back on his elbow and gnawed at the tough strong meat. His face was blank, but it was a man's face.

The bright evening light washed the eastern ridge, but the valley was darkening. Doves flew down from the hills to the spring, and the quail came running out of the brush and joined them, calling clearly to one another.

Out of the corner of his eye, Pepé saw a shadow grow out of the bushy crease. He turned his head slowly. A big spotted wildcat was creeping toward the spring, belly to the ground, moving like thought.

Pepé cocked his rifle and edged the muzzle slowly around. Then he looked apprehensively up the trail and dropped the hammer again. From the ground beside him he picked an oak twig and threw it toward the spring. The quail flew up with a roar, and the doves whistled away. The big cat stood up: for a long moment he looked at Pepé with cold yellow eyes, and then fearlessly walked back into the gulch.

The dusk gathered quickly in the deep valley. Pepé muttered his prayers, put his head down on his arm, and went instantly to sleep.

The moon came up and filled the valley with cold blue light, and the wind swept rustling down from the peaks. The owls worked up and down the slopes looking for rabbits. Down in the brush of the gulch, a coyote gabbled. The oak trees whispered softly in the night breeze.

Pepé started up, listening. His horse had whinnied. The moon was just slipping behind the western ridge, leaving the valley in darkness behind it. Pepé sat tensely gripping his rifle. From far up the trail, he heard an answering whinny and the crash of shod hoofs on the broken rock. He jumped to his feet, ran to his horse, and led it under the trees. He threw on the saddle and cinched it tight for the steep trail, caught the unwilling head and forced the bit into the mouth. He felt the saddle to make sure the water bag and the sack of jerky were there. Then he mounted and turned up the hill.

It was velvet-dark. The horse found the entrance to the trail where it left the flat, and started up, stumbling and slipping on the rocks. Pepé's hand rose up to his head. His hat was gone. He had left it under the oak tree.

The horse had struggled far up the trail when the first change of dawn came into the air, a steel grayness as light mixed thoroughly with dark. Gradually the sharp snaggled edge of the ridge stood out above them, rotten granite tortured and eaten by the winds of time. Pepé had dropped his reins on the horn, leaving direction to the horse. The brush grabbed at his legs in the dark until one knee of his jeans was ripped.

Gradually the light flowed down over the ridge. The starved brush and rocks stood out in the half-light, strange and lonely in high perspective. Then there came warmth into the light. Pepé drew up and looked back, but he could see nothing in the darker valley below. The sky turned blue over the coming sun. In the waste of the mountainside, the poor dry brush grew only three feet high. Here and there, big outcroppings of unrotted granite stood up like moldering houses. Pepé relaxed a little. He drank from his water bag and bit off a piece of jerky. A single eagle flew over, high in the light.

Without warning Pepé's horse screamed and fell on its side. He was almost down before the rifle crash echoed up from the valley. From a hole behind the struggling shoulder, a stream of bright crimson blood pumped and stopped and pumped and stopped. The hoofs threshed on the ground. Pepé lay half stunned beside the horse. He looked slowly down the hill. A piece of sage clipped off beside his head and another crash echoed up from side to side of the canyon. Pepé flung himself frantically behind a bush.

He crawled up the hill on his knees and one hand. His right hand held the rifle up off the ground and pushed it ahead of him. He moved with the instinctive care of an animal. Rapidly he wormed his way toward one of the big outcroppings of granite on the hill above him. Where the brush was high he doubled up and ran; but where the cover was slight he wriggled forward on his stomach, pushing the rifle ahead of him. In the last little distance there was no cover at all. Pepé poised and then he darted across the space and flashed around the corner of the rock.

He leaned panting against the stone. When his breath came easier, he moved along behind the big rock until he came to a narrow split that offered a thin section of vision down the hill. Pepé lay on his stomach and pushed the rifle barrel through the slit and waited.

The sun reddened the western ridges now. Already the buzzards were settling down toward the place where the horse lay. A small brown bird scratched in the dead sage leaves directly in front of the rifle muzzle. The coasting eagle flew back toward the rising sun.

Pepé saw a little movement in the brush far below. His grip tightened on the gun. A little brown doe stepped daintily out on the trail and crossed it and disappeared into the brush again. For a long time Pepé waited. Far below he could see the little flat and the oak trees and the slash of green. Suddenly his eyes flashed back at the trail again. A quarter of a mile down there had been a quick movement in the chaparral. The rifle swung over. The front sight nestled in the V of the rear sight. Pepé studied for a moment and then raised the rear sight a notch. The little movement in the brush came again. The sight settled on it. Pepé squeezed the trigger. The explosion crashed down the mountain and up the other side, and came rattling back. The whole side of the slope grew still. No more movement. And then a white streak cut into the granite of the slit and a bullet whined away and a crash sounded up from below. Pepé felt a sharp pain in his right hand. A sliver of granite was sticking out from between his first and second knuckles, and the point protruded from his palm. Carefully he pulled out the sliver of stone. The wound bled evenly and gently. No vein or artery was cut.

Pepé looked into a little dusty cave in the rock and gathered a handful of spider web, and he pressed the mass into the cut, plastering the soft web into the blood. The flow stopped almost at once.

The rifle was on the ground. Pepé picked it up, levered a new shell into the chamber. And then he slid into the brush on his stomach. Far to the right he crawled, and then up the hill, moving slowly and carefully, crawling to cover and resting and then crawling again.

In the mountains the sun is high in its arc before it penetrates the gorges. The hot face looked over the hill and brought instant heat with it. The white light beat on the rocks and reflected from them and rose up quivering from the earth again, and the rocks and bushes seemed to quiver behind the air.

Pepé crawled in the general direction of the ridge peak, zigzagging for cover. The deep cut between his knuckles began to throb. He crawled close to a rattlesnake before he saw it, and when it raised its dry head and made a soft beginning whir, he backed up and took another way. The quick gray lizards flashed in front of him, raising a tiny line of dust. He found another mass of spider web and pressed it against his throbbing hand.

Pepé was pushing the rifle with his left hand now. Little drops of sweat ran to the ends of his coarse black hair and rolled down his cheeks. His lips and tongue were growing thick and heavy. His lips writhed to draw saliva into his mouth. His little dark eyes were uneasy and suspicious. Once when a gray lizard paused in front of him on the parched ground and turned its head sideways, he crushed it flat with a stone.

When the sun slid past noon, he had not gone a mile. He crawled exhaustedly a last hundred yards to a patch of high sharp manzanita, crawled desperately, and when the patch was reached he wriggled in among the tough gnarly trunks and dropped his head on his left arm. There was little shade in the meager brush, but there was cover and safety. Pepé went to sleep as he lay and the sun beat on his back. A few little birds hopped close to him and peered and hopped away.

Pepé squirmed in his sleep, and he raised and dropped his wounded hand again and again.

The sun went down behind the peaks and the cool evening came, and then the dark. A coyote yelled from the hillside. Pepé started awake and looked about with misty eyes. His hand was swollen and heavy; a little thread of pain ran up the inside of his arm and settled in a pocket in his armpit. He peered about and then stood up, for the mountains were black and the moon had not yet risen. Pepé stood up in the dark. The coat of his father pressed on his arm. His tongue was swollen until it nearly filled his mouth. He wriggled out of the coat and dropped it in the brush, and then he struggled up the hill, falling over rocks and tearing his way through the brush. The rifle knocked against stones as he went. Little dry avalanches of gravel and shattered stone went whispering down the hill behind him.

After a while the old moon came up and showed the jagged ridge-top ahead of him. By moonlight Pepé traveled more easily. He bent forward so that his throbbing arm hung away from his body. The journey uphill was made in dashes and rests, a frantic rush up a few yards and then a rest. The wind coasted down the slope, rattling the dry stems of the bushes.

The moon was at meridian when Pepé came at last to the sharp backbone of the ridgetop. On the last hundred yards of the rise, no soil had clung under the wearing winds. The way was on solid rock. He clambered to the top and looked down on the other side. There was a draw like the last below him, misty with moonlight, brushed with dry struggling sage and chaparral. On the other side the hill rose up sharply, and at the top the jagged rotten teeth of the mountain showed against the sky. At the bottom of the cut, the brush was thick and dark.

Pepé stumbled down the hill. His throat was almost closed with thirst. At first he tried to run, but immediately he fell and rolled. After that he went more carefully. The moon was just disappearing behind the mountains when he came to the bottom. He crawled into the heavy brush, feeling with his fingers for water. There was no water in the bed of the stream, only damp earth. Pepé laid his gun down and scooped up a handful of mud and put it in his mouth, and then he spluttered and scraped the earth from his tongue with his finger, for the mud drew at his mouth like a poultice. He dug a hole in the stream bed with his fingers, dug a little basin to catch water; but before it was very deep his head fell forward on the damp ground and he slept.

The dawn came and the heat of the day fell on the earth, and still Pepé slept. Late in the afternoon his head jerked up. He looked slowly around. His eyes were slits of weariness. Twenty feet away in the heavy brush a big tawny mountain lion stood looking at him. Its long thick tail waved gracefully; its ears were erect with interest, not laid back dangerously. The lion squatted down on its stomach and watched him.

Pepé looked at the hole he had dug in the earth. A half inch of muddy water had collected in the bottom. He tore the sleeve from his hurt arm, with his teeth ripped out a little square, soaked it in the water and put it in his mouth. Over and over he filled the cloth and sucked it.

Still the lion sat and watched him. The evening came down, but there was no movement on the hills. No birds visited the dry bottom of the cut. Pepé looked occasionally at the lion. The eyes of the yellow beast drooped as though he were about to sleep. He yawned and his long, thin red tongue curled out. Suddenly his head jerked around, and his nostrils quivered. His big tail lashed. He stood up and slunk like a tawny shadow into the thick brush.

A moment later Pepé heard the sound, the faint far crash of horses' hoofs on gravel. And he heard something else, a high whining yelp of a dog.

Pepé took his rifle in his left hand, and he glided into the brush almost as quietly as the lion had. In the darkening evening he crouched up the hill toward the next ridge. Only when the dark came did he stand up. His energy was short. Once it was dark he fell over the rocks and slipped to his knees on the steep slope, but he moved on and on up the hill, climbing and scrambling over the broken hillside.

When he was far up toward the top, he lay down and slept for a little while. The withered moon, shining on his face, awakened him. He stood up and moved up the hill. Fifty yards away he stopped and turned back, for he had forgotten his rifle. He walked heavily down and poked about in the brush, but he could not find his gun. At last he lay down to rest. The pocket of pain in his armpit had grown more sharp. His arm seemed to swell out and fall with every heartbeat. There was no position lying down where the heavy arm did not press against his armpit.

With the effort of a hurt beast, Pepé got up and moved again toward the top of the ridge. He held his swollen arm away from his body with his left hand. Up the steep hill he dragged himself, a few steps and a rest, and a few more steps. At last he was nearing the top. The moon showed the uneven sharp back of it against the sky.

Pepé's brain spun in a big spiral up and away from him. He slumped to the ground and lay still. The rock ridgetop was only a hundred feet above him.

The moon moved over the sky. Pepé half turned on his back. His tongue tried to make words, but only a thick hissing came from between his lips.

When the dawn came, Pepé pulled himself up. His eyes were sane again. He drew his great puffed arm in front of him and looked at the angry wound. The black line ran up from his wrist to his armpit. Automatically he reached in his pocket for the big black knife, but it was not there. His eyes searched the ground. He picked up a sharp blade of stone and scraped at the wound, sawed at the proud flesh, and then squeezed the green juice out in big drops. Instantly he threw back his head and whined like a dog. His whole right side shuddered at the pain, but the pain cleared his head.

In the gray light he struggled up the last slope to the ridge and crawled over and lay down behind a line of rocks. Below him lay a deep canyon exactly like the last, waterless and desolate. There was no flat, no oak trees, not even heavy brush in the bottom of it. And on the other side a sharp ridge stood up, thinly brushed with starving sage, littered with broken granite. Strewn over the hill there were giant outcroppings, and on the top the granite teeth stood out against the sky.

The new day was light now. The flame of the sun came over the ridge and fell on Pepé where he lay on the ground. His coarse black hair was littered with twigs and bits of spider web. His eyes had retreated back into his head. Between his lips the tip of his black tongue showed.

He sat up and dragged his great arm into his lap and nursed it, rocking his body and moaning in his throat. He threw back his head and looked up into the pale sky. A big black bird circled nearly out of sight, and far to the left another was sailing near.

He lifted his head to listen, for a familiar sound had come to him from the valley he had climbed out of; it was the crying yelp of hounds, excited and feverish, on a trail.

Pepé bowed his head quickly. He tried to speak rapid words, but only a thick hiss came from his lips. He drew a shaky cross on his breast with his left hand. It was a long struggle to get to his feet. He crawled slowly and mechanically to the top of a big rock on the ridge peak. Once there, he arose slowly, swaying to his feet, and stood erect. Far below he could see the dark brush where he had slept. He braced his feet and stood there, black against the morning sky.

There came a ripping sound at his feet. A piece of stone flew up, and a bullet droned off into the next gorge. The hollow crash echoed up from below. Pepé looked down for a moment and then pulled himself straight again.

His body jarred back. His left hand fluttered helplessly toward his breast. The second crash sounded from below. Pepé swung forward and toppled from the rock. His body struck and rolled over and over, starting a little avalanche. And when at last he stopped against a bush, the avalanche slid slowly down and covered up his head.

FOR DISCUSSION

1. In naturalistic fiction (see Glossary, page 516, for a definition of *naturalism*), man is seen as a victim of his heritage and environment. His actions are not the result of his own choosing but, instead, are determined by natural forces beyond his control. To what extent is "Flight" an example of this naturalistic point of view? In answering this question, pay special attention to Pepé's crime and the motivation behind it.

2. Do you think Pepé makes the right decision to run away from the law? Why or why not? During the long chase, suspense is maintained by balancing the chances of Pepé's escape against the chances of his capture. What are the factors in Pepé's favor? What are the forces aligned against him? At what point in the story do you begin to sense the hopelessness of Pepé's situation?

3. Describe your reaction to the story's ending. How does it differ from your reaction to the ending of the usual stories about crime and punishment? Explain why this is the case.

4. Mama says, "A boy gets to be a man when a man is needed." Explain the relevance of this statement to the rest of the story. Does Pepé "get to be a man" as a result of his experience? Defend your answer by referring to specific passages within the story.

5. Steinbeck includes many descriptions of nature throughout the story. Which of these descriptive passages struck you as especially vivid? What purpose do they serve in terms of the rest of the story? Would the story have been improved or weakened if Steinbeck had omitted them? Explain your answer.

FOR COMPOSITION

1. Naturalistic fiction assumes that the average man is trapped by his economic or social background and is therefore not a free agent. Write a composition which discusses your attitude toward this idea. Refer to the protagonist of "Flight" to illustrate your viewpoint.

2. Write a short composition based on Mama Torres' idea that "a boy gets to be a man when a man is needed." Use an example from your own experience to support or refute this idea.

William Faulkner

William Faulkner has set his novels and short stories against the background of a decaying South with its changing social conditions. He himself was descended from a prominent Southern family that lost both its wealth and its position in the Civil War. "A Rose for Emily," about an aristocratic Southern lady who has grown up in the aftermath of the war, is written in the tradition of the Gothic horror tale (see page 515), which Edgar Allan Poe made famous in the nineteenth century. Faulkner is one of a long line of American authors who have found a fascination in the strange, the mysterious, and the macabre.

A Rose for Emily

When Miss Emily Grierson died, our whole town went to her funeral: the men through a sort of respectful affection for a fallen monument, the women mostly out of curiosity to see the inside of her house, which no one save an old manservant—a combined gardener and cook—had seen in at least ten years.

It was a big, squarish frame house that had once been white, decorated with cupolas and spires and scrolled balconies in the heavily lightsome style of the seventies, set on what had once been our most select street. But garages and cotton gins had encroached and obliterated even the august names of that neighborhood; only Miss Emily's house was left, lifting its stubborn and coquettish decay above the cotton wagons and the gasoline pumps—an eyesore among eyesores. And now Miss Emily had gone to join the representatives of those august names where they lay in the cedar-bemused cemetery among the ranked and anonymous graves of Union and Confederate soldiers who fell at the battle of Jefferson.

Alive, Miss Emily had been a tradition, a duty, and a care; a sort of hereditary obligation upon the town, dating from that day in 1894 when Colonel Sartoris, the mayor—he who fathered the edict that no Negro woman should appear on the streets without an apron—remitted her taxes, the dispensation dating from the death of her father on into perpetuity. Not that Miss Emily would have accepted charity. Colonel Sartoris invented an involved tale to the effect that Miss Emily's father had loaned money to the town, which the town, as a matter of business, preferred this way of repaying. Only a man of Colonel Sartoris' generation and thought could have invented it, and only a woman could have believed it.

When the next generation, with its more modern ideas, became mayors and aldermen, this arrangement created some little dissatisfaction. On the first of the year they mailed her a tax notice. February came, and there was no reply. They wrote her a formal letter, asking her to call at the sheriff's office at her convenience. A week later the mayor wrote her himself, offering to call or to send his car for her, and received in reply a note on paper of an archaic shape, in a thin, flowing calligraphy in faded ink, to the effect that she no longer went out at all. The tax notice was also enclosed, without comment.

They called a special meeting of the Board of Aldermen. A deputation waited upon her, knocked at the door through which no visitor had passed since she ceased giving china-painting lessons eight or ten years earlier. They were admitted by the old Negro into a dim hall from which a stairway mounted into still more shadow. It smelled of dust and disuse—a close, dank smell. The Negro led them into the parlor. It was furnished in heavy, leather-covered furniture. When the Negro opened the blinds of one window, they could see that the leather was cracked; and when they sat down, a faint dust rose sluggishly about their thighs, spinning with slow motes in the single sun-ray. On a tarnished gilt easel before the fireplace stood a crayon portrait of Miss Emily's father.

They rose when she entered—a small, fat woman in black, with a thin gold chain descending to her waist and vanishing into her belt, leaning on an ebony cane with a tarnished gold head. Her skeleton was small and spare; perhaps that was why what would have been merely plumpness in another was obesity in her. She looked bloated, like a body long submerged in motionless water, and of that pallid hue. Her eyes, lost in the fatty ridges of her face, looked like two small pieces of coal pressed into a lump of dough as they moved from one face to another while the visitors stated their errand.

She did not ask them to sit. She just stood in the door and listened quietly until the spokesman came to a stumbling halt. Then they could hear the invisible watch ticking at the end of the gold chain.

Her voice was dry and cold. "I have no taxes in Jefferson. Colonel Sartoris explained it to me. Perhaps one of you can gain access to the city records and satisfy yourselves."

"But we have. We are the city authorities, Miss Emily. Didn't you get a notice from the sheriff, signed by him?"

"I received a paper, yes," Miss Emily said. "Perhaps he considers himself the sheriff . . . I have no taxes in Jefferson."

"But there is nothing on the books to show that, you see. We must go by the—"

"See Colonel Sartoris. I have no taxes in Jefferson."

"But, Miss Emily—"

"See Colonel Sartoris." (Colonel Sartoris had been dead almost ten years.) "I have no taxes in Jefferson. Tobe!" The Negro appeared. "Show these gentlemen out."

II

So she vanquished them, horse and foot, just as she had vanquished their fathers thirty years before about the smell. That was two years after her father's death and a short time after her sweetheart—the one we believed would marry her— had deserted her. After her father's death she went out very little; after her sweetheart went away, people hardly saw her at all. A few of the ladies had the temerity to call, but were not received, and the only sign of life about the place was the Negro man—a young man then—going in and out with a market basket.

"Just as if a man – any man – could keep a kitchen properly," the ladies said; so they were not surprised when the smell developed. It was another link between the gross, teeming world and the high and mighty Griersons.

A neighbor, a woman, complained to the mayor, Judge Stevens, eighty years old.

"But what will you have me do about it, madam?" he said.

"Why, send her word to stop it," the woman said. "Isn't there a law?"

"I'm sure that won't be necessary," Judge Stevens said. "It's probably just a snake or a rat that nigger of hers killed in the yard. I'll speak to him about it."

The next day he received two more complaints, one from a man who came in diffident deprecation.[1] "We really must do something about it, Judge. I'd be the last one in the world to bother Miss Emily, but we've got to do something." That night the Board of Aldermen met – three graybeards and one younger man, a member of the rising generation.

"It's simple enough," he said. "Send her word to have her place cleaned up. Give her a certain time to do it in, and if she don't..."

"Dammit, sir," Judge Stevens said, "will you accuse a lady to her face of smelling bad?"

So the next night, after midnight, four men crossed Miss Emily's lawn and slunk about the house like burglars, sniffing along the base of the brickwork and at the cellar openings while one of them performed a regular sowing motion with his hand out of a sack slung from his shoulder. They broke open the cellar door and sprinkled lime there, and in all the outbuildings. As they recrossed the lawn, a window that had been dark was lighted and Miss Emily sat in it, the light behind her, and her upright torso motionless as that of an idol. They crept quietly across the lawn and into the shadow of the locusts that lined the street. After a week or two the smell went away.

That was when people had begun to feel really sorry for her. People in our town, remembering how old lady Wyatt, her

[1] *diffident deprecation:* shy disapproval or protest

great-aunt, had gone completely crazy at last, believed that the Griersons held themselves a little too high for what they really were. None of the young men were quite good enough for Miss Emily and such. We had long thought of them as a tableau,[2] Miss Emily a slender figure in white in the background, her father a spraddled silhouette in the foreground, his back to her and clutching a horsewhip, the two of them framed by the back-flung front door. So when she got to be thirty and was still single, we were not pleased exactly, but vindicated; even with insanity in the family she wouldn't have turned down all of her chances if they had really materialized.

When her father died, it got about that the house was all that was left to her; and in a way, people were glad. At last they could pity Miss Emily. Being left alone, and a pauper, she had become humanized. Now she too would know the old thrill and the old despair of a penny more or less.

The day after his death all the ladies prepared to call at the house and offer condolence and aid, as is our custom. Miss Emily met them at the door, dressed as usual and with no trace of grief on her face. She told them that her father was not dead. She did that for three days, with the ministers calling on her, and the doctors, trying to persuade her to let them dispose of the body. Just as they were about to resort to law and force, she broke down, and they buried her father quickly.

We did not say she was crazy then. We believed she had to do that. We remembered all the young men her father had driven away, and we knew that with nothing left, she would have to cling to that which had robbed her, as people will.

III

She was sick for a long time. When we saw her again her hair was cut short, making her look like a girl, with a vague resemblance to those angels in colored church windows—sort of tragic and serene.

The town had just let the contracts for paving the sidewalks, and in the summer after her father's death they began the

[2] *tableau:* picture

work. The construction company came with niggers and mules and machinery, and a foreman named Homer Barron, a Yankee —a big, dark, ready man, with a big voice and eyes lighter than his face. The little boys would follow in groups to hear him cuss the niggers, and the niggers singing in time to the rise and fall of picks. Pretty soon he knew everybody in town. Whenever you heard a lot of laughing anywhere about the square, Homer Barron would be in the center of the group. Presently we began to see him and Miss Emily on Sunday afternoons driving in the yellow-wheeled buggy and the matched team of bays from the livery stable.

At first we were glad that Miss Emily would have an interest, because the ladies all said, "Of course a Grierson would not think seriously of a Northerner, a day laborer." But there were still others, older people, who said that even grief could not cause a real lady to forget *noblesse oblige*[3] — without calling it *noblesse oblige*. They just said, "Poor Emily. Her kinsfolk should come to her." She had some kin in Alabama; but years ago her father had fallen out with them over the estate of old lady Wyatt, the crazy woman, and there was no communication between the two families. They had not even been represented at the funeral.

And as soon as the old people said, "Poor Emily," the whispering began. "Do you suppose it's really so?" they said to one another. "Of course it is. What else could . . ." This behind their hands; rustling of craned silk and satin behind jalousies closed upon the sun of Sunday afternoon as the thin, swift clop-clop-clop of the matched team passed: "Poor Emily."

She carried her head high enough — even when we believed that she was fallen. It was as if she demanded more than ever the recognition of her dignity as the last Grierson; as if it had wanted that touch of earthiness to reaffirm her imperviousness. Like when she bought the rat poison, the arsenic. That was over a year after they had begun to say "Poor Emily," and while the two female cousins were visiting her.

---

[3] *noblesse oblige:* the obligation of honorable, generous, and responsible behavior accompanying high birth or rank

"I want some poison," she said to the druggist. She was over thirty then, still a slight woman, though thinner than usual, with cold, haughty black eyes in a face the flesh of which was strained across the temples and about the eyesockets as you imagine a lighthouse-keeper's face ought to look. "I want some poison," she said.

"Yes, Miss Emily. What kind? For rats and such? I'd recom—"

"I want the best you have. I don't care what kind."

The druggist named several. "They'll kill anything up to an elephant. But what you want is—"

"Arsenic," Miss Emily said. "Is that a good one?"

"Is . . . arsenic? Yes, ma'am. But what you want—"

"I want arsenic."

The druggist looked down at her. She looked back at him, erect, her face like a strained flag. "Why, of course," the druggist said. "If that's what you want. But the law requires you to tell what you are going to use it for."

Miss Emily just stared at him, her head tilted back in order to look him eye for eye, until he looked away and went and got the arsenic and wrapped it up. The Negro delivery boy brought her the package; the druggist didn't come back. When she opened the package at home there was written on the box, under the skull and bones: "For rats."

IV

So the next day we all said, "She will kill herself"; and we said it would be the best thing. When she had first begun to be seen with Homer Barron, we had said, "She will marry him." Then we said, "She will persuade him yet," because Homer himself had remarked—he liked men, and it was known that he drank with the younger men in the Elks' Club —that he was not a marrying man. Later we said, "Poor Emily" behind the jalousies as they passed on Sunday afternoon in the glittering buggy, Miss Emily with her head high and Homer Barron with his hat cocked and a cigar in his teeth, reins and whip in a yellow glove.

Then some of the ladies began to say that it was a disgrace

to the town and a bad example to the young people. The men did not want to interfere, but at last the ladies forced the Baptist minister—Miss Emily's people were Episcopal—to call upon her. He would never divulge what happened during that interview, but he refused to go back again. The next Sunday they again drove about the streets, and the following day the minister's wife wrote to Miss Emily's relations in Alabama.

So she had blood-kin under her roof again and we sat back to watch developments. At first nothing happened. Then we were sure that they were to be married. We learned that Miss Emily had been to the jeweler's and ordered a man's toilet set in silver, with the letters H. B. on each piece. Two days later we learned that she had bought a complete outfit of men's clothing, including a nightshirt, and we said, "They are married." We were really glad. We were glad because the two female cousins were even more Grierson than Miss Emily had ever been.

So we were not surprised when Homer Barron—the streets had been finished some time since—was gone. We were a little disappointed that there was not a public blowing-off, but we believed that he had gone on to prepare for Miss Emily's coming, or to give her a chance to get rid of the cousins. (By that time it was a cabal,[4] and we were all Miss Emily's allies to help circumvent the cousins.) Sure enough, after another week they departed. And, as we had expected all along, within three days Homer Barron was back in town. A neighbor saw the Negro man admit him at the kitchen door at dusk one evening.

And that was the last we saw of Homer Barron. And of Miss Emily for some time. The Negro man went in and out with the market basket, but the front door remained closed. Now and then we would see her at a window for a moment, as the men did that night when they sprinkled the lime, but for almost six months she did not appear on the streets. Then we knew that this was to be expected too; as if that quality of her father which had thwarted her woman's life so many times had been too virulent and too furious to die.

[4]*cabal:* plot or intrigue

When we next saw Miss Emily, she had grown fat and her hair was turning gray. During the next few years it grew grayer and grayer until it attained an even pepper-and-salt iron-gray, when it ceased turning. Up to the day of her death at seventy-four it was still that vigorous iron-gray, like the hair of an active man.

From that time on her front door remained closed, save for a period of six or seven years, when she was about forty, during which she gave lessons in china-painting. She fitted up a studio in one of the downstairs rooms, where the daughters and granddaughters of Colonel Sartoris' contemporaries were sent to her with the same regularity and in the same spirit that they were sent to church on Sundays with a twenty-five-cent piece for the collection plate. Meanwhile her taxes had been remitted.

Then the newer generation became the backbone and the spirit of the town, and the painting pupils grew up and fell away and did not send their children to her with boxes of color and tedious brushes and pictures cut from the ladies' magazines. The front door closed upon the last one and remained closed for good. When the town got free postal delivery, Miss Emily alone refused to let them fasten the metal numbers above her door and attach a mailbox to it. She would not listen to them.

Daily, monthly, yearly we watched the Negro grow grayer and more stooped, going in and out with the market basket. Each December we sent her a tax notice, which would be returned by the post office a week later, unclaimed. Now and then we would see her in one of the downstairs windows — she had evidently shut up the top floor of the house — like the carven torso of an idol in a niche, looking or not looking at us, we could never tell which. Thus she passed from generation to generation — dear, inescapable, impervious, tranquil, and perverse.

And so she died. Fell ill in the house filled with dust and shadows, with only a doddering Negro man to wait on her. We did not even know she was sick; we had long since given up trying to get any information from the Negro. He talked to no one, probably not even to her, for his voice had grown harsh and rusty, as if from disuse.

She died in one of the downstairs rooms, in a heavy walnut bed with a curtain, her gray head propped on a pillow yellow and moldy with age and lack of sunlight.

V

The Negro met the first of the ladies at the front door and let them in, with their hushed, sibilant voices and their quick, curious glances, and then he disappeared. He walked right through the house and out the back and was not seen again.

The two female cousins came at once. They held the funeral on the second day, with the town coming to look at Miss Emily beneath a mass of bought flowers, with the crayon face of her father musing profoundly above the bier and the ladies sibilant and macabre; and the very old men — some in their brushed Confederate uniforms — on the porch and the lawn, talking of Miss Emily as if she had been a contemporary of theirs, believing that they had danced with her and courted her perhaps, confusing time with its mathematical progression, as the old do, to whom all the past is not a diminishing road but, instead, a huge meadow which no winter ever quite touches, divided from them now by the narrow bottle-neck of the most recent decade of years.

Already we knew that there was one room in that region above stairs which no one had seen in forty years, and which would have to be forced. They waited until Miss Emily was decently in the ground before they opened it.

The violence of breaking down the door seemed to fill this room with pervading dust. A thin, acrid pall as of the tomb seemed to lie everywhere upon this room decked and furnished as for a bridal: upon the valance curtains of faded rose color, upon the rose-shaded lights, upon the dressing table, upon the delicate array of crystal and the man's toilet things backed with tarnished silver, silver so tarnished that the monogram was obscured. Among them lay a collar and tie, as if they had just been removed, which, lifted, left upon the surface a pale crescent in the dust. Upon a chair hung the suit, carefully folded; beneath it the two mute shoes and the discarded socks.

The man himself lay in the bed.

For a long while we just stood there, looking down at the profound and fleshless grin. The body had apparently once lain in the attitude of an embrace, but now the long sleep that outlasts love, that conquers even the grimace of love, had cuckolded him. What was left of him, rotted beneath what was left of the nightshirt, had become inextricable from the bed in which he lay; and upon him and upon the pillow beside him lay that even coating of the patient and biding dust.

Then we noticed that in the second pillow was the indentation of a head. One of us lifted something from it, and leaning forward, that faint and invisible dust dry and acrid in the nostrils, we saw a long strand of iron-gray hair.

FOR DISCUSSION

1. You learn that Miss Emily has lost the ability to distinguish between reality and illusion. Through which incidents do you discover this fact?
2. The story is told from the point of view (see Glossary, page 517) of one of the townspeople. How do he and the community feel toward Miss Emily? What character traits of Miss Emily seem to set her "above" the rest of the community?
3. What effect did Miss Emily's father have upon her life and upon the course of the story?
4. What is the community's opinion of Homer Barron? In what sense is it characteristic of Miss Emily to choose such a man?
5. How does Miss Emily "keep Homer faithful"? In what respect is this action true to her character?
6. What circumstances occur during the course of the story that hint at the outcome? What later significance has Faulkner's careful description of Miss Emily's hair in Part IV?
7. What would you say is the mood of this story? Which details seem most important in creating this mood?
8. Faulkner's talent for painting a picture with words is apparent throughout the story, particularly in his descriptions of Miss Emily. Find several examples that you consider particularly good.

FOR COMPOSITION

1. Write a short composition in which you justify your own opinion of Miss Emily. Do you find her horrible or admirable?
2. Might this story be interpreted as a commentary on society in general? Develop a composition telling why you do or do not think so.

THE RISE OF A NATIONAL LITERATURE

Following the adoption of the Constitution in 1789, this country entered a period of expansion and change so rapid and far-reaching that it left Americans gasping. Three new states were added to the original thirteen before the turn of the century. By 1821 the number had grown to twenty-four. Canals, railroads, highways, and steamboats—plus such inventions as the reaper, the cotton gin, and the telegraph—helped to create a new empire out of the vast West, South, and Southwest. Settlements became small cities almost overnight, and so abundant were the natural resources that thoughtful men warned against this country's becoming "the land of the almighty dollar."

The cultural growth of the country was less spectacular. Nevertheless, the public school system was extended—often with government support—new colleges were established, and the three hundred printing presses existing in 1800 were more than tripled by 1825. Approximately a third of the books available to American readers were printed in this country, and the number of periodicals more than doubled. Meanwhile, libraries, museums, art galleries, and such institutions as the American Academy of Arts in New York and the Library of Congress in Washington, D.C., were being established. It is not surprising that the demand for a national literature became loud and insistent. Political independence—reaffirmed by the War of 1812—called for independence in cultural and intellectual matters as well. Moreover, there was a strong feeling that English literature was not suitable for the training of young Americans: it was thought to be undemocratic. What was needed was a literature based upon American ideals and of sufficient scope and stature to silence the ridicule of English critics.

The spirit of romanticism already had played an important part in America's denial of European authority and cultural influence, its pride in the "American ideals" which had created the Republic, and its delight in the infinite wealth, opportunities, and natural beauties of an unspoiled land.

Now this same spirit was to give America its first real literary motivation. That it should have come through the study and imitation of English poetry, fiction, drama, and essay is somewhat ironic, for many Americans resented the criticism and condescension of English observers and travelers. No doubt the English attitude intensified the determination of those American writers willing to meet the challenge. Could they create a literature that equalled or surpassed their English models in perfection of expression yet remained faithful to American ideals and experience? Having American things to say, could they discover an American way of saying them?

Two writers who met this challenge in the early 1800's were Washington Irving and James Fenimore Cooper. By 1825 both had established themselves as men of letters whose work was important enough to command the attention of cultivated Europeans. Each contributed to the rise of a national literature that, within a few years, had the stature and scope of the new democracy.

WASHINGTON IRVING was particularly suited to the role he

was to play in American literature: "the first purely cultural ambassador from the New World to the Old, the first American man of letters to gain international fame." Even his first book, *A History of New York*, was a financial success and brought praise from no less an English writer than Sir Walter Scott. His second, *The Sketch Book*, was an international best seller and reaffirmed his determination to earn his livelihood through writing. The purpose of this book is clearly stated in a letter he wrote to a friend:

> I have attempted no lofty theme nor sought to look wise and learned, which appears to be very much the fashion among our American writers at present. I have preferred addressing myself to the feeling & fancy of the reader, more than to his judgment. My writings may therefore appear light & trifling in our country of philosophers & politicians—but if they possess merit in the class of literature to which they belong it is all to which I aspire in the work. I seek only to blow a flute of accompaniment in the national concert, and leave others to play the fiddle & French Horn.

Irving wrote *The Sketch Book* in England, where he remained so long that he was criticized by sensitive Americans who wondered if he had lost all patriotic feeling. He did return to this country, however, in 1832, after visiting Spain and exploring its romantic history and legends. The materials he gathered there were used for *The Alhambra*, a collection of tales and sketches which, with *The Sketch Book*, set the romantic pattern for the American short story.

The contribution of JAMES FENIMORE COOPER to American literature was to create not one, but a whole shelf of distinctively American novels. His purpose was to acquaint all mankind with American facts and American ideas. *The Spy*, his first mature novel, appeared the same year as Irving's *The Sketch Book* and proved a remarkable success in England as well as in America. Sir Walter Scott's historical novels were then at the height of their popularity and no doubt influenced Cooper's choice of method. He did not, however, consider them his models. In his opinion, the only hope for American literature was to be emancipated from all English influence, relying upon its own "usable past" for events, characters, and themes and upon its own writers for suitable techniques of narration and style.

For his early and best novels – the Indian and sea tales – Cooper used only the recent past, which he could blend with his own memories and describe against a background he knew and loved. Here he found the stuff of romance – the unusual and the heroic – and, despite his shortcomings as a writer, turned it into novels that were more than mere adventure yarns. No one can deny that his style is serviceable rather than artistic, but it "never seriously clogs the movement of his stories; they [his tales] possess the elementary and yet fundamental virtue of activity. Their end is never really in doubt, but one wants to know what will happen next; fortunes change with dizzy abruptness, like a game of snakes-and-ladders, till the firm final throw."[1]

Cooper was too much the amateur to contribute, as Irving did, to the creation of an American standard of expression that future writers might follow. He did, however, make clear the direction that future American writing must take. If there was to be a new and characteristic literature, tradition and foreign controls must be abandoned. Moreover, such a literature must be created from the inside out – created from what is thought and felt and experienced firsthand to the form in which it is presented.

[1] Marcus Cunliffe, *The Literature of the United States* (Baltimore: Penguin Books, Inc., 1961), p. 62.

Washington Irving

At a time when the purpose of American letters was largely to make converts in religion or politics, Washington Irving chose as his purpose to entertain readers. He was determined, however, that his sketches and stories should have more than an interesting narrative to recommend them. He brought to them "characters, lightly yet expressively delineated . . . and a half concealed vein of humor." These qualities are to be seen in two of Irving's finest stories, "Rip Van Winkle" and "The Stout Gentleman." The following tale is in a different vein. It is based on a German legend, but with an original twist by Irving. In it one can see the beginnings of the Gothic tale in American literature more than a hundred years before Faulkner.

The Specter Bridegroom

On the summit of one of the heights of the Odenwald, a wild and romantic tract of Upper Germany, that lies not far from the confluence[1] of the Main and the Rhine, there stood, many, many years since, the Castle of the Baron Von Landshort. It is now quite fallen to decay, and almost buried among beech-trees and dark firs; above which, however, its old watchtower may still be seen, struggling, like the former possessor I have mentioned, to carry a high head, and look down upon the neighboring country.

The baron was a dry branch of the great family Katzenellenbogen,[2] and inherited the relics of the property, and all the

---

[1] *confluence:* meeting
[2] *Katzenellenbogen* (Cat's elbow): name given in compliment to one of the women of the family celebrated for her fine arm

pride of his ancestors. Though the warlike disposition of his predecessors had much impaired the family possessions, yet the baron still endeavored to keep up some show of former state. The times were peaceable, and the German nobles, in general, had abandoned their inconvenient old castles, perched like eagles' nests among the mountains, and had built more convenient residences in the valleys: still the baron remained proudly drawn up in his little fortress, cherishing, with hereditary inveteracy,[3] all the old family feuds; so that he was on ill terms with some of his nearest neighbors, on account of dispute that had happened between their great-great-grandfathers.

The baron had but one child, a daughter; but nature, when she grants but one child, always compensates by making it a prodigy; and so it was with the daughter of the baron. All the nurses, gossips, and country cousins assured her father that she had not her equal for beauty in all Germany; and who should know better than they? She had, moreover, been brought up with great care under the superintendence of two maiden aunts, who had spent some years of their early life at one of the little German courts, and were skilled in all the branches of knowledge necessary to the education of a fine lady. Under their instructions she became a miracle of accomplishments. By the time she was eighteen, she could embroider to admiration, and had worked whole histories of the saints in tapestry, with such strength of expression in their countenances, that they looked like so many souls in purgatory. She could read without great difficulty, and had spelled her way through several church legends, and almost all the chivalric wonders of the Heldenbuch.[4] She had even made considerable proficiency in writing; could sign her own name without missing a letter, and so legibly, that her aunts could read it without spectacles. She excelled in making little elegant good-for-nothing lady-like knickknacks of all kinds; was versed in the most abstruse[5] dancing of the day; played a

---

[3]*inveteracy:* deep-rooted characteristic
[4]*Heldenbuch:* Book of Heroes
[5]*abstruse:* difficult to understand

number of airs on the harp and guitar; and knew all the tender ballads of the Minnelieders[6] by heart.

Her aunts, too, having been great flirts and coquettes in their younger days, were admirably calculated to be vigilant guardians and strict censors of the conduct of their niece; for there is no duenna[7] so rigidly prudent, and inexorably decorous, as a superannuated coquette. She was rarely suffered out of their sight; never went beyond the domains of the castle, unless well attended, or rather well watched; had continual lectures read to her about strict decorum and implicit obedience; and, as to the men — pah! — she was taught to hold them at such a distance, and in such absolute distrust, that, unless properly authorized, she would not have cast a glance upon the handsomest cavalier in the world — no, not if he were even dying at her feet.

The good effects of this system were wonderfully apparent. The young lady was a pattern of docility and correctness. While others were wasting their sweetness in the glare of the world, and liable to be plucked and thrown aside by every hand, she was coyly blooming into fresh and lovely womanhood under the protection of those immaculate spinsters like a rose-bud blushing forth among guardian thorns. Her aunts looked upon her with pride and exultation and vaunted that though all the other young ladies in the world might go astray, yet, thank Heaven, nothing of the kind could happen to the heiress of Katzenellenbogen.

But, however scantily the Baron Von Landshort might be provided with children, his household was by no means a small one; for Providence had enriched him with abundance of poor relations. They, one and all, possessed the affectionate disposition common to humble relatives; were wonderfully attached to the baron, and took every possible occasion to come in swarms and enliven the castle. All family festivals were commemorated by these good people at the baron's expense; and when they were filled with good cheer, they would declare that there was nothing on earth so delightful as these family meetings, these jubilees of the heart.

[6] *Minnelieders:* a class of medieval German musicians and singers
[7] *duenna:* governess

The baron, though a small man, had a large soul, and it swelled with satisfaction at the consciousness of being the greatest man in the little world about him. He loved to tell long stories about the dark old warriors whose portraits looked grimly down from the walls around, and he found no listeners equal to those who fed at his expense. He was much given to the marvelous, and a firm believer in all those supernatural tales with which every mountain and valley in Germany abounds. The faith of his guests exceeded even his own: they listened to every tale of wonder with open eyes and mouth, and never failed to be astonished, even though repeated for the hundredth time. Thus lived the Baron Von Landshort, the oracle of his table, the absolute monarch of his little territory, and happy, above all things, in the persuasion that he was the wisest man of the age.

At the time of which my story treats, there was a great family-gathering at the castle, on an affair of the utmost importance: it was to receive the destined bridegroom of the baron's daughter. A negotiation had been carried on between the father and an old nobleman of Bavaria, to unite the dignity of their houses by the marriage of their children. The preliminaries had been conducted with proper punctilio.[8] The young people were betrothed without seeing each other; and the time was appointed for the marriage ceremony. The young Count Von Altenburg had been recalled from the army for the purpose, and was actually on his way to the baron's to receive his bride. Missives had even been received from him, from Würtzburg, where he was accidentally detained, mentioning the day and hour when he might be expected to arrive.

The castle was in a tumult of preparation to give him a suitable welcome. The fair bride had been decked out with uncommon care. The two aunts had superintended her toilet,[9] and quarreled the whole morning about every article of her dress. The young lady had taken advantage of their contest to follow the bent of her own taste; and fortunately it was a good one. She looked as lovely as a youthful bridegroom could

---

[8] *punctilio:* careful observance of ceremony and formality
[9] *toilet:* process of dressing, arranging the hair, etc.

desire; and the flutter of expectation heightened the luster of her charms.

The suffusions that mantled her face and neck, the gentle heaving of the bosom, the eye now and then lost in reverie, all betrayed the soft tumult that was going on in her little heart. The aunts were continually hovering around her; for maiden aunts are apt to take great interest in affairs of this nature. They were giving her a world of staid counsel how to deport herself, what to say, and in what manner to receive the expected lover.

The baron was no less busied in preparations. He had, in truth, nothing exactly to do; but he was naturally a fuming, bustling little man, and could not remain passive when all the world was in a hurry. He worried from top to bottom of the castle with an air of infinite anxiety; he continually called the servants from their work to exhort them to be diligent; and buzzed about every hall and chamber, as idly restless and importunate as a blue-bottle fly on a warm summer's day.

In the meantime the fatted calf had been killed; the forests had rung with the clamor of the huntsmen; the kitchen was crowded with good cheer; the cellars had yielded up whole oceans of *Rheinwein* and *Ferne-wein;*[10] and even the great Heidelberg tun[11] had been laid under contribution. Everything was ready to receive the distinguished guest with *Saus und Braus*[12] in the true spirit of German hospitality; — but the guest delayed to make his appearance. Hour rolled after hour. The sun, that had poured his downward rays upon the rich forest of the Odenwald, now just gleamed along the summits of the mountains. The baron mounted the highest tower, and strained his eyes in hope of catching a distant sight of the count and his attendants. Once he thought he beheld them; the sound of horns came floating from the valley, prolonged by the mountain echoes. A number of horsemen were seen far below, slowly advancing along the road; but when they had nearly reached the foot of the mountain, they sud-

---

[10] *Rheinwein and Ferne-wein:* German wines

[11] *tun:* huge cask for wine or beer

[12] *Saus und Braus:* hustle and bustle

denly struck off in a different direction. The last ray of sunshine departed, — the bats began to flit by in the twilight, — the road grew dimmer and dimmer to the view, and nothing appeared stirring in it but now and then a peasant lagging homeward from his labor.

While the old castle of Landshort was in this state of perplexity, a very interesting scene was transacting in a different part of the Odenwald.

The young Count Von Altenburg was tranquilly pursuing his route in that sober jog-trot way, in which a man travels toward matrimony when his friends have taken all the trouble and uncertainty of courtship off his hands, and a bride is waiting for him, as certainly as a dinner at the end of his journey. He had encountered at Würtzburg a youthful companion in arms, with whom he had seen some service on the frontiers, — Herman Von Starkenfaust, one of the stoutest hands and worthiest hearts of German chivalry, who was now returning from the army. His father's castle was not far distant from the old fortress of Landshort, although a hereditary feud rendered the families hostile, and strangers to each other.

In the warm-hearted moment of recognition, the young friends related all their past adventures and fortunes, and the count gave the whole history of his intended nuptials with a young lady whom he had never seen, but of whose charms he had received the most enrapturing descriptions.

As the route of the friends lay in the same direction, they agreed to perform the rest of their journey together; and, that they might do it the more leisurely, set off from Würtzburg at an early hour, the count having given directions for his retinue to follow and overtake him.

They beguiled their wayfaring with recollections of their military scenes and adventures; but the count was apt to be a little tedious, now and then, about the reputed charms of his bride, and the felicity that awaited him.

In this way they had entered among the mountains of the Odenwald, and were traversing one of its most lonely and thickly-wooded passes. It is well known that the forests of Germany have always been as much infested by robbers as its castles by specters; and, at this time, the former were particularly numerous, from the hordes of disbanded soldiers wandering about the country. It will not appear extraordinary, therefore, that the cavaliers were attacked by a gang of these stragglers, in the midst of the forest. They defended themselves with bravery, but were nearly overpowered, when the count's retinue arrived to their assistance. At sight of them the robbers fled, but not until the count had received a mortal wound. He was slowly and carefully conveyed back to the city of Würtzburg, and a friar summoned from a neighboring convent, who was famous for his skill in administering to both soul and body; but half of his skill was superfluous; the moments of the unfortunate count were numbered.

With his dying breath he entreated his friend to repair instantly to the castle of Landshort, and explain the fatal cause of his not keeping his appointment with his bride. Though not the most ardent of lovers, he was one of the most punctilious of men, and appeared earnestly solicitous that his mission should be speedily and courteously executed. "Unless this is done," said he, "I shall not sleep quietly in my grave!" He repeated these last words with peculiar solemnity. A request, at a moment so impressive, admitted no hesitation. Starkenfaust endeavored to soothe him to calmness; promised faithfully to execute his wish, and gave him his hand in solemn pledge. The dying man pressed it in acknowledgment, but soon lapsed into delirium—raved about his bride—his engagements—his plighted word; ordered his horse, that he might ride to the castle of Landshort; and expired in the fancied act of vaulting into the saddle.

Starkenfaust bestowed a sigh and a soldier's tear on the untimely fate of his comrade; and then pondered on the awkward mission he had undertaken. His heart was heavy, and his head perplexed; for he was to present himself an unbidden guest among hostile people, and to damp their festivity with tidings fatal to their hopes. Still there were certain whisperings of curiosity in his bosom to see this far-famed beauty of Katzenellenbogen, so cautiously shut up from the world; for he was a passionate admirer of the sex, and there was a dash of eccentricity and enterprise in his character that made him fond of all singular adventure.

Previous to his departure he made all due arrangements with the holy fraternity of the convent for the funeral solemnities of his friend, who was to be buried in the cathedral of Würtzburg, near some of his illustrious relatives; and the mourning retinue of the count took charge of his remains. It is now high time that we should return to the ancient family of Katzenellenbogen, who were impatient for their guest, and still more for their dinner; and to the worthy little baron, whom we left airing himself on the watchtower.

Night closed in, but still no guest arrived. The baron descended from the tower in despair. The banquet, which had been delayed from hour to hour, could no longer be postponed. The meats were already overdone; the cook in an agony; and the whole household had the look of a garrison that had been reduced by famine. The baron was obliged reluctantly to give orders for the feast without the presence of the guest. All were seated at the table, and just on the point of commencing, when the sound of a horn from without the gate gave notice of the approach of a stranger. Another long blast filled the old courts of the castle with its echoes, and was answered by the warder from the walls. The baron hastened to receive his future son-in-law.

The drawbridge had been let down, and the stranger was before the gate. He was a tall, gallant cavalier, mounted on a black steed. His countenance was pale, but he had a beaming, romantic eye, and an air of stately melancholy. The baron was a little mortified that he should have come in this simple, solitary style. His dignity for a moment was ruffled, and he felt disposed to consider it a want of proper respect for the important occasion, and the important family with which he was to be connected. He pacified himself, however, with the conclusion that it must have been youthful impatience which had induced him thus to spur on sooner than his attendants.

"I am sorry," said the stranger, "to break in upon you thus unseasonably" —

Here the baron interrupted him with a world of compliments and greetings; for, to tell the truth, he prided himself upon his courtesy and eloquence. The stranger attempted, once or twice, to stem the torrent of words, but in vain, so he bowed his head and suffered it to flow on. By the time the baron had come to a pause, they had reached the inner court of the castle; and the stranger was again about to speak, when he was once more interrupted by the appearance of the female part of the family, leading forth the shrinking and blushing bride. He gazed on her for a moment as one entranced; it seemed as if his whole soul beamed forth in the gaze, and rested upon that lovely form. One of the maiden aunts whispered something in her ear; she made an effort to speak; her moist blue eye was timidly raised; gave a shy glance of inquiry on the stranger; and was cast again to the ground. The words died away; but there was a sweet smile playing about her lips, and a soft dimpling of the cheek that showed her glance had not been unsatisfactory. It was impossible for a girl of the fond age of eighteen, highly predisposed for love and matrimony, not to be pleased with so gallant a cavalier.

The late hour at which the guest had arrived left no time for parley. The baron was peremptory, and deferred all particular conversation until the morning, and led the way to the untasted banquet.

It was served up in the great hall of the castle. Around the walls hung the hard-favored portraits of the heroes of the house of Katzenellenbogen, and the trophies which they had gained in the field and in the chase. Hacked corselets,[13] splintered jousting spears, and tattered banners were mingled with the spoils of sylvan warfare;[14] the jaws of the wolf, and the tusks of the boar, grinned horribly among cross-bows and battle-axes, and a huge pair of antlers branched immediately over the head of the youthful bridegroom.

The cavalier took but little notice of the company or the entertainment. He scarcely tasted the banquet, but seemed absorbed in admiration of his bride. He conversed in a low tone that could not be overheard—for the language of love is never loud; but where is the female ear so dull that it cannot catch the softer whisper of the lover? There was a mingled tenderness and gravity in his manner, that appeared to have a power-

[13] *corselets:* suits of armor
[14] *sylvan warfare:* hunting

ful effect upon the young lady. Her color came and went as she listened with deep attention. Now and then she made some blushing reply, and when his eye was turned away, she would steal a sidelong glance at his romantic countenance, and heave a gentle sigh of tender happiness. It was evident that the young couple were completely enamored. The aunts, who were deeply versed in the mysteries of the heart, declared that they had fallen in love with each other at first sight.

The feast went on merrily, or at least noisily, for the guests were all blessed with those keen appetites that attend upon light purses and mountain-air. The baron told his best and longest stories, and never had he told them so well, or with such great effect. If there was anything marvelous, his auditors were lost in astonishment; and if anything facetious, they were sure to laugh exactly in the right place. The baron, it is true, like most great men, was too dignified to utter any joke but a dull one; it was always enforced, however, by a bumper[15] of excellent Hockheimer; and even a dull joke, at one's own table, served up with jolly old wine, is irresistible. Many good things were said by poorer and keener wits, that would not bear repeating, except on similar occasions; many sly speeches whispered in ladies' ears, that almost convulsed them with suppressed laughter; and a song or two roared out by a poor, but merry and broad-faced cousin of the baron, that absolutely made the maiden aunts hold up their fans.

Amidst all this revelry, the stranger guest maintained a most singular and unseasonable gravity. His countenance assumed a deeper cast of dejection as the evening advanced; and, strange as it may appear, even the baron's jokes seemed only to render him the more melancholy. At times he was lost in thought, and at times there was a perturbed and restless wandering of the eye that bespoke a mind but ill at ease. His conversations with the bride became more and more earnest and mysterious. Lowering clouds began to steal over the fair serenity of her brow, and tremors to run through her tender frame.

[15] *bumper:* full cup or glass

All this could not escape the notice of the company. Their gayety was chilled by the unaccountable gloom of the bridegroom; their spirits were infected; whispers and glances were interchanged, accompanied by shrugs and dubious shakes of the head. The song and the laugh grew less and less frequent; there were dreary pauses in the conversation, which were at length succeeded by wild tales and supernatural legends. One dismal story produced another still more dismal, and the baron nearly frightened some of the ladies into hysterics with the history of the goblin horseman that carried away the fair Leonora; a dreadful story, which has since been put into excellent verse, and is read and believed by all the world.

The bridegroom listened to this tale with profound attention. He kept his eyes steadily fixed on the baron, and, as the story drew to a close, began gradually to rise from his seat, growing taller and taller, until, in the baron's entranced eye, he seemed almost to tower into a giant. The moment the tale was finished, he heaved a deep sigh, and took a solemn farewell of the company. They were all amazement. The baron was perfectly thunderstruck.

"What! going to leave the castle at midnight? why, everything was prepared for his reception; a chamber was ready for him if he wished to retire."

The stranger shook his head mournfully and mysteriously; "I must lay my head in a different chamber to-night!"

There was something in this reply, and the tone in which it was uttered, that made the baron's heart misgive him; but he rallied his forces, and repeated his hospitable entreaties.

The stranger shook his head silently, but positively, at every offer; and, waving his farewell to the company, stalked slowly out of the hall. The maiden aunts were absolutely petrified; the bride hung her head, and a tear stole to her eye.

The baron followed the stranger to the great court of the castle, where the black charger stood pawing the earth, and snorting with impatience.—When they had reached the portal, whose deep archway was dimly lighted by a cresset,[16] the

---

[16] *cresset:* torch

stranger paused, and addressed the baron in a hollow tone of voice, which the vaulted roof rendered still more sepulchral. "Now that we are alone," he said, "I will impart to you the reason of my going. I have a solemn, and indispensable engagement" —

"Why," said the baron, "cannot you send some one in your place?"

"It admits of no substitute — I must attend it in person — I must away to Würtzburg cathedral" —

"Ay," said the baron, plucking up spirit, "but not until to-morrow — to-morrow you shall take your bride there."

"No! no!" replied the stranger, with tenfold solemnity, "my engagement is with no bride — the worms! the worms expect me! I am a dead man — I have been slain by robbers — my body lies at Würtzburg — at midnight I am to be buried — the grave is waiting for me — I must keep my appointment!"

He sprang on his black charger, dashed over the drawbridge, and the clattering of his horse's hoofs was lost in the whistling of the night-blast.

The baron returned to the hall in the utmost consternation, and related what had passed. Two ladies fainted outright, others sickened at the idea of having banqueted with a specter. It was the opinion of some, that this might be the wild huntsman, famous in German legend. Some talked of mountain sprites, of wood-demons, and of other supernatural beings, with which the good people of Germany have been so grievously harassed since time immemorial. One of the poor relations ventured to suggest that it might be some sportive evasion of the young cavalier, and that the very gloominess of the caprice seemed to accord with so melancholy a personage. This, however, drew on him the indignation of the whole company, and especially of the baron, who looked upon him as little better than an infidel; so that he was fain to abjure[17] his heresy as speedily as possible, and come into the faith of the true believers.

But whatever may have been the doubts entertained, they were completely put to an end by the arrival, next day, of regular missives, confirming the intelligence of the young

[17] *abjure:* renounce publicly

count's murder, and his interment in Würtzburg cathedral.

The dismay at the castle may well be imagined. The baron shut himself up in his chamber. The guests, who had come to rejoice with him, could not think of abandoning him in his distress. They wandered about the courts, or collected in groups in the hall, shaking their heads and shrugging their shoulders, at the troubles of so good a man; and sat longer than ever at table, and ate and drank more stoutly than ever, by way of keeping up their spirits. But the situation of the widowed bride was the most pitiable. To have lost a husband before she had even embraced him—and such a husband! If the very specter could be so gracious and noble, what must have been the living man. She filled the house with lamentations.

On the night of the second day of her widowhood, she had retired to her chamber, accompanied by one of her aunts, who insisted on sleeping with her. The aunt, who was one of the best tellers of ghost-stories in all Germany, had just been recounting one of her longest, and had fallen asleep in the very midst of it. The chamber was remote, and overlooked a small garden. The niece lay pensively gazing at the beams of the rising moon, as they trembled on the leaves of an aspentree before the lattice. The castle clock had just tolled midnight, when a soft strain of music stole up from the garden. She rose hastily from her bed, and stepped lightly to the window. A tall figure stood among the shadows of the trees. As it raised its head, a beam of moonlight fell upon the countenance. Heaven and earth! she beheld the Specter Bridegroom! A loud shriek at that moment burst upon her ear, and her aunt, who had been awakened by the music, and had followed her silently to the window, fell into her arms. When she looked again, the specter had disappeared.

Of the two females, the aunt now required the most soothing, for she was perfectly beside herself with terror. As to the young lady, there was something, even in the specter of her lover, that seemed endearing. There was still the semblance of manly beauty; and though the shadow of a man is but little calculated to satisfy the affections of a lovesick girl yet, where the substance is not to be had, even that is consoling. The aunt declared she would never sleep in that chamber again; the niece, for once, was refractory,[18] and declared as strongly that she would sleep in no other in the castle: the consequence was, that she had to sleep in it alone; but she drew a promise from her aunt not to relate the story of the specter lest she should be denied the only melancholy pleasure left her on earth—that of inhabiting the chamber over which the guardian shade of her lover kept its nightly vigils.

How long the good old lady would have observed this promise is uncertain, for she dearly loved to talk of the marvelous, and there is triumph in being the first to tell a frightful story; it is, however, still quoted in the neighborhood, as a memorable instance of female secrecy, that she kept it to herself for a whole week; when she was suddenly absolved from all further restraint, by intelligence brought to the breakfast-table one morning that the young lady was not to be found. Her room was empty—the bed had not been slept in— the window was open, and the bird had flown!

The astonishment and concern with which the intelligence was received can only be imagined by those who have witnessed the agitation which the mishaps of a great man cause among his friends. Even the poor relations paused for a moment from the indefatigable labors of the trencher;[19] when the aunt, who had at first been struck speechless, wrung her hands, and shrieked out, "The goblin! the goblin! she's carried away by the goblin!"

In a few words she related the fearful scene of the garden, and concluded that the specter must have carried off his bride. Two of the domestics corroborated the opinion, for they had heard the clattering of a horse's hoofs down the mountain about midnight, and had no doubt that it was the specter on his black charger, bearing her away to the tomb. All present were struck with the direful probability; for events of the kind are extremely common in Germany, as many well-authenticated histories bear witness.

What a lamentable situation was that of the poor baron! What a heart-rending dilemma for a fond father, and a member

---

[18] *refractory:* stubborn
[19] *trencher:* hearty eater

of the great family of Katzenellenbogen! His only daughter had either been rapt[20] away to the grave, or he was to have some wood-demon for a son-in-law, and, perchance, a troop of goblin grandchildren. As usual, he was completely bewildered, and all the castle in an uproar. The men were ordered to take horse, and scour every road and path and glen of the Odenwald. The baron himself had just drawn on his jack-boots, girded on his sword and was about to mount his steed to sally forth on the doubtful quest, when he was brought to a pause by a new apparition. A lady was seen approaching the castle, mounted on a palfrey,[21] attended by a cavalier on horseback. She galloped up to the gate, sprang from her horse, and falling at the baron's feet, embraced his knees. It was his lost daughter, and her companion —the Specter Bridegroom! The baron was astounded. He looked at his daughter, then at the specter, and almost doubted the evidence of his senses. The latter, too, was wonderfully improved in his appearance since his visit to the world of spirits. His dress was splendid, and set off a noble figure of manly symmetry. He was no longer pale and melancholy. His fine countenance was flushed with the glow of youth, and joy rioted in his large dark eye.

The mystery was soon cleared up. The cavalier (for, in truth, as you must have known all the while, he was no goblin) announced himself as Sir Herman Von Starkenfaust. He related his adventure with the young count. He told how he had hastened to the castle to deliver the unwelcome tidings, but that the eloquence of the baron had interrupted him in every attempt to tell his tale. How the sight of the bride had completely captivated him, and that to pass a few hours near her, he had tacitly suffered the mistake to continue. How he had been sorely perplexed in what way to make a decent retreat, until the baron's goblin stories had suggested his eccentric exit. How, fearing the feudal hostility of the family, he had repeated his visits by stealth—had haunted the garden beneath the young lady's window—had wooed—had won—

---

[20] *rapt:* snatched
[21] *palfrey:* small saddle horse

had borne away in triumph—and, in a word, had wedded the fair.

Under any other circumstances the baron would have been inflexible, for he was tenacious of paternal authority, and devoutly obstinate in all family feuds; but he loved his daughter; he had lamented her as lost; he rejoiced to find her still alive; and, though her husband was of a hostile house, yet, thank Heaven, he was not a goblin. There was something, it must be acknowledged, that did not exactly accord with his notions of strict veracity, in the joke the knight had passed upon him of his being a dead man; but several old friends present, who had served in the wars, assured him that every stratagem was excusable in love, and that the cavalier was entitled to special privilege, having lately served as a trooper.

Matters, therefore, were happily arranged. The baron pardoned the young couple on the spot. The revels at the castle were resumed. The poor relations overwhelmed this new member of the family with loving-kindness; he was so gallant, so generous—and so rich. The aunts, it is true, were somewhat scandalized that their system of strict seclusion and passive obedience should be so badly exemplified, but attributed it all to their negligence in not having the windows grated. One of them was particularly mortified at having her marvelous story marred, and that the only specter she had ever seen should turn out a counterfeit; but the niece seemed perfectly happy at having found him, substantial flesh and blood—and so the story ends.

FOR DISCUSSION

1. What do you consider most important in this story: the events that tell what happened, the characters, the setting, or the manner in which the story is told? Tell why. Which interests you most and, in your opinion, is best presented?
2. From the title, you would expect the stranger to be the main character. Is he? Why do you think Irving devotes so much attention to the baron? What kind of person is he? How believable are the specter bridegroom and his bride? Do you think that Irving

expects you to take them seriously? Cite evidence from the story.

3. Several characteristics of the romantic spirit (see page 517) are revealed in the setting of this story, the choice of characters, and the suggestion of the supernatural. Point these out.

4. Throughout the story there is gentle humor in Irving's picturing of situations and characters, particularly the maiden aunts and the poor relatives, and in his commentaries on human nature and the customs of the Old World. Point out the comments and passages you enjoy most.

5. Critics generally consider the use of coincidence (see page 514) a weak literary device in creating a story plot. Where does it occur in this story and what purpose does it serve? If you think it detracts from the story, tell why. (Irving always considered the plot "merely as a frame on which to stretch my materials.")

6. Two scenes in the story are especially melodramatic. Where do they occur? Do you think that Irving was following the literary fashion of his day, or was he overplaying these emotional situations as part of the humor? If possible find evidence for your opinion in the story.

7. What qualities of style can you find in this story which reveal an "artist-like touch" and which you consider characteristic of Irving's descriptions?

FOR COMPOSITION

1. In a short composition, describe the qualities of character, the behavior, and the accomplishments which would be most valued in a baron's daughter. Use the story as your source of information.

2. Using the specter bridegroom as an example, write your impressions of a gallant cavalier. You may want to draw some comparisons between him and his modern counterpart, the movie or television idol.

James Fenimore Cooper

The romantic novels of James Fenimore Cooper made as important a contribution to American literature as did the stories of Washington Irving. However, Cooper's purpose was not just to entertain his readers, but to "put the whole of America, roots and all, into books." He achieved his purpose most notably in his series of novels, *The Leatherstocking Tales,* with its famous hero, called variously Leatherstocking, Natty Bumppo, and Hawkeye. In his idealization of the frontiersman — strong, silent, resourceful, fighting evil single-handed — Cooper created a hero, typically American, who has come down to the present day in many forms, not only in fiction but in the movies and on television. The following selection is a chapter from *The Deerslayer,* the novel which deals with Leatherstocking as a very young man.

Leatherstocking Kills His First Indian

Day had fairly dawned before the young man, whom we have left in the situation described in the last chapter,[1] again opened his eyes. This was no sooner done than he started up and looked about him with the eagerness of one who suddenly felt the importance of accurately ascertaining his precise position. His rest had been deep and undisturbed; and when he awoke, it was with a clearness of intellect and a readiness of resources that were much needed at that particular moment. The sun had not risen, it is true, but the vault of heaven was rich with the winning softness that "brings and shuts the day," while the whole air was filled with the carols of birds,

---

[1] The previous night, during a scouting trip, Deerslayer had waited in a canoe for his friends Hutter and Hurry. He saw them captured by the Indians but he managed to escape. He spent the night drifting in one canoe, with two more in tow, waiting until morning to attempt to rescue Hutter's daughters.

the hymns of the feathered tribe. These sounds first told Deerslayer the risks he ran. The air—for wind it could scarce be called—was still light, it is true, but it had increased a little in the course of the night, and as the canoes were mere feathers on the water, they had drifted twice the expected distance; and, what was still more dangerous, had approached so near the base of the mountain that here rose precipitously from the eastern shore, as to render the carols of the birds plainly audible. This was not the worst. The third canoe had taken the same direction, and was slowly drifting toward a point where it must inevitably touch, unless turned aside by a shift of wind or human hands. In other respects, nothing presented itself to attract attention or to awaken alarm. The castle stood on its shoal, nearly abreast of the canoes, for the drift had amounted to miles in the course of the night, and the ark lay fastened to its piles, as both had been left so many hours before.

As a matter of course, Deerslayer's attention was first given to the canoe ahead. It was already quite near the point, and a very few strokes of the paddle sufficed to tell him that it must touch before he could possibly overtake it. Just at this moment, too, the wind inopportunely freshened, rendering the drift of the light craft much more rapid and certain. Feeling the impossibility of preventing a contact with the land, the young man wisely determined not to heat himself with unnecessary exertions; but first looking to the priming of his piece,[2] he proceeded slowly and warily toward the point, taking care to make a little circuit, that he might be exposed on only one side as he approached.

The canoe adrift, being directed by no such intelligence, pursued its proper way and grounded on a small sunken rock, at the distance of three or four yards from the shore. Just at that moment, Deerslayer had got abreast of the point and turned the bows of his own boat to the land, first casting loose his tow, that his movements might be unencumbered. The canoe hung an instant on the rock; then it rose a hair's-breadth on an almost imperceptible swell of the water, swung round, floated clear, and reached the strand. All this the young man

[2] *piece*: rifle

noted, but it neither quickened his pulses nor hastened his hand. If anyone had been lying in wait for the arrival of the waif, he must be seen, and the utmost caution in approaching the shore became indispensable; if no one was in ambush, hurry was unnecessary. The point being nearly diagonally opposite to the Indian encampment, he hoped the last, though the former was not only possible, but probable; for the savages were prompt in adopting all the expedients of their particular modes of warfare, and quite likely had many scouts searching the shores for craft to carry them off to the castle. As a glance at the lake from any height or projection would expose the smallest object on its surface, there was little hope that either of the canoes could pass unseen; and Indian sagacity needed no instruction to tell which way a boat or a log would drift, when the direction of the wind was known. As Deerslayer drew nearer and nearer to the land, the stroke of his paddle grew slower, his eye became more watchful, and his ears and nostrils almost dilated with the effort to detect any lurking danger. 'Twas a trying moment for a novice, nor was there the encouragement which even the timid sometimes feel, when conscious of being observed and commended. He was entirely alone, thrown on his own resources, and was cheered by no friendly eye, emboldened by no encouraging voice. Notwithstanding all these circumstances, the most experienced veteran in forest warfare could not have behaved better. Equally free from recklessness and hesitation, his advance was marked by a sort of philosophical prudence that appeared to render him superior to all motives but those which were best calculated to effect his purpose. Such was the commencement of a career in forest exploits, that afterward rendered this man, in his way, and under the limits of his habits and opportunities, as renowned as many a hero whose name had adorned the pages of works more celebrated than legends simple as ours can ever become.

When about a hundred yards from the shore, Deerslayer rose in the canoe, gave three or four vigorous strokes with the paddle, sufficient of themselves to impel the bark to land, and then quickly laying aside the instrument of labor, he seized that of war. He was in the very act of raising the rifle, when a sharp report was followed by the buzz of a bullet that passed so near his body as to cause him involuntarily to start. The next instant Deerslayer staggered and fell his whole length in the bottom of the canoe. A yell—it came from a single voice—followed, and an Indian leaped from the bushes upon the open area of the point, bounding toward the canoe. This was the moment the young man desired. He rose on the instant and leveled his own rifle at his uncovered foe; but his finger hesitated about pulling the trigger on one whom he held at such a disadvantage. This little delay, probably, saved the life of the Indian, who bounded back into the cover as swiftly as he had broken out of it. In the meantime, Deerslayer had been swiftly approaching the land, and his own canoe reached the point just as his enemy disappeared. As its movements had not been directed, it touched the shore a few yards from the other boat; and though the rifle of his foe had to be loaded, there was not time to secure his prize and carry it beyond danger before he would be exposed to another shot. Under the circumstances, therefore, he did not pause an instant, but dashed into the woods and sought a cover.

On the immediate point there was a small open area, partly in native grass and partly beach, but a dense fringe of bushes lined its upper side. This narrow belt of dwarf vegetation passed, one issued immediately into the high and gloomy vaults of the forest. The land was tolerably level for a few hundred feet, and then it rose precipitously in a mountainside. The trees were tall, large, and so free from underbrush that they resembled vast columns, irregularly scattered, upholding a dome of leaves. Although they stood tolerably close together, for their ages and size, the eye could penetrate to considerable distances; and bodies of men, even, might have engaged beneath their cover with concert and intelligence.

Deerslayer knew that his adversary must be employed in reloading, unless he had fled. The former proved to be the case, for the young man had no sooner placed himself behind a tree than he caught a glimpse of the arm of the Indian, his body being concealed by an oak, in the very act of forcing the leathered bullet home. Nothing would have been easier than to spring forward and decide the affair by a close assault on

his unprepared foe; but every feeling of Deerslayer revolted
at such a step, although his own life had just been attempted
from a cover. He was yet unpracticed in the ruthless expedients of savage warfare, of which he knew nothing except by
tradition and theory, and it struck him as an unfair advantage
to assail an unarmed foe. His color had heightened, his eye
frowned, his lips were compressed, and all his energies were
collected and ready; but, instead of advancing to fire, he
dropped his rifle to the usual position of a sportsman in readiness to catch his aim, and muttered to himself, unconscious
that he was speaking:

"No, no—that may be redskin warfare, but it's not a Christian's gifts. Let the miscreant[3] charge, and then we'll take it
out like men; for the canoe he *must* not and *shall* not have.
No, no; let him have time to load, and God will take care of
the right!"

All this time the Indian had been so intent on his own movements that he was even ignorant that his enemy was in the
wood. His only apprehension was that the canoe would be recovered and carried away before he might be in readiness to
prevent it. He had sought the cover from habit, but was within
a few feet of the fringe of bushes, and could be at the margin
of the forest in readiness to fire in a moment. The distance
between him and his enemy was about fifty yards, and the
trees were so arranged by nature that the line of sight was not
interrupted, except by the particular trees behind which each
party stood.

His rifle was no sooner loaded than the savage glanced
around him, and advanced incautiously as regarded the real,
but stealthily as respected the fancied position of his enemy,
until he was fairly exposed. Then Deerslayer stepped from
behind his own cover and hailed him.

"Thisaway, redskin; thisaway, if you're looking for me," he
called out. "I'm young in war, but not so young as to stand on
an open beach to be shot down like an owl by daylight. It
rests on yourself whether it's peace or war atween us; for my
gifts are white gifts, and I'm not one of them that thinks it
valiant to slay human mortals singly in the woods."

[3] *miscreant:* villain

The savage was a good deal startled by this sudden discovery of the danger he ran. He had a little knowledge of English, however, and caught the drift of the other's meaning. He was also too well schooled to betray alarm, but, dropping the butt of his rifle to the earth with an air of confidence, he made a gesture of lofty courtesy. All this was done with the ease and self-possession of one accustomed to consider no man his superior. In the midst of this consummate acting, however, the volcano that raged within caused his eyes to glare and his nostrils to dilate, like those of some wild beast that is suddenly prevented from taking the fatal leap.

"Two canoes," he said, in the deep guttural tones of his race, holding up the number of fingers he mentioned, by way of preventing mistakes; "one for you—one for me."

"No, no, Mingo, that will never do. You own neither; and neither shall you have, as long as I can prevent it. I know it's war atween your people and mine, but that's no reason why human mortals should slay each other like savage creatur's that meet in the woods; go your way, then, and leave me to go mine. The world is large enough for us both; and when we meet fairly in battle, why, the Lord will order the fate of each of us."

"Good!" exclaimed the Indian; "my brother missionary— great talk; all about Manitou."[4]

"Not so—not so, warrior. I'm not good enough for the Moravians,[5] and am too good for most of the other vagabonds that preach about in the woods. No, no, I'm only a hunter, as yet, though afore the peace is made, 'tis like enough there'll be occasion to strike a blow at some of your people. Still, I wish it to be done in fair fight, and not in a quarrel about the ownership of a miserable canoe."

"Good! My brother very young—but he is very wise. Little warrior—great talker. Chief, sometimes, in council "

"I don't know this, nor do I say it, Injin," returned Deerslayer, coloring a little at the ill-concealed sarcasm of the

---

[4]*Manitou:* to the Indians, one of the powers which dominate the forces of nature

[5]*Moravians:* a Protestant religious sect

other's manner; "I look forward to a life in the woods, and I only hope it may be a peaceable one. All young men must go on the warpath when there's occasion, but war isn't needfully massacre. I've seen enough of the last, this very night, to know that Providence frowns on it; and I now invite you to go your own way, while I go mine; and hope that we may part fri'nds."

"Good! My brother has two scalp—gray hair under t'other. Old wisdom—young tongue."

Here the savage advanced with confidence, his hand extended, his face smiling, and his whole bearing denoting amity and respect. Deerslayer met his offered friendship in a proper spirit, and they shook hands cordially, each endeavoring to assure the other of his sincerity and desire to be at peace.

"All have his own," said the Indian; "my canoe, mine; your canoe, your'n. Go look; if your'n, you keep; if mine, I keep."

"That's just, redskin; though you must be wrong in thinking the canoe your property. However, seein' is believin', and we'll go down to the shore, where you may look with your own eyes; for it's likely you'll object to trustin' altogether to mine."

The Indian uttered his favorite exclamation of "good!" and then they walked side by side toward the shore. There was no apparent distrust in the manner of either, the Indian moving in advance, as if he wished to show his companion that he did not fear turning his back to him. As they reached the open ground the former pointed toward Deerslayer's boat, and said emphatically:

"No mine—paleface canoe. *This* red man's. No want other man's canoe—want his own."

"You're wrong, redskin, you're altogther wrong. This canoe was left in old Hutter's keeping, and is his'n according to all law, red or white, till its owner comes to claim it. Here's the seats and the stitching of the bark to speak for themselves. No man ever know'd an Injin to turn off such work."

"Good! My brother little old—big wisdom. Injin no make him. White man's work."

"I'm glad you think so, for holding out to the contrary might

have made ill blood atween us; everyone having a right to
take possession of his own. I'll just shove the canoe out of
reach of dispute at once, as the quickest way of settling
difficulties."

While Deerslayer was speaking, he put a foot against the
end of the light boat, and giving a vigorous shove, he sent it
out into the lake a hundred feet or more, where, taking the
true current, it would necessarily float past the point and be
in no further danger of coming ashore. The savage started
at this ready and decided expedient, and his companion saw
that he cast a hurried and fierce glance at his own canoe, or
that which contained the paddles. The change of manner,
however, was but momentary, and then the Iroquois resumed
his air of friendliness and a smile of satisfaction.

"Good!" he repeated, with stronger emphasis than ever.
"Young head, old mind. Know how to settle quarrel. Farewell, brother. He go to house in water—muskrat house—Injin
go to camp; tell chiefs no find canoe."

Deerslayer was not sorry to hear this proposal, for he felt
anxious to join the females, and he took the offered hand of
the Indian very willingly. The parting words were friendly,
and, while the red man walked calmly toward the wood, with
the rifle in the hollow of his arm, without once looking back
in uneasiness or distrust, the white man moved toward the
remaining canoe, carrying his piece in the same pacific manner, it is true, but keeping his eyes fastened on the movements
of the other. The distrust, however, seemed to be altogether
uncalled for, and as if ashamed to have entertained it, the
young man averted his look and stepped carelessly up to his
boat. Here he began to push the canoe from the shore and to
make his other preparations for departing. He might have
been thus employed a minute, when, happening to turn his
face toward the land, his quick and certain eye told him at a
glance the imminent jeopardy in which his life was placed.
The black, ferocious eyes of the savage were glancing on him,
like those of the crouching tiger, through a small opening in
the bushes, and the muzzle of his rifle seemed already to be
opening in a line with his own body.

Then, indeed, the long practice of Deerslayer, as a hunter,

did him good service. Accustomed to fire with the deer on the bound, and often when the precise position of the animal's body had in a manner to be guessed at, he used the same expedients here. To cock and poise his rifle were the acts of a single moment and a single motion; then, aiming almost without sighting, he fired into the bushes where he knew a body ought to be, in order to sustain the appalling countenance which alone was visible. There was not time to raise the piece any higher or to take a more deliberate aim. So rapid were his movements that both parties discharged their pieces at the same instant, the concussions mingling in one report. The mountains, indeed, gave back but a single echo. Deerslayer dropped his piece and stood, with head erect, steady as one of the pines in the calm of a June morning, watching the result; while the savage gave the yell that has become historical for its appalling influence, leaped through the bushes and came bounding across the open ground, flourishing a tomahawk. Still Deerslayer moved not, but stood with his unloaded rifle fallen against his shoulders, while, with a hunter's habits, his hands were mechanically feeling for the powder horn and charger. When about forty feet from his enemy, the savage hurled his keen weapon; but it was with an eye so vacant and a hand so unsteady and feeble that the young man caught it by the handle as it was flying past him. At that instant the Indian staggered and fell his whole length on the ground.

"I know'd it—I know'd it!" exclaimed Deerslayer, who was already preparing to force a fresh bullet into his rifle; "I know'd it must come to this, as soon as I had got the range from the creatur's eyes. A man sights suddenly and fires quick when his own life's in danger; yes, I know'd it would come to this. I was about the hundredth part of a second too quick for him, or it might have been bad for me! The riptyle's bullet has just grazed my side—but, say what you will for or ag'in 'em, a redskin is by no means as sartain with powder and ball as a white man. Their gifts don't seem to lie thataway. Even Chingachgook,[6] great as he is in other matters, isn't downright deadly with the rifle."

---

[6] *Chingachgook:* Indian friend of Deerslayer

By this time the piece was reloaded, and Deerslayer, after tossing the tomahawk into the canoe, advanced to his victim, and stood over him, leaning on his rifle, in melancholy attention. It was the first instance in which he had seen a man fall in battle—it was the first fellow creature against whom he had ever seriously raised his own hand. The sensations were novel; and regret, with the freshness of our better feelings, mingled with his triumph. The Indian was not dead, though shot directly through the body. He lay on his back motionless, but his eyes, now full of consciousness, watched each action of his victor—as the fallen bird regards the fowler—jealous of every movement. The man probably expected the fatal blow which was to precede the loss of his scalp; or perhaps he anticipated that this latter act of cruelty would precede his death. Deerslayer read his thoughts; and he found a melancholy satisfaction in relieving the apprehensions of the helpless savage.

"No, no, redskin," he said; "you've nothing more to fear from me. I am of a Christian stock, and scalping is not of my gifts. I'll just make sartain of your rifle and then come back and do you what sarvice I can. Though here, I can't stay much longer, as the crack of three rifles will be apt to bring some of your devils down upon me."

The close of this was said in a sort of a soliloquy, as the young man went in quest of the fallen rifle. The piece was found where its owner had dropped it, and was immediately put into the canoe. Laying his own rifle at its side, Deerslayer then returned and stood over the Indian again.

"All inmity atween you and me's at an ind, redskin," he said; "and you may set your heart at rest on the score of the scalp or any further injury. My gifts are white, as I've told you; and I hope my conduct will be white also!"

Could looks have conveyed all they meant, it is probable Deerslayer's innocent vanity on the subject of color would have been rebuked a little; but he comprehended the gratitude that was expressed in the eyes of the dying savage, without in the least detecting the bitter sarcasm that struggled with the better feeling.

"Water!" ejaculated the thirsty and unfortunate creature; "give poor Injin water."

"Aye, water you shall have, if you drink the lake dry. I'll just carry you down to it, that you may take your fill. This is the way, they tell me, with all wounded people—water is their greatest comfort and delight."

So saying, Deerslayer raised the Indian in his arms, and carried him to the lake. Here he first helped him to take an attitude in which he could appease his burning thirst; after which he seated himself on a stone and took the head of his wounded adversary in his own lap and endeavored to soothe his anguish in the best manner he could.

"It would be sinful in me to tell you your time hadn't come, warrior," he commenced, "and therefore I'll not say it. You've passed the middle age already, and, considerin' the sort of lives ye lead, your days have been pretty well filled. The principal thing now is to look forward to what comes next. Neither redskin nor paleface, on the whole, calculates much on sleepin' forever; but both expect to live in another world. Each has his gifts, and will be judged by 'em, and, I suppose, you've thought these matters over enough, not to stand in need of sarmons when the trial comes. You'll find your happy hunting grounds, if you've been a just Injin; if an onjust, you'll meet your desarts in another way. I've my own idees about these things; but you're too old and exper'enced to need any explanations from one as young as I."

"Good!" ejaculated the Indian, whose voice retained its depth even as life ebbed away; "young head—old wisdom!"

"It's sometimes a consolation, when the ind comes, to know that them we've harmed, or tried to harm, forgive us. I suppose natur' seeks this relief, by way of getting a pardon on 'arth; as we never can know whether He pardons, who is all in all, till judgment itself comes. It's soothing to know that *any* pardon at such times; and that, I conclude, is the secret. Now, as for myself, I overlook altogether your designs ag'in my life; first, because no harm came of 'em; next, because it's your gifts and natur' and trainin', and I ought not to have trusted you at all; and, finally and chiefly, because I can bear no ill will to a dying man, whether heathen or Christian. So put your heart at ease, so far as I'm consarned; you know best what other matters ought to trouble you, or what ought to give you satisfaction in so trying a moment."

It is probable that the Indian had some of the fearful glimpses of the unknown state of being which God, in mercy, seems at times to afford to all the human race; but they were necessarily in conformity with his habits and prejudices. Like most of his people, and like too many of our own, he thought more of dying in a way to gain applause among those he left than to secure a better state of existence hereafter. While Deerslayer was speaking, his mind was a little bewildered, though he felt that the intention was good; and when he had done, a regret passed over his spirit that none of his own tribe were present to witness his stoicism[7] under extreme bodily suffering and the firmness with which he met his end. With the high innate courtesy that so often distinguishes the Indian warrior before he becomes corrupted by too much intercourse with the worst class of the white men, he endeavored to express his thankfulness for the other's good intentions, and to let him understand that they were appreciated.

"Good!" he repeated, for this was an English word much used by the savages—"good! Young head; young *heart,* too. *Old* heart tough; no shed tear. Hear Indian when he die, and no want to lie—what he call him?"

"Deerslayer is the name I bear now, though the Delawares have said that when I get back from this warpath, I shall have a more manly title, provided I can 'arn one."

"That good name for boy—poor name for warrior. He get better quick. No fear *there"*—the savage had strength sufficient, under the strong excitement he felt, to raise a hand and tap the young man on his breast—"eye sartain—finger lightning—aim, death—great warrior soon. No Deerslayer—Hawkeye—Hawkeye—Hawkeye. Shake hand."

Deerslayer—or Hawkeye, as the youth was then first named, for in after years he bore the appellation throughout all that region—Deerslayer took the hand of the savage, whose last breath was drawn in that attitude, gazing in admiration at the countenance of a stranger, who had shown so much readiness, skill, and firmness, in a scene that was equally trying and

---

[7] *stoicism:* indifference to pain

novel. When the reader remembers it is the highest gratification an Indian can receive to see his enemy betray weakness, he will be better able to appreciate the conduct which had extorted so great a concession at such a moment.

"His spirit has fled!" said Deerslayer, in a suppressed, melancholy voice. "Ah's me! Well, to this we must all come, sooner or later; and he is happiest, let his skin be of what color it may, who is best fitted to meet it. Here lies the body of no doubt a brave warrior, and the soul is already flying toward its Heaven or Hell, whether that be a happy hunting ground, a place scant of game, regions of glory, according to Moravian doctrine, or flames or fire! So it happens, too, as regards other matters! Here have old Hutter and Hurry Harry got themselves into difficulty, if they hav'n't got themselves into torment and death, and all for a bounty that luck offers to me in what many would think a lawful and suitable manner. But not a farthing of such money shall cross my hand. White I was born, and white will I die; clinging to color to the last, even though the King's majesty, his governors, and all his councils, both at home and in the Colonies, forget from what they come, and where they hope to go, and all for a little advantage in warfare. No, no — warrior, hand of mine shall never molest your scalp, and so your soul may rest in peace on the p'int of making a decent appearance, when the body comes to join it, in your own land of spirits."

Deerslayer arose as soon as he had spoken. Then he placed the body of the dead man in a sitting posture, with its back against the little rock, taking the necessary care to prevent it from falling or in any way settling into an attitude that might be thought unseemly by the sensitive, though wild, notions of a savage. When this duty was performed, the young man stood gazing at the grim countenance of his fallen foe, in a sort of melancholy abstraction. As was his practice, however, a habit gained by living so much alone in the forest, he then began again to give utterance to his thoughts and feelings aloud.

"I didn't wish your life, redskin," he said, "but you left me no choice atween killing or being killed. Each party acted according to his gifts, I suppose, and blame can light on neither. You were treacherous, according to your natur' in war, and I was a little oversightful, as I'm apt to be in trusting others. Well, this is my first battle with a human mortal, though it's not likely to be the last. I have fou't most of the creatur's of the forest, such as bears, wolves, painters, and catamounts, but this is the beginning with the redskins. If I was Injin-born, now, I might tell of this, or carry in the scalp, and boast of the expl'ite afore the whole tribe; or, if my inimy had only been even a bear, 'twould have been nat'ral and proper to let everybody know what had happened; but I don't well see how I'm to let even Chingachgook into this secret, so long as it can be done only by boasting with a white tongue. And why should I wish to boast of it a'ter all? It's slaying a human, although he was a savage; and how do I know that he was a just Injin; and that he has not been taken away suddenly to anything but happy hunting grounds. When it's onsartain whether good or evil has been done, the wisest way is not to be boastful — still, I *should* like Chingachgook to know that I haven't discredited the Delawares or my training!". . .

FOR DISCUSSION

1. From the incident recounted in this chapter, what impression do you gain of the frontiersman, the "noble red men," and the relationship between them? Do you think that Cooper idealizes them? Explain.

2. Some critics consider Cooper a master storyteller. He must, therefore, have excelled (a) in creating dramatic situations that involve the characters in a conflict, (b) in building suspense, and (c) in keeping the action of the story moving rapidly forward. Point out examples which show that he does, or does not, possess these storytelling gifts.

3. What criticisms might be made of the way Cooper has his characters speak and of what he has them say? Would you say that the dialogue makes the characters seem more real or less so? Explain.

4. In the introduction to this section, it was stated that Cooper believed that literature must be created from the inside out. What the writer wanted to express — the ideas, feelings, and experiences — should determine how he expressed them. Try to find evidence of this belief in the chapter you have just read.

FOR COMPOSITION

1. Through the words, thoughts, and actions of Deerslayer, the author revealed his attitude toward the beliefs and practices of the so-called "savages." In a short composition, state what you think Cooper's attitude is. Give examples to support your statement.

2. Write a short essay — humorous if you like — in which you compare or contrast the incident recounted in this selection with a similar one you might see in a Western movie or television program.

THE ROMANTIC TRIUMPH

By 1855 America could boast of a national literature that was worthy to stand independently and proudly with the literature of the Old World. Actually, within five years, 1850 to 1855, American writers produced more works of quality and originality than have been produced in a similar period in the entire history of American literature. These works included four of the world's great literary masterpieces: *Representative Men* by Ralph Waldo Emerson, *Walden* by Henry Thoreau, *The Scarlet Letter* by Nathaniel Hawthorne, and *Moby Dick* by Herman Melville. They also included the poems, stories, and essays of Edgar Allan Poe, America's first distinguished Southern writer. The contribution of Poe, Hawthorne, and Melville was one of literary forms and techniques. No longer would American writers have to turn to the Old World for models of excellence.

The spirit of romanticism is as evident in the works of Poe, Hawthorne, and Melville as in the works of Irving and Cooper. These later writers also glorified nature and the common man, made use of the strange and unfamiliar, and were fascinated by the traditions, beliefs, and legends of the past. In addition, they explored the boundless universe of the fantastic and the supernatural — Poe to a greater extent than Hawthorne or Melville. Because they expressed themselves with such artistry and in such different forms and styles, their work represents "the romantic triumph" in the development of American literature.

The life of EDGAR ALLAN POE has inspired many fanciful legends that are as misleading as they are intriguing. Neither a misunderstood prophet nor a devil-in-disguise, Poe was, in fact, a thoroughly professional writer with all the practical sense of the man who depends wholly on his pen for a livelihood. A popular poet, critic, and writer of short stories, he called himself "essentially a magazinist" and had a businessman's knowledge of his market. He was, in addition, an outstanding reviewer and editor, and thus exerted an important influence on his literary contemporaries.

Poe's practical approach to literature made him contemptuous of most of the leading writers of his day — particularly of the New England writers. Calling Boston the "Frogpond," he viciously attacked the Transcendentalists and accused Longfellow of plagiarism. Emerson, in turn, referred to Poe as "the jingle man." Longfellow enraged him by simply ignoring his attacks. Between Poe and Hawthorne, however, there was no quarrel. Poe called this New England writer one of America's "few men of indisputable genius," and Hawthorne reciprocated by making public his admiration for the originality of Poe's tales.

In his countless reviews and in his essays on literary theory, Poe produced what one scholar has called "the first body of valuable aesthetic criticism on this side of the Atlantic." In his review of Hawthorne's *Twice-Told Tales*, he pointed out that every element in a short story should contribute to the story's single effect.

With a consistency unusual among literary men, Poe practiced what he preached. His stories of mystery and suspense, which had an important influence on European writers, are remarkable for their craftsmanship and consistency of tone and mood. In his search for beauty, Poe did not, in the manner of many romantic writers, simply wait to be inspired. He used all the powers of his intellect and imagination to create beauty.

NATHANIEL HAWTHORNE, like Poe, was constantly concerned with finding the literary forms and techniques best suited to the subjects and themes that interested him. He could not, however, agree with Poe that moral problems have no place in literature. Born of Puritan stock in Salem, Massachusetts, Hawthorne could never ignore the principle of evil and the part which evil plays in men's lives and in society. He did not, however, seek to dictate the morals and behavior of his readers as his Puritan ancestors had done. His task, as he saw it, was to analyze the effects of sin—whether thought or committed—on the human heart and mind. For Hawthorne, the Unpardonable Sin was that coldness of heart in man that causes him to separate himself from those around him, resulting in a deep sense of guilt.

He did not believe, however, that the writer who is concerned with conveying ideas can limit himself to the common incidents of common life. The real must be combined with the imaginary—even with the supernatural—and be made believable. One way was to create a setting for each tale that was unfamiliar to his readers, such as a seventeenth-century New England village. Another way was to use the supernatural in such a way that the reader could, if he chose, interpret it as a natural phenomenon. He achieved this by always having the supernatural reported by a character whose perceptions were unreliable, or having it witnessed at a moment so dramatic and emotional that a hallucination would be understandable. The viewers could have perceived sights or sounds that were not actually present. A third way was to create a mood that pervaded the entire tale, making the unreal seem real and the emotional, psychological, or fantastic effect of both seem more intense.

For even a master craftsman like Hawthorne the task of telling a story and, at the same time, dealing with complex spiritual problems was not easy. He was not the first American writer to make use of the symbol—an object which stands for an idea, belief, moral state, ambition, or the like. In "The Minister's Black Veil," for example, the veil is the central symbol, and during the course of the tale, it comes to have not one but several meanings. Hawthorne used symbols in most of his tales and novels, and with striking effect. Through them he portrayed some enduring, profound, genuine traits in human nature.

HERMAN MELVILLE recognized the existence of evil in the world and insisted that "virtues and vices alike depend upon a certain excess." In Hawthorne he found a fellow-American who was also concerned with "that which is beneath the seeming" and who shared his tragic view of life. When he first read Hawthorne's "dark tales" in the summer of 1850, he was deeply moved by them. Before that time, Melville had written conventional adventure tales and had experimented with allegory. Responding to Hawthorne's "deep intellect, which drops down into the universe like a plummet," Melville learned how a literary work can be romantic and tragic at the same time. The following year Melville wrote *Moby Dick*, which many critics consider America's greatest novel.

Melville's debt to Hawthorne must not be exaggerated, however. There were many more differences than similarities between the two men and, therefore, between their respective approaches to life and literature. Hawthorne was something of a recluse and drew on his native New England for subject matter; Melville was a wanderer and wrote about the sea and faraway places. Moreover, Hawthorne's restraint, moodiness, and aloofness contrast sharply with Melville's warm, democratic sympathy for all men. Melville's ultimate reference point was always "the essential dignity of man, which no legislator has a right to violate."

Melville found the basis of that dignity in man's capacity to accept defeat and to persevere. He believed that all men share the same lot: all live in the same hostile universe and all ultimately experience suffering. Accordingly, Melville's heroes and heroines are almost invariably humble people who gain wisdom and stature through failure and suffering. By combining the romantic spirit with a tragic view of life, Melville gave a new dimension to American literature.

Edgar Allan Poe

Through painstaking effort and stringent self-criticism, Edgar Allan Poe made himself a master craftsman of the short story. The originator of the American detective story, he also gave his imagination full freedom in creating a variety of supernatural tales in the Gothic tradition of horror and fantasy. One of the most brilliant is "The Masque[1] of the Red Death," which combines meticulous plot organization with a flair for dramatic effect.

The Masque of the Red Death

The "Red Death" had long devastated the country. No pestilence had ever been so fatal, or so hideous. Blood was its Avatar[2] and its seal—the redness and the horror of blood. There were sharp pains, and sudden dizziness, and then profuse bleeding at the pores, with dissolution.[3] The scarlet stains upon the body and especially upon the face of the victim, were the pest ban[4] which shut him out from the aid and from the sympathy of his fellowmen. And the whole seizure, progress and termination of the disease, were the incidents of half an hour.

But the Prince Prospero was happy and dauntless and sagacious.[5] When his dominions were half depopulated, he summoned to his presence a thousand hale and light-hearted friends from among the knights and dames of his court, and with these retired to the deep seclusion of one of his castellated abbeys. This was an extensive and magnificent struc-

---

[1] *masque:* a party at which masks and costumes are worn
[2] *Avatar:* bodily manifestation
[3] *dissolution:* death
[4] *pest ban:* plague curse
[5] *sagacious:* wise, shrewd

ture, the creation of the prince's own eccentric yet august taste. A strong and lofty wall girdled it in. This wall had gates of iron. The courtiers, having entered, brought furnaces and massy hammers and welded the bolts. They resolved to leave means neither of ingress or egress to the sudden impulses of despair or frenzy from within. The abbey was amply provisioned. With such precautions the courtiers might bid defiance to contagion. The external world could take care of itself. In the meantime it was folly to grieve, or to think. The prince had provided all the appliances of pleasure. There were buffoons, there were improvisatori,[6] there were ballet dancers, there were musicians, there was Beauty, there was wine. All these and security were within. Without was the "Red Death."

It was toward the close of the fifth or sixth month of his seclusion, and while the pestilence raged most furiously abroad, that the Prince Prospero entertained his thousand friends at a masked ball of the most unusual magnificence.

It was a voluptuous scene, that masquerade. But first let me tell of the rooms in which it was held. There were seven—an imperial suite. In many palaces, however, such suites form a long and straight vista, while the folding doors slide back nearly to the walls on either hand, so that the view of the whole extent is scarcely impeded. Here the case was very different; as might have been expected from the duke's love of the *bizarre.* The apartments were so irregularly disposed that the vision embraced but little more than one at a time. There was a sharp turn at every twenty or thirty yards, and at each turn a novel effect. To the right and left, in the middle of each wall, a tall and narrow Gothic window looked out upon a closed corridor which pursued the windings of the suite These windows were of stained glass whose color varied in accordance with the prevailing hue of the decorations of the chamber into which it opened. That at the eastern extremity was hung, for example, in blue—and vividly blue were its windows. The second chamber was purple in its ornaments and tapestries, and here the panes were purple. The third was green throughout, and so were the casements. The fourth

[6] *improvisatori:* composers and singers of extemporaneous songs

was furnished and lighted with orange — the fifth with white — the sixth with violet. The seventh apartment was closely shrouded in black velvet tapestries that hung all over the ceiling and down the walls, falling in heavy folds upon a carpet of the same material and hue. But in this chamber only, the color of the windows failed to correspond with the decorations. The panes here were scarlet — a deep blood color. Now in no one of the seven apartments was there any lamp or candelabrum, amid the profusion of golden ornaments that lay scattered to and fro or depended from the roof. There was no light of any kind emanating from lamp or candle within the suite of chambers. But in the corridors that followed the suite, there stood, opposite to each window a heavy tripod, bearing a brazier of fire, that projected its rays through the tinted glass and so glaringly illumined the room. And thus were produced a multitude of gaudy and fantastic appearances. But in the western or black chamber the effect of the fire-light that streamed upon the dark hangings through the blood-tinted panes, was ghastly in the extreme, and produced so wild a look upon the countenances of those who entered, that there were few of the company bold enough to set foot within its precincts at all.

It was in this apartment, also, that there stood against the western wall, a gigantic clock of ebony. Its pendulum swung to and fro with a dull, heavy, monotonous clang; and when the minute-hand made the circuit of the face, and the hour was to be stricken, there came from the brazen lungs of the clock a sound which was clear and loud and deep and exceedingly musical, but of so peculiar a note and emphasis that, at each lapse of an hour, the musicians of the orchestra were constrained to pause, momentarily, in their performance, to hearken to the sound; and thus the waltzers perforce ceased their evolutions; and there was a brief disconcert of the whole gay company; and, while the chimes of the clock yet rang, it was observed that the giddiest grew pale, and the more aged and sedate passed their hands over their brows as if in confused revery or meditation. But when the echoes had fully ceased, a light laughter at once pervaded the assembly; the musicians looked at each other and smiled as if at their own nervousness and folly, and made whispering vows, each to the other, that the next chiming of the clock should produce in them no similar emotion; and then, after the lapse of sixty minutes, (which embrace three thousand and six hundred seconds of the Time that flies,) there came yet another chiming of the clock, and then were the same disconcert and tremulousness and meditation as before.

But, in spite of these things, it was a gay and magnificent revel. The tastes of the duke were peculiar. He had a fine eye for colors and effects. He disregarded the *decora*[7] of mere fashion. His plans were bold and fiery, and his conceptions glowed with barbaric lustre. There are some who would have thought him mad. His followers felt that he was not. It was necessary to hear and see and touch him to be *sure* that he was not.

He had directed, in great part, the moveable embellishments of the seven chambers, upon occasion of this great *fête;* and it was his own guiding taste which had given character to the masqueraders. Be sure they were grotesque. There were much glare and glitter and piquancy and phantasm[8] — much of what has been since seen in *"Hernani."*[9] There were arabesque figures with unsuited[10] limbs and appointments. There were delirious fancies such as the madman fashions. There were much of the beautiful, much of the wanton, much of the *bizarre*, something of the terrible, and not a little of that which might have excited disgust. To and fro in the seven chambers there stalked, in fact, a multitude of dreams. And these — the dreams — writhed in and about, taking hue from the rooms, and causing the wild music of the orchestra to seem as the echo of their steps. And, anon, there strikes the ebony clock which stands in the hall of the velvet. And then, for a moment, all is still, and all is silent save the voice of the clock. The dreams are stiff-frozen as they stand. But the echoes of the chime die away — they have

[7] *decora:* accepted standards, proprieties
[8] *piquancy and phantasm:* liveliness and ghostliness
[9] *Hernani:* a romantic tragedy by Victor Hugo (French) in which lavish costumes were worn
[10] *unsuited:* unmatched

endured but an instant—and a light, half-subdued laughter floats after them as they depart. And now again the music swells, and the dreams live, and writhe to and fro more merrily than ever, taking hue from the many-tinted windows through which stream the rays from the tripods. But to the chamber which lies most westwardly of the seven, there are now none of the maskers who venture; for the night is waning away; and there flows a ruddier light through the blood-colored panes; and the blackness of the sable drapery appals; and to him whose foot falls upon the sable carpet, there comes from the near clock of ebony a muffled peal more solemnly emphatic than any which reaches *their* ears who indulge in the more remote gaieties of the other apartments.

But these other apartments were densely crowded, and in them beat feverishly the heart of life. And the revel went whirlingly on, until at length there commenced the sounding of midnight upon the clock. And then the music ceased, as I have told; and the evolutions of the waltzers were quieted; and there was an uneasy cessation of all things as before. But now there were twelve strokes to be sounded by the bell of the clock; and thus it happened, perhaps, that more of thought crept, with more of time, into the meditations of the thoughtful among those who revelled. And thus, too, it happened, perhaps, that before the last echoes of the last chime had utterly sunk into silence, there were many individuals in the crowd who had found leisure to become aware of the presence of a masked figure which had arrested the attention of no single individual before. And the rumor of this new presence having spread itself whisperingly around, there arose at length from the whole company a buzz, or murmur, expressive of disapprobation and surprise—then, finally, of terror, of horror, and of disgust.

In an assembly of phantasms such as I have painted, it may well be supposed that no ordinary appearance could have excited such sensation. In truth the masquerade license of the night was nearly unlimited; but the figure in question had out-Heroded Herod,[11] and gone beyond the bounds of even

---

[11] *out-Heroded Herod:* quotation from Shakespeare's *Hamlet,* meaning the masked figure had "gone beyond all limits"

the prince's indefinite decorum. There are chords in the hearts of the most reckless which cannot be touched without emotion. Even with the utterly lost, to whom life and death are equally jests, there are matters of which no jest can be made. The whole company, indeed, seemed now deeply to feel in the costume and bearing of the stranger neither wit nor propriety existed. The figure was tall and gaunt, and shrouded from head to foot in the habiliments of the grave. The mask which concealed the visage was made so nearly to resemble the countenance of a stiffened corpse that the closest scrutiny must have had difficulty in detecting the cheat. And yet all this might have been endured, if not approved, by the mad revellers around. But the mummer[12] had gone so far as to assume the type of the Red Death. His vesture was dabbled in *blood*—and his broad brow, with all the features of the face, was besprinkled with the scarlet horror.

When the eyes of Prince Prospero fell upon this spectral image (which with a slow and solemn movement, as if more fully to sustain its *rôle*, stalked to and fro among the waltzers) he was seen to be convulsed, in the first moment with a strong shudder either of terror or distaste; but, in the next, his brow reddened with rage.

"Who dares?" he demanded hoarsely of the courtiers who stood near him—"who dares insult us with this blasphemous mockery? Seize him and unmask him—that we may know whom we have to hang at sunrise, from the battlements!"

It was in the eastern or blue chamber in which stood the Prince Prospero as he uttered these words. They rang throughout the seven rooms loudly and clearly—for the prince was a bold and robust man, and the music had become hushed at the waving of his hand.

It was in the blue room where stood the prince, with a group of pale courtiers by his side. At first, as he spoke, there was a slight rushing movement of this group in the direction of the intruder, who at the moment was also near at hand, and now, with deliberate and stately step, made closer approach to the speaker. But from a certain nameless awe with which the mad assumptions of the mummer had inspired the whole

[12] *mummer:* one who goes merrymaking in disguise

party, there were found none who put forth hand to seize him; so that, unimpeded, he passed within a yard of the prince's person; and, while the vast assembly, as if with one impulse, shrank from the centres of the rooms to the walls, he made his way uninterruptedly, but with the same solemn and measured step which had distinguished him from the first, through the blue chamber to the purple — through the purple to the green — through the green to the orange — through this again to the white — and even thence to the violet, ere a decided movement had been made to arrest him. It was then, however, that the Prince Prospero, maddening with rage and the shame of his own momentary cowardice, rushed hurriedly through the six chambers, while none followed him on account of a deadly terror that had seized upon all. He bore aloft a drawn dagger, and had approached, in rapid impetuosity, to within three or four feet of the retreating figure, when the latter, having attained the extremity of the velvet apartment, turned suddenly and confronted his pursuer. There was a sharp cry — and the dagger dropped gleaming upon the sable carpet, upon which, instantly afterwards, fell prostrate in death the Prince Prospero. Then, summoning the wild courage of despair, a throng of the revellers at once threw themselves into the black apartment, and, seizing the mummer, whose tall figure stood erect and motionless within the shadow of the ebony clock, gasped in unutterable horror at finding the grave-cerements[13] and corpse-like mask which they handled with so violent a rudeness, untenanted by any tangible form.

And now was acknowledged the presence of the Red Death. He had come like a thief in the night. And one by one dropped the revellers in the blood-bedewed halls of their revel, and died each in the despairing posture of his fall. And the life of the ebony clock went out with that of the last of the gay. And the flames of the tripods expired. And Darkness and Decay and the Red Death held illimitable dominion over all.

[13] *grave-cerements:* burial clothes, shroud

FOR DISCUSSION

1. Poe says of the skillful story writer: "Having conceived, with deliberate care, a certain unique or single *effect* to be wrought out, he then invents such incidents . . . as may best aid him in establishing this preconceived effect. If his very initial sentence tend not to the outbringing of this effect, then he has failed in his first step." What "single effect" do you think he intends to create in "The Masque of the Red Death"? Is his initial sentence in keeping with this purpose? Which details of the story seem particularly important in building Poe's preconceived effect?
2. At the beginning of the story, Prince Prospero takes elaborate precaution to shut out the Red Death. Why is the outcome of the story ironical?
3. This tale has been called an allegory—a narrative in which people, objects, or events symbolize certain truths about human experience. What is the real identity of the masked stranger? What "truth about human experience" is the underlying theme of the story? What do the masked ball, the brazier fires, and the clock represent?
4. In keeping with the allegorical idea of the story, why do you suppose the hourly striking of the clock is upsetting to the revellers?
5. Poe's stories often show a distinctive flair for the dramatic. How is it evident in his description of the seven chambers? Why is the decor of the seventh chamber appropriate for what later takes place there? Find other examples of Poe's use of dramatic effect.
6. Throughout the story Poe uses contrast in both ideas and description to heighten the bizarre effect. Note, for example, the contrast between the Prince's gleaming dagger and the sable carpet on which it falls as he dies. Point out further examples of Poe's effective use of contrast.

FOR COMPOSITION

1. After reviewing "The Romantic Triumph" (page 84), write a short paragraph on "The Masque of the Red Death" as a reflection of the Romantic spirit.
2. From the bits of information that Poe scatters throughout the story, piece together a character study of Prince Prospero. In your opinion, is he mad? Be sure to give evidence to support your opinion.

Nathaniel Hawthorne

In Nathaniel Hawthorne's tales, with their chill New England setting, the major characters are frequently obsessed by a single idea, which makes them lonely or in some way sets them apart from their fellow men. Often they have a strong sense of guilt and remorse arising from a deep moral cause. Hawthorne's major contribution to American literature was his infusion of a central idea about good and evil into a story through the use of symbols. This, together with an admirable style of restrained intensity, has made him one of America's major writers of fiction.

The Minister's Black Veil

The sexton stood in the porch of Milford meeting-house, pulling busily at the bell-rope. The old people of the village came stooping along the street. Children, with bright faces, tripped merrily beside their parents, or mimicked a graver gait, in the conscious dignity of their Sunday clothes. Spruce bachelors looked sidelong at the pretty maidens, and fancied that the Sabbath sunshine made them prettier than on week days. When the throng had mostly streamed into the porch, the sexton began to toll the bell, keeping his eye on the Reverend Mr. Hooper's door. The first glimpse of the clergyman's figure was the signal for the bell to cease its summons.

"But what has good Parson Hooper got upon his face?" cried the sexton in astonishment.

All within hearing immediately turned about, and beheld the semblance of Mr. Hooper, pacing slowly his meditative way towards the meeting-house. With one accord they started, expressing more wonder than if some strange minister were coming to dust the cushions of Mr. Hooper's pulpit.

"Are you sure it is our parson?" inquired Goodman Gray of the sexton.

"Of a certainty it is good Mr. Hooper," replied the sexton. "He was to have exchanged pulpits with Parson Shute, of Westbury; but Parson Shute sent to excuse himself yesterday, being to preach a funeral sermon."

The cause of so much amazement may appear sufficiently slight. Mr. Hooper, a gentlemanly person, of about thirty, though still a bachelor, was dressed with due clerical neatness, as if a careful wife had starched his band, and brushed the weekly dust from his Sunday's garb. There was but one thing remarkable in his appearance. Swathed about his forehead, and hanging down over his face, so low as to be shaken by his breath, Mr. Hooper had on a black veil. On a nearer view it seemed to consist of two folds of crape, which entirely concealed his features, except the mouth and chin, but probably did not intercept his sight, further than to give a darkened aspect to all living and inanimate things. With this gloomy shade before him, good Mr. Hooper walked onward, at a slow and quiet pace, stooping somewhat, and looking on the ground, as is customary with abstracted men, yet nodding kindly to those of his parishioners who still waited on the meeting-house steps. But so wonderstruck were they that his greeting hardly met with a return.

"I can't really feel as if good Mr. Hooper's face was behind that piece of crape," said the sexton.

"I don't like it," muttered an old woman, as she hobbled into the meeting-house. "He has changed himself into something awful, only by hiding his face."

"Our parson has gone mad!" cried Goodman Gray, following him across the threshold!

A rumor of some unaccountable phenomenon had preceded Mr. Hooper into the meeting-house, and set all the congregation astir. Few could refrain from twisting their heads towards the door; many stood upright, and turned directly about; while several little boys clambered upon the seats, and came down again with a terrible racket. There was a general bustle, a rustling of the women's gowns and shuffling of the men's feet, greatly at variance with that hushed repose which should

attend the entrance of the minister. But Mr. Hooper appeared
not to notice the perturbation of his people. He entered with
an almost noiseless step, bent his head mildly to the pews on
each side, and bowed as he passed his oldest parishioner, a
white-haired great-grandsire, who occupied an arm-chair in
the center of the aisle. It was strange to observe how slowly
this venerable man became conscious of something singular
in the appearance of his pastor. He seemed not fully to partake
of the prevailing wonder, till Mr. Hooper had ascended the
stairs, and showed himself in the pulpit, face to face with his
congregation, except for the black veil. That mysterious emblem was never once withdrawn. It shook with the measured
breath, as he gave out the psalm; it threw its obscurity between him and the holy page, as he read the Scriptures; and
while he prayed, the veil lay heavily on his uplifted
countenance. Did he seek to hide it from the dread Being
whom he was addressing?

Such was the effect of this simple piece of crape that more
than one woman of delicate nerves was forced to leave the
meeting-house. Yet perhaps the pale-faced congregation was
almost as fearful a sight to the minister as his black veil to
them.

Mr. Hooper had the reputation of a good preacher, but not
an energetic one: he strove to win his people heavenward by
mild, persuasive influences, rather than to drive them thither
by the thunders of the Word. The sermon which he now
delivered was marked by the same characteristics of style and
manner as the general series of his pulpit oratory. But there
was something either in the sentiment of the discourse itself,
or in the imagination of the auditors, which made it greatly the
most powerful effort that they had ever heard from their
pastor's lips. It was tinged rather more darkly than usual with
the gentle gloom of Mr. Hooper's temperament. The subject
had reference to secret sin, and those sad mysteries which we
hide from our nearest and dearest and would fain conceal
from our own consciousness, even forgetting that the Omniscient can detect them. A subtle power was breathed into his
words. Each member of the congregation, the most innocent
girl and the man of hardened breast, felt as if the preacher

had crept upon them behind his awful veil, and discovered their hoarded iniquity of deed or thought. Many spread their clasped hands on their bosoms. There was nothing terrible in what Mr. Hooper said, at least, no violence; and yet, with every tremor of his melancholy voice the hearers quaked. An unsought pathos came hand in hand with awe. So sensible were the audience of some unwonted attribute in their minister that they longed for a breath of wind to blow aside the veil, almost believing that a stranger's visage would be discovered, though the form, gesture, and voice were those of Mr. Hooper.

At the close of the service the people hurried out with indecorous confusion, eager to communicate their pent-up amazement, and conscious of lighter spirits the moment they lost sight of the black veil. Some gathered in little circles, huddled closely together, with their mouths all whispering in the center; some went homeward alone, wrapped in silent meditation; some talked loudly, and profaned the Sabbath day with ostentatious[1] laughter. A few shook their sagacious heads, intimating that they could penetrate the mystery; while one or two affirmed that there was no mystery at all, but only that Mr. Hooper's eyes were so weakened by the midnight lamp, as to require a shade. After a brief interval, forth came good Mr. Hooper also, in the rear of his flock. Turning his veiled face from one group to another, he paid due reverence to the hoary heads, saluted the middle-aged with kind dignity as their friend and spiritual guide, greeted the young with mingled authority and love, and laid his hands on the little children's heads to bless them. Such was always his custom on the Sabbath day. Strange and bewildered looks repaid him for his courtesy. None, as on former occasions, aspired to the honor of walking by their pastor's side. Old Squire Saunders, doubtless by an accidental lapse of memory, neglected to invite Mr. Hooper to his table, where the good clergyman had been wont to bless the food, almost every Sunday since his settlement. He returned, therefore, to the parsonage, and, at the moment of closing the door, was observed to look back upon the people, all of whom had their eyes fixed upon the

[1] *ostentatious:* showy

minister. A sad smile gleamed faintly from beneath the black veil, and flickered about his mouth, glimmering as he disappeared.

"How strange," said a lady, "that a simple black veil, such as any woman might wear on her bonnet, should become such a terrible thing on Mr. Hooper's face!"

"Something must surely be amiss with Mr. Hooper's intellects," observed her husband, the physician of the village. "But the strangest part of the affair is the effect of this vagary,[2] even on a sober-minded man like myself. The black veil, though it covers only our pastor's face, throws its influence over his whole person, and makes him ghost-like from head to foot. Do you not feel it so?"

"Truly do I," replied the lady; "and I would not be alone with him for the world. I wonder he is not afraid to be alone with himself!"

"Men sometimes are so," said her husband.

The afternoon service was attended with similar circumstances. At its conclusion, the bell tolled for the funeral of a young lady. The relatives and friends were assembled in the house, and the more distant acquaintances stood about the door, speaking of the good qualities of the deceased, when their talk was interrupted by the appearance of Mr. Hooper, still covered with his black veil. It was now an appropriate emblem. The clergyman stepped into the room where the corpse was laid, and bent over the coffin, to take a last farewell of his deceased parishioner. As he stooped, the veil hung straight down from his forehead, so that, if her eyelids had not been closed forever, the dead maiden might have seen his face. Could Mr. Hooper be fearful of her glance, that he so hastily caught back the black veil? A person who watched the interview between the dead and living scrupled not to affirm that, at the instant when the clergyman's features were disclosed, the corpse had slightly shuddered, rustling the shroud and muslin cap, though the countenance retained the composure of death. A superstitious old woman was the only witness of this prodigy. From the coffin Mr. Hooper passed into the chamber of the mourners, and thence to the head of

[2] *vagary:* oddity, eccentric action

the staircase, to make the funeral prayer. It was a tender and heart-dissolving prayer, full of sorrow, yet so imbued with celestial hopes that the music of a heavenly harp, swept by the fingers of the dead, seemed faintly to be heard among the saddest accents of the minister. The people trembled, though they but darkly understood him, when he prayed that they, and himself, and all of mortal race, might be ready, as he trusted this young maiden had been, for the dreadful hour that should snatch the veil from their faces. The bearers went heavily forth, and the mourners followed, saddening all the street, with the dead before them and Mr. Hooper in the black veil behind.

"Why do you look back?" said one in the procession to his partner.

"I had a fancy," replied she, "that the minister and the maiden's spirit were walking hand in hand."

"And so had I at the same moment," said the other.

That night the handsomest couple in Milford village were to be joined in wedlock. Though reckoned a melancholy man, Mr. Hooper had a placid cheerfulness for such occasions which often excited a sympathetic smile where livelier merriment would have been thrown away. There was no quality of his disposition which made him more beloved than this. The company at the wedding awaited his arrival with impatience, trusting that the strange awe which had gathered over him throughout the day would now be dispelled. But such was not the result. When Mr. Hooper came, the first thing that their eyes rested on was the same horrible black veil, which had added deeper gloom to the funeral and could portend[3] nothing but evil to the wedding. Such was its immediate effect on the guests that a cloud seemed to have rolled duskily from beneath the black crape and dimmed the light of the candles. The bridal pair stood up before the minister. But the bride's cold fingers quivered in the tremulous hand of the bridegroom, and her deathlike paleness caused a whisper that the maiden who had been buried a few hours before was come from her grave to be married. If ever another wedding were so dismal, it was that famous one where they tolled the

---

[3] *portend:* be a warning of, foreshadow

wedding knell. After performing the ceremony, Mr. Hooper raised a glass of wine to his lips, wishing happiness to the new-married couple in a strain of mild pleasantry that ought to have brightened the features of the guests, like a cheerful gleam from the hearth. At that instant, catching a glimpse of his figure in the looking-glass, the black veil involved his own spirit in the horror with which it overwhelmed all others. His frame shuddered, his lips grew white, he spilt the untasted wine upon the carpet, and rushed forth into the darkness. For the Earth, too, had on her Black Veil.

The next day, the whole village of Milford talked of little else than Parson Hooper's black veil. That, and the mystery concealed behind it, supplied a topic for discussion between acquaintances meeting in the street, and good women gossiping at their open windows. It was the first item of news that the tavern-keeper told to his guests. The children babbled of it on their way to school. One imitative little imp covered his face with an old black handkerchief, thereby so affrighting his playmates that the panic seized himself, and he well-nigh lost his wits by his own waggery.

It was remarkable that of all the busybodies and impertinent people in the parish, not one ventured to put the plain question to Mr. Hooper, wherefore he did this thing. Hitherto, whenever there appeared the slightest call for such interference, he had never lacked advisers, nor shown himself averse to be guided by their judgment. If he erred at all, it was by so painful a degree of self-distrust, that even the mildest censure would lead him to consider an indifferent action as a crime. Yet, though so well acquainted with this amiable weakness, no individual among his parishioners chose to make the black veil a subject of friendly remonstrance. There was a feeling of dread, neither plainly confessed nor carefully concealed, which caused each to shift the responsibility upon another, till at length it was found expedient to send a deputation of the church, in order to deal with Mr. Hooper about the mystery, before it should grow into a scandal. Never did an embassy so ill discharge its duties. The minister received them with friendly courtesy, but became silent, after they were seated, leaving to his visitors the whole burden of introducing their important business. The topic, it might be supposed, was obvious enough. There was the black veil swathed round Mr. Hooper's forehead and concealing every feature above his placid mouth, on which at times they could perceive the glimmering of a melancholy smile. But that piece of crape, to their imagination, seemed to hang down before his heart, the symbol of a fearful secret between him and them. Were the veil but cast aside they might speak freely of it, but not till then. Thus they sat a considerable time, speechless, confused, and shrinking uneasily from Mr. Hooper's eye, which they felt to be fixed upon them with an invisible glance. Finally, the deputies returned abashed to their constituents, pronouncing the matter too weighty to be handled, except by a council of the churches, if indeed it might not require a general synod.

But there was one person in the village unappalled by the awe with which the black veil had impressed all beside herself. When the deputies returned without an explanation, or even venturing to demand one, she, with the calm energy of her character, determined to chase away the strange cloud that appeared to be settling round Mr. Hooper, every moment more darkly than before. As his plighted wife, it should be her privilege to know what the black veil concealed. At the minister's first visit, therefore, she entered upon the subject with a direct simplicity which made the task easier both for him and her. After he had seated himself, she fixed her eyes steadily upon the veil, but could discern nothing of the dreadful gloom that had so overawed the multitude: it was but a double fold of crape, hanging down from his forehead to his mouth, and slightly stirring with his breath.

"No," said she, aloud and smiling, "there is nothing terrible in this piece of crape, except that it hides a face which I am always glad to look upon. Come, good sir, let the sun shine from behind the cloud. First lay aside your black veil, then tell me why you put it on."

Mr. Hooper's smile glimmered faintly.

"There is an hour to come," said he, "when all of us shall cast aside our veils. Take it not amiss, beloved friend, if I wear this piece of crape till then."

"Your words are a mystery too," returned the young lady. "Take away the veil from them at least."

"Elizabeth, I will," said he, "so far as my vow may suffer me. Know, then, this veil is a type and a symbol, and I am bound to wear it ever, both in light and darkness, in solitude and before the gaze of multitudes, and as with strangers, so with my familiar friends. No mortal eye will see it withdrawn. This dismal shade must separate me from the world: even you, Elizabeth, can never come behind it!"

"What grievous affliction hath befallen you," she earnestly inquired, "that you should thus darken your eyes forever?"

"If it be a sign of mourning," replied Mr. Hooper, "I, perhaps, like most other mortals, have sorrows dark enough to be typified by a black veil."

"But what if the world will not believe that it is the type of an innocent sorrow?" urged Elizabeth. "Beloved and respected as you are, there may be whispers that you hide your face under the consciousness of secret sin. For the sake of your holy office, do away this scandal!"

The color rose into her cheeks as she intimated the nature of the rumors that were already abroad in the village. But Mr. Hooper's mildness did not forsake him. He even smiled again —that same sad smile, which always appeared like a faint glimmering of light, proceeding from the obscurity beneath the veil.

"If I hide my face for sorrow, there is cause enough," he merely replied, "and if I cover it for secret sin, what mortal might not do the same?"

And with this gentle, but unconquerable obstinacy did he resist all her entreaties. At length Elizabeth sat silent. For a few moments she appeared lost in thought, considering, probably, what new methods might be tried to withdraw her lover from so dark a fantasy, which, if it had no other meaning, was perhaps a symptom of mental disease. Though of a firmer character than his own, the tears rolled down her cheeks. But, in an instant, as it were, a new feeling took the place of sorrow: her eyes were fixed insensibly on the black veil, when, like a sudden twilight in the air, its terrors fell around her. She arose, and stood trembling before him.

"And do you feel it then, at last?" said he mournfully.

She made no reply, but covered her eyes with her hand, and turned to leave the room. He rushed forward and caught her arm.

"Have patience with me, Elizabeth!" cried he, passionately. "Do not desert me, though this veil must be between us here on earth. Be mine, and hereafter there shall be no veil over my face, no darkness between our souls! It is but a mortal veil—it is not for eternity! O! you know not how lonely I am, and how frightened, to be alone behind my black veil. Do not leave me in this miserable obscurity forever!"

"Lift the veil at once and look me in the face," said she.

"Never! It cannot be!" replied Mr. Hooper.

"Then, farewell!" said Elizabeth.

She withdrew her arm from his grasp and slowly departed, pausing at the door to give one long, shuddering gaze, that seemed almost to penetrate the mystery of the black veil. But even amid his grief Mr. Hooper smiled to think that only a material emblem had separated him from happiness, though the horrors which it shadowed forth must be drawn darkly between the fondest of lovers.

From that time no attempts were made to remove Mr. Hooper's black veil, or, by a direct appeal, to discover the secret which it was supposed to hide. By persons who claimed a superiority to popular prejudice it was reckoned merely an eccentric whim, such as often mingles with the sober actions of men otherwise rational, and tinges them all with its own semblance of insanity. But with the multitude good Mr. Hooper was irreparably a bugbear.[4] He could not walk the streets with any peace of mind, so conscious was he that the gentle and timid would turn aside to avoid him, and that others would make it a point of hardihood to throw themselves in his way. The impertinence of the latter class compelled him to give up his customary walk at sunset to the burial ground; for when he leaned pensively over the gate, there would always be faces behind the gravestones peeping at his black veil. A fable went the rounds that the stare of the dead people drove him thence. It grieved him to the very depth of his kind heart

---

[4] *bugbear:* anything causing seemingly needless or excessive fear or anxiety

to observe how the children fled from his approach, breaking up their merriest sports while his melancholy figure was yet afar off. Their instinctive dread caused him to feel more strongly than aught else that a preternatural horror was interwoven with the threads of the black crape. In truth, his own antipathy to the veil was known to be so great that he never willingly passed before a mirror, nor stooped to drink at a still fountain, lest in its peaceful bosom he should be affrighted by himself. This was what gave plausibility to the whispers that Mr. Hooper's conscience tortured him for some great crime too horrible to be entirely concealed, or otherwise than so obscurely intimated. Thus, from beneath the black veil, there rolled a cloud into the sunshine, an ambiguity of sin or sorrow, which enveloped the poor minister, so that love or sympathy could never reach him. It was said the ghost and fiend consorted with him there. With self-shudderings and outward terrors, he walked continually in its shadow, groping darkly within his own soul, or gazing through a medium that saddened the whole world. Even the lawless wind, it was believed, respected his dreadful secret, and never blew aside the veil. But still good Mr. Hooper sadly smiled at the pale visages of the worldly throng as he passed by.

Among all its bad influences, the black veil had the one desirable effect, of making its wearer a very efficient clergyman. By the aid of his mysterious emblem—for there was no other apparent cause—he became a man of awful power over souls that were in agony for sin. His converts always regarded him with a dread peculiar to themselves, affirming, though but figuratively, that, before he brought them to celestial light, they had been with him behind the black veil. Its gloom, indeed, enabled him to sympathize with all dark affections. Dying sinners cried aloud for Mr. Hooper, and would not yield their breath till he appeared; though ever, as he stooped to whisper consolation, they shuddered at the veiled face so near their own. Such were the terrors of the black veil, even when Death had bared his visage! Strangers came long distances to attend service at his church, with the mere idle purpose of gazing at his figure, because it was forbidden them to behold his face. But many were made to quake ere they departed! Once, during Governor Belcher's administration, Mr. Hooper was appointed to preach the election sermon. Covered with his black veil, he stood before the chief magistrate, the council, and the representatives, and wrought so deep an impression, that the legislative measures of that year were characterized by all the gloom and piety of our earliest ancestral sway.

In this manner Mr. Hooper spent a long life, irreproachable in outward act, yet shrouded in dismal suspicions; kind and loving, though unloved, and dimly feared; a man apart from men, shunned in their health and joy, but ever summoned to their aid in mortal anguish. As years wore on, shedding their snows above his sable veil, he acquired a name throughout the New England churches, and they called him Father Hooper. Nearly all his parishioners, who were of mature age when he was settled, had been borne away by many a funeral: he had one congregation in the church, and a more crowded one in the church-yard; and having wrought so late into the evening, and done his work so well, it was now good Father Hooper's turn to rest.

Several persons were visible by the shaded candlelight in the death chamber of the old clergyman. Natural connections he had none. But there was the decorously grave though unmoved physician, seeking only to mitigate[5] the last pangs of the patient whom he could not save. There were the deacons and other eminently pious members of his church. There, also, was the Reverend Mr. Clark, of Westbury, a young and zealous divine, who had ridden in haste to pray by the bedside of the expiring minister. There was the nurse, no hired handmaiden of death, but one whose calm affection had endured thus long in secrecy, in solitude, amid the chill of age, and would not perish, even at the dying hour. Who, but Elizabeth! And there lay the hoary head of good Father Hooper upon the death pillow, with the black veil still swathed about his brow and reaching down over his face, so that each more difficult gasp of his faint breath caused it to stir. All through life that piece of crape had hung between him and the world: it had separated him from cheerful brotherhood and woman's love, and

[5] *mitigate:* make less painful or severe

kept him in that saddest of all prisons, his own heart; and still it lay upon his face, as if to deepen the gloom of his darksome chamber, and shade him from the sunshine of eternity.

For some time previous his mind had been confused, wavering doubtfully between the past and the present, and hovering forward, as it were, at intervals, into the indistinctness of the world to come. There had been feverish turns, which tossed him from side to side, and wore away what little strength he had. But in his most convulsive struggles, and in the wildest vagaries of his intellect, when no other thought retained its sober influence, he still showed an awful solicitude lest the black veil should slip aside. Even if his bewildered soul could have forgotten, there was a faithful woman at his pillow, who, with averted eyes, would have covered that aged face, which she had last beheld in the comeliness of manhood. At length the death-stricken old man lay quietly in the torpor of mental and bodily exhaustion, with an imperceptible pulse, and breath that grew fainter and fainter, except when a long, deep, and irregular inspiration seemed to prelude the flight of his spirit.

The minister of Westbury approached the bedside.

"Venerable Father Hooper," said he, "the moment of your release is at hand. Are you ready for the lifting of the veil that shuts in time from eternity?"

Father Hooper at first replied merely by a feeble motion of his head; then, apprehensive, perhaps, that his meaning might be doubtful, he exerted himself to speak.

"Yea," said he, in faint accents, "my soul hath a patient weariness until that veil be lifted."

"And is it fitting," resumed the Reverend Mr. Clark, "that a man so given to prayer, of such a blameless example, holy in deed and thought, so far as mortal judgment may pronounce; is it fitting that a father in the church should leave a shadow on his memory, that may seem to blacken a life so pure? I pray you, my venerable brother, let not this thing be! Suffer us to be gladdened by your triumphant aspect as you go to your reward. Before the veil of eternity be lifted, let me cast aside this black veil from your face!"

And thus speaking, the Reverend Mr. Clark bent forward to

reveal the mystery of so many years. But, exerting a sudden energy, that made all the beholders stand aghast, Father Hooper snatched both his hands from beneath the bedclothes, and pressed them strongly on the black veil, resolute to struggle, if the minister of Westbury would contend with a dying man.

"Never!" cried the veiled clergyman. "On earth, never!"

"Dark old man!" exclaimed the affrighted minister, "with what horrible crime upon your soul are you now passing to the judgment?"

Father Hooper's breath heaved; it rattled in his throat; but, with a mighty effort, grasping forward with his hands, he caught hold of life, and held it back till he should speak. He even raised himself in bed; and there he sat, shivering with the arms of death around him, while the black veil hung down, awful, at that last moment, in the gathered errors of a lifetime. And yet the faint, sad smile, so often there, now seemed to glimmer from its obscurity, and linger on Father Hooper's lips.

"Why do you tremble at me alone?" cried he, turning his veiled face round the circle of pale spectators. "Tremble also at each other! Have men avoided me, and women shown no pity, and children screamed and fled, only for my black veil? What, but the mystery which it obscurely typifies, has made this piece of crape so awful? When the friend shows his inmost heart to his friend; the lover to his best beloved; when man does not vainly shrink from the eye of his Creator, loathsomely treasuring up the secret of his sin; then deem me a monster, for the symbol beneath which I have lived, and die! I look around me, and, lo! on every visage a Black Veil!"

While his auditors shrank from one another in mutual affright, Father Hooper fell back upon his pillow, a veiled corpse, with a faint smile lingering on the lips. Still veiled, they laid him in his coffin, and a veiled corpse they bore him to the grave. The grass of many years has sprung up and withered on that grave, the burial stone is moss-grown, and good Mr. Hooper's face is dust; but awful is still the thought that it moldered beneath the black veil.

FOR DISCUSSION

1. When Mr. Hooper first appears with the veil over his face, how do the villagers react? In what ways does his strange behavior affect his life in the community? How does the veil lessen or increase his effectiveness as a preacher? Cite incidents from the story as evidence.
2. Each time Mr. Hooper is asked to remove the veil, how does he react and why does he refuse? What does he lose by insisting upon wearing it? Does he behave strangely in other ways? What kind of person is he?
3. In your opinion, why is the reader never told the exact nature of the "secret sin" for which Mr. Hooper was atoning? Would the story be more effective if that information had been provided? Would the story have the same meaning? Explain.
4. How important is the supernatural in revealing the character of the minister and the beliefs and attitudes of the townspeople? What does it contribute to the over-all mood of the story? Discuss the incidents in which Hawthorne uses it and tell why they—and the entire action of the story—would, or would not, be as dramatic without the supernatural.
5. At the end of the story, Mr. Hooper says, "I look around me, and, lo! on every visage a Black Veil!" Is he simply having a deathbed hallucination? If not, what does he mean by this statement?
6. The veil—the symbol that governs the entire story—has several levels of meaning. Note the various uses of the word *veil*. In each use, what does the word stand for or symbolize?
7. Select one or two passages in the story which impress you as particularly good examples of Hawthorne's style. Point out the qualities of this style and tell why it is well suited to this kind of story.

FOR COMPOSITION

1. Write a character sketch of Mr. Hooper as he is revealed by what he says and does, by what others say about him or the way they react to him, and by what the author tells you. Focus primarily on the kind of person he is, with just a brief description of his appearance.
2. Choose two of the incidents in the story which suggest the supernatural, and describe them briefly in your own words. Then give

what you consider a satisfactory natural explanation of each. Also tell why you think that the townspeople would, or would not, accept a natural explanation. Limit your analysis to three carefully planned paragraphs.

Herman Melville

In a letter to Hawthorne in 1851, Herman Melville wrote, "What I feel most moved to write, that is banned—it will not pay. Yet altogether, write the *other* way I cannot." At the time, he was working on his great novel, *Moby Dick*, which won him praise from literary men and critics, but few readers. These few deserted him when he published *Pierre*, another "thought-driving" book, but more shocking. Melville then turned to the writing of short pieces for magazines, among them the sketches which he called *The Encantadas, or, The Enchanted Isles*. About these isles, Melville wrote, "In no world but a fallen one could such lands exist." His portrayal of these lands, and of the strange people and events connected with them, reveal Melville at his best. In these sketches he is a master in the creation of mood and in the use of imagery and symbol. Some critics consider *The Encantadas* almost equal to *Moby Dick* in literary excellence.

Norfolk Isle and the Chola Widow

Sketch Eighth

"At last they in an island did espy
A seemly woman sitting by the shore,
That with great sorrow and sad agony
Seemed some great misfortune to deplore,
And loud to them for succor called evermore."

"Black his eye as the midnight sky,
White his neck as the driven snow,
Red his cheek as the morning light;—
Cold he lies in the ground below.

My love is dead,
Gone to his death-bed,
All under the cactus tree."

"Each lonely scene shall thee restore,
For thee the tear be duly shed;
Belov'd till life can charm no more,
And mourned till Pity's self be dead."

Far to the northeast of Charles's Isle,[1] sequestered from the rest, lies Norfolk Isle; and, however insignificant to most voyagers, to me, through sympathy, that lone island has become a spot made sacred by the strangest trials of humanity.

It was my first visit to the Encantadas. Two days had been spent ashore in hunting tortoises. There was not time to capture many; so on the third afternoon we loosed our sails. We were just in the act of getting under way, the uprooted anchor yet suspended and invisibly swaying beneath the wave, as the good ship gradually turned her heel to leave the isle behind, when the seaman who heaved with me at the windlass paused suddenly, and directed my attention to something moving on the land, not along the beach, but somewhat back, fluttering from a height.

In view of the sequel of this little story, be it here narrated how it came to pass, that an object which partly from its being so small was quite lost to every other man on board, still caught the eye of my handspike companion. The rest of the crew, myself included, merely stood up to our spikes in heaving, whereas, unwontedly exhilarated, at every turn of the ponderous windlass, my belted comrade leaped atop of it, with might and main giving a downward, thewy,[2] perpendicular heave, his raised eye bent in cheery animation upon the slowly receding shore. Being high lifted above all others was the reason he perceived the object, otherwise unperceivable; and this elevation of his eye was owing to the eleva-

---

[1] *Charles's Isle, Norfolk Isle:* two of the islands in the Encantadas, or the Galapagos Islands, located in the eastern Pacific

[2] *thewy:* muscular

tion of his spirits; and this again—for truth must out—to a dram of Peruvian pisco,[3] in guerdon[4] for some kindness done, secretly administered to him that morning by our mulatto steward. Now, certainly, pisco does a deal of mischief in the world; yet seeing that, in the present case, it was the means, though indirect, of rescuing a human being from the most dreadful fate, must we not also needs admit that sometimes pisco does a deal of good?

Glancing across the water in the direction pointed out, I saw some white thing hanging from an inland rock, perhaps half a mile from the sea.

"It is a bird; a white-winged bird; perhaps a—no; it is—it is a handkerchief!"

"Aye, a handkerchief!" echoed my comrade, and with a louder shout apprised[5] the captain.

Quickly now—like the running out and training of a great gun—the long cabin spy-glass was thrust through the mizzen-rigging from the high platform of the poop;[6] whereupon a human figure was plainly seen upon the inland rock, eagerly waving towards us what seemed to be the handkerchief.

Our captain was a prompt, good fellow. Dropping the glass, he lustily ran forward, ordering the anchor to be dropped again; hands to stand by a boat, and lower away.

In a half-hour's time the swift boat returned. It went with six and came with seven; and the seventh was a woman.

It is not artistic heartlessness, but I wish I could but draw in crayons; for this woman was a most touching sight; and crayons, tracing softly melancholy lines, would best depict the mournful image of the dark-damasked Chola widow.

Her story was soon told, and though given in her own strange language was as quickly understood; for our captain, from long trading on the Chilean coast, was well versed in the Spanish. A Cholo, or half-breed Indian woman of Payta in Peru, three years gone by, with her young new-wedded

---

[3] *pisco:* a South American brandy
[4] *guerdon:* reward
[5] *apprised:* informed
[6] *poop:* raised deck at the stern of a sailing ship

husband Felipe, of pure Castilian blood, and her one only Indian brother, Truxill, Hunilla had taken passage on the main in a French whaler, commanded by a joyous man; which vessel, bound to the cruising grounds beyond the Enchanted Isles, proposed passing close by their vicinity. The object of the little party was to procure tortoise oil, a fluid which for its great purity and delicacy is held in high estimation wherever known; and it is well known all along this part of the Pacific coast. With a chest of clothes, tools, cooking utensils, a rude apparatus for trying out the oil, some casks of biscuit, and other things, not omitting two favorite dogs, of which faithful animal all the Cholos are very fond, Hunilla and her companions were safely landed at their chosen place; the Frenchman, according to the contract made ere sailing, engaged to take them off upon returning from a four months' cruise in the westward seas; which interval the three adventurers deemed quite sufficient for their purposes.

On the isle's lone beach they paid him in silver for their passage out, the stranger having declined to carry them at all except upon that condition; though willing to take every means to insure the due fulfillment of his promise. Felipe had striven hard to have this payment put off to the period of the ship's return. But in vain. Still they thought they had, in another way, ample pledge of the good faith of the Frenchman. It was arranged that the expenses of the passage home should not be payable in silver, but in tortoises; one hundred tortoises ready captured to the returning captain's hand. These the Cholos meant to secure after their own work was done, against the probable time of the Frenchman's coming back; and no doubt in prospect already felt, that in those hundred tortoises—now somewhere ranging the isle's interior—they possessed one hundred hostages. Enough: the vessel sailed; the gazing three on shore answered the loud glee of the singing crew; and ere evening, the French craft was hull down in the distant sea, its masts three faintest lines which quickly faded from Hunilla's eye.

The stranger had given a blithesome promise, and anchored it with oaths; but oaths and anchors equally will drag; naught else abides on fickle earth but unkept promises of joy. Contrary winds from out unstable skies, or contrary moods of his more varying mind, or shipwreck and sudden death in solitary waves; whatever was the cause, the blithe stranger never was seen again.

Yet, however dire a calamity was here in store, misgivings of it ere due time never disturbed the Cholos' busy minds, now all intent upon the toilsome matter which had brought them hither. Nay, by swift doom coming like the thief at night, ere seven weeks went by, two of the little party were removed from all anxieties of land or sea. No more they sought to gaze with feverish fear, or still more feverish hope, beyond the present's horizon line; but into the furthest future their own silent spirits sailed. By perservering labor beneath that burning sun, Felipe and Truxill had brought down to their hut many scores of tortoises, and tried out the oil, when, elated with their good success, and to reward themselves for such hard work, they, too hastily, made a catamaran, or Indian raft, much used on the Spanish main, and merrily started on a fishing trip, just without a long reef with many jagged gaps, running parallel with the shore, about half a mile from it. By some bad tide or hap, or natural negligence of joyfulness (for though they could not be heard, yet by their gestures they seemed singing at the time), forced in deep water against that iron bar, the ill-made catamaran was overset, and came all to pieces; when dashed by broad-chested swells between their broken logs and the sharp teeth of the reef, both adventurers perished before Hunilla's eyes.

Before Hunilla's eyes they sank. The real woe of this event passed before her sight as some sham tragedy on the stage. She was seated in a rude bower among the withered thickets, crowning a lofty cliff, a little back from the beach. The thickets were so disposed, that in looking upon the sea at large she peered out from among the branches as from the lattice of a high balcony. But upon the day we speak of here, the better to watch the adventure of those two hearts she loved, Hunilla had withdrawn the branches to one side, and held them so. They formed an oval frame, through which the bluely boundless sea rolled like a painted one. And there, the invisible painter painted to her view the wave-tossed and disjointed raft, its once level logs slantingly upheaved, as raking masts, and the four struggling arms undistinguishable among them; and then all subsided into smooth-flowing creamy waters, slowly drifting the splintered wreck; while first and last, no sound of any sort was heard. Death in a silent picture; a dream of the eye; such vanishing shapes as the mirage shows.

So instant was the scene, so trance-like its mild pictorial effect, so distant from her blasted bower and her common sense of things, that Hunilla gazed and gazed, nor raised a finger or a wail. But as good to sit thus dumb, in stupor staring on that dumb show, for all that otherwise might be done. With half a mile of sea between, how could her two enchanted arms aid those four fated ones? The distance long, the time one sand. After the lightning is beheld, what fool shall stay the thunder-bolt? Felipe's body was washed ashore, but Truxill's never came; only his gay, braided hat of golden straw — that same sunflower thing he waved to her, pushing from the strand — and now, to the last gallant, it still saluted her. But Felipe's body floated to the marge,[7] with one arm encirclingly outstretched. Lock-jawed in grim death, the lover-husband softly clasped his bride, true to her even in death's dream. Ah, Heaven, when man thus keeps his faith, wilt Thou be faithless who created the faithful one? But they cannot break faith who never plighted it.

It needs not to be said what nameless misery now wrapped the lonely widow. In telling her own story she passed this almost entirely over, simply recounting the event. Construe[8] the comment of her features as you might, from her mere words little would you have weened[9] that Hunilla was herself the heroine of her tale. But not thus did she defraud us of our tears. All hearts bled that grief could be so brave.

She but showed us her soul's lid, and the strange ciphers thereon engraved; all within, with pride's timidity, was withheld. Yet was there one exception. Holding out her small olive hand before her captain, she said in mild and slowest Spanish, "Señor, I buried him," then paused, struggled as

---

[7] *marge:* edge, margin
[8] *construe:* interpret
[9] *weened:* imagined, thought

against the writhed coiling of a snake, and cringing suddenly, leaped up, repeating in impassioned pain, "I buried him, my life, my soul!"

Doubtless, it was by half-unconscious, automatic motions of her hands, that this heavy-hearted one performed the final office for Felipe, and planted a rude cross of withered sticks — no green ones might be had — at the head of that lonely grave, where rested now in lasting uncomplaint and quiet haven he whom untranquil seas had overthrown.

But some dull sense of another body that should be interred, of another cross that should hallow another grave — unmade as yet — some dull anxiety and pain touching her undiscovered brother, now haunted the oppressed Hunilla. Her hands fresh from the burial earth, she slowly went back to the beach, with unshaped purposes wandering there, her spell-bound eye bent upon the incessant waves. But they bore nothing to her but a dirge, which maddened her to think that murderers should mourn. As time went by, and these things came less dreamingly to her mind, the strong persuasions of her Romish[10] faith, which sets peculiar store by consecrated urns, prompted her to resume in waking earnest that pious search which had but been begun as in somnambulism.[11] Day after day, week after week, she trod the cindery beach, till at length a double motive edged every eager glance. With equal longing she now looked for the living and the dead; the brother and the captain; alike vanished, never to return. Little accurate note of time had Hunilla taken under such emotions as were hers, and little, outside herself, served for calendar or dial. As to poor Crusoe in the self-same sea, no saint's bell pealed forth the lapse of week or month; each day went by unchallenged; no chanticleer[12] announced those sultry dawns, no lowing herds those poisonous nights. All wonted[13] and steadily recurring sounds, human, or humanized by sweet fellowship with man, but one stirred that torrid trance — the cry of dogs; save which naught but the rolling sea invaded it,

---

[10] *Romish:* Roman Catholic
[11] *somnambulism:* sleepwalking
[12] *chanticleer:* rooster
[13] *wonted:* accustomed

an all-pervading monotone; and to the widow that was the least loved voice she could have heard.

No wonder, that as her thoughts now wandered to the un-returning ship, and were beaten back again, the hope against hope so struggled in her soul, that at length she desperately said, "Not yet, not yet; my foolish heart runs on too fast." So she forced patience for some further weeks. But to those whom earth's sure indraft[14] draws, patience or impatience is still the same.

Hunilla now sought to settle precisely in her mind, to an hour, how long it was since the ship had sailed; and then, with the same precision, how long a space remained to pass. But this proved impossible. What present day or month it was she could not say. Time was her labyrinth, in which Hunilla was entirely lost.

And now follows — —

Against my own purposes a pause descends upon me here. One knows not whether nature doth not impose some secrecy upon him who has been privy to[15] certain things. At least, it is to be doubted whether it be good to blazon such. If some books are deemed most baneful and their sale forbid, how, then, with deadlier facts, not dreams of doting men? Those whom books will hurt will not be proof against events. Events, not books, should be forbid. But in all things man sows upon the wind, which bloweth just there whither it listeth; for ill or good, man cannot know. Often ill comes from the good, as good from ill.

When Hunilla — —

Dire sight it is to see some silken beast long dally with a golden lizard ere she devour. More terrible, to see how feline fate will sometimes dally with a human soul, and by a name-less magic make it repulse a sane despair with a hope which is but mad. Unwittingly I imp[16] this cat-like thing, sporting with the heart of him who reads; for if he feel not he reads in vain.

— "The ship sails this day, today," at last said Hunilla to herself; "this gives me certain time to stand on; without cer-

---

[14] *indraft:* inward current or pull
[15] *privy to:* secretly or privately informed about
[16] *imp:* mimic

tainty I go mad. In loose ignorance I have hoped and hoped; now in firm knowledge I will but wait. Now I live and no longer perish in bewilderings. Holy Virgin, aid me! Thou wilt waft back the ship. Oh, past length of weary weeks—all to be dragged over—to buy the certainty of to-day, I freely give ye, though I tear ye from me!"

As mariners, tost in tempest on some desolate ledge, patch them a boat out of the remnants of their vessel's wreck, and launch it in the self-same waves, see here Hunilla, this lone shipwrecked soul, out of treachery invoking trust. Humanity, thou strong thing, I worship thee, not in the laureled victor, but in this vanquished one.

Truly Hunilla leaned upon a reed, a real one; no metaphor: a real Eastern reed. A piece of hollow cane, drifted from unknown isles, and found upon the beach, its once jagged ends rubbed smoothly even as by sand-paper; its golden glazing gone. Long ground between the sea and land, upper and nether stone, the unvarnished substance was filed bare, and wore another polish now, one with itself, the polish of its agony. Circular lines at intervals cut all round this surface, divided it into six panels of unequal length. In the first were scored the days, each tenth one marked by a longer and deeper notch; the second was scored for the number of sea-fowl eggs for sustenance, picked out from the rocky nests; the third, how many fish had been caught from the shore; the fourth, how many small tortoises found inland; the fifth, how many days of sun; the sixth, of clouds; which last, of the two, was the greater one. Long night of busy numbering, misery's mathematics, to weary her too-wakeful soul to sleep; yet sleep for that was none.

The panel of the days was deeply worn—the long tenth notches half effaced, as alphabets of the blind. Ten thousand times the longing widow had traced her finger over the bamboo—dull flute, which played on, gave no sound—as if counting birds flown by in air would hasten tortoises creeping through the woods.

After the one hundred and eightieth day no further mark was seen; that last one was the faintest, as the first the deepest.

"There were more days," said our Captain; "many, many

more; why did you not go on and notch them, too, Hunilla?"

"Señor, ask me not."

"And meantime, did no other vessel pass the isle?"

"Nay, señor; — but — —"

"You do not speak; but *what*, Hunilla?"

"Ask me not, Señor."

"You saw ships pass, far away; you waved to them; they passed on; — was that it, Hunilla?"

"Señor, be it as you say."

Braced against her woe, Hunilla would not, durst not trust the weakness of her tongue. Then when our Captain asked whether any whale-boats had — —

But no, I will not file this thing complete for scoffing souls to quote, and call it firm proof upon their side. The half shall here remain untold. Those two unnamed events which befell Hunilla on this isle, let them abide between her and her God. In nature, as in law, it may be libelous to speak some truths.

Still, how it was that, although our vessel had lain three days anchored nigh the isle, its one human tenant should not have discovered us till just upon the point of sailing, never to revisit so lone and far a spot, this needs explaining ere the sequel come.

The place where the French captain had landed the little party was on the further and opposite end of the isle. There, too, it was that they had afterwards built their hut. Nor did the widow in her solitude desert the spot where her loved ones had dwelt with her, and where the dearest of the twain now slept his last long sleep, and all her plaints awaked him not, and he of husbands the most faithful during life.

Now, high broken land rises between the opposite extremities of the isle. A ship anchored at one side is invisible from the other. Neither is the isle so small, but a considerable company might wander for days through the wilderness of one side, and never be seen, or their halloos heard, by any stranger holding aloof on the other. Hence Hunilla, who naturally associated the possible coming of ships with her own part of the isle, might to the end have remained quite ignorant of the presence of our vessel, were it not for a mysterious presentiment, borne to her, so our mariners averred, by this isle's enchanted air. Nor did the widow's answer undo the thought.

"How did you come to cross the isle this morning, then, Hunilla?" said our Captain.

"Señor, something came flitting by me. It touched my cheek, my heart, Señor."

"What do you say, Hunilla?"

"I have said, Señor, something came through the air."

It was a narrow chance. For when in crossing the isle Hunilla gained the high land in the center, she must then for the first have perceived our masts, and also marked that their sails were being loosed, perhaps even heard the echoing chorus of the windlass song. The strange ship was about to sail, and she behind. With all haste she now descends the height on the hither side, but soon loses sight of the ship among the sunken jungles at the mountain's base. She struggles on through the withered branches, which seek at every step to bar her path, till she comes to the isolated rock, still some way from the water. This she climbs, to reassure herself. The ship is still in plainest sight. But now, worn out with over-tension, Hunilla all but faints; she fears to step down from her giddy perch; she is fain to pause, there where she is, and as a last resort catches the turban from her head, unfurls and waves it over the jungles towards us.

During the telling of her story the mariners formed a voiceless circle round Hunilla and the Captain; and when at length the word was given to man the fastest boat, and pull around to the isle's thither side, to bring away Hunilla's chest and the tortoise oil, such alacrity[17] of both cheery and sad obedience seldom before was seen. Little ado was made. Already the anchor had been recommitted to the bottom, and the ship swung calmly to it.

But Hunilla insisted upon accompanying the boat as indispensable pilot to her hidden hut. So being refreshed with the best the steward could supply, she started with us. Nor did ever any wife of the most famous admiral, in her husband's barge, receive more silent reverence of respect than poor Hunilla from this boat's crew.

[17] *alacrity:* liveliness

Rounding many a vitreous cape and bluff, in two hours' time we shot inside the fatal reef; wound into a secret cove, looked up along a green many-gabled lava wall, and saw the island's solitary dwelling.

It hung upon an impending cliff, sheltered on two sides by tangled thickets, and half-screened from view in front by juttings of the rude stairway, which climbed the precipice from the sea. Built of canes, it was thatched with long, mildewed grass. It seemed an abandoned hay-rick, whose haymakers were now no more. The roof inclined but one way; the eaves coming to within two feet of the ground. And here was a simple apparatus to collect the dews, or rather doubly-distilled and finest winnowed rains, which, in mercy or in mockery, the night-skies sometimes drop upon these blighted Encantadas. All along beneath the eaves, a spotted sheet, quite weather-stained, was spread, pinned to short, upright stakes, set in the shallow sand. A small clinker, thrown into the cloth, weighed its middle down, thereby straining all moisture into a calabash[18] placed below. This vessel supplied each drop of water ever drunk upon the isle by the Cholos. Hunilla told us the calabash would sometimes, but not often, be half filled overnight. It held six quarts, perhaps. "But," said she, "we were used to thirst. At sandy Payta, where I live, no shower from heaven ever fell; all the water there is brought on mules from the inland vales."

Tied among the thickets were some twenty moaning tortoises, supplying Hunilla's lonely larder; while hundreds of vast tableted black bucklers,[19] like displaced, shattered tombstones of dark slate, were also scattered round. These were the skeleton backs of those great tortoises from which Felipe and Truxill had made their precious oil. Several large calabashes and two goodly kegs were filled with it. In a pot near by were the caked crusts of a quantity which had been permitted to evaporate. "They meant to have strained it off next day," said Hunilla, as she turned aside.

I forgot to mention the most singular sight of all, though the first that greeted us after landing.

---

[18] *calabash:* a type of gourd
[19] *bucklers:* round shields

Some ten small, soft-haired ringleted dogs, of a beautiful breed, peculiar to Peru, set up a concert of glad welcomings when we gained the beach, which was responded to by Hunilla. Some of these dogs had, since her widowhood, been born upon the isle, the progeny of the two brought from Payta. Owing to the jagged steeps and pitfalls, tortuous thickets, sunken clefts and perilous intricacies of all sorts in the interior, Hunilla, admonished by the loss of one favorite among them, never allowed these delicate creatures to follow her in her occasional birds'-nests climbs and other wanderings; so that, through long habituation, they offered not to follow, when that morning she crossed the land, and her own soul was then too full of other things to heed their lingering behind. Yet, all along she had so clung to them, that, besides what moisture they lapped up at early daybreak from the small scoop-holes among the adjacent rocks, she had shared the dew of her calabash among them; never laying by any considerable store against those prolonged and utter droughts which, in some disastrous seasons, warp these isles.

Having pointed out, at our desire, what few things she would like transported to the ship—her chest, the oil, not omitting the live tortoises which she intended for a grateful present to our Captain—we immediately set to work, carrying them to the boat down the long, sloping stair of deeply-shadowed rock. While my comrades were thus employed, I looked and Hunilla had disappeared.

It was not curiosity alone, but, it seems to me, something different mingled with it, which prompted me to drop my tortoise, and once more gaze slowly around. I remembered the husband buried by Hunilla's hands. A narrow pathway led into a dense part of the thickets. Following it through many mazes, I came out upon a small, round, open space, deeply chambered there.

The mound rose in the middle; a bare heap of finest sand, like that unverdured[20] heap found at the bottom of an hour-glass run out. At its head stood the cross of withered sticks; the dry, peeled bark still fraying from it; its transverse limb

---

[20] *unverdured:* devoid of green vegetation

tied up with rope, and forlornly adroop in the silent air.

Hunilla was partly prostrate upon the grave; her dark head bowed, and lost in her long, loosened Indian hair; her hands extended to the cross-foot, with a little brass crucifix clasped between; a crucifix worn featureless, like an ancient graven knocker long plied in vain. She did not see me, and I made no noise, but slid aside, and left the spot.

A few moments ere all was ready for our going, she re-appeared among us. I looked into her eyes, but saw no tear. There was something which seemed strangely haughty in her air, and yet it was the air of woe. A Spanish and an Indian grief, which would not visibly lament. Pride's height in vain abased to proneness on the rack;[21] nature's pride subduing nature's torture.

Like pages the small and silken dogs surrounded her, as she slowly descended towards the beach. She caught the two most eager creatures in her arms — *"Tita mia! Tomotita mia!"* — and fondling them, inquired how many could we take on board.

The mate commanded the boat's crew; not a hard-hearted man, but his way of life had been such that in most things, even in the smallest, simple utility was his leading motive.

"We cannot take them all, Hunilla; our supplies are short; the winds are unreliable; we may be a good many days going to Tumbez. So take those you have, Hunilla; but no more."

She was in the boat; the oarsmen, too, were seated, all save one, who stood ready to push off and then spring himself. With the sagacity of their race, the dogs now seemed aware that they were in the very instant of being deserted upon a barren strand. The gunwales of the boat were high; its prow — presented inland — was lifted; so owing to the water, which they seemed instinctively to shun, the dogs could not well leap into the little craft. But their busy paws hard scraped the prow, as it had been some farmer's door shutting them out from shelter in a winter storm. A clamorous agony of alarm. They did not howl, or whine; they all but spoke.

"Push off! Give way!" cried the mate. The boat gave one

---

[21]*rack:* an instrument of torture

heavy drag and lurch, and next moment shot swiftly from the beach, turned on her heel, and sped. The dogs ran howling along the water's marge; now pausing to gaze at the flying boat, then motioning as if to leap in chase, but mysteriously withheld themselves; and again ran howling along the beach. Had they been human beings, hardly would they have more vividly inspired the sense of desolation. The oars were plied as confederate feathers of two wings. No one spoke. I looked back upon the beach, and then upon Hunilla, but her face was set in a stern dusky calm. The dogs crouching in her lap vainly licked her rigid hands. She never looked behind her, but sat motionless, till we turned a promontory of the coast and lost all sights and sounds astern. She seemed as one who, having experienced the sharpest of mortal pangs, was henceforth content to have all lesser heart-strings riven, one by one. To Hunilla, pain seemed so necessary, that pain in other beings, though by love and sympathy made her own, was unrepiningly[22] to be borne. A heart of yearning in a frame of steel. A heart of earthly yearning, frozen by the frost which falleth from the sky.

The sequel is soon told. After a long passage, vexed by calms and baffling winds, we made the little port of Tumbez in Peru, there to recruit the ship. Payta was not very distant. Our captain sold the tortoise oil to a Tumbez merchant; and adding to the silver a contribution from all hands, gave it to our silent passenger, who knew not what the mariners had done.

The last seen of lone Hunilla she was passing into Payta town, riding upon a small gray ass; and before her on the ass's shoulders, she eyed the jointed workings of the beast's armorial cross.

[22] *unrepiningly:* uncomplainingly

FOR DISCUSSION

1. At the beginning of this selection, the narrator says, "through sympathy, that lone island has become a spot made sacred by the strangest trials of humanity." What were these trials? Why were they so strange? What do you think the narrator means by the word *sacred*?

2. What impressions do you gain of Hunilla and from which details, incidents, and remarks provided in this selection? What effect does she have on the captain and the crew? How do you think she feels toward them? What evidence can you find that she is still capable of deep human emotions?

3. How do you account for the strange "something" that leads Hunilla to cross the isle and see the ship that rescues her? At what point in the sketch does the narrator leave part of the story untold? What effect does this create?

4. During the narrator's retelling of Hunilla's tale, he interjects that "in all things man sows upon the wind . . . ." What does he mean? Find other passages in which he comments on man's lot and discuss their meaning.

5. Throughout the sketch there are frequent references to the cross. Sometimes it represents an object, such as the cross of withered sticks which Hunilla places on her husband's grave. Sometimes it represents more than an object; it is a symbol. What idea, belief, quality, or attitude toward life does the cross symbolize in this sketch? Note especially the use of this symbol in the last line. Discuss the meaning of this line.

6. In all the sketches included in *The Encantadas,* Melville is concerned with the same question: At how low a level can human existence go on, and what qualities are necessary for this existence? What is the level of existence on Norfolk Isle? What qualities would such an existence call forth? Why is the tortoise a symbol both of the level of existence and of the qualities? How does Melville's use of the tortoise symbol help you to understand Hunilla's predicament?

7. The style of a literary work is characteristic of the author and, to some extent, of the period in which he wrote. If Hemingway, for example, had written this sketch, the style would have been different both because he does not write like Melville and because he is a modern writer. After some member of the class has read the third paragraph of this sketch aloud, discuss the qualities of

Melville's style. Which qualities do you think are characteristic of his way of writing? Which are characteristic of the writing of his day?

FOR COMPOSITION

1. From the details given in this sketch, write a description of Norfolk Isle. Try to bring out the over-all impression which you think Melville intended to convey. Decide first whether it is barren, desolate, wild, brooding, lonely — perhaps none of these or a combination of two or more.
2. In a short composition explain both why Hunilla decides to keep a record of the days and how she keeps it. Suggest what you think could be the reason she stops.

THE REGIONAL OUTLOOK

By the middle of the nineteenth century, this country could be justly proud of its achievements, literary as well as economic and political. Europeans were not only reading American books; they were also praising them for their excellence. America now had a tradition of its own, from which future writers could draw inspiration, and to which they could turn for models. They even had a new model in the short tale or story perfected by Poe and Hawthorne. One must remember, however, that this tradition developed along the Atlantic seaboard, principally in and around Boston and New York, the oldest centers of culture in the United States. It was a conservative and aristocratic culture, concerned primarily with preserving the heritage of the past and fostering an interest in the literature and art of the Old World. It made a tremendous contribution to American thought, education and literature, but it represented only one segment of American life. Even as Hawthorne, Melville, and Poe were publishing their literary masterpieces, a new culture was developing to the south and west of the Allegheny Mountains. In time it would replace the mature culture of the East and produce a more "American" literary tradition, because it was not modeled on, and had no close link with, the culture of the Old World.

To understand this new culture, one must be aware of the forces which, by 1850, had already begun to change the face of America. Perhaps the most important force was expansion. Scarcely had this nation won its independence than men like Daniel Boone began to explore and settle unclaimed land to the south and west. In sixty-five years, this country had grown in size from thirteen Atlantic states to a sprawling nation that stretched as far west as the Pacific coast and as far south as the Mexican border.

The key to the momentous development of the frontier was the railroads. By 1850 they spread from the Alleghenies to the Mississippi River; by 1869 they stretched from coast to coast. Now books, magazines, and newspapers—as well as professional men, printing presses, and the ever-popular lecturer—began to move in quantity and with speed from the Eastern and Middle Border states to the Far West. "Now American writers began to explore their country; now Americans began to know themselves as a single people and at the same time a diverse people, one large pattern full of endless variations."[1]

Bret Harte was the founder of the new literature which flourished in the sixties and seventies. It came to be known as "local color" or regional literature because its aim was to paint the scenery, manners, and characters peculiar to the more picturesque areas of the continental United States. It was romantic in its concern with the glamorous past, the picturesque and unfamiliar, the common man—rogue or hero—and the ideals of independence and self-reliance. Yet its "very focusing of attention on definite parts of the country and on specific types of character, specific dialects, specific dress, made for that careful scrutiny of the realities of life which constituted the prime demand of the out-and-out realist."[2] Thus, regional literature was both romantic and realistic.

[1] Wallace Stegner, "Western Record and Romance." *Literary History of the United States*, p. 862.

[2] Louis Wann, *The Rise of Realism: 1860-1900* (New York: The Macmillan Company, 1961), p. 11.

The motivation for this literature was the national interest in the American scene and the desire of the reading public to have this scene presented faithfully, including the racy language and rough ways of mining camps and river towns. Writers from North and South, East and West, historians, journalists, poets, novelists, and artists of the short story—all took part in a literary movement that for decades attracted almost as much attention in the Old World as in the New. Four writers who made an outstanding contribution to this movement by their works or influence were Bret Harte, Mark Twain, Sarah Orne Jewett, and George Washington Cable.

By birth and early environment, BRET HARTE was an Easterner, and though he made his fame by portraying the rough and tumble life of the Far West, he used only a small part of the literary material that this region offered. As editor of the California magazine, the *Overland Monthly*, he decided it should include something about the region. Several of his stories had already appeared in various magazines, including the *Atlantic Monthly*, but the one he wrote for the *Overland*, "The Luck of Roaring Camp," proved to be the great popular "hit" of the decade. Within three years he had won such a nation-wide reputation that the *Atlantic* offered him ten thousand dollars a year to write California stories. He accepted, moved to the East, and for several years continued to write voluminously and, at times, brilliantly. "Already, however, his truly creative work was done. Clever and theatrical rather than great, he proved unable to develop the field he had discovered."[3] His significant work narrows down to a handful of stories and poems produced between 1869, the year of his first triumph, and 1871.

MARK TWAIN won recognition as a major writer with the publication of his Mississippi River books. Only recently, however, has his enormous contribution to American and world literature been fairly evaluated and fully appreciated. Once considered chiefly a writer of regional literature and of children's stories, he is now considered one of the most distinguished authors America has produced. Bernard DeVoto,

[3]Walter Fuller Taylor, *The Story of American Letters* (Chicago: Henry Regnery Company, 1956), p. 233.

the well-known critic and historian, has claimed that Twain "had a greater effect than any other American writer on the evolution of American prose." Ernest Hemingway, one of the giants of twentieth-century American fiction, contended that, "All modern American literature comes from one book by Mark Twain called *Huckleberry Finn*. . . . There was nothing before. There has been nothing as good since."

Twain himself would certainly have been surprised by such extravagant praise from the critics and creators of modern fiction. He knew that he was a "phunny phellow" and that he had a talent for "authentic" writing, but he was almost proud of being un-literary. Late in his career he wrote a letter to a friend which reads almost like a direct refutation of Long-fellow and the genteel tradition: "I have never tried in even one single instance, to help cultivate the cultivated classes. . . . And I never had any ambition in that direction, but always hunted for bigger game—the masses. I have seldom deliberately tried to instruct them, but have done my best to entertain them. . . . Yes, you see, I have always catered for the Belly and the Members."

Perhaps Twain's importance to such men as DeVoto and Hemingway lay precisely in his avoidance of the conventionally "literary." Ignoring traditional models, he proved finally that great and enduring literature could be created from purely American materials and expressed in a purely American style. The outstanding characteristics of Twain's writing were derived from native folk sources rather than from a recognized literary tradition. His particular sense of the dramatic, his ability to see romance in American subjects, and his masterful use of exaggeration for comic effect are all present, in embryonic form, in the "tall tales" of the old West. His style, moreover, reflects his early training in the straight-forward yet colorful writing that characterized American journalism in the nineteenth century.

Perhaps the most striking testimony to Twain's ability to say profound and moving things in an apparently simple way is the fact that he can be read with equal pleasure and profit by both the young and the mature.

SARAH ORNE JEWETT was a product of aristocratic New England culture. Yet she was concerned neither with re-creating the American past nor with making Americans aware of the culture of the Old World. Accompanying her doctor father on his professional calls, she came to know firsthand the town and country people of Maine and to resent the lack of understanding and the condescending attitude of the summer visitors from the city. "I wanted the world to know their grand, simple lives," she later wrote, "and, so far as I had a mission, when I first began to write, I think that was it." Her stories about these "beloved village folks" appeared first in leading magazines and then in two collections, *Deephaven* and *A White Heron, and Other Stories.*

Miss Jewett's New England had been left behind by history. While the West was being conquered and cities such as New York were becoming the centers of American life, she chose to picture a twilight world—a world of quiet, subdued colors in which a chance encounter with a woods animal or a conversation with a friend could make a whole day worthwhile.

She observed and pictured nature with such acuteness and sensitivity that her natural settings seem almost to have personalities of their own. Yet she was interested in the natural world only insofar as it affected human beings. "Miss Jewett's landscapes had always figures in the foreground, for people were always in the foreground of her consciousness."[4]

GEORGE WASHINGTON CABLE'S native New Orleans fur-nished the picturesque setting for most of his stories and for his first and best novel, *The Grandissimes.* By teaching him-self to read French, he was able to study the city archives, drawing material for his stories from the old Creole records. Though his settings, action, and characters are essentially romantic, Cable's treatment of them is realistic. His char-acters are psychologically believable human beings, usually of Creole background, and their Creole dialect is accurately and faithfully rendered. His descriptions are colorful while

[4] Carlos Baker, "Delineation of Life and Character," *Literary History of the United States,* p. 846.

presenting careful and accurate details. The charm of his stories, underlined by a quiet, unobtrusive humor, made Cable a leading figure among the regional writers.

A serious social thinker, Cable was concerned with the prevalent social injustice to both Creoles and Negroes, even though he was able to sympathize with the troubled South. More and more, his writing tended to reflect the social reformer rather than the storyteller. As a result, his novels and later writings never matched the charm of his early stories.

Bret Harte

Guilty at times of sentimentality and exaggeration, Bret Harte was, nevertheless, a master at portraying the picturesque California life in the era following the gold rush and at blending this picturesqueness with Western humor. He took delight in those grotesque contrasts of character and situation which keep interest taut by swift change and by unexpected turns. His major contribution to the short story was his ability to create a swift forward movement to a climactic ending, sometimes a surprise ending as in Poe's stories. His strength as a writer lay in his clean and disciplined style, his ear for language and dialect, his humor, and his avoidance of prudery and preaching.

The Boom in the Calaveras Clarion

The editorial sanctum of the *Calaveras Clarion* opened upon the "composing-room" of that paper on the one side, and gave apparently upon the rest of Calaveras County upon the other. For, situated on the very outskirts of the settlement and the summit of a very steep hill, the pines sloped away from the editorial windows to the long valley of the South Fork and—infinity. The little wooden building had invaded Nature without subduing it. It was filled night and day with the murmur of pines and their fragrance. Squirrels scampered over its roof when it was not preoccupied by woodpeckers, and a printer's devil[1] had once seen a nest-building blue jay enter a window in the composing-room, flutter before one of the slanting type-cases with an air of deliberate selection, and then fly off with a vowel in its bill.

Amidst these sylvan surroundings the temporary editor of the *Clarion* sat at his sanctum, reading the proofs of an edi-

[1]*printer's devil:* apprentice or errand boy in a printing office

135

torial. As he was occupying that position during a six weeks'
absence of the *bona fide*[2] editor and proprietor, he was consequently reading the proof with some anxiety and responsibility. It had been suggested to him by certain citizens that
the *Clarion* needed a firmer and more aggressive policy towards the Bill before the Legislature for the wagon road to
the South Fork. Several Assembly men had been "got at" by
the rival settlement of Liberty Hill, and a scathing exposure
and denunciation of such methods was necessary. The interests of their own township were also to be "whooped up." All
this had been vigorously explained to him, and he had grasped
the spirit, if not always the facts, of his informants. It is to be
feared, therefore, that he was perusing his article more with
reference to its vigor than his own convictions. And yet he
was not so greatly absorbed as to be unmindful of the murmur
of the pines without, his half-savage environment, and the
lazy talk of his sole companions, — the foreman and printer in
the adjoining room.

"Bet your life! I've always said that a man *inside* a newspaper office could hold his own agin any outsider that wanted
to play rough or tried to raid the office! Thar's the press, and
thar's the printin' ink and roller! Folks talk a heap o' the power
o' the Press! — I tell ye, ye don't half know it. Why, when old
Kernel Fish was editin' the *Sierra Banner,* one o' them bullies
that he'd lampooned[3] in the *Banner* fought his way past the
Kernel in the office, into the composin'-room, to wreck every-
thin' and 'pye'[4] all the types. Spoffrel — ye don't remember
Spoffrel? — little red-haired man? — was foreman. Spoffrel
fended him off with the roller and got one good dab inter his
eyes that blinded him, and then Spoffrel sorter skirmished him
over to the press, — a plain lever just like ours, — whar the
locked-up form of the inside was still a-lyin'! Then, quick as
lightnin', Spoffrel tilts him over agin it, and *he* throws out his
hand and ketches hold o' the form to steady himself, when
Spoffrel just runs the form and the hand under the press and
down with the lever! And that held the feller fast as grim

[2] *bona fide:* real, actual
[3] *lampooned:* ridiculed
[4] *pye:* jumble

death! And when at last he begs off, and Spoff lets him loose, the hull o' that 'ere lampooning article he objected to was printed right onto the skin o' his hand! Fact, and it wouldn't come off, either."

"Gosh, but I'd like to hev seen it," said the printer. "There ain't any chance, I reckon, o' such a sight here. The boss don't take no risks lampoonin', and he" (the editor knew he was being indicated by some unseen gesture of the unseen workman) "ain't that style."

"Ye never kin tell," said the foreman didactically,[5] "what might happen! I've known editors to get into a fight jest for a little innercent bedevilin' o' the opposite party. Sometimes for a misprint. Old man Pritchard of the *Argus* oncet had a hole blown through his arm because his proof-reader had called Colonel Starbottle's speech an 'ignominious'[6] defense, when the old man hed written 'ingenuous'[7] defense."

The editor paused in his proof-reading. He had just come upon the sentence: "We cannot congratulate Liberty Hill—in its superior elevation—upon the ignominious silence of the representative of all Calaveras when this infamous Bill was introduced." He referred to his copy. Yes! He had certainly written "ignominious,"—that was what his informants had suggested. But was he sure they were right? He had a vague recollection, also, that the representative alluded to—Senator Bradley—had fought two duels, and was a "good" though somewhat impulsive shot! He might alter the word to "ingenuous" or "ingenious," either would be finely sarcastic, but then—there was his foreman, who would detect it! He would wait until he had finished the entire article. In that occupation he became oblivious of the next room, of a silence, a whispered conversation, which ended with a rapping at the door and the appearance of the foreman in the doorway.

"There's a man in the office who wants to see the editor," he said.

"Show him in," replied the editor briefly. He was, however, conscious that there was a singular significance in his fore-

---

[5] *didactically:* in a teaching manner
[6] *ignominious:* disgraceful
[7] *ingenuous:* naive, innocent

man's manner, and an eager apparition of the other printer over the foreman's shoulder.

"He's carryin' a shot-gun, and is a man twice as big as you be," said the foreman gravely.

The editor quickly recalled his own brief and as yet blameless record in the *Clarion*. "Perhaps," he said tentatively, with a gentle smile, "he's looking for Captain Brush" (the absent editor).

"I told him all that," said the foreman grimly, "and he said he wanted to see the man in charge."

In proportion as the editor's heart sank his outward crest arose. "Show him in," he said loftily.

"We *kin* keep him out," suggested the foreman, lingering a moment; "me and him," indicating the expectant printer behind him, "is enough for that."

"Show him up," repeated the editor firmly.

The foreman withdrew; the editor seated himself and again took up his proof. The doubtful word "ignominious" seemed to stand out of the paragraph before him; it certainly *was* a strong expression! He was about to run his pencil through it when he heard the heavy step of his visitor approaching. A sudden instinct of belligerency[8] took possession of him, and he wrathfully threw the pencil down.

The burly form of the stranger blocked the doorway. He was dressed like a miner, but his build and general physiognomy were quite distinct from the local variety. His upper lip and chin were clean-shaven, still showing the blue-black roots of the beard which covered the rest of his face and deepened in a thick fleece under his throat. He carried a small bundle tied up in a silk handkerchief in one hand, and a "shot-gun" in the other, perilously at half-cock. Entering the sanctum, he put down his bundle and quietly closed the door behind him. He then drew an empty chair towards him and dropped heavily into it with his gun on his knees. The editor's heart dropped almost as heavily, although he quite composedly held out his hand.

"Shall I relieve you of your gun?"

"Thank ye, lad—noa. It's moor coomfortable wi' me, and

8 *belligerency:* state of being warlike

it's main dangersome to handle on the half-cock. That's why I didn't leave 'im on the horse outside!"

At the sound of his voice and occasional accent a flash of intelligence relieved the editor's mind. He remembered that twenty miles away, in the illimitable vista from his windows, lay a settlement of English north-country miners, who, while faithfully adopting the methods, customs, and even slang of the Californians, retained many of their native peculiarities. The gun he carried on his knee, however, was evidently part of the Californian imitation.

"Can I do anything for you?" said the editor blandly.

"Ay! I've coom here to bill ma woife."

"I—don't think I understand," hesitated the editor, with a smile.

"I've coom here to get ye to put into your paper a warnin', a notiss, that onless she returns to my house in four weeks, I'll have nowt to do wi' her again."

"Oh!" said the editor, now perfectly reassured, "you want an advertisement? That's the business of the foreman; I'll call him." He was rising from his seat when the stranger laid a heavy hand on his shoulder and gently forced him down again.

"Noa, lad! I don't want noa foreman nor understrappers to take this job, I want to talk it over wi' you. *Sabe?*[9] My woife she bin up and awaa these six months. We had a bit of difference, that ain't here nor there, but she skedaddled outer my house. I want to give her fair warning, and let her know I ain't payin' any debts o' hers arter this notiss, and I ain't takin' her back arter four weeks from date."

"I see," said the editor glibly. "What's your wife's name?"

"Eliza Jane Dimmidge."

"Good," continued the editor, scribbling on the paper before him; "something like this will do: 'Whereas my wife, Eliza Jane Dimmidge having left my bed and board without just cause or provocation, this is to give notice that I shall not be responsible for any debts of her contracting on or after this date.'"

"Ye must be a lawyer," said Mr. Dimmidge admiringly.

[9] *sabe:* understand

It was an old enough form of advertisement, and the remark showed incontestably that Mr. Dimmidge was not a native; but the editor smiled patronizingly and went on: "'And I further give notice that if she does not return within the period of four weeks from this date, I shall take such proceedings for relief as the law affords.'"

"Coom, lad, I didn't say *that*."

"But you said you wouldn't take her back."

"Ay."

"And you can't prevent her without legal proceedings. She's your wife. But you needn't take proceedings, you know. It's only a warning."

Mr. Dimmidge nodded approvingly. "That's so."

"You'll want it published for four weeks, until date?" asked the editor.

"Mebbe longer, lad."

The editor wrote "till forbid" in the margin of the paper and smiled.

"How big will it be?" said Mr. Dimmidge.

The editor took up a copy of the *Clarion* and indicated about an inch of space. Mr. Dimmidge's face fell.

"I want it bigger,—in large letters, like a play-card,"[10] he said. "That's no good for a warning."

"You can have half a column or a whole column if you like," said the editor airily.

"I'll take a whole one," said Mr. Dimmidge simply.

The editor laughed. "Why! it would cost you a hundred dollars."

"I'll take it," repeated Mr. Dimmidge.

"But," said the editor gravely, "the same notice in a small space will serve your purpose and be quite legal."

"Never you mind that, lad! It's the looks of the thing I'm arter, and not the expense. I'll take that column."

The editor called in the foreman and showed him the copy. "Can you display that so as to fill a column?"

The foreman grasped the situation promptly. It would be big business for the paper. "Yes," he said meditatively, "that bold-faced election type will do it."

[10] *play-card:* (placard) poster

Mr. Dimmidge's face brightened. The expression "bold-faced" pleased him. "That's it! I told you. I want to bill her in a portion of the paper."

"I might put in a cut," said the foreman suggestively; "something like this." He took a venerable woodcut from the case. I grieve to say it was one which, until the middle of the present century, was common enough in the news-paper offices in the Southwest. It showed the running figure of a Negro woman carrying her personal property in a knotted handkerchief slung from a stick over her shoulder, and was supposed to represent "a fugitive slave."

Mr. Dimmidge's eyes brightened. "I'll take that, too. It's a little dark-complected for Mrs. D., but it will do. Now roon away, lad," he said to the foreman, as he quietly pushed him into the outer office again and closed the door. Then, facing the surprised editor, he said, "Theer's another notiss I want ye to put in your paper; but that's atween *us*. Not a word to *them*," he indicated the banished foreman with a jerk of his thumb. "*Sabe?* I want you to put this in another part o' your paper, quite innocent-like, ye know." He drew from his pocket a gray wallet, and taking a slip of paper read from it gravely, "'If this should meet the eye of R. B., look out for M. J. D. He is on your track. When this you see write a line to E. J. D., Elktown Post Office.' I want this to go in as 'Personal and Private'—*sabe?* like them notisses in the big 'Frisco papers."

"I see," said the editor, laying it aside. "It shall go in the same issue in another column."

Apparently Mr. Dimmidge expected something more than this reply, for after a moment's hesitation he said with an odd smile:—

"Ye ain't seein' the meanin' o' that, lad?"

"No," said the editor lightly; "but I suppose R. B. does, and it isn't intended that any one else should."

"Mebbe it is, and mebbe it isn't," said Mr. Dimmidge, with a self-satisfied air. "I don't mind saying atween us that R. B. is the man as I've suspicioned as havin' something to do with my wife goin' away; and ye see, if he writes to E. J. D. —that's my wife's initials—at Elktown, *I'll* get that letter and so make sure."

"But suppose your wife goes there first, or sends?"

"Then I'll ketch her or her messenger. Ye see?"

The editor did not see fit to oppose any argument to this phenomenal simplicity, and Mr. Dimmidge, after settling his bill with the foreman, and enjoining the editor to the strictest secrecy regarding the origin of the "personal notice," took up his gun and departed, leaving the treasury of the *Clarion* unprecedentedly enriched, and the editor to his proofs.

The paper duly appeared the next morning with the column advertisement, the personal notice, and the weighty editorial on the wagon road. There was a singular demand for the paper, the edition was speedily exhausted, and the editor was proportionately flattered, although he was surprised to receive neither praise nor criticism from his subscribers. Before evening, however, he learned to his astonishment that the excitement was caused by the column advertisement. Nobody knew Mr. Dimmidge, nor his domestic infelicities,[11] and the editor and foreman, being equally in the dark, took refuge in a mysterious and impressive evasion of all inquiry. Never since the last San Francisco Vigilance Committee had the office been so besieged. The editor, foreman, and even the apprentice were buttonholed and "treated" at the bar, but to no effect. All that could be learned was that it was a *bona fide* advertisement, for which one hundred dollars had been received! There were great discussions and conflicting theories as to whether the value of the wife, or the husband's anxiety to get rid of her, justified the enormous expense and ostentatious display. She was supposed to be an exceedingly beautiful woman by some, by others a perfect Sycorax;[12] in one breath Mr. Dimmidge was a weak, uxorious[13] spouse, wasting his substance on a creature who did not care for him, and in another a maddened, distracted, henpecked man, content to purchase peace and rest at any price. Certainly, never was advertisement more effective in its publicity, or cheaper in proportion to the circulation it commanded. It was copied

---

[11]*infelicities:* misfortunes
[12]*Sycorax:* a foul witch in Shakespeare's *The Tempest*
[13]*uxorious:* irrationally fond of one's wife

throughout the whole Pacific slope; mighty San Francisco papers described its size and setting under the attractive head-line, "How they Advertise a Wife in the Mountains!" It reappeared in the Eastern journals, under the title of "Whim-sicalities of the Western Press." It was believed to have crossed to England as a specimen of "Transatlantic Savagery." The real editor of the *Clarion* awoke one morning, in San Francisco, to find his paper famous. Its advertising columns were eagerly sought for; he at once advanced the rates. People bought excessive issues to gaze upon this monumental record of extravagance. A singular idea, which, however, brought further fortune to the paper, was advanced by an astute critic at the Eureka Saloon. "My opinion, gentlemen, is that the whole blamed thing is a bluff! There ain't no Mr. Dimmidge; there ain't no Mrs. Dimmidge; there ain't no desertion! The whole rotten thing is an *advertisement* o' suthin'! Ye'll find afore ye get through with it that that there wife won't come back until that blamed husband buys Somebody's Soap, or treats her to Somebody's particular Starch or Patent Medicine! Ye jest watch and see!" The idea was startling, and seized upon the mercantile mind. The principal merchant of the town, and purveyor to the mining settlements beyond, appeared the next morning at the office of the *Clarion*. "Ye wouldn't mind puttin' this 'ad' in a column alongside o' the Dimmidge one, would ye?" The young editor glanced at it, and then, with a serpent-like sagacity, veiled, however, by the suavity[14] of the dove, pointed out that the original advertiser might think it called his *bona fides*[15] into question and withdraw his advertisement. "But if we secured you by an offer of double the amount per column?" urged the mer-chant. "That," responded the *locum tenens*,[16] "was for the actual editor and proprietor in San Francisco to determine. He would telegraph." He did so. The response was, "Put it in." Whereupon in the next issue, side by side with Mr. Dim-midge's protracted warning, appeared a column with the

---

[14] *suavity:* smooth politeness
[15] *bona fides:* good faith, honesty
[16] *locum tenens:* temporary substitute

announcement, in large letters, "WE HAVEN'T LOST ANY
WIFE, but WE are prepared to furnish the following goods
at a lower rate than any other advertiser in the county," followed by the usual price list of the merchant's wares. There
was an unprecedented demand for that issue. The reputation
of the *Clarion*, both as a shrewd advertising medium and a
comic paper, was established at once. For a few days the editor waited with some apprehension for a remonstrance from
the absent Dimmidge, but none came. Whether Mr. Dimmidge recognized that this new advertisement gave extra
publicity to his own, or that he was already on the track of the
fugitive, the editor did not know. The few curious citizens
who had, early in the excitement, penetrated the settlement
of the English miners twenty miles away in search of information, found that Mr. Dimmidge had gone away, and that Mrs.
Dimmidge had *never* resided there with him!

Six weeks passed. The limit of Mr. Dimmidge's advertisement had been reached, and, as it was not renewed, it had
passed out of the pages of the *Clarion*, and with it the merchant's advertisement in the next column. The excitement
had subsided, although its influence was still felt in the
circulation of the paper and its advertising popularity. The
temporary editor was also nearing the limit of his incumbency,[17] but had so far participated in the good fortune of the
Clarion as to receive an offer from one of the San Francisco
dailies.

It was a warm night, and he was alone in his sanctum. The
rest of the building was dark and deserted, and his solitary
light, flashing out through the open window, fell upon the
nearer pines and was lost in the dark, indefinable slope below.
He had reached the sanctum by the rear, and a door which he
also left open to enjoy the freshness of the aromatic air. Nor
did it in the least mar his privacy. Rather the solitude of the
great woods without seemed to enter through that door and
encompassed him with its protecting loneliness. There was
occasionally a faint "peep" in the scant eaves, or a "pat-pat,"
ending in a frightened scurry across the roof, or the slow flap

---

[17] *incumbency:* term of office

of a heavy wing in the darkness below. These gentle disturbances did not, however, interrupt his work on "The True Functions of the County Newspaper," the editorial on which he was engaged.

Presently a more distinct rustling against the straggling blackberry bushes beside the door attracted his attention. It was followed by a light tapping against the side of the house. The editor started and turned quickly towards the open door. Two outside steps led to the ground. Standing upon the lower one was a woman. The upper part of her figure, illuminated by the light from the door, was thrown into greater relief by the dark background of the pines. Her face was unknown to him, but it was a pleasant one, marked by a certain good-humored determination.

"May I come in?" she said confidently.

"Certainly," said the editor. "I am working here alone because it is so quiet." He thought he would precipitate some explanation from her by excusing himself.

"That's the reason why I came," she said, with a quiet smile.

She came up the next step and entered the room. She was plainly but neatly dressed, and now that her figure was revealed he saw that she was wearing a linsey-woolsey riding skirt, and carried a serviceable raw-hide whip in her cotton-gauntleted hand. She took the chair he offered her and sat down sideways on it, her whip hand now also holding up her skirt, and permitting a hem of clean white petticoat and a smart, well-shaped boot to be seen.

"I don't remember to have had the pleasure of seeing you in Calaveras before," said the editor tentatively.

"No. I never was here before," she said composedly, "but you've heard enough of me, I reckon. I'm Mrs. Dimmidge." She threw one hand over the back of the chair, and with the other tapped her riding-whip on the floor.

The editor started. Mrs. Dimmidge! Then she was not a myth. An absurd similarity between her attitude with the whip and her husband's entrance with his gun six weeks before forced itself upon him and made her an invincible presence.

"Then you have returned to your husband?" he said hesitatingly.

"Not much!" she returned, with a slight curl of her lip "But you read his advertisement?"

"I saw that column of fool nonsense he put in your paper — ef that's what you mean," she said with decision, "but I didn't come here to see *him* — but *you*."

The editor looked at her with a forced smile, but vague misgiving. He was alone at night in a deserted part of the settlement, with a plump, self-possessed woman who had a contralto voice, a horsewhip, and — he could not help feeling — an evident grievance.

"To see me?" he repeated, with a faint attempt at gallantry. "You are paying me a great compliment, but really" —

"When I tell you I've come three thousand miles from Kansas straight here without stopping, ye kin reckon it's so," she replied firmly.

"Three thousand miles!" echoed the editor wonderingly.

"Yes. Three thousand miles from my own folks' home in Kansas, where six years ago I married Mr. Dimmidge, — a British furriner as could scarcely make himself understood in any Christian language! Well, he got round me and dad, allowin' he was a reg'lar out-and-out profeshnal miner, — had lived in mines ever since he was a boy; and so, not knowin' what kind o' mines, and dad just bilin' over with the gold fever, we were married and kem across the plains to Californy. He was a good enough man to look at, but it warn't three months before I discovered that he allowed a wife was no better nor a slave, and he the master. That made me open my eyes; but then, as he didn't drink, and didn't gamble, and didn't swear, and was a good provider and laid by money, why, I shifted along with him as best I could. We drifted down the first year to Sonora, at Red Dog, where there wasn't another woman. Well, I did the slave business, — never stirring out o' the settlement, never seein' a town or a crowd o' decent people, — and he did the lord and master! We played that game for two years, and I got tired. But when at last he allowed he'd go up to Elktown Hill, where there was a passel o' his countrymen at work, with never a sign o' any other folks,

and leave me alone at Red Dog until he fixed up a place for
me at Elktown Hill, — I kicked! I gave him fair warning! I did
as other slaves did, — I ran away!"

A recollection of the wretched woodcut which Mr. Dimmidge had selected to personify his wife flashed upon the
editor with a new meaning. Yet perhaps she had not seen it,
and had only read a copy of the advertisement. What could
she want? The *Calaveras Clarion*, although a "Palladium"[18]
and a "Sentinel upon the Heights of Freedom" in reference
to wagon roads, was not a redresser of domestic wrongs, —
except through its advertising columns! Her next words
intensified that suggestion.

"I've come here to put an advertisement in your paper."

The editor heaved a sigh of relief, as once before. "Certainly," he said briskly. "But that's another department of
the paper, and the printers have gone home. Come to-morrow
morning early."

"To-morrow morning I shall be miles away," she said de-
cisively, "and what I want done has got to be done *now!* I
don't want to see no printers; I don't want *anybody* to know
I've been here but you. That's why I kem here at night, and
rode all the way from Sawyer's Station, and wouldn't take the
stagecoach. And when we've settled about the advertisement,
I'm going to mount my horse, out thar in the bushes, and scoot
outer the settlement."

"Very good," said the editor resignedly. "Of course I can
deliver your instructions to the foreman. And now — let me
see — I suppose you wish to intimate in a personal notice to
your husband that you've returned."

"Nothin' o' the kind!" said Mrs. Dimmidge coolly. "I want
to placard him as he did me. I've got it all written out
here. *Sabe?*"

She took from her pocket a folded paper, and spreading it
out on the editor's desk, with a certain pride of authorship,
read as follows: —

"Whereas my husband, Micah J. Dimmidge, having given
out that I have left his bed and board, — the same being a bunk

in a log cabin and pork and molasses three times a day, — and having advertised that he'd pay no debts of *my* contractin', — which, as thar ain't any, might be easier collected than debts of his own contractin', — this is to certify that unless he returns from Elktown Hill to his only home in Sonora in one week from date, payin' the cost of this advertisement, I'll know the reason why. — Eliza Jane Dimmidge."

"Thàr," she added, drawing a long breath, "put that in a column of the *Clarion*, same size as the last, and let it work, and that's all I want of you."

"A column?" repeated the editor. "Do you know the cost is very expensive, and I *could* put it in a single paragraph?"

"I reckon I kin pay the same as Mr. Dimmidge did for *his*," said the lady complacently. "I didn't see your paper myself, but the paper as copied it — one of them big New York dailies — said that it took up a whole column."

The editor breathed more freely; she had not seen the infamous woodcut which her husband had selected. At the same moment he was struck with a sense of retribution, justice, and compensation.

"Would you," he asked hesitatingly, — "would you like it illustrated — by a cut?"

"With which?"

"Wait a moment; I'll show you."

He went into the dark composing-room, lit a candle, and rummaging in a drawer sacred to weather-beaten, old-fashioned electrotyped advertising symbols of various trades, finally selected one and brought it to Mrs. Dimmidge. It represented a bare and exceedingly stalwart arm wielding a large hammer.

"Your husband being a miner, — a quartz miner, — would that do?" he asked. (It had been previously used to advertise a blacksmith, a gold-beater, and a stone-mason.)

The lady examined it critically.

"It does look a little like Micah's arm," she said meditatively. "Well — you kin put it in."

The editor was so pleased with his success that he must needs make another suggestion. "I suppose," he said ingenuously, "that you don't want to answer the 'Personal'?"

"'Personal'?" she repeated quickly, "what's that? I ain't seen no 'Personal.'"

The editor saw his blunder. She, of course, had never seen Mr. Dimmidge's artful "Personal"; *that* the big dailies naturally had not noticed nor copied. But it was too late to withdraw now. He brought out a file of the *Clarion*, and snipping out the paragraph with his scissors, laid it before the lady.

She stared at it with wrinkled brows and a darkening face.

"And *this* was in the same paper?—put in by Mr. Dimmidge?" she asked breathlessly.

The editor, somewhat alarmed, stammered "Yes." But the next moment he was reassured. The wrinkles disappeared, a dozen dimples broke out where they had been, and the determined, matter-of-fact Mrs. Dimmidge burst into a fit of rosy merriment. Again and again she laughed, shaking the building, startling the sedate, melancholy woods beyond, until the editor himself laughed in sheer vacant sympathy.

"Lordy!" she said at last, gasping, and wiping the laughter from her wet eyes. "I never thought of *that*."

"No," explained the editor smilingly; "of course you didn't. Don't you see, the papers that copied the big advertisement never saw that little paragraph, or if they did, they never connected the two together."

"Oh, it ain't that," said Mrs. Dimmidge, trying to regain her composure and holding her sides. "It's that blessed *dear* old dunderhead of a Dimmidge I'm thinking of. That gets me. I see it all now. Only, sakes alive! I never thought *that* of him. Oh, it's just too much!" and she again relapsed behind her handkerchief.

"Then I suppose you don't want to reply to it," said the editor.

Her laughter instantly ceased. "Don't I?" she said, wiping her face into its previous complacent determination. "Well, young man, I reckon that's just what I *want* to do! Now, wait a moment; let's see what he said," she went on, taking up and reperusing[19] the "Personal" paragraph. "Well, then," she went on, after a moment's silent composition with moving lips, "you just put these lines in."

[19] *reperusing:* rereading

The editor took up his pencil.

"To Mr. M. J. Dimmidge.—Hope you're still on R. B.'s tracks. Keep there!—E.J.D."

The editor wrote down the line, and then, remembering Mr. Dimmidge's voluntary explanation of *his* "Personal," waited with some confidence for a like frankness from Mrs Dimmidge. But he was mistaken.

"You think that he—R.B.—or Mr. Dimmidge—will understand this?" he at last asked tentatively. "Is it enough?"

"Quite enough," said Mrs. Dimmidge emphatically. She took a roll of greenbacks from her pocket, selected a hundred-dollar bill and then a five, and laid them before the editor. "Young man," she said, with a certain demure gravity, "you've done me a heap o' good. I never spent money with more satisfaction than this. I never thought much o' the 'power o' the Press,' as you call it, afore. But this has been a right comfortable visit, and I'm glad I ketched you alone. But you understand one thing: this yer visit, and *who* I am, is betwixt you and me only."

"Of course I must say that the advertisement was *authorized*," returned the editor. "I'm only the temporary editor. The proprietor is away."

"So much the better," said the lady complacently. "You just say you found it on your desk with the money; but don't you give me away."

"I can promise you that the secret of your personal visit is safe with me," said the young man, with a bow, as Mrs. Dimmidge rose. "Let me see you to your horse," he added. "It's quite dark in the woods."

"I can see well enough alone, and it's just as well you shouldn't know *how* I kem or *how* I went away. Enough for you to know that I'll be miles away before that paper comes out. So stay where you are."

She pressed his hand frankly and firmly, gathered up her riding-skirt, slipped backwards to the door, and the next moment rustled away into the darkness.

Early the next morning the editor handed Mrs. Dimmidge's advertisement, and the woodcut he had selected, to his foreman. He was purposely brief in his directions, so as to avoid inquiry, and retired to his sanctum. In the space of a few moments the foreman entered with a slight embarrassment of manner.

"You'll excuse my speaking to you, sir," he said, with a singular mixture of humility and cunning. "It's no business of mine, I know; but I thought I ought to tell you that this yer kind o' thing won't pay any more,—it's about played out!"

"I don't think I understand you," said the editor loftily, but with an inward misgiving. "You don't mean to say that a regular, actual advertisement"—

"Of course, I know all that," said the foreman, with a peculiar smile; "and I'm ready to back you up in it, and so's the boy; but it won't pay."

"It *has* paid a hundred and five dollars," said the editor, taking the notes from his pocket; "so I'd advise you to simply attend to your duty and set it up."

A look of surprise, followed, however, by a kind of pitying smile, passed over the foreman's face. "Of course, sir, *that's* all right, and you know your own business; but if you think that the new advertisement will pay this time as the other one did, and whoop up another column from an advertiser, I'm afraid you'll slip up. It's a little 'off color' now,—not 'up to date,'—if it ain't a regular 'back number,' as you'll see."

"Meantime I'll dispense with your advice," said the editor curtly, "and I think you had better let our subscribers and advertisers do the same, or the *Clarion* might also be obliged to dispense with your *services.*"

"I ain't no blab," said the foreman, in an aggrieved manner, "and I don't intend to give the show away even if it don't *pay.* But I thought I'd tell you, because I know the folks round here better than you do."

He was right. No sooner had the advertisement appeared than the editor found that everybody believed it to be a sheer invention of his own to "once more boom" the *Clarion.* If they had doubted *Mr.* Dimmidge, they utterly rejected *Mrs.* Dimmidge as an advertiser! It was a stale joke that nobody would follow up; and on the heels of this came a letter from the editor-in-chief.

My dear Boy,—You meant well, I know, but the second

Dimmidge "ad" was a mistake. Still, it was a big bluff of yours
to show the money, and I send you back your hundred dollars,
hoping you won't "do it again." Of course you'll have to keep
the advertisement in the paper for two issues, just as if it were
a real thing, and it's lucky that there's just now no pressure in
our columns. You might have told a better story than that hogwash about your finding the "ad" and a hundred dollars lying
loose on your desk one morning. It was rather thin, and I don't
wonder the foreman kicked.

The young editor was in despair. At first he thought of writing to Mrs. Dimmidge at the Elktown Post-Office, asking her
to relieve him of his vow of secrecy; but his pride forbade.
There was a humorous concern, not without a touch of pity,
in the faces of his contributors as he passed; a few affected to
believe in the new advertisement, and asked him vague, per-
functory questions about it. His position was trying, and he
was not sorry when the term of his engagement expired the
next week, and he left Calaveras to take his new position on
the San Francisco paper.

He was standing in the saloon[20] of the Sacramento boat
when he felt a sudden heavy pressure on his shoulder, and
looking round sharply, beheld not only the black-bearded
face of Mr. Dimmidge, lit up by a smile, but beside it the
beaming, buxom face of Mrs. Dimmidge, overflowing with
good-humor. Still a little sore from his past experience, he
was about to address them abruptly, when he was utterly
vanquished by the hearty pressure of their hands and the
unmistakable look of gratitude in their eyes.

"I was just saying to 'Lizy Jane," began Mr. Dimmidge
breathlessly, "if I could only meet that young man o' the
Clarion what brought us together again" —

"You'd be willin' to pay four times the amount we both
paid him," interpolated the laughing Mrs. Dimmidge.

"But I didn't bring you together," burst out the dazed young
man, "and I'd like to know, in the name of Heaven, what
brought you together now?"

"Don't you see, lad," said the imperturbable Mr. Dim-

[20] *saloon:* main cabin or lounge

midge, "'Lizy Jane and myself had qua'led, and we just unpacked our fool nonsense in your paper and let the hull world know it! And we both felt kinder skeert and shamed like, and it looked such small hogwash, and of so little account, for all the talk it made, that we kinder felt lonely as two separated fools that really ought to share their foolishness together."

"And that ain't all," said Mrs. Dimmidge, with a sly glance at her spouse, "for I found out from that 'Personal' you showed me that this particular old fool was actooally jealous!—*jealous!*"

"And then?" said the editor impatiently.

"And then I *knew* he loved me all the time."

FOR DISCUSSION

1. A surprise ending can add to the enjoyment of a story only if it is believable and consistent with what the author has led the reader to expect. In your opinion, how well does the ending of this story fulfill these requirements? What clues might have led you to expect a reconciliation between the Dimmidges?

2. What reason do you have for believing that Mr. Dimmidge does, or does not, intend his first notice to be simply a formal ultimatum to his wife before taking legal action against her? Why does he want the notice to occupy a full column? Why does he also place the "personal" item? How do you explain Mrs. Dimmidge's full-column notice and her reaction to her husband's personal notice?

3. What effects does the Dimmidges' personal quarrel have on the *Clarion* and on the career of the temporary editor? Does the editor have any choice in the way he handles this unusual situation? Would a more experienced editor handle it differently? Would a present-day editor ever face a similar situation? Give reasons to support your answers.

4. How do the people of Calaveras react to Mr. Dimmidge's full-column notice and to Mrs. Dimmidge's reply? Toward the end of the story, why is the temporary editor so happy to be leaving Calaveras?

5. What impression do you gain of Mr. Dimmidge from the way he enters the *Clarion* office and from the young editor's reaction? What further insights into his character are revealed through what he says and does, through what his wife says about him, and

through what the author tells you? Cite evidence from the story to support your answers.

6. What kind of person is Mrs. Dimmidge? What reasons do you have for believing that she is, or is not, a typical frontier woman? Point out how her basic femininity is revealed.

7. How does each of the following contribute to the humor of the story: (a) the temporary editor's unfamiliarity with the ways of frontier towns, (b) the nature of the woodcuts chosen for the two notices, (c) the various reactions to the first notice, and (d) the nature of Mrs. Dimmidge's replies to her husband's full-column notice and to his personal item? Point out examples of exaggeration which also add to the humor.

8. How important is setting in this story? What does the author mean when he remarks that the *Clarion* building "had invaded Nature without subduing it?"

9. In his day, Bret Harte was considered a master craftsman in the short story form. Why, in your opinion, would this story have appealed particularly to Eastern readers? In what way does it reveal his special talents for (a) portraying character, (b) creating suspense, and (c) picturing one part of the American scene?

FOR COMPOSITION

1. Write a character sketch of Mr. Dimmidge, Mrs. Dimmidge, or the editor. In addition to describing his or her appearance, bring out the qualities and traits which best reveal his or her character.

2. Suppose that you were helping to prepare a television play based on this story. Write a description of the setting you think would picture the time and place in which the events occur. Use the details given in the story. Invent others if they are needed.

Mark Twain

Mark Twain once said, ". . . the end and aim of my ambition is to be authentic—is to be considered authentic." This word *authentic*, if interpreted broadly, is the key to much of what is great in Twain's works. He reproduced regional dialects more accurately than any other writer of the "local color" era; he described natural phenomena with the care and thoroughness of a naturalist; he created complex characters with equal attention to their good and their bad qualities.

Most important, he presented his material in a clear, direct way. His style is pure and uncluttered. His images are so apt and his use of language so skillful that the reader feels as though he were being *shown* the world, not being *told* about it.

Buck Fanshaw's Funeral

Somebody has said that in order to know a community, one must observe the style of its funerals and know what manner of men they bury with most ceremony. I cannot say which class we buried with most éclat[1] in our "flush times," the distinguished public benefactor or the distinguished rough— possibly the two chief grades or grand divisions of society honored their illustrious dead about equally; and hence, no doubt, the philosopher I have quoted from would have needed to see two representative funerals in Virginia[2] before forming his estimate of the people.

There was a grand time over Buck Fanshaw when he died. He was a representative citizen. He had "killed his man"— not in his own quarrel, it is true, but in defense of a stranger unfairly beset by numbers. He had kept a sumptuous saloon.

[1] *éclat:* acclaim
[2] *Virginia:* Virginia City, Nevada, former center of gold and silver mining

155

He had been the proprietor of a dashing helpmeet whom he could have discarded without the formality of a divorce. He had held a high position in the fire department and been a very Warwick[3] in politics. When he died there was great lamentation throughout the town, but especially in the vast bottom-stratum of society.

On the inquest it was shown that Buck Fanshaw, in the delirium of a wasting typhoid fever, had taken arsenic, shot himself through the body, cut his throat, and jumped out of a four-story window and broken his neck—and after due deliberation, the jury, sad and tearful, but with intelligence unblinded by its sorrow, brought in a verdict of death "by the visitation of God." What could the world do without juries?

Prodigious preparations were made for the funeral. All the vehicles in town were hired, all the saloons put in mourning, all the municipal and fire-company flags hung at half-mast, and all the firemen ordered to muster in uniform and bring their machines duly draped in black. Now—let us remark in parentheses—as all the peoples of the earth had representative adventurers in the Silverland, and as each adventurer had brought the slang of his nation or his locality with him, the combination made the slang of Nevada the richest and the most infinitely varied and copious that had ever existed anywhere in the world, perhaps, except in the mines of California in the "early days." Slang was the language of Nevada. It was hard to preach a sermon without it, and be understood. Such phrases as "You bet!" "Oh, no, I reckon not!" "No Irish need apply," and a hundred others, became so common as to fall from the lips of a speaker unconsciously—and very often when they did not touch the subject under discussion and consequently failed to mean anything.

After Buck Fanshaw's inquest, a meeting of the short-haired brotherhood was held, for nothing can be done on the Pacific coast without a public meeting and an expression of sentiment. Regretful resolutions were passed and various committees appointed; among others, a committee of one was

---

[3]*Warwick:* Earl of Warwick, a very influential English statesman of the fifteenth century

deputed to call on the minister, a fragile, gentle, spirituel new fledgling from an Eastern theological seminary, and as yet unacquainted with the ways of the mines. The committee-man, "Scotty" Briggs, made his visit; and in after days it was worth something to hear the minister tell about it. Scotty was a stalwart rough, whose customary suit, when on weighty official business, like committee work, was a fire-helmet, flaming red flannel shirt, patent-leather belt with spanner[4] and revolver attached, coat hung over arm, and pants stuffed into boot-tops. He formed something of a contrast to the pale theological student. It is fair to say of Scotty, however, in passing, that he had a warm heart, and a strong love for his friends, and never entered into a quarrel when he could reasonably keep out of it. Indeed, it was commonly said that whenever one of Scotty's fights was investigated, it always turned out that it had originally been no affair of his, but that out of native good-heartedness he had dropped in of his own accord to help the man who was getting the worst of it. He and Buck Fanshaw were bosom friends for years, and had often taken adventurous "pot-luck" together. On one occasion, they had thrown off their coats and taken the weaker side in a fight among strangers, and after gaining a hard-earned victory, turned and found that the men they were helping had deserted early, and not only that, but had stolen their coats and made off with them. But to return to Scotty's visit to the minister. He was on a sorrowful mission, now, and his face was the picture of woe. Being admitted to the presence he sat down before the clergyman, placed his fire-hat on an unfinished manuscript sermon under the minister's nose, took from it a red silk handkerchief, wiped his brow and heaved a sigh of dismal impressiveness, explanatory of his business. He choked, and even shed tears; but with an effort he mastered his voice and said in lugubrious[5] tones:

"Are you the duck that runs the gospel-mill next door?"

"Am I the—pardon me, I believe I do not understand?"

With another sigh and a half-sob, Scotty rejoined:

"Why you see we are in a bit of trouble, and the boys

[4] *spanner:* wrench
[5] *lugubrious:* mournful to the point of being ridiculous

thought maybe you would give us a lift, if we'd tackle you—
that is, if I've got the rights of it and you are the head clerk oi
the doxology-works next door."

"I am the shepherd in charge of the flock whose fold is
next door."

"The which?"

"The spiritual adviser of the little company of believers
whose sanctuary adjoins these premises."

Scotty scratched his head, reflected a moment, and then
said:

"You ruther hold over me, pard. I reckon I can't call that
hand. Ante and pass the buck."

"How? I beg pardon. What did I understand you to say?"

"Well, you've ruther got the bulge on me. Or maybe we've
both got the bulge, somehow. You don't smoke me and I
don't smoke you. You see, one of the boys has passed in his
checks, and we want to give him a good send-off, and so the
thing I'm on now is to roust out somebody to jerk a little chin-
music for us and waltz him through handsome."

"My friend, I seem to grow more and more bewildered.
Your observations are wholly incomprehensible to me. Cannot you simplify them in some way? At first I thought perhaps
I understood you, but I grope now. Would it not expedite[6]
matters if you restricted yourself to categorical[7] statements
of fact unencumbered with obstructing accumulations of
metaphor and allegory?"

Another pause, and more reflection. Then, said Scotty:

"I'll have to pass, I judge."

"How?"

"You've raised me out, pard."

"I still fail to catch your meaning."

"Why, that last lead of yourn is too many for me—that's
the idea. I can't neither trump nor follow suit."

The clergyman sank back in his chair perplexed. Scotty
leaned his head on his hand and gave himself up to thought.
Presently his face came up, sorrowful but confident.

---

[6] *expedite:* speed up the progress of
[7] *categorical:* direct, unqualified

"I've got it now, so's you can savvy,"[8] he said. "What we want is a gospel-sharp. See?"

"A what?"

"Gospel-sharp. Parson."

"Oh! Why did you not say so before? I am a clergyman — a parson."

"Now you talk! You see my blind and straddle it like a man. Put it there!" — extending a brawny paw, which closed over the minister's small hand and gave it a shake indicative of fraternal sympathy and fervent gratification.

"Now we're all right, pard. Let's start fresh. Don't you mind my snuffling a little — becuz we're in a power of trouble. You see, one of the boys has gone up the flume —"

"Gone where?"

"Up the flume — throwed up the sponge, you understand."

"Thrown up the sponge?"

"Yes — kicked the bucket —"

"Ah — has departed to that mysterious country from whose bourne no traveler returns."[9]

"Return! I reckon not. Why, pard, he's *dead!*"

"Yes, I understand."

"Oh, you do? Well I thought maybe you might be getting tangled some more. Yes, you see he's dead again —"

"*Again!* Why, has he ever been dead before?"

"Dead before? No! Do you reckon a man has got as many lives as a cat? But you bet you he's awful dead now, poor old boy, and I wish I'd never seen this day. I don't want no better friend than Buck Fanshaw. I knowed him by the back: and when I know a man and like him, I freeze to him — you hear *me*. Take him all round, pard, there never was a bullier man in the mines. No man ever knowed Buck Fanshaw to go back on a friend. But it's all up, you know, it's all up. It ain't no use. They've scooped him."

"Scooped him?"

"Yes — death has. Well, well, well, we've got to give him up. Yes, indeed. It's a kind of a hard world, after all, *ain't* it?

[8] *savvy:* understand

[9] *mysterious country . . . returns:* He is quoting from Hamlet's soliloquy in Shakespeare's play.

But pard, he was a rustler! You ought to seen him get started
once. He was a bully boy with a glass eye! Just spit in his
face and give him room according to his strength, and it was
just beautiful to see him peel and go in. He was the worst
son of a thief that ever drawed breath. Pard, he was *on* it!
He was on it bigger than an Injun!"

"On it? On what?"

"On the shoot. On the shoulder. On the fight, you understand. *He* didn't give a continental for *any*body. *Beg* your
pardon, friend, for coming so near saying a cuss-word — but
you see I'm on an awful strain, in this palaver,[10] on account
of having to cramp down and draw everything so mild. But
we've got to give him up. There ain't any getting around that,
I don't reckon. Now if we can get you to help plant him —"

"Preach the funeral discourse? Assist at the obsequies?"[11]

"Obs'quies is good. Yes. That's it — that's our little game.
We are going to get the thing up regardless, you know. He
was always nifty himself, and so you bet you his funeral ain't
going to be no slouch — solid-silver door-plate on his coffin,
six plumes on the hearse, and a nigger on the box in a biled[12]
shirt and a plug hat — how's that for high? And we'll take care
of *you*, pard. We'll fix you all right. There'll be a kerridge
for you; and whatever you want, you just 'scape out and we'll
'tend to it. We've got a shebang fixed up for you to stand
behind, in No. 1's house, and don't you be afraid. Just go in
and toot your horn, if you don't sell a clam. Put Buck through
as bully as you can, pard, for anybody that knowed him will
tell you that he was one of the whitest[13] men that was ever in
the mines. You can't draw it too strong. He never could
stand it to see things going wrong. He's done more to make
this town quiet and peaceable than any man in it. I've seen
him lick four Greasers in eleven minutes, myself. If a thing
wanted regulating, *he* warn't a man to go browsing around
after somebody to do it, but he would prance in and regulate
it himself. He warn't a Catholic. Scasely. He was down on 'em.

---

[10] *palaver:* talk, conversation
[11] *obsequies:* funeral rites
[12] *biled:* boiled
[13] *whitest:* fairest, most impartial

His word was, "No Irish need apply!" But it didn't make no difference about that when it came down to what a man's rights was—and so, when some roughs jumped the Catholic boneyard and started in to stake out town lots in it he *went* for 'em! And he *cleaned* 'em, too! I was there, pard, and I seen it myself."

"That was very well indeed—at least the impulse was—whether the act was strictly defensible or not. Had deceased any religious convictions? That is to say, did he feel a dependence upon, or acknowledge alliance to a higher power?"

More reflection.

"I reckon you've stumped me again, pard. Could you say it over once more, and say it slow?"

"Well, to simplify it somewhat, was he, or rather had he ever been connected with any organization sequestered[14] from secular concerns and devoted to self-sacrifice in the interests of morality?"

"All down but nine—set 'em up on the other alley, pard."

"What did I understand you to say?"

"Why, you're most too many for me, you know. When you get in with your left I hunt grass every time. Every time you draw, you fill; but I don't seem to have any luck. Let's have a new deal."

"How? Begin again?"

"That's it."

"Very well. Was he a good man, and—"

"There—I see that; don't put up another chip till I look at my hand. A good man, says you? Pard, it ain't no name for it. He was the best man that ever—pard, you would have doted on that man. He could lam any galoot of his inches in America. It was him that put down the riot last election before it got a start; and everybody said he was the only man that could have done it. He waltzed in with a spanner in one hand and a trumpet in the other, and sent fourteen men home on a shutter in less than three minutes. He had that riot all broke up and prevented nice before anybody ever got a chance to strike a blow. He was always for peace, and he would *have* peace—he could not stand disturbances. Pard, he was a great

[14] *sequestered:* secluded, isolated

loss to this town. It would please the boys if you could chip in something like that and do him justice. Here once when the Micks got to throwing stones through the Methodis' Sunday-school windows, Buck Fanshaw, all of his own notion, shut up his saloon and took a couple of six-shooters and mounted guard over the Sunday-school. Says he, 'No Irish need apply!'" And they didn't. He was the bulliest man in the mountains, pard! He could run faster, jump higher, hit harder, and hold more tanglefoot whisky without spilling it than any man in seventeen counties. Put that in, pard—it'll please the boys more than anything you could say. And you can say, pard, that he never shook his mother."

"Never shook his mother?"

"That's it—any of the boys will tell you so."

"Well, but why *should* he shake her?"

"That's what *I* say—but some people does."

"Not people of any repute?"

"Well, some that averages pretty so-so."

"In my opinion the man that would offer personal violence to his own mother, ought to—"

"Cheese it, pard; you've banked your ball clean outside the string. What I was a drivin' at, was, that he never *throwed* off on his mother—don't you see? No indeedy. He give her a house to live in, and town lots, and plenty of money; and he looked after her and took care of her all the time; and when she was down with the smallpox I'm d—d if he didn't set up and nuss her himself! *Beg* your pardon for saying it, but it hopped out too quick for yours truly. You've treated me like a gentleman, pard, and I ain't the man to hurt your feelings intentional. I think you're a square man, pard. I like you, and I'll lick any man that don't. I'll lick him till he can't tell himself from a last year's corpse! Put it *there!*" (Another fraternal handshake—and exit.)

The obsequies were all that "the boys" could desire. Such a marvel of funeral pomp had never been seen in Virginia. The plumed hearse, the dirge-breathing brass-bands, the closed marts of business, the flags drooping at half-mast, the long, plodding procession of uniformed secret societies, military battalions and fire companies, draped engines, carriages of officials, and citizens in vehicles and on foot, attracted multitudes of spectators to the sidewalks, roofs, and windows; and for years afterward, the degree of grandeur attained by any civic display in Virginia was determined by comparison with Buck Fanshaw's funeral.

Scotty Briggs, as a pall-bearer and a mourner, occupied a prominent place at the funeral, and when the sermon was finished and the last sentence of the prayer for the dead man's soul ascended, he responded, in a low voice, but with feeling:

"AMEN. No Irish need apply."

As the bulk of the response was without apparent relevancy, it was probably nothing more than a humble tribute to the memory of the friend that was gone; for, as Scotty had once said, it was "his word."

Scotty Briggs, in after days, achieved the distinction of becoming the only convert to religion that was ever gathered from the Virginia roughs; and it transpired that the man who had it in him to espouse the quarrel of the weak out of inborn nobility of spirit was no mean timber whereof to construct a Christian. The making him one did not warp his generosity or diminish his courage; on the contrary it gave intelligent direction to the one and a broader field to the other. If his Sunday-school class progressed faster than the other classes, was it matter for wonder? I think not. He talked to his pioneer small-fry in a language they understood! It was my large privilege, a month before he died, to hear him tell the beautiful story of Joseph and his brethren to his class "without looking at the book." I leave it to the reader to fancy what it was like, as it fell, riddled with slang, from the lips of that grave, earnest teacher, and was listened to by his little learners with a consuming interest that showed that they were as unconscious as he was that any violence was being done to the sacred proprieties![15]

---

[15] *proprieties:* accepted standards of behavior

FOR DISCUSSION

1. What was the general conception of a "good" man in the "vast bottom-stratum" of Virginia City society? How would you characterize Buck Fanshaw and Scotty Briggs?
2. In what sense is Buck Fanshaw a "representative citizen" of Virginia City? From Scotty's description of the election riot, what is your opinion of Buck as a "peacemaker"?
3. Contrast the parson with Scotty Briggs. How is he different in background, appearance, and personality?
4. Mark Twain was extremely accurate in his reproduction of regional slang and dialect. What information does he give you about the characteristic speech of Nevada in the early days? What are the obvious differences between the speech of Scotty and that of the parson? How is the language of each consistent with his background?
5. In Scotty's description of the funeral "obsequies," what does he mean by "No. 1's house" and "the Catholic boneyard"?
6. What "distinction" does Scotty achieve some years after the funeral? Why is he unusually successful?
7. Twain used exaggeration to add humor to his stories and novels, particularly when he was poking fun at the foolishness of men. What do you think were his opinions on juries, public meetings and committees, the language used by clergymen and Sunday-school teachers? What part does exaggeration play in making Scotty and the parson humorous characters?

FOR COMPOSITION

1. In a short composition give your impression of the life and people of Virginia City at the time of this story. What do you think was the over-all mood of the time and place?
2. In two or three paragraphs discuss the speech of either Scotty or the parson. Which expressions do you find particularly amusing? What are some of the possible sources of each man's words or expressions?

Sarah Orne Jewett

Miss Jewett's characters and settings reflect her native New England. Her stories revolve not around heroes and villains, but around ordinary people facing and overcoming the conflicts of everyday life. Even her most incidental characters are treated with great care, and her settings are described with painstaking accuracy and attention to detail. Moreover, she was able to reproduce the subtlest rhythms and inflections of country speech accurately and authentically. These qualities, for which Miss Jewett has often been called the finest of the nineteenth century "local colorists," are reflected in the following story of a young girl's conflict of loyalties.

A White Heron

I

The woods were already filled with shadows one June evening, just before eight o'clock, though a bright sunset still glimmered faintly among the trunks of the trees. A little girl was driving home her cow, a plodding, dilatory,[1] provoking creature in her behavior, but a valued companion for all that. They were going away from the western light, and striking deep into the dark woods, but their feet were familiar with the path, and it was no matter whether their eyes could see it or not.

There was hardly a night the summer through when the old cow could be found waiting at the pasture bars; on the contrary, it was her greatest pleasure to hide herself away among the high huckleberry bushes, and though she wore a loud bell she had made the discovery that if one stood perfectly still it would not ring. So Sylvia had to hunt for her until

---

[1] *dilatory:* slow

she found her, and call Co'! Co'! with never an answering
Moo, until her childish patience was quite spent. If the
creature had not given good milk and plenty of it, the case
would have seemed very different to her owners. Besides,
Sylvia had all the time there was, and very little use to make
of it. Sometimes in pleasant weather it was a consolation to
look upon the cow's pranks as an intelligent attempt to play
hide and seek, and as the child had no playmates she lent
herself to this amusement with a good deal of zest. Though
this chase had been so long that the wary animal herself had
given an unusual signal of her whereabouts, Sylvia had only
laughed when she came upon Mistress Moolly at the swamp-
side, and urged her affectionately homeward with a twig of
birch leaves. The old cow was not inclined to wander farther,
she even turned in the right direction for once as they left the
pasture, and stepped along the road at a good pace. She was
quite ready to be milked now, and seldom stopped to browse.
Sylvia wondered what her grandmother would say because
they were so late. It was a great while since she had left home
at half past five o'clock, but everybody knew the difficulty of
making this errand a short one. Mrs. Tilley had chased the
hornéd torment too many summer evenings herself to blame
any one else for lingering, and was only thankful as she waited
that she had Sylvia, nowadays, to give such valuable assistance. The good woman suspected that Sylvia loitered
occasionally on her own account; there never was such a
child for straying about out-of-doors since the world was
made! Everybody said that it was a good change for a little
maid who had tried to grow for eight years in a crowded
manufacturing town, but, as for Sylvia herself, it seemed as
if she never had been alive at all before she came to live at
the farm. She thought often with wistful compassion of a
wretched dry geranium that belonged to a town neighbor.

"'Afraid of folks,'" old Mrs. Tilley said to herself, with a
smile, after she had made the unlikely choice of Sylvia from
her daughter's houseful of children, and was returning to the
farm. "'Afraid of folks,' they said! I guess she won't be troubled no great with 'em up to the old place!" When they
reached the door of the lonely house and stopped to unlock

it, and the cat came to purr loudly, and rub against them, a deserted pussy, indeed, but fat with young robins, Sylvia whispered that this was a beautiful place to live in, and she never should wish to go home. The companions followed the shady woodroad, the cow taking slow steps, and the child very fast ones. The cow stopped long at the brook to drink, as if the pasture were not half a swamp, and Sylvia stood still and waited, letting her bare feet cool themselves in the shoal² water, while the great twilight moths struck softly against her. She waded on through the brook as the cow moved away, and listened to the thrushes with a heart that beat fast with pleasure. There was a stirring in the great boughs overhead. They were full of little birds and beasts that seemed to be wide-awake, and going about their world, or else saying goodnight to each other in sleepy twitters. Sylvia herself felt sleepy as she walked along. However, it was not much farther to the house, and the air was soft and sweet. She was not often in the woods so late as this, and it made her feel as if she were a part of the gray shadows and the moving leaves. She was just thinking how long it seemed since she first came to the farm a year ago, and wondering if everything went on in the noisy town just the same as when she was there; the thought of the great red-faced boy who used to chase and frighten her made her hurry along the path to escape from the shadow of the trees.

Suddenly this little woods-girl is horror-stricken to hear a clear whistle not very far away. Not a bird's whistle, which would have a sort of friendliness, but a boy's whistle, determined, and somewhat aggressive. Sylvia left the cow to whatever sad fate might await her, and stepped discreetly aside into the bushes, but she was just too late. The enemy had discovered her, and called out in a very cheerful and persuasive tone, "Halloa, little girl, how far is it to the road?" and trembling Sylvia answered almost inaudibly, "A good ways."

She did not dare to look boldly at the tall young man, who carried a gun over his shoulder, but she came out of her bush and again followed the cow, while he walked alongside.

"I have been hunting for some birds," the stranger said

²*shoal:* shallow

kindly, "and I have lost my way, and need a friend very much. Don't be afraid," he added gallantly. "Speak up and tell me what your name is, and whether you think I can spend the night at your house, and go out gunning early in the morning."

Sylvia was more alarmed than before. Would not her grandmother consider her to blame? But who could have foreseen such an accident as this? It did not appear to be her fault, and she hung her head as if the stem of it were broken, but managed to answer "Sylvy," with much effort when her companion again asked her name.

Mrs. Tilley was standing in the doorway when the trio came into view. The cow gave a loud moo by way of explanation.

"Yes, you'd better speak up for yourself, you old trial! Where'd she tuck herself away this time, Sylvy?" Sylvia kept an awed silence; she knew by instinct that her grandmother did not comprehend the gravity of the situation. She must be mistaking the stranger for one of the farmer-lads of the region.

The young man stood his gun beside the door, and dropped a heavy game-bag beside it; then he bade Mrs. Tilley good-evening, and repeated his wayfarer's story, and asked if he could have a night's lodging.

"Put me anywhere you like," he said, "I must be off early in the morning, before day; but I am very hungry, indeed. You can give me some milk at any rate, that's plain."

"Dear sakes, yes," responded the hostess, whose long slumbering hospitality seemed to be easily awakened. "You might fare better if you went out on the main road a mile or so, but you're welcome to what we've got. I'll milk right off, and you make yourself at home. You can sleep on husks or feathers," she proffered graciously. "I raised them all myself. There's good pasturing for geese just below here towards the ma'sh. Now step round and set a plate for the gentleman, Sylvy!" And Sylvia promptly stepped. She was glad to have something to do, and she was hungry herself.

It was a surprise to find so clean and comfortable a little dwelling in this New England wilderness. The young man had known the horrors of its most primitive housekeeping,

and the dreary squalor of that level of society which does
not rebel at the companionship of hens. This was the best
thrift of an old-fashioned farmstead, though on such a small
scale that it seemed like a hermitage. He listened eagerly
to the old woman's quaint talk, he watched Sylvia's pale
face and shining gray eyes with ever growing enthusiasm,
and insisted that this was the best supper he had eaten for
a month; then, afterward, the new-made friends sat down
in the doorway together while the moon came up.

Soon it would be berry-time, and Sylvia was a great help
at picking. The cow was a good milker, though a plaguy³
thing to keep track of, the hostess gossiped frankly, adding
presently that she had buried four children, so that Sylvia's
mother, and a son (who might be dead) in California were
all the children she had left. "Dan, my boy, was a great hand
to go gunning," she explained sadly. "I never wanted for
pa'tridges or gray squer'ls while he was to home. He's been
a great wand'rer, I expect, and he's no hand to write letters.
There, I don't blame him, I'd ha' seen the world myself if
it had been so I could.

"Sylvia takes after him," the grandmother continued
affectionately, after a minute's pause. "There ain't a foot o'
ground she don't know her way over, and the wild creatur's
counts her one o' themselves. Squer'ls she'll tame to come an'
feed right out o' her hands, and all sorts o' birds. Last winter
she got the jay-birds to bangeing⁴ here, and I believe she'd
'a' scanted herself of her own meals to have plenty to throw
out amongst 'em, if I hadn't kep' watch. Anything but crows,
I tell her, I'm willin' to help support, — though Dan he went
an' tamed one o' them that did seem to have reason same as
folks. It was round here a good spell after he went away.
Dan an' his father they didn't hitch, — but he never held up
his head ag'in after Dan had dared him an' gone off."

The guest did not notice this hint of family sorrows in his
eager interest in something else.

"So Sylvy knows all about birds, does she?" he exclaimed,
as he looked round at the little girl who sat, very demure

³*plaguy:* annoying
⁴*bangeing:* lounging about

but increasingly sleepy, in the moonlight. "I am making a collection of birds myself. I have been at it ever since I was a boy." (Mrs. Tilley smiled.) "There are two or three very rare ones I have been hunting for these five years. I mean to get them on my own ground if they can be found."

"Do you cage 'em up?" asked Mrs. Tilley doubtfully, in response to this enthusiastic announcement.

"Oh, no, they're stuffed and preserved, dozens and dozens of them," said the ornithologist,[5] "and I have shot or snared every one myself. I caught a glimpse of a white heron three miles from here on Saturday, and I have followed it in this direction. They have never been found in this district at all. The little white heron, it is," and he turned again to look at Sylvia with the hope of discovering that the rare bird was one of her acquaintances.

But Sylvia was watching a hop-toad in the narrow footpath.

"You would know the heron if you saw it," the stranger continued eagerly. "A queer tall white bird with soft feathers and long thin legs. And it would have a nest perhaps in the top of a high tree, made of sticks, something like a hawk's nest."

Sylvia's heart gave a wild beat; she knew that strange white bird, and had once stolen softly near where it stood in some bright green swamp grass, away over at the other side of the woods. There was an open place where the sunshine always seemed strangely yellow and hot, where tall, nodding rushes grew, and her grandmother had warned her that she might sink in the soft black mud underneath and never be heard of more. Not far beyond were the salt marshes and beyond those was the sea, the sea which Sylvia wondered and dreamed about, but never had looked upon, though its great voice could often be heard above the noise of the woods on stormy nights.

"I can't think of anything I should like so much as to find that heron's nest," the handsome stranger was saying. "I would give ten dollars to anybody who could show it to me," he added desperately, "and I mean to spend my whole vacation hunting for it if need be. Perhaps it was only migrating,

[5] *ornithologist:* one who studies birds

or had been chased out of its own region by some bird of prey."

Mrs. Tilley gave amazed attention to all this, but Sylvia still watched the toad, not divining, as she might have done at some calmer time, that the creature wished to get to its hole under the doorstep, and was much hindered by the unusual spectators at that hour of the evening. No amount of thought, that night, could decide how many wished-for treasures the ten dollars, so lightly spoken of, would buy.

The next day the young sportsman hovered about the woods, and Sylvia kept him company, having lost her first fear of the friendly lad, who proved to be most kind and sympathetic. He told her many things about the birds and what they knew and where they lived and what they did with themselves. And he gave her a jack-knife, which she thought as great a treasure as if she were a desert-islander. All day long he did not once make her troubled or afraid except when he brought down some unsuspecting singing creature from its bough. Sylvia would have liked him vastly better without his gun; she could not understand why he killed the very birds he seemed to like so much. But as the day waned, Sylvia still watched the young man with loving admiration. She had never seen anybody so charming and delightful; the woman's heart, asleep in the child, was vaguely thrilled by a dream of love. Some premonition of that great power stirred and swayed these young foresters who traversed the solemn woodlands with soft-footed silent care. They stopped to listen to a bird's song; they pressed forward again eagerly, parting the branches, — speaking to each other rarely and in whispers; the young man going first and Sylvia following, fascinated, a few steps behind, with her gray eyes dark with excitement.

She grieved because the longed-for white heron was elusive, but she did not lead the guest, she only followed, and there was no such thing as speaking first. The sound of her own unquestioned voice would have terrified her, — it was hard enough to answer yes or no when there was need of that. At last evening began to fall, and they drove the cow home together, and Sylvia smiled with pleasure when they came to the place where she heard the whistle and was afraid only the night before.

II

Half a mile from home, at the farther edge of the woods, where the land was highest, a great pine-tree stood, the last of its generation. Whether it was left for a boundary mark, or for what reason, no one could say; the woodchoppers who had felled its mates were dead and gone long ago, and a whole forest of sturdy trees, pines and oaks and maples, had grown again. But the stately head of this old pine towered above them all and made a landmark for sea and shore miles and miles away. Sylvia knew it well. She had always believed that whoever climbed to the top of it could see the ocean; and the little girl had often laid her hand on the great rough trunk and looked up wistfully at those dark boughs that the wind always stirred, no matter how hot and still the air might be below. Now she thought of the tree with a new excitement, for why, if one climbed it at break of day, could not one see all the world, and easily discover whence the white heron flew, and mark the place, and find the hidden nest?

What a spirit of adventure, what wild ambition! What fancied triumph and delight and glory for the later morning when she could make known the secret! It was almost too real and too great for the childish heart to bear.

All night the door of the little house stood open, and the whippoorwills came and sang upon the very step. The young sportsman and his old hostess were sound asleep, but Sylvia's great design kept her broad awake and watching. She forgot to think of sleep. The short summer night seemed as long as the winter darkness, and at last when the whippoorwills ceased, and she was afraid the morning would after all come too soon, she stole out of the house and followed the pasture path through the woods, hastening toward the open ground beyond, listening with a sense of comfort and companionship to the drowsy twitter of a half-awakened bird, whose perch she had jarred in passing. Alas, if the great wave of human interest which flooded for the first time this dull little life should sweep away the satisfactions of an existence heart to heart with nature and the dumb life of the forest!

There was the huge tree asleep yet in the paling moonlight, and small and hopeful Sylvia began with utmost bravery to mount to the top of it, with tingling, eager blood coursing the channels of her whole frame, with her bare feet and fingers, that pinched and held like bird's claws to the monstrous ladder reaching up, up, almost to the sky itself. First she must mount the white oak tree that grew alongside, where she was almost lost among the dark branches and the green leaves heavy and wet with dew; a bird fluttered off its nest, and a red squirrel ran to and fro and scolded pettishly at the harmless housebreaker. Sylvia felt her way easily. She had often climbed there, and knew that higher still one of the oak's upper branches chafed against the pine trunk, just where its lower boughs were set close together. There, when she made the dangerous pass from one tree to the other, the great enterprise would really begin.

She crept out along the swaying oak limb at last, and took the daring step across into the old pine-tree. The way was harder than she thought; she must reach far and hold fast, the sharp dry twigs caught and held her and scratched her like angry talons, the pitch made her thin little fingers clumsy and stiff as she went round and round the tree's great stem, higher and higher upward. The sparrows and robins in the woods below were beginning to wake and twitter to the dawn, yet it seemed much lighter there aloft in the pine-tree, and the child knew that she must hurry if her project were to be of any use.

The tree seemed to lengthen itself out as she went up, and to reach farther and farther upward. It was like a great mainmast to the voyaging earth; it must truly have been amazed that morning through all its ponderous frame as it felt this determined spark of human spirit creeping and climbing from higher branch to branch. Who knows how steadily the least twigs held themselves to advantage[6] this light, weak creature on her way! The old pine must have loved his new

---

[6] *advantage:* to help

dependent. More than all the hawks, and bats, and moths, and even the sweet-voiced thrushes, was the brave, beating heart of the solitary gray-eyed child. And the tree stood still and held away the winds that June morning while the dawn grew bright in the east.

Sylvia's face was like a pale star, if one had seen it from the ground, when the last thorny bough was past, and she stood trembling and tired but wholly triumphant, high in the tree-top. Yes, there was the sea with the dawning sun making a golden dazzle over it, and toward that glorious east flew two hawks with slow-moving pinions.[7] How low they looked in the air from that height when before one had only seen them far up, and dark against the blue sky. Their gray feathers were as soft as moths; they seemed only a little way from the tree, and Sylvia felt as if she too could go flying away among the clouds. Westward, the woodlands and farms reached miles and miles into the distance; here and there were church steeples, and white villages; truly it was a vast and awesome world.

The birds sang louder and louder. At last the sun came up bewilderingly bright. Sylvia could see the white sails of ships out at sea, and the clouds that were purple and rose-colored and yellow at first began to fade away. Where was the white heron's nest in the sea of green branches, and was this wonderful sight and pageant of the world the only reward for having climbed to such a giddy height? Now look down again, Sylvia, where the green marsh is set among the shining birches and dark hemlocks; there where you saw the white heron once you will see him again; look, look! a white spot of him like a single floating feather comes up from the dead hemlock and grows larger, and rises, and comes close at last, and goes by the landmark pine with steady sweep of wing and outstretched slender neck and crested head. And wait! wait! do not move a foot or a finger, little girl, do not send an arrow of light and consciousness from your two eager eyes, for the heron has perched on a pine bough not far beyond yours, and cries back to his mate on the nest, and plumes his feathers for the new day!

[7] *pinions:* wings

The child gives a long sigh a minute later when a company of shouting cat-birds comes also to the tree, and vexed by their fluttering and lawlessness the solemn heron goes away. She knows his secret now, the wild, light, slender bird that floats and wavers, and goes back like an arrow presently to his home in the green world beneath. Then Sylvia, well satisfied, makes her perilous way down again, not daring to look far below the branch she stands on, ready to cry sometimes because her fingers ache and her lamed feet slip. Wondering over and over again what the stranger would say to her, and what he would think when she told him how to find his way straight to the heron's nest.

"Sylvy, Sylvy!" called the busy old grandmother again and again, but nobody answered, and the small husk bed was empty, and Sylvia had disappeared.

The guest waked from a dream, and remembering his day's pleasure hurried to dress himself that it might sooner begin. He was sure from the way the shy little girl looked once or twice yesterday that she had at least seen the white heron, and now she must really be persuaded to tell. Here she comes now, paler than ever, and her worn old frock is torn and tattered, and smeared with pine pitch. The grandmother and the sportsman stand in the door together and question her, and the splendid moment has come to speak of the dead hemlock-tree by the green marsh.

But Sylvia does not speak after all, though the old grandmother fretfully rebukes her, and the young man's kind appealing eyes are looking straight in her own. He can make them rich with money; he has promised it, and they are poor now. He is so well worth making happy, and he waits to hear the story she can tell.

No, she must keep silence! What is it that suddenly forbids her and makes her dumb? Has she been nine years growing, and now, when the great world for the first time puts out a hand to her, must she thrust it aside for a bird's sake? The murmur of the pine's green branches is in her ears, she remembers how the white heron came flying through the golden air and how they watched the sea and the morning together, and Sylvia cannot speak; she cannot tell the heron's secret and give its life away.

Dear loyalty, that suffered a sharp pang as the guest went away disappointed later in the day, that could have served and followed him and loved him as a dog loves! Many a night Sylvia heard the echo of his whistle haunting the pasture path as she came home with the loitering cow. She forgot even her sorrow at the sharp report of his gun and the piteous sight of thrushes and sparrows dropping silent to the ground, their songs hushed and their pretty feathers stained and wet with blood. Were the birds better friends than their hunter might have been,—who can tell? Whatever treasures were lost to her, woodlands and summer-time, remember! Bring your gifts and graces and tell your secrets to this lonely country child!

FOR DISCUSSION

1. Sylvia has to choose between two deeply felt loyalties. What are these loyalties? Why is it so difficult for her to choose between them? In your opinion, what leads her to choose as she does? What clues are you given that foreshadow her final decision?
2. Why, in your opinion, is Sylvia "afraid of folks"? How is this fear revealed in the story? In what way does she demonstrate a degree of courage unusual in a girl of nine? How do you account for the fact that she could be frightened at one time and courageous at another?
3. How would you describe Sylvia's relationship with Nature? In what ways is this relationship brought out in the tree-climbing scene? Why should "woodlands and summer-time" tell their "secrets to this lonely country child"?
4. What kind of person is the young man? What single misgiving does Sylvia have about him? Would you consider him the antagonist in the story? Explain. What does the end of the story reveal about him?
5. How would you describe Mrs. Tilley? What does the bare mention of her husband and her son Dan contribute to your understanding of her? What is the nature of her relationship with Sylvia?
6. In what ways does the author create suspense in the tree-climbing scene? How does she suggest the little girl's fear?
7. How important is the setting in "A White Heron"? Show why you think Miss Jewett does, or does not, romanticize Nature.

FOR COMPOSITION

1. Write a character sketch of Sylvia. Be sure to show the effects of her earlier city life and her later woodland life upon her feelings, character, and personality.
2. In a short composition, tell how you, as an older person, might have reacted in Sylvia's situation. Might your feelings have been different in any way?

George Washington Cable

George Washington Cable found the materials for his colorful stories among the city archives of his native New Orleans. The part-French, part-Spanish flavor of the quaint old city provided a romantic setting for his realistically-drawn characters. His skillful and accurate rendering of the Creole dialect, as in the following story, lends an exotic touch to this nineteenth-century narrative about the mysterious Creole, Jean Poquelin.

Jean-ah Poquelin

In the first decade of the present century, when the newly established American Government was the most hateful thing in Louisiana—when the Creoles[1] were still kicking at such vile innovations as the trial by jury, American dances, anti-smuggling laws, and the printing of the Governor's proclamation in English—when the Anglo-American flood that was presently to burst in a crevasse[2] of immigration upon the delta had thus far been felt only as slippery seepage which made the Creole tremble for his footing—there stood, a short distance above what is now Canal Street, and considerably back from the line of villas which fringed the riverbank on Tchoupitoulas Road, an old colonial plantation house half in ruin.

It stood aloof from civilization, the tracts that had once been its indigo[3] fields given over to their first noxious wild-

[1] *Creoles:* descendants of the French or Spanish settlers of Louisiana and New Orleans
[2] *crevasse:* a deep crack
[3] *indigo:* plants of the pea family that yield a deep violet-blue dye

178

ness, and grown up into one of the horridest marshes within a circuit of fifty miles.

The house was of heavy cypress, lifted up on pillars, grim, solid, and spiritless, its massive build a strong reminder of days still earlier, when every man had been his own peace officer and the insurrection of the blacks a daily contingency. Its dark, weather-beaten roof and sides were hoisted up above the jungly plain in a distracted way, like a gigantic ammunition wagon stuck in the mud and abandoned by some retreating army. Around it was a dense growth of low water willows, with half a hundred sorts of thorny or fetid[4] bushes, savage strangers alike to the "language of flowers" and to the botanist's Greek. They were hung with countless strands of discolored and prickly smilax, and the impassable mud below bristled with *chevaux de frise*[5] of the dwarf palmetto. Two lone forest trees, dead cypresses, stood in the center of the marsh, dotted with roosting vultures. The shallow strips of water were hid by myriads of aquatic plants, under whose coarse and spiritless flowers, could one have seen it, was a harbor of reptiles, great and small, to make one shudder to the end of his days.

The house was on a slightly raised spot, the levee of a draining canal. The waters of this canal did not run; they crawled, and were full of big, ravening fish and alligators that held it against all comers.

Such was the home of old Jean Marie Poquelin, once an opulent indigo planter, standing high in the esteem of his small, proud circle of exclusively male acquaintances in the old city; now a hermit, alike shunned by and shunning all who had ever known him. "The last of his line," said the gossips. His father lies under the floor of the St. Louis Cathedral, with the wife of his youth on one side, and the wife of his old age on the other. Old Jean visits the spot daily. His half brother—alas! there was a mystery; no one knew what had become of the gentle, young half brother, more than thirty

---

[4]*fetid:* stinking
[5]*chevaux de frise:* The thorny stems of the dwarf palmetto resemble the ancient weapons of this name, pieces of wood with projecting spikes. (French)

years his junior, whom once he seemed so fondly to love, but who, seven years ago, had disappeared suddenly, once for all, and left no clue of his fate.

They had seemed to live so happily in each other's love. No father, mother, wife to either, no kindred upon earth. The elder a bold, frank, impetuous, chivalric adventurer; the younger a gentle, studious, book-loving recluse; they lived upon the ancestral estate like mated birds, one always on the wing, the other always in the nest.

There was no trait in Jean Marie Poquelin, said the old gossips, for which he was so well known among his few friends as his apparent fondness for his "little brother." "Jacques said this," and "Jacques said that"; he "would leave this or that, or any thing to Jacques," for Jacques was a scholar, and "Jacques was good," or "wise," or "just," or "farsighted," as the nature of the case required; and "he should ask Jacques as soon as he got home," since Jacques was never elsewhere to be seen.

It was between the roving character of the one brother, and the bookishness of the other, that the estate fell into decay. Jean Marie, generous gentleman, gambled the slaves away one by one, until none was left, man or woman, but one old African mute.

The indigo fields and vats of Louisiana had been generally abandoned as unremunerative. Certain enterprising men had substituted the culture of sugar; but while the recluse was too apathetic to take so active a course, the other saw larger, and, at that time, equally respectable profits, first in smuggling, and later in the African slave trade. What harm could he see in it? The whole people said it was vitally necessary, and to minister to a vital public necessity—good enough, certainly, and so he laid up many a doubloon,[6] that made him none the worse in the public regard.

One day old Jean Marie was about to start upon a voyage that was to be longer, much longer, than any that he had yet made. Jacques had begged him hard for many days not to go, but he laughed him off, and finally said, kissing him:

---

[6] *doubloon:* old Spanish coin worth about eight dollars

"*Adieu, petit frère.*"[7]

"No," said Jacques, "I shall go with you."

They left the old hulk of a house in the sole care of the African mute, and went away to the Guinea coast together.

Two years after, old Poquelin came home without his vessel. He must have arrived at his house by night. No one saw him come. No one saw "his little brother"; rumor whispered that he, too, had returned, but he had never been seen again.

A dark suspicion fell upon the old slave trader. No matter that the few kept the many reminded of the tenderness that had ever marked his bearing to the missing man. The many shook their heads. "You know he has a quick and fearful temper"; and "why does he cover his loss with mystery?" "Grief would out with the truth."

"But," said the charitable few, "look in his face; see that expression of true humanity." The many did look in his face, and, as he looked in theirs, he read the silent question: "Where is thy brother Abel?"[8] The few were silenced, his former friends died off, and the name of Jean Marie Poquelin became a symbol of witchery, devilish crime, and hideous nursery fictions.

The man and his house were alike shunned. The snipe and duck hunters forsook the marsh, and the woodcutters abandoned the canal. Sometimes the hardier boys who ventured out there snake-shooting heard a low thumping of oarlocks on the canal. They would look at each other for a moment half in consternation, half in glee, then rush from their sport in wanton haste to assail with their gibes the unoffending, withered old man who, in rusty attire, sat in the stern of a skiff, rowed homeward by his white-headed African mute.

"O Jean-ah Poquelin! O Jean-ah! Jean-ah Poquelin!"

It was not necessary to utter more than that. No hint of wickedness, deformity, or any physical or moral demerit; merely the name and tone of mockery: "Oh, Jean-ah Poquelin!" and while they tumbled one over another in their

---

[7] *Adieu, petit frère:* Good-by, little brother. (French)
[8] *Abel:* in the Bible, the son of Adam and Eve, killed by his brother Cain

needless haste to fly, he would rise carefully from his seat, while the aged mute, with downcast face, went on rowing, and, rolling up his brown fist and extending it toward the urchins, would pour forth such an unholy broadside of French imprecation and invective as would all but craze them with delight.

Among both blacks and whites the house was the object of a thousand superstitions. Every midnight, they affirmed, the *feu follet*[9] came out of the marsh and ran in and out of the rooms, flashing from window to window. The story of some lads, whose word in ordinary statements was worthless, was generally credited, that the night they camped in the woods, rather than pass the place after dark, they saw, about sunset, every window blood-red, and on each of the four chimneys an owl sitting, which turned his head three times round, and moaned and laughed with a human voice. There was a bottomless well, everybody professed to know, beneath the sill of the big front door under the rotten veranda; whoever set his foot upon that threshold disappeared forever in the depth below.

What wonder the marsh grew as wild as Africa! Take all the Faubourg[10] Ste. Marie, and half the ancient city, you would not find one graceless daredevil reckless enough to pass within a hundred yards of the house after midnight.

The alien races pouring into old New Orleans began to find the few streets named for the Bourbon[11] princes too strait for them. The wheel of fortune, beginning to whirl, threw them off beyond the ancient corporation lines, and sowed civilization and even trade upon the lands of the Graviers and Girods.[12] Fields became roads, roads streets. Everywhere the leveler[13] was peering through his glass, rodsmen were whacking their way through willow brakes

---

[9] *feu follet:* will-o'-the-wisp (French)

[10] *Faubourg:* a suburb or district within a city (French)

[11] *Bourbon:* ruling family of both France and Spain at various times between 1589 and 1931

[12] *Graviers and Girods:* prominent families of New Orleans

[13] *leveler:* surveyor

and rose hedges, and the sweating Irishmen tossed the blue clay up with their long-handled shovels.

"Ha! that is all very well," quoth the Jean-Baptistes, feeling the reproach of an enterprise that asked neither cooperation nor advice of them, "but wait till they come yonder to Jean Poquelin's marsh; ha! ha! ha!" The supposed predicament so delighted them, that they put on a mock terror and whirled about in an assumed stampede, then caught their clasped hands between their knees in excess of mirth, and laughed till the tears ran; for whether the streetmakers mired in the marsh, or contrived to cut through old "Jean-ah's" property, either event would be joyful. Meantime a line of tiny rods, with bits of white paper in their split tops, gradually extended its way straight through the haunted ground, and across the canal diagonally.

"We shall fill that ditch," said the men in mud boots, and brushed close along the chained and padlocked gate of the haunted mansion. Ah, Jean-ah Poquelin, those were not Creole boys, to be stampeded with a little hard swearing.

He went to the Governor. That official scanned the odd figure with no slight interest. Jean Poquelin was of short, broad frame, with a bronzed leonine face. His brow was ample and deeply furrowed. His eye, large and black, was bold and open like that of a war horse, and his jaws shut together with the firmness of iron. He was dressed in a suit of Attakapas cottonade, and his shirt unbuttoned and thrown back from the throat and bosom, sailorwise, showed a herculean breast, hard and grizzled. There was no fierceness or defiance in his look, no harsh ungentleness, no symptom of his unlawful life or violent temper; but rather a peaceful and peaceable fearlessness. Across the whole face, not marked in one or another feature, but as it were laid softly upon the countenance like an almost imperceptible veil, was the imprint of some great grief. A careless eye might easily overlook it, but, once seen, there it hung—faint, but unmistakable.

The Governor bowed.

"*Parlez-vous français?*"[14] asked the figure.

---

[14] *Parlez-vous français?* Do you speak French?

"I would rather talk English, if you can do so," said the Governor.

"My name, Jean Poquelin."

"How can I serve you, Mr. Poquelin?"

"My 'ouse is yond'; *dans le marais là-bas.*"[15]

The Governor bowed.

"Dat *marais* billong to me."

"Yes, sir."

"To me; Jean Poquelin; I hown 'im meself."

"Well, sir?"

"He don't billong to you; I get him from me father."

"That is perfectly true, Mr. Poquelin, as far as I am aware."

"You want to make strit pass yond'?"

"I do not know, sir; it is quite probable; but the city will indemnify you for any loss you may suffer—you will get paid, you understand."

"Strit can't pass dare."

"You will have to see the municipal authorities about that, Mr. Poquelin."

A bitter smile came upon the old man's face.

"*Pardon, Monsieur,* you is not *le Gouverneur?*"

"Yes."

"*Mais,*[16] yes. You har *le Gouverneur*—yes. Veh-well. I come to you. I tell you, strit can't pass at me 'ouse."

"But you will have to see—"

"I come to you. You is *le Gouverneur.* I know not the new laws. I ham a Fr-r-rench-a-man! Fr-rench-a-man have something *aller au contraire*[17]—he come at his *Gouverneur.* I come at you. If me not had been bought from me king like *bossals*[18] in the hold time, ze king gof—France would-a-show *Monsieur le Gouverneur* to take care his men to make strit in right places. *Mais,* I know; we billong to *Monsieur le President.* I want you do somesin for me, eh?"

"What is it?" asked the patient Governor.

---

[15]*dans le marais là-bas:* in the marsh over there
[16]*Mais:* but
[17]*aller au contraire:* to go or speak against
[18]*bossals:* slaves, vassals

"I want you tell *Monsieur le President,* strit—can't—pass
—at—me—'ouse."

"Have a chair, Mr. Poquelin"; but the old man did not
stir. The Governor took a quill and wrote a line to a city
official, introducing Mr. Poquelin, and asking for him every
possible courtesy. He handed it to him, instructing him
where to present it.

"Mr. Poquelin," he said, with a conciliatory smile, "tell
me, is it your house that our Creole citizens tell such odd
stories about?"

The old man glared sternly upon the speaker, and with
immovable features said:

"You don't see me trade some Guinea nigga'?"

"Oh, no."

"You don't see me make some smugglin'?"

"No, sir; not at all."

"But, I am Jean Marie Poquelin. I mine me hown bizniss.
Dat all right? Adieu."

He put his hat on and withdrew. By and by he stood, letter
in hand, before the person to whom it was addressed. This
person employed an interpreter.

"He says," said the interpreter to the officer, "he come to
make you the fair warning how you muz not make the street
pas' at his 'ouse."

The officer remarked that "such impudence was refresh-
ing"; but the experienced interpreter translated freely.

"He says: 'Why you don't want?'" said the interpreter.

The old slave trader answered at some length.

"He says," said the interpreter, again turning to the officer,
"the morass is a too unhealth' for peopl' to live."

"But we expect to drain his old marsh; it's not going to be
a marsh."

"*Il dit*"[19]—the interpreter explained in French.

The old man answered tersely.

"He says the canal is a private," said the interpreter.

"Oh! *that* old ditch; that's to be filled up. Tell the old man
we're going to fix him up nicely."

[19] *Il dit:* He says

Translation being duly made, the man in power was amused to see a thundercloud gathering on the old man's face.

"Tell him," he added, "by the time we finish, there'll not be a ghost left in his shanty."

The interpreter began to translate, but—

"*J' comprends, j' comprends,*"[20] said the old man, with an impatient gesture, and burst forth, pouring curses upon the United States, the President, the Territory of Orleans, Congress, the Governor and all his subordinates, striding out of the apartment as he cursed, while the object of his maledictions roared with merriment and rammed the floor with his foot.

"Why, it will make his old place worth ten dollars to one," said the official to the interpreter.

"'Tis not for de worse of de property," said the interpreter.

"I should guess not," said the other, whittling his chair— "seems to me as if some of these old Creoles would liever[21] live in a crawfish hole than to have a neighbor."

"You know what make old Jean Poquelin make like that? I will tell you. You know—"

The interpreter was rolling a cigarette, and paused to light his tinder; then, as the smoke poured in a thick double stream from his nostrils, he said, in a solemn whisper:

"He is a witch."

"Ho, ho, ho!" laughed the other.

"You don't believe it? What you want to bet?" cried the interpreter, jerking himself half up and thrusting out one arm while he bared it of its coat sleeve with the hand of the other. "What you want to bet?"

"How do you know?" asked the official.

"Dass what I goin' to tell you. You know, one evening I was shooting some *grosbec.*[22] I killed three, but I had trouble to find them, it was becoming so dark. When I have them I start' to come home; then I got to pas' at Jean Poquelin's house."

---

[20] *J' comprends:* I understand
[21] *liever:* rather, sooner
[22] *grosbec:* grosbeak, bird with a thick, conical bill

"Ho, ho, ho!" laughed the other, throwing his leg over the arm of his chair.

"Wait," said the interpreter. "I come along slow, not making some noises; still, still —"

"And scared," said the smiling one.

"*Mais*, wait. I get all pas' the 'ouse. 'Ah!' I say; 'all right!' Then I see two thing' before! Hah! I get as cold and *humide*,[23] and shake like a leaf. You think it was nothing? There I see, so plain as can be (though it was making nearly dark), I see Jean — Marie — Po-que-lin walkin' right in front, and right there beside of him was something like a man — but not a man — white like paint! — I dropp' on the grass from scared — they pass'; so sure as I live 'twas the ghos' of Jacques Poquelin, his brother!"

"Pooh!" said the listener.

"I'll put my han' in the fire," said the interpreter.

"But did you never think," asked the other, "that that might be Jack Poquelin, as you call him, alive and well, and for some cause hid away by his brother?"

"But there har' no cause!" said the other, and the entrance of third parties changed the subject.

Some months passed and the street was opened. A canal was first dug through the marsh, the small one which passed so close to Jean Poquelin's house was filled, and the street, or rather a sunny road, just touched a corner of the old mansion's dooryard. The morass ran dry. Its venomous denizens[24] slipped away through the bulrushes; the cattle roaming freely upon its hardened surface trampled the superabundant undergrowth. The bellowing frogs croaked to westward. Lilies and the flower-de-luce sprang up in the place of reeds; smilax and poison oak gave way to the purple-plumed ironweed and pink spiderwort; the bindweeds ran everywhere blooming as they ran, and on one of the dead cypresses a giant creeper hung its green burden of foliage and lifted its scarlet trumpets. Sparrows and redbirds flitted through the bushes, and dewberries grew ripe beneath. Over all these came a sweet, dry

[23] *humide:* wet, damp
[24] *denizens:* inhabitants

smell of salubrity[25] which the place had not known since the sediments of the Mississippi first lifted it from the sea.

But its owner did not build. Over the willow brakes, and down the vista of the open street, bright new houses, some singly, some by ranks, were prying in upon the old man's privacy. They even settled down toward his southern side. First a woodcutter's hut or two, then a market gardener's shanty, then a painted cottage, and all at once the *faubourg* had flanked and half surrounded him and his dried-up marsh.

Ah! then the common people began to hate him. "The old tyrant!" "You don't mean an old *tyrant?*" "Well, then, why don't he build when the public need demands it? What does he live in that unneighborly way for?" "The old pirate!" "The old kidnaper!" How easily even the most ultra Louisianians put on the imported virtues of the North when they could be brought to bear against the hermit. "There he goes, with the boys after him! Ah! ha! ha! Jean-ah Poquelin! Ah! Jean-ah! Aha! aha! Jean-ah Marie! Jean-ah Poquelin! The old villain!" How merrily the swarming *Americains* echo the spirit of persecution! "The old fraud," they say—"pretends to live in a haunted house, does he? We'll tar and feather him someday. Guess we can fix him."

He cannot be rowed home along the old canal now; he walks. He has broken sadly of late, and the street urchins are ever at his heels. It is like the days when they cried: "Go up, thou baldhead," and the old man now and then turns and delivers ineffectual curses.

To the Creoles—to the incoming lower class of superstitious Germans, Irish, Sicilians, and others—he became an omen and embodiment of public and private ill fortune. Upon him all the vagaries of their superstitions gathered and grew. If a house caught fire, it was imputed to his machinations. Did a woman go off in a fit, he had bewitched her. Did a child stray off for an hour, the mother shivered with the apprehension that Jean Poquelin had offered him to strange gods. The house was the subject of every bad boy's invention who loved to contrive ghostly lies. "As long as that house

[25] *salubrity:* healthfulness, wholesomeness

stands we shall have bad luck. Do you not see our pease and beans dying, our cabbages and lettuce going to seed and our gardens turning to dust, while every day you can see it raining in the woods? The rain will never pass old Poquelin's house. He keeps a fetich.[26] He has conjured the whole Faubourg Ste. Marie. And why, the old wretch? Simply because our playful and innocent children call after him as he passes."

A "Building and Improvement Company," which had not yet got its charter, "but was going to," and which had not, indeed, any tangible capital yet, but "was going to have some," joined the "Jean-ah Poquelin" war. The haunted property would be such a capital site for a market house! They sent a deputation to the old mansion to ask its occupant to sell. The deputation never got beyond the chained gate and a very barren interview with the African mute. The President of the Board was then empowered (for he had studied French in Pennsylvania and was considered qualified) to call and persuade M. Poquelin to subscribe to the company's stock; but— —

"Fact is, gentlemen," he said at the next meeting, "it would take us at least twelve months to make Mr. Pokaleen understand the rather original features of our system, and he wouldn't subscribe when we'd done; besides, the only way to see him is to stop him on the street."

There was a great laugh from the Board; they couldn't help it. "Better meet a bear robbed of her whelps," said one.

"You're mistaken as to that," said the President. "I did meet him, and stopped him, and found him quite polite. But I could get no satisfaction from him; the fellow wouldn't talk in French, and when I spoke in English he hoisted his old shoulders up, and gave the same answer to everything I said."

"And that was—?" asked one or two, impatient of the pause.

"That it 'don't worse w'ile?'"

One of the Board said: "Mr. President, this market-house project, as I take it, is not altogether a selfish one; the com-

---

[26] *fetich:* an object believed to have magic power

munity is to be benefited by it. We may feel that we are working in the public interest [the Board smiled knowingly], if we employ all possible means to oust this old nuisance from among us. You may know that at the time the street was cut through, this old Poquelann did all he could to prevent it. It was owing to a certain connection which I had with that affair that I heard a ghost story [smiles, followed by a sudden dignified check]—ghost story, which, of course, I am not going to relate; but I *may* say that my profound conviction, arising from a prolonged study of that story, is, that this old villain, John Poquelann, has his brother locked up in that old house. Now if this is so, and we can fix it on him, I merely *suggest* that we can make the matter highly useful. I don't know," he added, beginning to sit down, "but that it is an action we owe to the community—hem!"

"How do you propose to handle the subject?" asked the President.

"I was thinking," said the speaker, "that, as a Board of Directors, it would be unadvisable for us to authorize any action involving trespass; but if you, for instance, Mr. President, should, as it were, for mere curiosity, *request* someone, as, for instance, our excellent Secretary, simply as a personal favor, to look into the matter—this is merely a suggestion."

The Secretary smiled sufficiently to be understood that, while he certainly did not consider such preposterous service a part of his duties as secretary, he might, notwithstanding, accede to the President's request; and the Board adjourned.

Little White, as the Secretary was called, was a mild, kind-hearted little man, who, nevertheless, had no fear of anything, unless it was the fear of being unkind.

"I tell you frankly," he privately said to the President, "I go into this purely for reasons of my own."

The next day, a little after nightfall, one might have descried this little man slipping along the rear fence of the Poquelin place, preparatory to vaulting over into the rank, grass-grown yard, and bearing himself altogether more after the manner of a collector of rare chickens than according to the usage of secretaries.

The picture presented to his eye was not calculated to

enliven his mind. The old mansion stood out against the western sky, black and silent. One long, lurid pencil stroke along a sky of slate was all that was left of daylight. No sign of life was apparent; no light at any window, unless it might have been on the side of the house hidden from view. No owls were on the chimneys, no dogs were in the yard.

He entered the place, and ventured up behind a small cabin which stood apart from the house. Through one of its many crannies he easily detected the African mute crouched before a flickering pine knot, his head on his knees, fast asleep.

He concluded to enter the mansion, and, with that view, stood and scanned it. The broad rear steps of the veranda would not serve him; he might meet someone midway. He was measuring, with his eye, the proportions of one of the pillars which supported it, and estimating the practicability of climbing it, when he heard a footstep. Someone dragged a chair out toward the railing, then seemed to change his mind and began to pace the veranda, his footfalls resounding on the dry boards with singular loudness. Little White drew a step backward, got the figure between himself and the sky, and at once recognized the short, broad-shouldered form of old Jean Poquelin.

He sat down upon a billet of wood, and, to escape the stings of a whining cloud of mosquitoes, shrouded his face and neck in his handkerchief, leaving his eyes uncovered.

He had sat there but a moment when he noticed a strange, sickening odor, faint, as if coming from a distance, but loathesome and horrid.

Whence could it come? Not from the cabin; not from the marsh, for it was as dry as powder. It was not in the air; it seemed to come from the ground.

Rising up, he noticed, for the first time, a few steps before him a narrow footpath leading toward the house. He glanced down it—ha! right there was someone coming—ghostly white!

Quick as thought, and as noiselessly, he lay down at full length against the cabin. It was bold strategy, and yet, there was no denying it, little White felt that he was frightened. "It is not a ghost," he said to himself. "I *know* it cannot be a ghost"; but the perspiration burst out at every pore, and the air seemed to thicken with heat. "It is a living man," he said in his thoughts. "I hear his footstep, and I hear old Poquelin's footsteps, too, separately, over on the veranda. I am not discovered; the thing has passed; there is that odor again; what a smell of death! Is it coming back? Yes. It stops at the door of the cabin. Is it peering in at the sleeping mute? It moves away. It is in the path again. Now it is gone." He shuddered. "Now, if I dare venture, the mystery is solved." He rose cautiously, close against the cabin, and peered along the path.

The figure of a man, a presence if not a body — but whether clad in some white stuff or naked, the darkness would not allow him to determine — had turned, and now, with a seeming painful gait, moved slowly from him. "Great Heaven! can it be that the dead do walk?" He withdrew again the hands which had gone to his eyes. The dreadful object passed between two pillars and under the house. He listened. There was a faint sound as of feet within a staircase; then all was still except the measured tread of Jean Poquelin walking on the veranda, and the heavy respirations of the mute slumbering in the cabin.

The little Secretary was about to retreat; but as he looked once more toward the haunted house a dim light appeared in the crack of a closed window, and presently old Jean Poquelin came, dragging his chair, and sat down close against the shining cranny. He spoke in a low, tender tone in the French tongue, making some inquiry. An answer came from within. Was it the voice of a human? So unnatural was it — so hollow, so discordant, so unearthly — that the stealthy listener shuddered again from head to foot; and when something stirred in some bushes nearby — though it may have been nothing more than a rat — and came scuttling through the grass, the little Secretary actually turned and fled. As he left the enclosure he moved with bolder leisure through the bushes; yet now and then he spoke aloud: "Oh, oh! I see, I understand!" and shut his eyes in his hands.

How strange that henceforth little White was the champion of Jean Poquelin! In season and out of season — wherever a word was uttered against him — the Secretary, with a quiet, aggressive force that instantly arrested gossip, demanded upon what authority the statement or conjecture was made;

but as he did not condescend to explain his own remarkable attitude, it was not long before the disrelish and suspicion which had followed Jean Poquelin so many years fell also upon him.

It was only the next evening but one after his adventure that he made himself a source of sullen amazement to one hundred and fifty boys, by ordering them to desist from their wanton hallooing. Old Jean Poquelin, standing and shaking his cane, rolling out his long-drawn maledictions, paused and stared, then gave the Secretary a courteous bow and started on. The boys, save one, from pure astonishment, ceased; but a ruffianly little Irish lad, more daring than any had yet been, threw a big hurtling clod that struck old Poquelin between the shoulders and burst like a shell. The enraged old man wheeled with uplifted staff to give chase to the scampering vagabond; and—he may have tripped, or he may not, but he fell full length. Little White hastened to help him up, but he waved him off with a fierce imprecation and, staggering to his feet, resumed his way homeward. His lips were reddened with blood.

Little White was on his way to the meeting of the Board. He would have given all he dared spend to have stayed away, for he felt both too fierce and too tremulous to brook the criticisms that were likely to be made.

"I can't help it, gentlemen; I can't help you to make a case against the old man, and I'm not going to."

"We did not expect this disappointment, Mr. White."

"I can't help that, sir. No, sir; you had better not appoint any more investigations. Somebody'll investigate himself into trouble. No, sir; it isn't a threat, it is only my advice, but I warn you that whoever takes the task in hand will rue it to his dying day—which may be hastened, too."

The President expressed himself surprised.

"I don't care a rush," answered little White, wildly and foolishly. "I don't care a rush if you are, sir. No, my nerves are not disordered; my head's as clear as a bell. No, I'm *not* excited."

A Director remarked that the Secretary looked as though he had waked from a nightmare.

"Well, sir, if you want to know the fact, I have; and if you choose to cultivate old Poquelin's society you can have one, too."

"White," called a facetious member, but White did not notice. "White," he called again.

"What?" demanded White, with a scowl.

"Did you see the ghost?"

"Yes, sir; I did," cried White, hitting the table, and handing the President a paper which brought the Board to other business.

The story got among the gossips that somebody (they were afraid to say little White) had been to the Poquelin mansion by night and beheld something appalling. The rumor was but a shadow of the truth, magnified and distorted as in the manner of shadows. He had seen skeletons walking, and had barely escaped the clutches of one by making the sign of the cross.

Some madcap boys with an appetite for the horrible plucked up courage to venture through the dried marsh by the cattle path, and come before the house at a spectral hour when the air was full of bats. Something which they but half saw—half a sight was enough—sent them tearing back through the willow brakes and acacia bushes to their homes, where they fairly dropped down, and cried:

"Was it white?" "No—yes—nearly so—we can't tell—but we saw it." And one could hardly doubt, to look at their ashen faces, that they had, whatever it was.

"If that old rascal lived in the country we come from," said certain *Americains*, "he'd have been tarred and feathered before now, wouldn't he, Sanders?"

"Well, now he just would."

"And we'd have rid him on a rail, wouldn't we?"

"That's what I allow."

"Tell you what you *could* do." They were talking to some rollicking Creoles who had assumed an absolute necessity for doing *something*. "What is it you call this thing where an old man marries a young girl, and you come out with horns and—"

"Charivari?"[27] asked the Creoles.

"Yes, that's it. Why don't you shivaree him?" Felicitous suggestion.

Little White, with his wife beside him, was sitting on their doorsteps on the sidewalk, as Creole custom had taught them, looking toward the sunset. They had moved into the lately opened street. The view was not attractive on the score of beauty. The houses were small and scattered, and across the flat commons, spite of the lofty tangle of weeds and bushes, and spite of the thickets of acacia, they needs must see the dismal old Poquelin mansion, tilted awry and shutting out the declining sun. The moon, white and slender, was hanging the tip of its horn over one of the chimneys.

"And you say," said the Secretary, "the old black man has been going by here alone? Patty, suppose old Poquelin should be concocting some mischief; he don't lack provocation; the way that clod hit him the other day was enough to have killed him. Why, Patty, he dropped as quick as *that!* No wonder you haven't seen him. I wonder if they haven't heard something about him up at the drugstore. Suppose I go and see."

"Do," said his wife.

She sat alone for half an hour, watching that sudden going out of the day peculiar to the latitude.

"That moon is ghost enough for one house," she said, as her husband returned. "It has gone right down the chimney."

"Patty," said little White, "the drug clerk says the boys are going to shivaree old Poquelin tonight. I'm going to try to stop it."

"Why, White," said his wife, "you'd better not. You'll get hurt."

"No, I'll not."

"Yes, you will."

"I'm going to sit out here until they come along. They're compelled to pass right by here."

"Why, White, it may be midnight before they start; you're not going to sit out here till then."

"Yes, I am."

[27]*charivari:* a mock serenade

"Well, you're very foolish," said Mrs. White in an undertone, looking anxious, and tapping one of the steps with her foot.

They sat a very long time talking over little family matters.

"What's that?" at last said Mrs. White.

"That's the nine-o'clock gun," said White, and they relapsed into a long-sustained, drowsy silence.

"Patty, you'd better go in and go to bed," said he at last.

"I'm not sleepy."

"Well, you're very foolish," quietly remarked little White, and again silence fell upon them.

"Patty, suppose I walk out to the old house and see if I can find out anything."

"Suppose," said she, "you don't do any such—listen!"

Down the street arose a great hubbub. Dogs and boys were howling and barking; men were laughing, shouting, groaning, and blowing horns, whooping, and clanking cowbells, whinnying, and howling, and rattling pots and pans.

"They are coming this way," said little White. "You had better go into the house, Patty."

"So had you."

"No. I'm going to see if I can't stop them."

"Why, White!"

"I'll be back in a minute," said White, and went toward the noise.

In a few moments the little Secretary met the mob. The pen hesitates on the word, for there is a respectable difference, measurable only on the scale of the half century, between a mob and a *charivari*. Little White lifted his ineffectual voice. He faced the head of the disorderly column, and cast himself about as if he were made of wood and moved by the jerk of a string. He rushed to one who seemed, from the size and clatter of his tin pan, to be a leader. *"Stop these fellows, Bienvenu, stop them just a minute, till I tell them something."* Bienvenu turned and brandished his instruments of discord in an imploring way to the crowd. They slackened their pace, two or three hushed their horns and joined the prayer of little White and Bienvenu for silence. The throng halted. The hush was delicious.

"Bienvenu," said little White, "don't shivaree old Poquelin tonight; he's ——"

"My fwang," said the swaying Bienvenu, "who tail you I goin' to chahivahi somebody, eh? You sink bickause I make a little playfool wiz siz tin pan zat I am *dhonk?*"

"Oh, no, Bienvenu, old fellow, you're all right. I was afraid you might not know that old Poquelin was sick, you know, but you're not going there, are you?"

"My fwang, I vay soy to tail you zat you ah dhonk as de dev'. I am *shem* of you. I ham ze servan' of *ze publique.* Zese citoyens[28] goin' to wickwest Jean Poquelin to give to the Ursuline'[29] two hondred fifty dolla' — —"

"*Hé quoi!*" cried a listener. "*Cinq cent piastres, oui!*[30]

"*Oui!*" said Bienvenu, "and if he wiffuse we make him some lit' *musique; ta-ra-ta!*" He hoisted a merry hand and foot, then frowning, added: "Old Poquelin got o bizniz dhink s'much w'isky."

"But, gentlemen," said little White, around whom a circle had gathered, "the old man is very sick."

"My faith!" cried a tiny Creole, "we did not make him to be sick. "W'en we have say we going make *le charivari,* do you want that we hall tell a lie? My faith! 'sfools!"

"But you can shivaree somebody else," said desperate little White.

"*Oui!*" cried Bienvenu, "*et chahivahi* Jean-ah Poquelin tomo'w!"

"Let us go to Madame Schneider!" cried two or three, and amid huzzas and confused cries, among which was heard a stentorian Celtic call for drinks, the crowd again began to move.

"*Cent piastres pour l'hôpital de charité!*"[31]

"Hurrah!"

"One hongred dolla' for Charity Hospital!"

"Hurrah!"

---

[28] *citoyens:* citizens
[29] *Ursulines:* nuns of the Ursuline order
[30] *Hé quoi! Cinq cent piastres, oui!* Hey what! Five hundred dollars, yes!
[31] *Cent piastres pour l'hôpital de charité!* A hundred dollars for the charity hospital!

"Whang!" went a tin pan, the crowd yelled, and Pandemonium gaped again. They were off at a right angle.

Nodding, Mrs. White looked at the mantel clock.

"Well, if it isn't away after midnight."

The hideous noise downstreet was passing beyond earshot. She raised a sash and listened. For a moment there was silence. Someone came to the door.

"Is that you, White?"

"Yes. They've gone down to shivaree the old Dutchwoman who married her stepdaughter's sweetheart. They say she has got to pay a hundred dollars to the hospital before they stop."

The couple retired, and Mrs. White slumbered. She was awakened by her husband snapping the lid of his watch.

"What time?" she asked.

"Half past three. Patty, I haven't slept a wink. Those fellows are out yet. Don't you hear them?"

"Why, White, they're coming this way!"

"I know they are," said White, sliding out of bed and drawing on his clothes, "and they're coming fast. You'd better go away from that window, Patty! My! what a clatter!"

"Here they are," said Mrs. White, but her husband was gone. Two or three hundred men and boys pass the place at a rapid walk straight down the broad, new street, toward the hated house of ghosts. The din was terrific. She saw little White at the head of the rabble brandishing his arms and trying in vain to make himself heard; but they only shook their heads, laughing and hooting the louder, and so passed, bearing him on before them.

Swiftly they pass out from among the houses, away from the dim oil lamps of the street, out into the broad starlit commons, and enter the willowy jungles of the haunted ground. Some hearts fail and their owners lag behind and turn back, suddenly remembering how near morning it is. But the most part push on, tearing the air with their clamor.

Down ahead of them in the long, thicket-darkened way there is — singularly enough — a faint dancing light. It must be very near the old house; it is. It has stopped now. It is a lantern, and is under a well-known sapling which has grown up on the wayside since the canal was filled. Now it swings mysteriously to and fro. A goodly number of the more ghost-fearing give up the sport; but a full hundred move forward at a run, doubling their devilish howling and banging.

Yes; it is a lantern, and there are two persons under the tree. The crowd draws near—drops into a walk; one of the two is the old African mute; he lifts the lantern up so that it shines on the other; the crowd recoils; there is a hush of all clangor, and all at once, with a cry of mingled fright and horror from every throat, the whole throng rushes back, dropping everything, sweeping past little White and hurrying on, never stopping until the jungle is left behind, and then to find that not one in ten has seen the cause of the stampede, and not one of the tenth is certain what it was.

There is one huge fellow among them who looks capable of any villainy. He finds something to mount on, and, in the Creole *patois*,[32] calls a general halt. Bienvenu sinks down, and, vainly trying to recline gracefully, resigns the leadership. The herd gather round the speaker; he assures them that they have been outraged. Their right peaceably to traverse the public streets has been trampled upon. Shall such encroachments be endured? It is now daybreak. Let them go now by the open light of day and force a free passage of the public highway!

A scattering consent was the response, and the crowd, thinned now and drowsy, straggled quietly down toward the old house. Some drifted ahead, others sauntered behind, but everyone, as he again neared the tree, came to a standstill. Little White sat upon a bank of turf on the opposite side of the way looking very stern and sad. To each newcomer he put the same question:

"Did you come here to go to old Poquelin's?"

"Yes."

"He's dead." And if the shocked hearer started away he would say: "Don't go away."

"Why not?"

"I want you to go to the funeral presently."

---

[32] *patois:* dialect

If some Louisianian, too loyal to dear France or Spain to understand English, looked bewildered, someone would interpret for him; and presently they went. Little White led the van, the crowd trooping after him down the middle of the way. The gate, that had never been seen before unchained, was open. Stern little White stopped a short distance from it; the rabble stopped behind him. Something was moving out from under the veranda. The many whisperers stretched upward to see. The African mute came very slowly toward the gate, leading by a cord in the nose a small brown bull, which was harnessed to a rude cart. On the flat body of the cart, under a black cloth, were seen the outlines of a long box.

"Hats off, gentlemen," said little White, as the box came in view, and the crowd silently uncovered.

"Gentlemen," said little White, "here come the last remains of Jean Marie Poquelin, a better man, I'm afraid, with all his sins—yes, a better—a kinder man to his blood—a man of more self-forgetful goodness—than all of you put together will ever dare to be."

There was a profound hush as the vehicle came creaking through the gate; but when it turned away from them toward the forest, those in front started suddenly. There was a backward rush, then all stood still again staring one way; for there, behind the bier, with eyes cast down and labored step, walked the living remains—all that was left—of little Jacques Poquelin, the long-hidden brother—a leper, as white as snow.

Dumb with horror, the cringing crowd gazed upon the walking death. They watched, in silent awe, the slow *cortège*[33] creep down the long, straight road and lessen on the view, until by and by it stopped where a wild, unfrequented path branched off into the undergrowth toward the rear of the ancient city.

"They are going to the *Terre aux Lépreux*,"[34] said one in the crowd. The rest watched them in silence.

The little bull was set free; the mute, with the strength of an ape, lifted the long box to his shoulder. For a moment more

[33] *cortège:* procession
[34] *Terre aux Lépreux:* Land of the Lepers

the mute and the leper stood in sight, while the former adjusted his heavy burden; then, without one backward glance upon the unkind human world, turning their faces toward the ridge in the depths of the swamp known as the Leper's Land, they stepped into the jungle, disappeared, and were never seen again.

FOR DISCUSSION

1. Contrast the personality of Jean with that of his younger half-brother Jacques. What is Jean's attitude toward Jacques?
2. After the decline of his estate, how does Jean make his living? Why is this fact important to the plot of the story?
3. How does the general public feel toward the brothers before Jacques' mysterious disappearance? In what ways does public opinion change toward Jean after Jacques' disappearance? What are "the many" implying in their silent question to Jean, "Where is thy brother Abel?"
4. Why does Jean regard the work of the levelers and the "streetmakers" as a threat? What is the result of his appeal to the Governor and the city official?
5. Little White is the first person to understand the situation fully, but the fate of Jacques is not totally unexpected if you have been attentive to details during the course of the story. What hints have you been given that Jacques is still alive and living with Jean? Have you been given any indications of his disease?
6. What sort of man is Little White? How is he different from the other Americans in the story? Why do you suppose he keeps Jean's secret instead of telling the other Board members? How do you interpret his statement to the mob that Jean was "a better man than all of you put together will ever be"?
7. The story dramatizes the conflict between two civilizations, that of the old-world Creoles and that of the Americans. What particular aspects of the newly-established American Government make it seem "the most hateful thing in Louisiana" to the Creoles? Do you feel that the actions of the Americans in this story justify the Creole resentment against them? Why or why not?
8. Cable was one of the first American writers to use dialect realistically. How is the Creole *patois* different from other American dialects you have read or heard? Why is Bienvenu's speech harder to understand than that of the other Creoles?

9. Though Cable's characters and settings are largely romantic in
   nature, his dialogues and descriptions are realistic. Examine his
   descriptions of the Poquelin mansion and its surrounding marsh.
   What other passages do you find that you consider particularly
   realistic?

FOR COMPOSITION

1. To Cable, New Orleans was romantic and picturesque. From his
   descriptions of parts of the city, do you think you would have liked
   the city at the time this story took place? Write a short composition
   telling why or why not.
2. The story tells you a good deal more about Jean than about his
   brother. Write a composition giving a brief character sketch of
   Jacques and then tell how you think he might have reacted to
   what happened. Be sure to consider such things as his feelings
   toward his older brother and toward the people of the city, also
   his reactions to his disease and to his brother's death.

THE GROWTH OF REALISM

Even as the regional American writers were portraying the quaint, picturesque, and adventurous American scene, it was rapidly disappearing. The great days of the Mississippi riverboats had come to an end, and the New England fishing villages were more deserted than ever. An increasing number of Americans and immigrants from Southern Europe were crowding into sprawling cities to work in factories and offices. Still others—industrialists and financiers—were intent on finding legal and socially acceptable ways of exploiting the vast natural and human resources of this nation, usually for personal gain.

As late as 1870, the spirit of romanticism was still strong in America. The country continued to assume as its peculiar and major responsibility the creation of a larger, better life for the common man. It continued to believe that intellectual and spiritual matters were more important than material possessions. Yet the surge of modern industrialism began to alter the American way of thinking.

The focus of American literature began gradually to shift

from a concern with the past, the picturesque, and the genteel, to a concern with the present, the everyday, and even the sordid—no matter how disillusioning. This shift was neither sudden nor complete, as the literature of the period clearly illustrates; however, it did much to change the traditional and puritanical attitudes of American readers toward what was rightly the subject matter and purpose of literature. Thus the writers of the period exercised greater freedom both in what they chose to write about and in the frank way they presented it.

Even if the meaning of the terms *romantic* and *realistic* could be clearly defined, any classification of the writers of this period as strictly romantic or realistic would be misleading, if not impossible. Whatever distinction can be made is one of degree. An author's early work could, for example, be more romantic than his later work. Often the subject matter of the work, and the author's attitude toward it, determined the degree to which the work itself was primarily romantic or realistic.

William Dean Howells, editor-in-chief of the influential *Atlantic Monthly* during the 1870's, became the primary spokesman for "realism" as a literary point of view. He defined it as "nothing more and nothing less than the truthful treatment of material." By this definition, a literary work was considered realistic to the extent that it was a "truthful treatment," no matter when it was written or by what author. The term *realism* also came to stand for an attitude—a reaction against the prudishness and shallow optimism of a romanticism which had gone to seed. Four writers who shared this attitude were Hamlin Garland, Frank Norris, Stephen Crane, and Jack London. With the courage of their convictions, they set out to explore and expose such "realities" as the grimness of life in small towns and on debt-ridden farms, the many inequities in the social system of the time, the unheroic, ugly nature of war, the dehumanizing effects of industrialization, and the depths to which men can sink under extreme hardship. Some of these writers used fiction as a medium for social protest; others did not. Yet all believed that life, in all its aspects, was their subject matter.

HAMLIN GARLAND chose as his subject matter the plight of his own people — the midwestern farmers — who were the victims of economic forces which neither they nor he clearly understood. As a young man he had left his parents' Dakota farm to educate himself in Boston and, if possible, to become a writer. On a visit to his homeland in 1887, he felt so indignant at the poverty and suffering of farm families, and so repelled by the squalid futility of their lives, that he determined to present these grim facts in fiction. His stories were so truthful in subject and treatment that only the most liberal magazines would print them.

The motivation for most of Garland's writing was his humanitarian concern with social injustice and his determination to awaken the public to the need for reform. As a result, his themes of social protest were too often overstated rather than suggested to the reader. Thus, he was not always successful in achieving a fusion of content and form that characterizes great literature and that provides the reader with a memorable and significant literary experience. Nevertheless, his stories brought a new vigor to American literature.

FRANK NORRIS modified some of the assumptions of his fellow realists to suit his own ideas about life and art. First, he rejected Howells' idea that fiction should be simply an imitation of life. "Life," he maintained, "is not always true to life. . . . In the fine arts we do not care one little bit about what life actually is, but what it looks like to an interesting, impressionable man." Second, he challenged the assumption that the writer should simply observe the world and report his observations. Norris could not be the kind of realist who "notes only the surface of things."

For Norris, the only important novel was "the novel with a 'Purpose.'" Moreover, he believed that fiction is at its best when it is sociological; that is, when it dramatizes the relationships between people of different social and economic classes. He hated special privilege and, like Garland, devoted much of his creative energy to exposing corruption and unfairness in the social system of his day. In style he was much influenced by the naturalism (see page 516) of the French writer, Emile Zola.

In 1900, with his reputation already secure, Norris set out to write a trilogy—a series of three novels—dealing with the growing, marketing, and exporting of American wheat. This "Epic of the Wheat" was never completed; the third novel, *The Wolf*, was in the planning stage when Norris died. The major concern of the trilogy is clearly revealed in the first two novels, *The Octopus* and *The Pit*; namely, the "world-old war between Freedom and Tyranny." Here the wheat symbolized what he called the "Life Force"; the railroads that carried the wheat symbolized the tyranny of the machine. These two novels secured Norris' place in American fiction; and in his use of naturalism he foreshadowed Faulkner's unflinching use of sordid detail, Hemingway's use of brutality, and Thomas Wolfe's poetic sweep and fervor.

STEPHEN CRANE was, in a sense, discovered by Hamlin Garland, who recognized in this young man the "artist he could describe but could not himself become." American readers could neither accept nor ignore Crane's first novel, *Maggie: A Girl of the Streets*, with its brutal yet honest picture of life in the slums of New York. Crane said that his purpose was "to show that environment is a tremendous thing in the world, and frequently shapes lives regardless." Environment is an equally "tremendous thing" in *The Red Badge of Courage*, Crane's great novel of the Civil War, and in his classic short story, "The Open Boat."

Crane had learned something about graphic writing from his experiences as a newspaper correspondent and something about the artistic possibilities of realism from his occasional reading in nineteenth-century French novels, but so had several of his contemporaries associated with American realism. What, then, were the sources of his greatness? One was his extraordinary ability to express profound observations about life in everyday language and in simple yet startling images and comparisons. Another was his concern with man's struggles within his own heart and mind as well as with outside forces. He believed that life itself was essentially tragic and that all men—rich and poor—were motivated primarily by fear. He saw irony in man's self-importance and self-pity in a universe that was essentially indifferent to man.

Crane's best work, which was his earlier work, shows his great interest in and mastery of technical form. Through simplicity, economy, and restraint, he achieved a sense of wonder and universality which, together with his naturalistic themes, affected the work of such later writers as Hemingway, Faulkner, and Steinbeck.

JACK LONDON lived as eventful and unconventional a life as any of his most unorthodox characters. By his own account, before he was nineteen he had shipped to Japan as a common seaman, traveled across the United States with little or no money, worked sixteen hours a day in a cannery, and spent thirty days in the Niagara Falls jail for vagrancy. According to all evidence, he did not slow his pace even in adulthood. Critics have suggested, in fact, that he seems to have behaved as though his life was one of his own adventure stories.

One of the most prolific writers of his generation, London achieved enormous popular success with some forty-nine volumes of fiction, some of them admittedly potboilers. His artistic achievement, however, is represented by only a small body of writing—two or three novels and a handful of stories.

In these works, London managed to achieve a fine balance between adventure and excitement on the one hand, and serious philosophical speculation on the other. Because he was greatly influenced by the scientific spirit that dominated European and American thought at the turn of the century, he was struck by the idea that human life may be subject to the same laws that govern the rest of the natural world. He was both intrigued and depressed by the possibility that man is ultimately driven by certain basic instincts, especially the need for food. Consequently, he based story after story on the theme that life is essentially a struggle for survival and that, under trying conditions, man is guided principally by his instinct for self-preservation. His work as a whole is characterized by a tremendous power and vitality, which compensates, in part, for his lack of complete artistic control.

Hamlin Garland

Hamlin Garland combined the realist's passion for accurate, truthful observation of life with the regionalist's knowledge of his area and its people. He had a keen eye for the kind of detail that creates pictures in the mind, and a keen ear for the dialect and colloquial speech of Midwestern farm folk. Whether he was reconstructing and interpreting a personal experience, as in his semi-autobiographical Middle Border novels, or creating a dramatic and carefully structured story like "Under the Lion's Paw," he left his readers with the conviction that he was a competent witness who intended to tell the whole truth.

Under the Lion's Paw

I

It was the last of autumn and first day of winter coming together. All day long the ploughmen on their prairie farms had moved to and fro in their wide level fields through the falling snow, which melted as it fell, wetting them to the skin —all day, notwithstanding the frequent squalls of snow, the dripping, desolate clouds, and the muck of the furrows, black and tenacious as tar.

Under their dripping harness the horses swung to and fro silently, with that marvelous uncomplaining patience which marks the horse. All day the wild geese, honking wildly, as they sprawled sidewise down the wind, seemed to be fleeing from an enemy behind, and with neck outthrust and wings extended, sailed down the wind, soon lost to sight.

Yet the ploughman behind his plough, though the snow lay on his ragged great-coat, and the cold clinging mud rose on his heavy boots, fettering him like gyves,[1] whistled in the very beard of the gale. As day passed, the snow, ceasing to melt, lay along the ploughed land, and lodged in the depth of the stubble, till on each slow round the last furrow stood out black and shining as jet between the ploughed land and the gray stubble.

When night began to fall, and the geese, flying low, began to alight invisibly in the near corn-field, Stephen Council was still at work "finishing a land." He rode on his sulky[2] plow when going with the wind, but walked when facing it. Sitting bent and cold but cheery under his slouch hat, he talked encouragingly to his four-in-hand.

"Come round there, boys!—Round agin! We got t'finish this land. Come in there, Dan! *Stiddy*, Kate,—stiddy! None o' y'r tantrums, Kittie. It's purty tuff, but it got a be did. *Tchk! tchk!* Step along, Pete! Don't let Kate git y'r single-tree[3] on the wheel. Once more!"

They seemed to know what he meant, and that this was the last round, for they worked with greater vigor than before.

"Once more, boys, an' then, sez I, oats an' a nice warm stall, an' sleep f'r all."

By the time the last furrow was turned on the land it was too dark to see the house, and the snow was changing to rain again. The tired and hungry man could see the light from the kitchen shining through the leafless hedge, and he lifted a great shout, "Supper f'r a half a dozen!"

It was nearly eight o'clock by the time he had finished his chores and started for supper. He was picking his way carefully through the mud, when the tall form of a man loomed up before him with a premonitory cough.

"Waddy ye want?" was the rather startled question of the farmer.

"Well, ye see," began the stranger, in a deprecating tone, "we'd like t' git in f'r the night. We've tried every house f'r the last two miles, but they hadn't any room f'r us. My wife's jest about sick, 'n' the children are cold and hungry—"

[1] *gyves:* shackles or chains for the feet
[2] *sulky:* having two wheels and a seat
[3] *single-tree:* crossbar to which a harnessed horse is fastened

"Oh, y' want 'o stay all night, eh?"

"Yes, sir; it 'ud be a great accom—"

"Waal, I don't make it a practice t' turn anybuddy way hungry, not on sech nights as this. Drive right in. We ain't got much, but sech as it is—"

But the stranger had disappeared. And soon his steaming, weary team, with drooping heads and swinging single-trees, moved past the well to the block beside the path. Council stood at the side of the "schooner"⁴ and helped the children out—two little half-sleeping children—and then a small woman with a babe in her arms.

"There ye go!" he shouted jovially, to the children. "Now we're all right! Run right along to the house there, an' tell Mam' Council you wants sumpthin' t' eat. Right this way, Mis'—keep right off t' the right there. I'll go and git a lantern. Come," he said to the dazed and silent group at his side.

"Mother," he shouted, as he neared the fragrant and warmly lighted kitchen, "here are some wayfarers an' folks who need sumpthin' t' eat an' a place t' snooze." He ended by pushing them all in.

Mrs. Council, a large, jolly, rather coarse-looking woman, took the children in her arms. "Come right in, you little rabbits. 'Most asleep, hey? Now here's a drink o' milk f'r each o' ye. I'll have s'm tea in a minute. Take off y'r things and set up t' the fire."

While she set the children to drinking milk, Council got out his lantern and went out to the barn to help the stranger about his team, where his loud, hearty voice could be heard as it came and went between the haymow and the stalls.

The woman came to light as a small, timid, and discouraged-looking woman, but still pretty, in a thin and sorrowful way.

"Land sakes! An' you've traveled all the way from Clear Lake t'day in this mud! Waal! waal! No wonder you're all tired out. Don't wait f'r the men, Mis'—" She hesitated, waiting for the name.

"Haskins."

"Mis' Haskins, set right up to the table an' take a good swig

⁴*schooner:* (prairie schooner) large covered wagon

o'tea whilst I make y s'm toast. It's green tea, an' it's good. I tell Council as I git older I don't seem to enjoy Young Hyson n'r Gunpowder.[5] I want the reel green tea, jest as it comes off'n the vines. Seems t' have more heart in it, some way. Don't s'pose it has. Council says it's all in m' eye."

Going on in this easy way, she soon had the children filled with bread and milk and the woman thoroughly at home, eating some toast and sweet-melon pickles, and sipping the tea.

"See the little rats!" she laughed at the children. "They're full as they can stick now, and they want to go to bed. Now, don't git up, Mis' Haskins; set right where you are an' let me look after 'em. I know all about young ones, though I'm all alone now. Jane went an' married last fall. But, as I tell Council, it's lucky we keep our health. Set right there, Mis' Haskins; I won't have you stir a finger."

It was an unmeasured pleasure to sit there in the warm, homely kitchen, the jovial chatter of the house-wife driving out and holding at bay the growl of the impotent, cheated wind.

The little woman's eyes filled with tears which fell down upon the sleeping baby in her arms. The world was not so desolate and cold and hopeless, after all.

"Now I hope Council won't stop out there and talk politics all night. He's the greatest man to talk politics an' read the *Tribune* — How old is it?"

She broke off and peered down at the face of the babe.

"Two months 'n' five days," said the mother, with a mother's exactness.

"Ye don't say! I want o' know! The dear little pudzy-wudzy!" she went on, stirring it up in the neighborhood of the ribs with her fat forefinger.

"Pooty tough on 'oo to go gallivant n' 'cross lots this way—"

"Yes, that's so; a man can't lift a mountain," said Council, entering the door. "Mother, this is Mr. Haskins, from Kansas. He's been eat up 'n' drove out by grasshoppers."

"Glad t' see yeh! — Pa, empty that wash-basin 'n' give him a chance t' wash."

[5] *Young Hyson . . . Gunpowder:* kinds of tea

Haskins was a tall man, with a thin, gloomy face. His hair was a reddish brown, like his coat, and seemed equally faded by the wind and sun, and his sallow face, though hard and set, was pathetic somehow. You would have felt that he had suffered much by the line of his mouth showing under his thin, yellow mustache.

"Hain't Ike got home yet, Sairy?"

"Hain't see 'im."

"W-a-a-l, set right up, Mr. Haskins; wade right into what we've got; 'tain't much, but we manage to live on it—she gits fat on it," laughed Council, pointing his thumb at his wife.

After supper, while the women put the children to bed, Haskins and Council talked on, seated near the huge cooking-stove, the steam rising from their wet clothing. In the Western fashion Council told as much of his own life as he drew from his guest. He asked but few questions, but by and by the story of Haskins' struggles and defeat came out. The story was a terrible one, but he told it quietly, seated with his elbows on his knees, gazing most of the time at the hearth.

"I didn't like the looks of the country, anyhow," Haskins said, partly rising and glancing at his wife. "I was ust t' northern Ingyannie, where we have lots o' timber 'n' lots of rain 'n' I didn't like the looks o' that dry prairie. What galled me the worst was goin' s' far away acrosst so much fine land layin' all through here vacant."

"And the 'hoppers eat ye four years, hand runnin', did they?"

"Eat! They wiped us out. They chawed everything that was green. They jest set around waitin' f'r us to die t' eat us, too. I ust t' dream of 'em sittin' 'round on the bedpost, six feet long, workin' their jaws. They et the fork-handles. They got worse 'n' worse till they jest rolled on one another, piled up like snow in winter. Well, it ain't no use. If I was t' talk all winter I couldn't tell nawthin'. But all the while I couldn't help thinkin' of all that land back here that nobuddy was usin' that I ought o' had 'stead o' bein' out there in that cussed country."

"Waal, why didn't ye stop an' settle here?" asked Ike, who had come in and was eating his supper.

"Fer the simple reason that you fellers wantid ten 'r fifteen dollars an acre fer the bare land, and I hadn't no money for that kind o' thing."

"Yes, I do my own work," Mrs. Council was heard to say in the pause which followed. "I'm a gettin' purty heavy t' be on m' laigs all day, but we can't afford t' hire, so I keep rackin' around somehow, like a foundered horse. S' lame—I tell Council he can't tell how lame I am, f'r I'm jest as lame in one laig as t'other." And the good soul laughed at the joke on herself as she took a handful of flour and dusted the biscuit-board to keep the dough from sticking.

"Well, I hain't *never* been very strong," said Mrs. Haskins. "Our folks was Canadians an' small-boned, and then since my last child I hain't got up again fairly. I don't like t' complain. Tim has about all he can bear now—but they was days this week when I jest wanted to lay right down an' die."

"Waal, now, I'll tell ye," said Council, from his side of the stove, silencing everybody with his good-natured roar, "I'd go down and *see* Butler, *anyway*, if I was you. I guess he'd let you have his place purty cheap; the farm's all run down. He's been anxious t'let t' somebuddy next year. It 'ud be a good chance fer you. Anyhow, you go to bed and sleep like a babe. I've got some ploughin' to' do, anyhow, an' we'll see if somethin' can't be done about your case. Ike, you go out an' see if the horses is all right, an' I'll show the folks t' bed."

When the tired husband and wife were lying under the generous quilts of the spare bed, Haskins listened a moment to the wind in the eaves, and then said, with a slow and solemn tone.

"There are people in this world who are good enough t' be angels, an' only haff t' die to *be* angels."

II

Jim Butler was one of those men called in the West "land poor." Early in the history of Rock River he had come into the town and started in the grocery business in a small way, occupying a small building in a mean part of the town. At this period of his life he earned all he got, and was up early and late sorting beans, working over butter, and carting his goods

to and from the station. But a change came over him at the end
of the second year, when he sold a lot of land for four times
what he paid for it. From that time forward he believed in
land speculation as the surest way of getting rich. Every cent
he could save or spare from his trade he put into land at forced
sale, or mortgages on land, which were "just as good as the
wheat," he was accustomed to say.

Farm after farm fell into his hands, until he was recognized
as one of the leading landowners of the country. His mortgages were scattered all over Cedar County, and as they
slowly but surely fell in he sought usually to retain the former
owner as tenant.

He was not ready to foreclose; indeed, he had the name of
being one of the "easiest" men in the town. He let the debtor
off again and again, extending the time whenever possible.

"I don't want y'r land," he said. "All I'm after is the int'rest
on my money—that's all. Now, if y' want 'o stay on the farm,
why, I'll give y' a good chance. I can't have the land layin'
vacant." And in many cases the owner remained as tenant.

In the meantime he had sold his store; he couldn't spend
time in it; he was mainly occupied now with sitting around
town on rainy days smoking and "gassin' with the boys," or
in riding to and from his farms. In fishing-time he fished a
good deal. Doc Grimes, Ben Ashley, and Cal Cheatham were
his cronies on these fishing excursions or hunting trips in the
time of chickens or partridges. In winter they went to northern
Wisconsin to shoot deer.

In spite of all these signs of easy life Butler persisted in
saying he "hadn't enough money to pay taxes on his land,"
and was careful to convey the impression that he was poor in
spite of his twenty farms. At one time he was said to be worth
fifty thousand dollars, but land had been a little slow of sale
of late, so that he was not worth so much.

A fine farm, known as the Higley place, had fallen into his
hands in the usual way the previous year, and he had not been
able to find a tenant for it. Poor Higley, after working himself
nearly to death on it in the attempt to lift the mortgage, had
gone off to Dakota, leaving the farm and his curse to Butler.

This was the farm which Council advised Haskins to apply

for; and the next day Council hitched up his team and drove down town to see Butler.

"You jest let *me* do the talkin'," he said. "We'll find him wearin' out his pants on some salt barrel somew'ers; and if he thought you *wanted* a place he'd sock it to you hot and heavy. You jest keep quiet; I'll fix 'im."

Butler was seated in Ben Ashley's store telling fish yarns when Council sauntered in casually.

"Hello, But; lyin' agin, hey?"

"Hellow, Steve! how goes it?"

"Oh, so-so. Too dang much rain these days. I thought it was goin' t' freeze up f'r good last night. Tight squeak if I get m' ploughin' done. How's farmin' with you these days?"

"Bad. Ploughin' ain't half done."

"It 'ud be a religious idee f'r you t' go out an' take a hand y'rself."

"I don't haff to," said Butler, with a wink.

"Got anybody on the Higley place?"

"No. Know of anybody?"

"Waal, no: not eggsackly. I've got a relation back t' Michigan who's bent hot an' cold on the idee o' comin' West f'r some time. *Might* come if he could get a good lay-out. What do you talk on the farm?"

"Well, I d' know. I'll rent it on shares or I'll rent it money rent."

"Waal, how much money, say?"

"Well, say ten percent, on the price—two-fufty."

"Waal, that ain't bad. Wait on 'im till 'e threshes?"

Haskins listened eagerly to this important question, but Council was coolly eating a dried apple which he had speared out of a barrel with his knife. Butler studied him carefully.

"Well, knocks me out of twenty-five dollars interest."

"My relation'll need all he's got t' git his crops in," said Council, in the safe, indifferent way.

"Well, all right; say wait." concluded Butler.

"All right; this is the man. Haskins, this is Mr. Butler—no relation to Ben—the hardest-working man in Cedar County."

On the way home Haskins said: "I ain't much better off. I'd like that farm; it's a good farm, but it's all run down, an' so 'm I. I could make a good farm of it if I had half a show. But I can't stock it n'r seed it."

"Waal, now, don't you worry," roared Council in his ear. "We'll pull y' through somehow till next harvest. He's agreed t' hire it ploughed, an' you can earn a hundred dollars plough-in' an' y' c'n git the seed o' me, an' pay me back when y' can."

Haskins was silent with emotion, but at last he said, "I ain't got nothin t' live on."

"Now, do't you worry 'bout that. You jest make your head-quarters at ol' Steve Council's. Mother'll take a pile o' comfort in havin' y'r wife an' children 'round. Y' see, Jane's married off lately, an' Ike's away a good 'eal, so we'll be darn glad t' have y' stop with us this winter. Nex' spring, we'll see if y' can't git a start agin." And he chirruped to the team, which sprang forward with the rumbling, clattering wagon.

"Say, looky here, Council, you can't do this. I never saw—" shouted Haskins in his neighbor's ear.

Council moved about uneasily in his seat and stopped his stammering gratitude by saying: "Hold on, now; don't make such a fuss over a little thing. When I see a man down, an' things all on top of 'im, I jest like t' kick 'em off an' help 'im up. That's the kind of religion I got, an' it's about the *only* kind."

They rode the rest of the way home in silence. And when the red light of the lamp shone out into the darkness of the cold and windy night, and he thought of this refuge for his children and wife, Haskins could have put his arm around the neck of his burly companion and squeezed him like a lover. But he contented himself with saying, "Steve Council, you'll git y'r pay f'r this some day."

"Don't want any pay. My religion ain't run on such business principles."

The wind was growing colder, and the ground was covered with a white frost, as they turned into the gate of the Council farm, and the children came rushing out, shouting, "Papa's come." They hardly looked like the same children who had sat at the table the night before. Their torpidity,[6] under the

---

[6] *torpidity:* sluggishness

influence of sunshine and Mother Council, had given way to a sort of spasmodic cheerfulness, as insects in winter revive when laid on the hearth.

III

Haskins worked like a fiend, and his wife, like the heroic woman that she was, bore also uncomplainingly the most terrible burdens. They rose early and toiled without intermission till the darkness fell on the plain, then tumbled into bed, every bone and muscle aching with fatigue, to rise with the sun next morning to the same round of the same ferocity of labor.

The eldest boy drove a team all through the spring, ploughing and seeding, milked the cows, and did chores innumerable, in most ways taking the place of a man.

An infinitely pathetic but common figure—this boy on the American farm, where there is no law against child labor. To see him in his coarse clothing, his huge boots, and his ragged cap, as he staggered with a pail of water from the well, or trudged in the cold and cheerless dawn into the frosty field behind his team, gave the city-bred visitor a sharp pang of sympathetic pain. Yet Haskins loved his boy, and would have saved him from this if he could, but he could not.

By June the first year the result of such Herculean toil began to show on the farm. The yard was cleaned up and sown to grass, the garden ploughed and planted, and the house mended.

Council had given them four of his cows.

"Take 'em an' run 'em on shares. I don't want 'o milk s' many. Ike's away s' much now, Sat'd'ys an' Sund'ys, I can't stand the bother anyhow."

Other men, seeing the confidence of Council in the newcomer, had sold him tools on time; and as he was really an able farmer, he soon had round him many evidences of his care and thrift. At the advice of Council he had taken the farm for three years, with the privilege of re-renting or buying at the end of the term.

"It's a good bargain, an' y' want 'o nail it," said Council,

"If you have any kind ov a crop, you c'n pay y'r debts, an' keep seed an' bread."

The new hope which now sprang up in the heart of Haskins and his wife grew great almost as a pain by the time the wide field of wheat began to wave and rustle and swirl in the winds of July. Day after day he would snatch a few moments after supper to go and look at it.

"Have ye seen the wheat t'-day, Nettie?" he asked one night as he rose from supper.

"No, Tim, I ain't had time."

"Well, take time now. Le's go look at it."

She threw an old hat on her head—Tommy's hat—and looking almost pretty in her thin, sad way, went out with her husband to the hedge.

"Ain't it grand, Nettie? Just look at it."

It was grand. Level, russet here and there, heavy-headed, wide as a lake, and full of multitudinous whispers and gleams of wealth, it stretched away before the gazers like the fabled field of the cloth of gold.

"Oh, I think—I *hope* we'll have a good crop, Tim; and oh, how good the people have been to us!"

"Yes; I don't know where we'd be t'-day if it hadn't been f'r Council and his wife."

"They're the best people in the world," said the little woman, with a great sob of gratitude.

"We'll be in the field on Monday, sure," said Haskins, gripping the rail on the fence as if already at the work of the harvest.

The harvest came, bounteous, glorious, but the winds came and blew it into tangles, and the rain matted it here and there close to the ground, increasing the work of gathering it threefold.

Oh, how they toiled in those glorious days! Clothing dripping with sweat, arms aching, filled with briers, fingers raw and bleeding, backs broken with the weight of heavy bundles, Haskins and his man toiled on. Tommy drove the harvester, while his father and a hired man bound on the machine. In this way they cut ten acres every day, and almost every night after supper, when the hand went to bed, Haskins returned to the field, shocking[7] the bound grain in the light of the moon. Many a night he worked till his anxious wife came out at ten o'clock to call him in to rest and lunch.

At the same time she cooked for the men, took care of the children, washed and ironed, milked the cows at night, made the butter, and sometimes fed the horses and watered them while her husband kept at the shocking.

No slave in the Roman galleys could have toiled so frightfully and lived, for this man thought himself a free man, and that he was working for his wife and babes.

When he sank into his bed with a deep groan of relief, too tired to change his grimy, dripping clothing, he felt that he was getting nearer and nearer to a home of his own, and pushing the wolf of want a little farther from his door.

There is no despair so deep as the despair of a homeless man or woman. To roam the roads of the country or the streets of the city, to feel there is no rood[8] of ground on which the feet can rest, to halt weary and hungry outside lighted windows, and hear laughter and song within,—these are the hungers and rebellions that drive men to crime and women to shame.

It was the memory of his homelessness, and the fear of its coming again, that spurred Timothy Haskins and Nettie, his wife, to such ferocious labor during that first year.

IV

"M, yes; 'm, yes; first-rate," said Butler, as his eye took in the neat garden, the pig-pen, and the well-filled barnyard. "You're gitt'n' quite a stock around yeh. Done well, eh?"

Haskins was showing Butler around the place. He had not seen it for a year, having spent the year in Washington and Boston with Ashley, his brother-in-law, who had been elected to Congress.

"Yes, I've laid out a good deal of money durin' the last three years. I've paid out three hundred dollars f'r fencin'."

"Um-h'm! I see, I see," said Butler, while Haskins went on:

[7] *shocking:* stacking grain sheaves together in piles to dry
[8] *rood:* a measure of area, usually a quarter-acre

"The kitchen there cost two hundred; the barn ain't cost much in money, but I've put a lot o' time on it. I've dug a new well, and I—"

"Yes, yes, I see. You've done well. Stock worth a thousand dollars," said Butler, picking his teeth with a straw.

"About that," said Haskins, modestly. "We begin to feel 's if we was gitt'n' a home f'r ourselves; but we've worked hard. I tell you we begin to feel it, Mr. Butler, and we're goin' t' begin to ease up purty soon. We've been kind o' plannin' a trip back t' *her* folks after the fall ploughin's done."

"*Eggs-actly!*" said Butler, who was evidently thinking of something else. "I suppose you've kind o' calc'lated on stayin' here three years more?"

"Well, yes, Fact is, I think I c'n buy the farm this fall, if you'll give me a reasonable show."

"Um-m! What do you call a reasonable show?"

"Well, say a quarter down and three years' time."

Butler looked at the huge stacks of wheat, which filled the yard, over which the chickens were fluttering and crawling, catching grasshoppers, and out of which the crickets were singing innumerably. He smiled in a peculiar way as he said, "Oh, I won't be hard on yeh. But what did you expect to pay f'r the place?"

"Why, about what you offered it for before, two thousand five hundred, or *possibly* three thousand dollars," he added quickly as he saw the owner shake his head.

"This farm is worth five thousand and five hundred dollars," said Butler, in a careless and decided voice.

"*What!*" almost shrieked the astounded Haskins. "What's that? Five thousand? Why, that's double what you offered it for three years ago."

"Of course, and it's worth it. It was all run down then; now it's in good shape. You've laid out fifteen hundred dollars in improvements, according to your own story."

"But you had nothin' t' do about that. It's my work an' my money."

"You bet it was; but it's my land."

"But what's to pay me for all my—"

"Ain't you had the use of 'em?" replied Butler, smiling calmly into his face.

Haskins was like a man struck on the head with a sandbag; he couldn't think; he stammered as he tried to say: "But—I never'd git the use—You'd rob me! More'n that: you agreed—you promised that I could buy or rent at the end of three years at—"

"That's all right. But I didn't say I'd let you carry off the improvements, nor that I'd go on renting the farm at two-fifty. The land is doubled in value, it don't matter how; it don't enter into the question; an' now you can pay me five hundred dollars a year rent, or take it on your own terms at fifty-five hundred, or—git out."

He was turning away, when Haskins, the sweat pouring from his face, fronted him, saying again:

"But you've done nothing to make it so. You hain't added a cent. I put it all there myself, expectin' to buy. I worked an' sweat to improve it. I was workin' for myself an' babes—"

"Well, why didn't you buy when I offered to sell? What y' kickin' about?"

"I'm kickin' about payin' you twice f'r my own things—my own fences, my own kitchen, my own garden."

Butler laughed. "You're too green t' eat, young feller. Your improvements! The law will sing another tune."

"But I trusted your word."

"Never trust anybody, my friend. Besides, I didn't promise not to do this thing. Why, man, don't look at me like that. Don't take me for a thief. It's the law. The reg'lar thing. Everybody does it."

"I don't care if they do. It's stealin' jest the same. You take three thousand dollars of my money—the work o' my hands and my wife's." He broke down at this point. He was not a strong man mentally. He could face hardship, ceaseless toil, but he could not face the cold and sneering face of Butler.

"But I don't take it," said Butler, coolly. "All you've got to do is to go on jest as you've been a-doin', or give me a thousand dollars down, and a mortgage at ten percent on the rest."

Haskins sat down blindly on a bundle of oats near by, and with staring eyes and dropping head went over the situation. He was under the lion's paw. He felt a horrible numbness in his heart and limbs. He was hid in a mist, and there was no path out.

Butler walked about, looking at the huge stacks of grain, and pulling now and again a few handfuls out, shelling the heads in his hands and blowing the chaff⁹ away. He hummed a little tune as he did so. He had an accommodating air of waiting. Haskins was in the midst of the terrible toil of the last year. He was walking again in the rain and the mud behind his plough; he felt the dust and dirt of the threshing. The ferocious husking-time, with its cutting wind and biting, clinging snows, lay hard upon him. Then he thought of his wife, how she had cheerfully cooked and baked, without holiday and without rest.

"Well, what do you think of it?" inquired the cool, mocking, insinuating voice of Butler.

"I think you're a thief and a liar!" shouted Haskins, leaping up. "A black-hearted houn'!" Butler's smile maddened him; with a sudden leap he caught a fork in his hands, and whirled it in the air. "You'll never rob another man, damn ye!" he grated through his teeth, a look of pitiless ferocity in his accusing eyes.

Butler shrank and quivered, expecting the blow; stood, held hypnotized by the eyes of the man he had a moment before despised—a man transformed into an avenging demon. But in the deadly hush between the lift of the weapon and its fall there came a gush of faint, childish laughter and then across the range of his vision, far away and dim, he saw the sun-bright head of his baby girl, as, with the pretty, tottering run of a two-year-old, she moved across the grass of the door-yard. His hands relaxed; the fork fell to the ground; his head lowered.

"Make out y'r deed an' mor'gage, an' git off'n my land, an' don't ye never cross my line agin: if y' do, I'll kill ye."

Butler backed away from the man in wild haste, and climbing into his buggy with trembling limbs drove off down the road, leaving Haskins seated dumbly on the sunny piles of sheaves, his head sunk into his hands.

⁹*chaff*: threshed or winnowed husks of grain

FOR DISCUSSION

1. Why is Haskins "under the lion's paw"? Is he a victim of circumstances or of his own actions and misguided trust? Give evidence to support your answer.
2. Legally, Butler could charge whatever he thought he could get either for the sale or rental of the land. From the information given in the story, is Haskins justified in calling him a thief and a liar? If Haskins had not lost control of himself, do you think he might have been able to force Butler to make more reasonable terms? Give reasons for your answer.
3. Garland devotes the first part of the story to the exposition (see page 514). What do you learn about the hardships of prairie life, the history of the two families, and the main characters?
4. Why does Council suggest that Haskins take Butler's offer? What drives Haskins and his wife to work like slaves in a Roman galley? Why do you think that Garland describes their struggle in such a dramatic way? What kind of reforms do you think he felt this story might help to bring about?
5. In this story, do you think the "message" of social injustice interferes with the telling of a moving and believable story? How does Garland make it seem real? Do you think he gives a truthful representation of the situation and people he chose to write about? Cite evidence from the story to support your statement. Also cite evidence that he does, or does not, have a keen eye for detail and a keen ear for the speech of midwestern country people of the last part of the nineteenth century.

FOR COMPOSITION

1. One test of a well-portrayed character is that his behavior throughout the story is consistent with the author's characterization of him. Choose one of the three male characters. In a short composition, tell why you think he is, or is not, well-portrayed. Cite examples from the story to support your opinion.
2. In a short essay, express your own thoughts and feelings on what you consider some of the social injustices of your own time to which people should be awakened.

Frank Norris

Frank Norris, like the later writer John Steinbeck, approached the novel from a naturalistic viewpoint, regarding man pessimistically as the victim of his economic and social environment. Unlike Steinbeck, Norris' characters are usually outlined types rather than individual personalities and are subordinated to his detailed studies of their social background. In a surge of rhythmical prose, his novel, *The Octopus*, portrays the struggle of a group of wheat farmers for survival against a monopolistic railroad. In the following chapters from the novel, two men—bitter enemies—are unwittingly drawn into different yet related struggles for survival.

from The Octopus

The ex-engineer reached the Post Office in Bonneville[1] towards eleven o'clock, but he did not at once present his notice of the arrival of his consignment at Ruggles's office. It entertained him to indulge in an hour's lounging about the streets. It was seldom he got into town, and when he did he permitted himself the luxury of enjoying his evident popularity. He met friends everywhere, in the Post Office, in the drug store, in the barber shop and around the court-house. With each one he held a moment's conversation; almost invariably this ended in the same way:

"Come on 'n have a drink."

"Well, I don't care if I do."

And the friends proceeded to the Yosemite bar, pledging each other with punctilious[2] ceremony. Dyke, however, was a strictly temperate man. His life on the engine had trained

[1] *Bonneville:* town in California
[2] *punctilious:* very exact, scrupulous

him well. Alcohol he never touched, drinking instead ginger ale, sarsaparilla-and-iron — soft drinks.

At the drug store, which also kept a stock of miscellaneous stationery, his eye was caught by a "transparent slate," a child's toy, where upon a little pane of frosted glass one could trace with considerable elaboration outline figures of cows, ploughs, bunches of fruit and even rural water mills that were printed on slips of paper underneath.

"Now, there's an idea, Jim," he observed to the boy behind the soda-water fountain: "I know a little tad that would just about jump out of her skin for that. Think I'll have to take it with me."

"How's Sidney getting along?" the other asked, while wrapping up the package.

Dyke's enthusiasm had made of his little girl a celebrity throughout Bonneville.

The ex-engineer promptly became voluble, assertive, doggedly emphatic.

"Smartest little tad in all Tulare County, and more fun! A regular whole show in herself."

"And the hops?" inquired the other.

"Bully," declared Dyke, with the good-natured man's readiness to talk of his private affairs to anyone who would listen. "Bully. I'm dead sure of a bonanza crop by now. The rain came *just* right. I actually don't know that I can store the crop in those barns I built, it's going to be so big. That foreman of mine was a daisy. Jim, I'm going to make money in that deal. After I've paid off the mortgage — you know I had to mortgage, yes, crop and homestead, both, but I can pay it off and all the interest to boot, lovely, — well, as I was saying, after all expenses are paid off I'll clear big money, m'son. Yes, sir. I knew there was boodle in hops. You know the crop is contracted for already. Sure, the foreman managed that. He's a daisy. Chap in San Francisco will take it all and at the advanced price. I wanted to hang on, to see if it wouldn't go to six cents, but the foreman said, 'No, that's good enough.' So I signed. Ain't it bully, hey?"

"Then what'll you do?"

"Well, I don't know. I'll have a lay-off for a month or so and

take the little tad and mother up and show 'em the city—
'Frisco—until it's time for the schools to open, and then we'll
put Sid in the seminary at Marysville. Catch on?"

"I suppose you'll stay right by hops now?"

"Right you are, m'son. I know a good thing when I see it.
There's plenty of others going into hops next season—I set
'em the example. Wouldn't be surprised if it came to be a
regular industry hereabouts. I'm planning ahead for next year
already. I can let the foreman go, now that I've learned the
game myself, and I think I'll buy a piece of land off Quien
Sabe and get a bigger crop, and build a couple more barns,
and, by George, in about five years' time I'll have things
humming. I'm going to make *money*, Jim."

He emerged once more into the street and went up the block
leisurely, planting his feet squarely. He fancied that he could
feel that he was considered of more importance nowadays. He
was no longer a subordinate, an employee. He was his own
man, a proprietor, an owner of land, furthering a successful
enterprise. No one had helped him; he had followed no one's
lead. He had struck out unaided for himself, and his success
was due solely to his own intelligence, industry, and foresight.
He squared his great shoulders till the blue gingham of his
jumper all but cracked. Of late, his great blond beard had
grown and work in the sun had made his face very red. Under
the visor of his cap—relic of his engineering days—his blue
eyes twinkled with vast good-nature. He felt that he made a
fine figure as he went by a group of young girls in lawns and
muslins and garden hats on their way to the Post Office. He
wondered if they looked after him, wondered if they had
heard he was in a fair way to become rich.

But the chronometer[3] in the window of the jewelry store
warned him that time was passing. He turned about, and,
crossing the street, took his way to Ruggles's office, which
was the freight as well as the land office of the P. and S. W.
Railroad.

As he stood for a moment at the counter in front of the wire
partition, waiting for the clerk to make out the order for the

---

[3]*chronometer:* a highly accurate clock

freight agent at the depot, Dyke was surprised to see a familiar figure in conference with Ruggles himself, by a desk inside the railing.

The figure was that of a middle-aged man, fat, with a great stomach, which he stroked from time to time. As he turned about, addressing a remark to the clerk, Dyke recognized S. Behrman. The banker, railroad agent, and political manipulator seemed to the ex-engineer's eyes to be more gross than ever. His smooth-shaven jowl stood out big and tremulous on either side of his face; the roll of fat on the nape of his neck, sprinkled with sparse, stiff hairs, bulged out with greater prominence. His great stomach, covered with a light brown linen vest, stamped with innumerable interlocked horseshoes, protruded far in advance, enormous, aggressive. He wore his inevitable round-topped hat of stiff brown straw, varnished so bright that it reflected the light of the office windows like a helmet, and even from where he stood Dyke could hear his loud breathing and the clink of the hollow links of his watch chain upon the vest buttons of imitation pearl, as his stomach rose and fell.

Dyke looked at him with attention. There was the enemy, the representative of the Trust with which Derrick's League was locking horns. The great struggle had begun to invest the combatants with interest. Daily, almost hourly, Dyke was in touch with the ranchers, the wheat-growers, he heard their denunciations, their growls of exasperation and defiance. Here was the other side—this placid, fat man, with a stiff straw hat and linen vest, who never lost his temper, who smiled affably upon his enemies, giving them good advice, commiserating[4] with them in one defeat after another, never ruffled, never excited, sure of his power, conscious that back of him was the Machine, the colossal force, the inexhaustible coffers of a mighty organization, vomiting millions to the League's thousands.

The League was clamorous, ubiquitous,[5] its objects known to every urchin on the streets, but the Trust was silent, its ways inscrutable, the public saw only the results. It worked

[4]*commiserating:* sympathizing
[5]*ubiquitous:* present everywhere at once

on in the dark, calm, disciplined, irresistible. Abruptly Dyke received the impression of the multitudinous ramifications of the colossus. Under his feet the ground seemed mined; down there below him in the dark the huge tentacles were silently twisting and advancing, spreading out in every direction, sapping the strength of all opposition, quiet, gradual, biding the time to reach up and out and grip with a sudden unleashing of gigantic strength.

"I'll be wanting some cars of you people before the summer is out," observed Dyke to the clerk as he folded up and put away the order that the other had handed him. He remembered perfectly well that he had arranged the matter of transporting his crop some months before, but his rôle of proprietor amused him and he liked to busy himself again and again with the details of his undertaking.

"I suppose," he added, "you'll be able to give 'em to me. There'll be a big wheat crop to move this year and I don't want to be caught in any car famine."

"Oh, you'll get your cars," murmured the other.

"I'll be the means of bringing business your way." Dyke went on; "I've done so well with my hops that there are a lot of others going into the business next season. Suppose," he continued, struck with an idea, "suppose we went into some sort of pool, a sort of shippers' organization, could you give us special rates, cheaper rates — say a cent and a half?"

The other looked up.

"A cent and a half! Say *four* cents and a half and maybe I'll talk business with you."

"Four cents and a half," returned Dyke. "I don't see it. Why, the regular rate is only two cents."

"No, it isn't," answered the clerk, looking him gravely in the eye, "it's five cents."

"Well, there's where you are wrong, m'son," Dyke retorted, genially. "You look it up. You'll find the freight on hops from Bonneville to 'Frisco is two cents a pound for car load lots. You told me that yourself last fall."

"That was last fall," observed the clerk. There was a silence. Dyke shot a glance of suspicion at the other. Then, reassured, he remarked:

"You look it up. You'll see I'm right."

S. Behrman came forward and shook hands politely with the ex-engineer.

"Anything I can do for you, Mr. Dyke?"

Dyke explained. When he had done speaking, the clerk turned to S. Behrman and observed, respectfully:

"Our regular rate on hops is five cents."

"Yes," answered S. Behrman, pausing to reflect; "yes, Mr. Dyke, that's right—five cents."

The clerk brought forward a folder of yellow paper and handed it to Dyke. It was inscribed at the top "Tariff Schedule No. 8," and underneath these words, in brackets, was a smaller inscription, *"Supersedes No. 7 of Aug. 1."*

"See for yourself," said S. Behrman. He indicated an item under the head of "Miscellany."

"The following rates for carriage of hops in car load lots," read Dyke, "take effect June 1, and will remain in force until superseded by a later tariff. Those quoted beyond Stockton are subject to changes in traffic arrangements with carriers by water from that point."

In the list that was printed below, Dyke saw that the rate for hops between Bonneville or Guadalajara and San Francisco was five cents.

For a moment Dyke was confused. Then swiftly the matter became clear in his mind. The Railroad had raised the rate on hops from two cents to five.

All his calculations as to a profit on his little investment he had based on a freight rate of two cents a pound. He was under contract to deliver his crop. He could not draw back. The new rate ate up every cent of his gains. He stood there ruined.

"Why, what do you mean?" he burst out. "You promised me a rate of two cents and I went ahead with my business with that understanding. What do you mean?"

S. Behrman and the clerk watched him from the other side of the counter.

"The rate is five cents," declared the clerk doggedly.

"Well, that ruins me," shouted Dyke. "Do you understand?

I won't make fifty cents. *Make?* Why, I will *owe,*—I'll be—be— That ruins me, do you understand?"

The other raised a shoulder.

"We don't force you to ship. You can do as you like. The rate is five cents."

"Well—but—damn you, I'm under contract to deliver. What am I going to do? Why, you told me—you promised me a two-cent rate."

"I don't remember it," said the clerk. "I don't know anything about that. But I know this: I know that hops have gone up. I know the German crop was a failure and that the crop in New York wasn't worth the hauling. Hops have gone up to nearly a dollar. You don't suppose we don't know that, do you, Mr. Dyke?"

"What's the price of hops got to do with you?"

"It's got *this* to do with us," returned the other with sudden aggressiveness, "that the freight rate has gone up to meet the price. We're not doing business for our health. My orders are to raise your rate to five cents, and I think you are getting off easy."

Dyke stared in blank astonishment. For the moment, the audacity of the affair was what most appealed to him. He forgot its personal application.

"Good Lord," he murmured, "good Lord! What will you people do next? Look here. What's your basis of applying freight rates, anyhow?" he suddenly vociferated[6] with furious sarcasm. "What's your rule? What are you guided by?"

But at the words, S. Behrman, who had kept silent during the heat of the discussion, leaned abruptly forward. For the only time in his knowledge, Dyke saw his face inflamed with anger and with the enmity and contempt of all this farming element with whom he was contending.

"Yes, what's your rule? What's your basis?" demanded Dyke turning swiftly to him.

S. Behrman emphasized each word of his reply with a tap of one forefinger on the counter before him:

"All—the—traffic—will—bear."

---

[6]*vociferated:* shouted

❀ ❀ ❀ ❀ ❀

S. Behrman went forward to the hatch that opened down into the vast hold of the ship. A great iron chute connected this hatch with the elevator,[7] and through it was rushing a veritable cataract of wheat.

It came from some gigantic bin within the elevator itself, rushing down the confines of the chute to plunge into the roomy, gloomy interior of the hold with an incessant, metallic roar, persistent, steady, inevitable. No men were in sight. The place was deserted. No human agency seemed to be back of the movement of the wheat. Rather, the grain seemed impelled with a force of its own, a resistless, huge force, eager, vivid, impatient for the sea.

S. Behrman stood watching, his ears deafened with the roar of the hard grains against the metallic lining of the chute. He put his hand once into the rushing tide, and the contact rasped the flesh of his fingers and, like an undertow, drew his hand after it in its impetuous dash.

Cautiously he peered down into the hold. A musty odor rose to his nostrils, the vigorous, pungent aroma of the raw cereal. It was dark. He could see nothing; but all about and over the opening of the hatch the air was full of a fine, impalpable dust that blinded the eyes and choked the throat and nostrils.

As his eyes became used to the shadows of the cavern below him, he began to distinguish the gray mass of the wheat, a great expanse, almost liquid in its texture, which, as the cataract from above plunged into it, moved and shifted in long, slow eddies. As he stood there, this cataract on a sudden increased in volume. He turned about, casting his eyes upward toward the elevator to discover the cause. His foot caught in a coil of rope, and he fell head foremost into the hold.

The fall was a long one, and he struck the surface of the wheat with the sodden impact of a bundle of damp clothes. For the moment he was stunned. All the breath was driven from his body. He could neither move nor cry out. But, by degrees, his wits steadied themselves and his breath returned

[7] *elevator:* a warehouse for storing grain

to him. He looked about and above him. The daylight in the hold was dimmed and clouded by the thick chaff-dust thrown off by the pour of grain, and even this dimness dwindled to twilight at a short distance from the opening of the hatch, while the remotest quarters were lost in impenetrable blackness. He got upon his feet, only to find that he sunk ankle-deep in the loose-packed mass underfoot.

"Hell," he muttered, "here's a fix."

Directly underneath the chute, the wheat, as it poured in, raised itself in a conical mound, but from the sides of this mound it shunted away incessantly in thick layers, flowing in all directions with the nimbleness of water. Even as S. Behrman spoke, a wave of grain poured around his legs and rose rapidly to the level of his knees. He stepped quickly back To stay near the chute would soon bury him to the waist.

No doubt there was some other exit from the hold, some companion-ladder that led up to the deck. He scuffled and waded across the wheat, groping in the dark with outstretched hands. With every inhalation he choked, filling his mouth and nostrils more with dust than with air. At times he could not breathe at all, but gagged and gasped, his lips distended. But search as he would, he could find no outlet to the hold, no stairway, no companion-ladder. Again and again, staggering along in the black darkness, he bruised his knuckles and forehead against the iron sides of the ship. He gave up the attempt to find any interior means of escape and returned laboriously to the space under the open hatchway. Already he could see that the level of the wheat was raised.

"God," he said, "this isn't going to do at all." He uttered a great shout. "Hello, on deck there, somebody. For God's sake!"

The steady, metallic roar of the pouring wheat drowned out his voice. He could scarcely hear it himself above the rush of the cataract. Besides this, he found it impossible to stay under the hatch. The flying grains of wheat, spattering as they fell, stung his face like wind-driven particles of ice. It was a veritable torture; his hands smarted with it. Once he was all but blinded. Furthermore, the succeeding waves of wheat, rolling from the mound under the chute, beat him back, swirling and dashing against his legs and knees, mounting swiftly higher, carrying him off his feet.

Once more he retreated, drawing back from beneath the hatch. He stood still for a moment and shouted again. It was in vain. His voice returned upon him, unable to penetrate the thunder of the chute, and horrified, he discovered that so soon as he stood motionless upon the wheat, he sank into it. Before he knew it, he was knee-deep again, and a long swirl of grain sweeping outward from the ever-breaking, ever-reforming pyramid below the chute poured around his thighs, immobilizing him.

A frenzy of terror suddenly leaped to life within him. The horror of death, the Fear of the Trap, shook him like a dry reed. Shouting, he tore himself free of the wheat and once more scrambled and struggled toward the hatchway. He stumbled as he reached it and fell directly beneath the pour. Like a storm of small shot, mercilessly, pitilessly, the unnumbered multitude of hurtling grains flagellated and beat and tore his flesh. Blood streamed from his forehead and, thickening with the powder-like chaff-dust, blinded his eyes. He struggled to his feet once more. An avalanche from the cone of wheat buried him to his thighs. He was forced back and back and back, beating the air, falling, rising, howling for aid. He could no longer see; his eyes, crammed with dust, smarted as if transfixed with needles whenever he opened them. His mouth was full of the dust, his lips were dry with it; thirst tortured him, while his outcries choked and gagged in his rasped throat.

And all the while, without stop, incessantly, inexorably, the wheat, as if moving with a force all its own, shot downward in a prolonged roar, persistent, steady, inevitable.

He retreated to a far corner of the hold and sat down with his back against the iron hull of the ship, and tried to collect his thoughts, to calm himself. Surely there must be some way of escape; surely he was not to die like this, die in this dreadful substance that was neither solid nor fluid. What was he to do? How make himself heard?

But even as he thought about this, the cone under the chute broke again and sent a great layer of grain rippling and tumbling toward him. It reached him where he sat and buried his hand and one foot.

He sprang up trembling and made for another corner.

Once more the level of the wheat rose and the grains began piling deeper about him. Once more he retreated. Once more he crawled staggering to the foot of the cataract, screaming till his ears sang and his eyeballs strained in their sockets, and once more the relentless tide drove him back.

Then began the terrible dance of death; the man dodging, doubling, squirming, hunted from one corner to another, the wheat slowly, inexorably flowing, rising, spreading to every angle, to every nook and cranny. It reached his middle. Furious and with bleeding hands and broken nails, he dug his way out to fall backward, all but exhausted, gasping for breath in the dust-thickened air. Roused again by the slow advance of the tide, he leaped up and stumbled away, blinded with the agony in his eyes, only to crash against the metal hull of the vessel. He turned about, the blood streaming from his face, and paused to collect his senses, and with a rush, another wave swirled about his ankles and knees. Exhaustion grew upon him. To stand still meant to sink; to lie or sit meant to be buried the quicker; and all this in the dark, all this in an air that could scarcely be breathed, all this while he fought an enemy that could not be gripped, toiling in a sea that could not be stayed.

Guided by the sound of the falling wheat, S. Behrman crawled on hands and knees toward the hatchway. Once more he raised his voice in a shout for help. His bleeding throat and raw, parched lips refused to utter but a wheezing moan. Once more he tried to look toward the one patch of faint light above him. His eyelids, clogged with chaff, could no longer open. The wheat poured about his waist as he raised himself upon his knees.

Reason fled. Deafened with the roar of the grain, blinded and made dumb with its chaff, he threw himself forward with clutching fingers, rolling upon his back, and lay there, moving feebly, the head rolling from side to side. The wheat, leaping continuously from the chute, poured around him. It filled the pockets of the coat, it crept up the sleeves and trouser legs, it covered the great, protuberant stomach, it ran at last in rivulets into the distended gasping mouth. It covered the face.

Upon the surface of the wheat, under the chute, nothing moved but the wheat itself. There was no sign of life. Then, for an instant, the surface stirred. A hand, fat with short fingers and swollen veins, reached up, clutching, then fell limp and prone. In another instant it was covered. In the hold of the *Swanhilda* there was no movement but the widening ripples that spread flowing from the ever-breaking, ever-reforming cone; no sound, but the rushing of the wheat that continued to plunge incessantly from the iron chute in a prolonged roar, persistent, steady, inevitable.

FOR DISCUSSION

1. Why doesn't either Dyke or Behrman stand a chance of winning in the struggle for survival? Are the forces which destroy them unrelated, or is each force just another aspect of the "machine"? Explain.
2. Why does the octopus so perfectly symbolize the colossal force against which the ranchers and farmers struggled? Contrast the tactics of the League with those of the Trust. Which were more effective? Why?
3. Dyke has no reason to anticipate trouble when he comes to Bonneville. What is his purpose in coming? Why is he in such good spirits? What impression do you gain of him from what he says and does and from the reactions of the townspeople to him?
4. To Dyke, and others like him, Behrman is the enemy—the other side. What kind of person is he? How do his appearance, manner, and attitude toward the farming element reveal his true character? Cite evidence from the selection to support your answer.
5. What reasons can you give for Behrman's presence at the elevator and his fascination with the cataract of wheat pouring into the ship's hold? Is his fall into the hold entirely accidental or is he in part responsible? Is his first reaction (when he recovered his breath) consistent with his earlier attitude and behavior? Explain.
6. In describing Behrman's struggle for survival, Norris uses the expressions "Fear of the Trap" and "terrible dance of death." Discuss both the literal meaning and the figurative, metaphorical meaning of each expression. How does Behrman feel about the trap he set for Dyke? Who or what is responsible for the trap in which he is caught? Why is his fate ironic? Explain.

7. As Norris portrays Dyke and Behrman, is each primarily a type of person or is he a distinct individual? How believable are they? Why do you, or do you not, care what happens to them?
8. Point out passages in this selection which illustrate Norris' skill in using words (a) to create a mood, (b) to suggest a change of pace – slow, normal, rapid – and (c) to picture a scene or person.

FOR COMPOSITION

1. Look back at the various attempts which Behrman makes to escape from the hold of the ship. In a short composition, tell why you believe he does, or does not, have a chance to escape. Point out those actions which you think lessen or destroy his chance to escape.
2. Norris' characterization is very different from that of John Steinbeck, a more recent writer; yet both writers share a similar view of man in relation to his environment. Using examples from "Flight" and from the Norris selection, write a short composition comparing their views.

Stephen Crane

Stephen Crane studied the emotion of fear with the curiosity and analytic precision of a scientist. One of his characteristic procedures—as seen in "The Open Boat"—was to invent, or adapt from his own experience, a situation in which a group of characters had to face extreme hardship or death. Then, with extraordinary psychological insight, he revealed the effect of this situation on the characters and the effect of their words and actions on each other. He looked into the minds and hearts of his characters to reveal their innermost thoughts and feelings.

Unlike many of the other realists, he resisted the temptation to overwrite. Instead, he created suspense and dramatic intensity through understatement and implication. The images and figures of speech he used to convey emotion and to create mood are strikingly simple, yet powerful in their appeal to the senses and to the imagination.

The Open Boat

A Tale Intended to Be After the Fact:
Being the Experience of Four Men from
the Sunk Steamer *Commodore*

I

None of them knew the color of the sky. Their eyes glanced level, and were fastened upon the waves that swept toward them. These waves were of the hue of slate, save for the tops, which were of foaming white, and all of the men knew the colors of the sea. The horizon narrowed and widened, and dipped and rose, and at all times its edge was jagged with waves that seemed thrust up in points like rocks.

Many a man ought to have a bathtub larger than the boat

which here rode upon the sea. These waves were most wrong-
fully and barbarously abrupt and tall, and each froth-top was
a problem in small-boat navigation.

The cook squatted in the bottom, and looked with both eyes
at the six inches of gunwale which separated him from the
ocean. His sleeves were rolled over his fat forearms, and the
two flaps of his unbuttoned vest dangled as he bent to bail
out the boat. Often he said, "Boy! that was a narrow clip." As
he remarked it he invariably gazed eastward over the
broken sea.

The oiler,[1] steering with one of the two oars in the boat,
sometimes raised himself suddenly to keep clear of water
that swirled in over the stern. It was a thin little oar, and it
seemed often ready to snap.

The correspondent, pulling at the other oar, watched the
waves and wondered why he was there.

The injured captain, lying in the bow, was at this time
buried in that profound dejection and indifference which
comes, temporarily at least, to even the bravest and most enduring when, willy-nilly, the firm fails, the army loses, the
ship goes down. The mind of the master of a vessel is rooted
deep in the timbers of her, though he command for a day or a
decade; and this captain had on him the stern impression of a
scene in the greys of dawn of seven turned faces, and later a
stump of a top-mast with a white ball on it, that slashed to and
fro at the waves, went low and lower, and down. Thereafter
there was something strange in his voice. Although steady,
it was deep with mourning, and of a quality beyond oration
or tears.

"Keep 'er a little more south, Billie," said he.

"A little more south, sir" said the oiler in the stern.

A seat in this boat was not unlike a seat upon a bucking
broncho, and by the same token a broncho is not much smaller.
The craft pranced and reared and plunged like an animal. As
each wave came, and she rose for it, she seemed like a horse
making at a fence outrageously high. The manner of her
scramble over these walls of water is a mystic thing, and,

---

[1] *oiler:* one who greases the machinery in a ship's engine room

moreover, at the top of them were ordinarily these problems in white water, the foam racing down from the summit of each wave requiring a new leap, and a leap from the air. Then, after scornfully bumping a crest, she would slide and race and splash down a long incline, and arrive bobbing and nodding in front of the next menace.

A singular disadvantage of the sea lies in the fact that after successfully surmounting one wave you discover that there is another behind it just as important and just as nervously anxious to do something effective in the way of swamping boats. In a ten-foot dinghy one can get an idea of the resources of the sea in the line of waves that is not probable to the average experience which is never at sea in a dinghy. As each salty wall of water approached, it shut all else from the view of the men in the boat, and it was not difficult to imagine that this particular wave was the final outburst of the ocean, the last effort of the grim water. There was a terrible grace in the move of the waves, and they came in silence, save for the snarling of the crests.

In the wan light the faces of the men must have been grey. Their eyes must have glinted in strange ways as they gazed steadily astern. Viewed from a balcony, the whole thing would doubtless have been weirdly picturesque. But the men in the boat had no time to see it, and if they had had leisure, there were other things to occupy their minds. The sun swung steadily up the sky, and they knew it was broad day because the color of the sea changed from slate to emerald green streaked with amber lights, and the foam was like tumbling snow. The process of the breaking day was unknown to them. They were aware only of this effect upon the color of the waves that rolled toward them.

In disjointed sentences the cook and the correspondent argued as to the difference between a life-saving station and a house of refuge. The cook had said: "There's a house of refuge just north of the Mosquito Inlet Light, and as soon as they see us they'll come off in their boat and pick us up."

"As soon as who see us?" said the correspondent.

"The crew," said the cook.

"Houses of refuge don't have crews," said the correspondent. "As I understand them, they are only places where clothes and grub are stored for the benefit of shipwrecked people. They don't carry crews."

"Oh, yes, they do," said the cook.

"No, they don't," said the correspondent.

"Well, we're not there yet, anyhow," said the oiler, in the stern.

"Well," said the cook, "perhaps it's not a house of refuge that I'm thinking of as being near Mosquito Inlet Light; perhaps it's a lifesaving station."

II

As the boat bounced from the top of each wave, the wind tore through the hair of the hatless men, and as the craft plopped her stern down again the spray slashed past them. The crest of each of these waves was a hill, from the top of which the men surveyed for a moment a broad tumultuous expanse, shining and wind-driven. It was probably splendid, it was probably glorious, this play of the free sea, wild with lights of emerald and white and amber.

"Bully good thing it's an on-shore wind," said the cook. "If not, where would we be? Wouldn't have a show."

"That's right," said the correspondent.

The busy oiler nodded his assent.

Then the captain, in the bow, chuckled in a way that expressed humour, contempt, tragedy, all in one. "Do you think we've got much of a show now, boys?" said he.

Whereupon the three were silent, save for a trifle of hemming and hawing. To express any particular optimism at this time they felt to be childish and stupid, but they all doubtless possessed this sense of the situation in their minds. A young man thinks doggedly at such times. On the other hand, the ethics of their condition was decidedly against any open suggestion of hopelessness. So they were silent.

"Oh, well," said the captain, soothing his children, "we'll get ashore all right."

But there was that in his tone which made them think; so the oiler quoth, "Yes! if this wind holds."

The cook was bailing. "Yes! if we don't catch hell in the surf."

Canton-flannel gulls flew near and far. Sometimes they sat down on the sea, near patches of brown seaweed that rolled over the waves with a movement like carpets on a line in a gale. The birds sat comfortably in groups, and they were envied by some in the dinghy, for the wrath of the sea was no more to them than it was to a covey of prairie chickens a thousand miles inland. Often they came very close and stared at the men with black bead-like eyes. At these times they were uncanny and sinister in their unblinking scrutiny, and the men hooted angrily at them, telling them to be gone. One came, and evidently decided to alight on the top of the captain's head. The bird flew parallel to the boat and did not circle, but made short sidelong jumps in the air in chicken-fashion. His black eyes were wistfully fixed upon the captain's head. "Ugly brute," said the oiler to the bird. "You look as if you were made with a jackknife." The cook and the correspondent swore darkly at the creature. The captain naturally wished to knock it away with the end of the heavy painter,[2] but he did not dare do it, because anything resembling an emphatic gesture would have capsized this freighted boat; and so, with his open hand, the captain gently and carefully waved the gull away. After it had been discouraged from the pursuit the captain breathed easier on account of his hair, and others breathed easier because the bird struck their minds at this time as being somehow gruesome and ominous.

In the meantime the oiler and the correspondent rowed. And also they rowed. They sat together in the same seat, and each rowed an oar. Then the oiler took both oars; then the correspondent took both oars; then the oiler; then the correspondent. They rowed and they rowed. The very ticklish part of the business was when the time came for the reclining one in the stern to take his turn at the oars. By the very last star of truth, it is easier to steal eggs from under a hen than it was to change seats in the dinghy. First the man in the stern

[2] *painter:* rope attached to bow of boat for mooring

slid his hand along the thwart[3] and moved with care, as if he were of Sèvres.[4] Then the man in the rowing-seat slid his hand along the other thwart. It was all done with the most extraordinary care. As the two sidled past each other, the whole party kept watchful eyes on the coming wave, and the captain cried· "Look out, now! Steady, there!"

The brown mats of seaweed that appeared from time to time were like islands, bits of earth. They were traveling, apparently, neither one way nor the other. They were, to all intents, stationary. They informed the men in the boat that it was making progress slowly toward the land.

The captain, rearing cautiously in the bow after the dinghy soared on a great swell, said that he had seen the lighthouse at Mosquito Inlet. Presently the cook remarked that he had seen it. The correspondent was at the oars then, and for some reason he too wished to look at the lighthouse; but his back was toward the far shore, and the waves were important, and for some time he could not seize an opportunity to turn his head. But at last there came a wave more gentle than the others, and when at the crest of it he swiftly scoured the western horizon.

"See it?" said the captain.

"No," said the correspondent, slowly; "I didn't see anything."

"Look again," said the captain. He pointed. "It's exactly in that direction."

At the top of another wave the correspondent did as he was bid, and this time his eyes chanced on a small, still thing on the edge of the swaying horizon. It was precisely like the point of a pin. It took an anxious eye to find a lighthouse so tiny.

"Think we'll make it, Captain?"

"If this wind holds and the boat don't swamp, we can't do much else," said the captain.

The little boat, lifted by each towering sea and splashed viciously by the crests, made progress that in the absence of seaweed was not apparent to those in her. She seemed just a

---

[3] *thwart:* rower's seat
[4] *Sèvres:* delicate porcelain, made at Sèvres, France

wee thing wallowing, miraculously top up, at the mercy of five oceans. Occasionally a great spread of water, like white flames, swarmed into her.

"Bail her, cook," said the captain, serenely.

"All right, Captain," said the cheerful cook.

III

It would be difficult to describe the subtle brotherhood of men that was here established on the seas. No one said that it was so. No one mentioned it. But it dwelt in the boat, and each man felt it warm him. They were a captain, an oiler, a cook, and a correspondent, and they were friends—friends in a more curiously iron-bound degree than may be common. The hurt captain, lying against the water-jar in the bow, spoke always in a low voice and calmly; but he could never command a more ready and swiftly obedient crew than the motley three of the dinghy. It was more than a mere recognition of what was best for the common safety. There was surely in it a quality that was personal and heart-felt. And after this devotion to the commander of the boat, there was this comradeship, that the correspondent, for instance, who had been taught to be cynical of men, knew even at the time was the best experience of his life. But no one said that it was so. No one mentioned it.

"I wish we had a sail," remarked the captain. "We might try my overcoat on the end of an oar, and give you two boys a chance to rest." So the cook and the correspondent held the mast and spread wide the overcoat; the oiler steered; and the little boat made good way with her new rig. Sometimes the oiler had to scull[5] sharply to keep a sea from breaking into the boat, but otherwise sailing was a success.

Meanwhile the lighthouse had been growing slowly larger. It had now almost assumed color, and appeared like a little grey shadow on the sky. The man at the oars could not be prevented from turning his head rather often to try for a glimpse of this little grey shadow.

[5]*scull:* to propel by using an oar over the stern of the boat

At last, from the top of each wave, the men in the tossing boat could see land. Even as the lighthouse was an upright shadow on the sky, this land seemed but a long black shadow on the sea. It certainly was thinner than paper. "We must be about opposite New Smyrna,"[6] said the cook, who had coasted this shore often in schooners. "Captain, by the way, I believe they abandoned that life-saving station there about a year ago."

"Did they?" said the captain.

The wind slowly died away. The cook and the correspondent were not now obliged to slave in order to hold high the oar. But the waves continued their old impetuous swooping at the dinghy, and the little craft, no longer under way, struggled woundily[7] over them. The oiler or the correspondent took the oars again.

Shipwrecks are apropos of nothing. If men could only train for them and have them occur when the men had reached pink condition, there would be less drowning at sea. Of the four in the dinghy none had slept any time worth mentioning for two days and two nights previous to embarking in the dinghy, and in the excitement of clambering about the deck of a foundering ship they had also forgotten to eat heartily.

For these reasons, and for others, neither the oiler nor the correspondent was fond of rowing at this time. The correspondent wondered ingenuously[8] how in the name of all that was sane could there be people who thought it amusing to row a boat. It was not an amusement; it was a diabolical punishment, and even a genius of mental aberrations[9] could never conclude that it was anything but a horror to the muscles and a crime against the back. He mentioned to the boat in general how the amusement of rowing struck him, and the weary-faced oiler smiled in full sympathy. Previously to the foundering, by the way, the oiler had worked a double watch in the engine-room of the ship.

"Take her easy now, boys," said the captain. "Don't spend

[6] *New Smyrna:* town on the east coast of Florida
[7] *woundily:* excessively
[8] *ingenuously:* candidly, frankly
[9] *genius . . . aberrations:* twister of ideas

yourselves. If we have to run a surf you'll need all your strength, because we'll sure have to swim for it. Take your time."

Slowly the land arose from the sea. From a black line it became a line of black and a line of white—trees and sand. Finally the captain said that he could make out a house on the shore. "That's the house of refuge, sure," said the cook. "They'll see us before long, and come out after us."

The distant lighthouse reared high. "The keeper ought to be able to make us out now, if he's looking through a glass," said the captain. "He'll notify the life-saving people."

"None of those other boats could have got ashore to give word of this wreck," said the oiler, in a low voice, "else the life-boat would be out hunting us."

Slowly and beautifully the land loomed out of the sea. The wind came again. It had veered from the north-east to the south-east. Finally a new sound struck the ears of the men in the boat. It was the low thunder of the surf on the shore. "We'll never be able to make the lighthouse now," said the captain. "Swing her head a little more north, Billie."

"A little more north, sir," said the oiler.

Whereupon the little boat turned her nose once more down the wind, and all but the oarsman watched the shore grow. Under the influence of this expansion doubt and direful apprehension were leaving the minds of the men. The management of the boat was still most absorbing, but it could not prevent a quiet cheerfulness. In an hour, perhaps, they would be ashore.

Their backbones had become thoroughly used to balancing in the boat, and they now rode this wild colt of a dinghy like circus men. The correspondent thought that he had been drenched to the skin, but happening to feel in the top pocket of his coat, he found therein eight cigars. Four of them were soaked with sea-water; four were perfectly scatheless. After a search, somebody produced three dry matches; and thereupon the four waifs rode impudently in their little boat and, with an assurance of an impending rescue shining in their eyes, puffed at the big cigars, and judged well and ill of all men. Everybody took a drink of water.

IV

"Cook," remarked the captain, "there don't seem to be any signs of life about your house of refuge."

"No," replied the cook. "Funny they don't see us!"

A broad stretch of lowly coast lay before the eyes of the men. It was of low dunes topped with dark vegetation. The roar of the surf was plain, and sometimes they could see the white lip of a wave as it spun up the beach. A tiny house was blocked out black upon the sky. Southward, the slim lighthouse lifted its little grey length.

Tide, wind, and waves were swinging the dinghy northward. "Funny they don't see us," said the men.

The surf's roar was here dulled, but its tone was nevertheless thunderous and mighty. As the boat swam over the great rollers the men sat listening to this roar. "We'll swamp sure," said everybody.

It is fair to say here that there was not a life-saving station within twenty miles in either direction; but the men did not know this fact, and in consequence they made dark and opprobrious[10] remarks concerning the eyesight of the nation's life-savers. Four scowling men sat in the dinghy and surpassed records in the invention of epithets.[11]

"Funny they don't see us."

The light-heartedness of a former time had completely faded. To their sharpened minds it was easy to conjure pictures of all kinds of incompetency and blindness and, indeed, cowardice. There was the shore of the populous land, and it was bitter and bitter to them that from it came no sign.

"Well," said the captain, ultimately; "I suppose we'll have to make a try for ourselves. If we stay out here too long, we'll none of us have strength left to swim after the boat swamps."

And so the oiler, who was at the oars, turned the boat straight for the shore. There was a sudden tightening of muscles. There was some thinking.

---

[10]*opprobrious:* abusive, disrespectful

[11]*epithets:* descriptive names or phrases expressing some characteristic quality of a person or thing

"If we don't all get ashore," said the captain—"if we don't all get ashore, I suppose you fellows know where to send news of my finish?"

They then briefly exchanged some addresses and admonitions. As for the reflections of the men, there was a great deal of rage in them. Perchance they might be formulated thus: "If I am going to be drowned—if I am going to be drowned—if I am going to be drowned, why, in the name of the seven mad gods who rule the sea, was I allowed to come thus far and contemplate sand and trees? Was I brought here merely to have my nose dragged away as I was about to nibble the sacred cheese of life? It is preposterous. If this old ninny-woman, Fate, cannot do better than this, she should be deprived of the management of men's fortunes. She is an old hen who knows not her intention. If she has decided to drown me, why did she not do it in the beginning and save me all this trouble? The whole affair is absurd.—But no; she cannot mean to drown me. She dare not drown me. She cannot drown me. Not after all this work." Afterward the man might have had an impulse to shake his fist at the clouds. "Just you drown me, now, and then hear what I call you!"

The billows that came at this time were more formidable. They seemed always just about to break and roll over the little boat in a turmoil of foam. There was a preparatory and long growl in the speech of them. No mind unused to the sea would have concluded that the dinghy could ascend these sheer heights in time. The shore was still afar. The oiler was a wily surfman. "Boys," he said swiftly, "she won't live three minutes more, and we're too far out to swim. Shall I take her to sea again, Captain?"

"Yes; go ahead!" said the captain.

This oiler, by a series of quick miracles and fast and steady oarsmanship, turned the boat in the middle of the surf and took her safely to sea again.

There was a considerable silence as the boat bumped over the furrowed sea to deeper water. Then somebody in gloom spoke: "Well, anyhow, they must have seen us from the shore by now."

The gulls went in slanting flight up the wind toward the

grey, desolate east. A squall, marked by dingy clouds and clouds brick-red like smoke from a burning building, appeared from the south-east.

"What do you think of those life-saving people? Ain't they peaches?"

"Funny they haven't seen us."

"Maybe they think we're out here for sport! Maybe they think we're fishin'. Maybe they think we're damned fools."

It was a long afternoon. A changed tide tried to force them southward, but wind and wave said northward. Far ahead, where coastline, sea, and sky formed their mighty angle, there were little dots which seemed to indicate a city on the shore.

"St. Augustine?"

The captain shook his head. "Too near Mosquito Inlet."

And the oiler rowed, and then the correspondent rowed; then the oiler rowed. It was a weary business. The human back can become the seat of more aches and pains than are registered in books for the composite anatomy of a regiment. It is a limited area, but it can become the theater of innumerable muscular conflicts, tangles, wrenches, knots, and other comforts.

"Did you ever like to row, Billie?" asked the correspondent.

"No," said the oiler; "hang it!"

When one exchanged the rowing-seat for a place in the bottom of the boat, he suffered a bodily depression that caused him to be careless of everything save an obligation to wiggle one finger. There was cold sea-water swashing to and fro in the boat, and he lay in it. His head, pillowed on a thwart, was within an inch of the swirl of a wave-crest, and sometimes a particularly obstreperous[12] sea came inboard and drenched him once more. But these matters did not annoy him. It is almost certain that if the boat had capsized he would have tumbled comfortably out upon the ocean as if he felt sure that it was a great soft mattress.

"Look! There's a man on the shore!"

"Where?"

"There! See 'im? See 'im?"

---

[12] *obstreperous:* noisy and unruly

"Yes, sure! He's walking along."

"Now he's stopped. Look! He's facing us!"

"He's waving at us!"

"So he is! By thunder!"

"Ah, now we're all right! Now we're all right! There'll be a boat out here for us in half an hour."

"He's going on. He's running. He's going up to that house there."

The remote beach seemed lower than the sea, and it required a searching glance to discern the like black figure. The captain saw a floating stick, and they rowed to it. A bath towel was by some weird chance in the boat, and, tying this on the stick, the captain waved it. The oarsman did not dare turn his head, so he was obliged to ask questions.

"What's he doing now?"

"He's standing still again. He's looking, I think.—There he goes again—toward the house.—Now he's stopped again."

"Is he waving at us?"

"No, not now; he was, though."

"Look! There comes another man!"

"He's running."

"Look at him go, would you!"

"Why, he's on a bicycle. Now he's met the other man. They're both waving at us. Look!"

"There comes something up the beach."

"What the devil is that thing?"

"Why, it looks like a boat."

"Why, certainly, it's a boat."

"No; it's on wheels."

"Yes, so it is. Well, that must be the life-boat. They drag them along shore on a wagon."

"That's the life-boat, sure."

"No, it's—it's an omnibus."

"I tell you it's a life-boat."

"It is not! It's an omnibus. I can see it plain. See? One of these big hotel omnibuses."

"By thunder, you're right. It's an omnibus, sure as fate. What do you suppose they are doing with an omnibus? Maybe they are going around collecting the life-crew, hey?"

"That's it, likely. Look! There's a fellow waving a little black flag. He's standing on the steps of the omnibus. There come those other two fellows. Now they're all talking together. Look at the fellow with the flag. Maybe he ain't waving it!"

"That ain't a flag, is it? That's his coat. Why, certainly, that's his coat."

"So it is; it's his coat. He's taken it off and is waving it around his head. But would you look at him swing it!"

"Oh, say, there isn't any life-saving station there. That's just a winter-resort hotel omnibus that has brought over some of the boarders to see us drown."

"What's that idiot with the coat mean? What's he signaling, anyhow?"

"It looks as if he were trying to tell us to go north. There must be a life-saving station up there."

"No; he thinks we're fishing. Just giving us a merry hand. See? Ah, there, Willie!"

"Well, I wish I could make something out of those signals. What do you suppose he means?"

"He don't mean anything; he's just playing."

"Well, if he'd just signal us to try the surf again, or to go to sea and wait, or go north, or go south, or go to hell, there would be some reason in it. But look at him! He just stands there and keeps his coat revolving like a wheel. The ass!"

"There come more people."

"Now there's quite a mob. Look! Isn't that a boat?"

"Where? Oh, I see where you mean. No, that's no boat."

"That fellow is still waving his coat."

"He must think we like to see him do that. Why don't he quit it? It don't mean anything."

"I don't know. I think he is trying to make us go north. It must be that there's a life-saving station there somewhere."

"Say, he ain't tired yet. Look at 'im wave!"

"Wonder how long he can keep that up. He's been revolving his coat ever since he caught sight of us. He's an idiot. Why aren't they getting men to bring a boat out? A fishing-boat—one of those big yawls—could come out here all right. Why don't he do something?"

"Oh, it's all right now."

"They'll have a boat out here for us in less than no time, now that they've seen us."

A faint yellow tone came into the sky over the low land. The shadows on the sea slowly deepened. The wind bore coldness with it, and the men began to shiver.

"Holy smoke!" said one, allowing his voice to express his impious mood, "if we keep on monkeying out here! If we've got to flounder out here all night!"

"Oh, we'll never have to stay here all night! Don't you worry. They've seen us now, and it won't be long before they'll come chasing out after us."

The shore grew dusky. The man waving a coat blended gradually into this gloom, and it swallowed in the same manner the omnibus and the group of people. The spray, when it dashed uproariously over the side, made the voyagers shrink and swear like men who were being branded.

"I'd like to catch the chump who waved the coat. I feel like socking him one, just for luck."

"Why? What did he do?"

"Oh, nothing, but then he seemed so damned cheerful."

In the meantime the oiler rowed, and then the correspondent rowed, and then the oiler rowed. Grey-faced and bowed forward, they mechanically, turn by turn, plied the leaden oars. The form of the lighthouse had vanished from the southern horizon, but finally a pale star appeared, just lifting from the sea. The streaked saffron in the west passed before the all-merging darkness, and the sea to the east was black. The land had vanished, and was expressed only by the low and drear thunder of the surf.

"If I am going to be drowned—if I am going to be drowned—if I am going to be drowned, why, in the name of the seven mad gods who rule the sea, was I allowed to come thus far and contemplate sand and trees? Was I brought here merely to have my nose dragged away as I was about to nibble the sacred cheese of life?"

The patient captain, drooped over the water-jar, was sometimes obliged to speak to the oarsman.

"Keep her head up! Keep her head up!"

"Keep her head up, sir." The voices were weary and low. This was surely a quiet evening. All save the oarsman lay heavily and listlessly in the boat's bottom. As for him, his eyes were just capable of noting the tall black waves that swept forward in a most sinister silence, save for an occasional subdued growl of a crest.

The cook's head was on a thwart, and he looked without interest at the water under his nose. He was deep in other scenes. Finally he spoke. "Billie," he murmured, dreamily, "what kind of pie do you like best?"

V

"Pie!" said the oiler and the correspondent, agitatedly. "Don't talk about those things, blast you!"

"Well," said the cook, "I was just thinking about ham sandwiches, and—"

A night on the sea in an open boat is a long night. As darkness settled finally, the shine of the light, lifting from the sea in the south, changed to full gold. On the northern horizon a new light appeared, a small bluish gleam on the edge of the waters. These two lights were the furniture of the world. Otherwise there was nothing but waves.

Two men huddled in the stern, and distances were so magnificent in the dinghy that the rower was enabled to keep his feet partly warm by thrusting them under his companions. Their legs indeed extended far under the rowing-seat until they touched the feet of the captain forward. Sometimes, despite the efforts of the tired oarsman, a wave came piling into the boat, an icy wave of the night, and the chilling water soaked them anew. They would twist their bodies for a moment and groan, and sleep the dead sleep once more, while the water in the boat gurgled about them as the craft rocked.

The plan of the oiler and the correspondent was for one to row until he lost the ability, and then arouse the other from his sea-water couch in the bottom of the boat.

The oiler plied the oars until his head drooped forward and the overpowering sleep blinded him; and he rowed yet afterward. Then he touched a man in the bottom of the boat, and called his name. "Will you spell[13] me for a little while?" he said meekly.

"Sure, Billie," said the correspondent, awaking and dragging himself to a sitting position. They exchanged places carefully, and the oiler, cuddling down in the sea-water at the cook's side, seemed to go to sleep instantly.

The particular violence of the sea had ceased. The waves came without snarling. The obligation of the man at the oars was to keep the boat headed so that the tilt of the rollers would not capsize her, and to preserve her from filling when the crests rushed past. The black waves were silent and hard to be seen in the darkness. Often one was almost upon the boat before the oarsman was aware.

In a low voice the correspondent addressed the captain. He was not sure that the captain was awake, although this iron man seemed to be always awake. "Captain, shall I keep her making for that light north, sir?"

The same steady voice answered him. "Yes. Keep it about two points off the port bow."

The cook had tied a life-belt around himself in order to get even the warmth which this clumsy cork contrivance could donate, and he seemed almost stove-like when a rower, whose teeth invariably chattered wildly as soon as he ceased his labour, dropped down to sleep.

The correspondent, as he rowed, looked down at the two men sleeping underfoot. The cook's arm was around the oiler's shoulders, and, with their fragmentary clothing and haggard faces, they were the babes of the sea—a grotesque rendering of the old babes in the wood.

Later he must have grown stupid at his work, for suddenly there was a growling of water, and a crest came with a roar and a swash into the boat, and it was a wonder that it did not set the cook afloat in his life-belt. The cook continued to sleep, but the oiler sat up, blinking his eyes and shaking with the new cold.

"Oh, I'm awful sorry, Billie," said the correspondent, contritely.

[13] *spell:* to relieve by giving a period of rest to

"That's all right, old boy," said the oiler, and lay down again and was asleep.

Presently it seemed that even the captain dozed, and the correspondent thought that he was the one man afloat on all the ocean. The wind had a voice as it came over the waves, and it was sadder than the end.

There was a long, loud swishing astern of the boat, and a gleaming trail of phosphorescence, like blue flame, was furrowed on the black waters. It might have been made by a monstrous knife.

Then there came a stillness, while the correspondent breathed with open mouth and looked at the sea.

Suddenly there was another swish and another long flash of bluish light, and this time it was alongside the boat, and might almost have been reached with an oar. The correspondent saw an enormous fin speed like a shadow through the water, hurling the crystalline spray and leaving the long glowing trail.

The correspondent looked over his shoulder at the captain. His face was hidden, and he seemed to be asleep. He looked at the babes of the sea. They certainly were asleep. So, being bereft of sympathy, he leaned a little way to one side and swore softly into the sea.

But the thing did not then leave the vicinity of the boat. Ahead or astern, on one side or the other, at intervals long or short, fled the long sparkling streak, and there was to be heard the *whirroo* of the dark fin. The speed and power of the thing was greatly to be admired. It cut the water like a gigantic and keen projectile.

The presence of this biding thing did not affect the man with the same horror that it would if he had been a picnicker. He simply looked at the sea dully and swore in an undertone.

Nevertheless, it is true that he did not wish to be alone with the thing. He wished one of his companions to awake by chance and keep him company with it. But the captain hung motionless over the water-jar, and the oiler and the cook in the bottom of the boat were plunged in slumber.

VI

"If I am going to be drowned—if I am going to be drowned —if I am going to be drowned, why, in the name of the seven mad gods who rule the sea, was I allowed to come thus far and contemplate sand and trees?"

During this dismal night, it may be remarked that a man would conclude that it was really the intention of the seven mad gods to drown him, despite the abominable injustice of it. For it was certainly an abominable injustice to drown a man who had worked so hard, so hard. The man felt it would be a crime most unnatural. Other people had drowned at sea since galleys swarmed with painted sails, but still—

When it occurs to a man that nature does not regard him as important, and that she feels she would not maim the universe by disposing of him, he at first wishes to throw bricks at the temple, and he hates deeply the fact that there are no bricks and no temples. Any visible expression of nature would surely be pelleted with his jeers.

Then, if there be no tangible thing to hoot, he feels, perhaps, the desire to confront a personification and indulge in pleas, bowed to one knee, and with hands supplicant, saying, "Yes, but I love myself."

A high cold star on a winter's night is the word he feels that she says to him. Thereafter he knows the pathos of his situation.

The men in the dinghy had not discussed these matters, but each had, no doubt, reflected upon them in silence and according to his mind. There was seldom any expression upon their faces save the general one of complete weariness. Speech was devoted to the business of the boat.

To chime the notes of his emotion, a verse mysteriously entered the correspondent's head. He had even forgotten that he had forgotten this verse, but it suddenly was in his mind.

A soldier of the Legion lay dying in Algiers;
There was lack of woman's nursing, there was dearth of
woman's tears;

But a comrade stood beside him, and he took that comrade's
   hand,
And he said, "I never more shall see my own, my native land."[14]

In his childhood the correspondent had been made acquainted with the fact that a soldier of the Legion lay dying
in Algiers, but he had never regarded the fact as important.
Myriads of his school fellows had informed him of the soldier's plight, but the dinning had naturally ended by making
him perfectly indifferent. He had never considered it his affair that a soldier of the Legion lay dying in Algiers, nor had
it appeared to him as a matter for sorrow. It was less to him
than the breaking of a pencil's point.

Now, however, it quaintly came to him as a human, living
thing. It was no longer merely a picture of a few throes in the
breast of a poet, meanwhile drinking tea and warming his
feet at the grate; it was an actuality — stern, mournful, and fine.

The correspondent plainly saw the soldier. He lay on the
sand with his feet out straight and still. While his pale left
hand was upon his chest in an attempt to thwart the going of
his life, the blood came between his fingers. In the far Al-
gerian distance, a city of low square forms was set against a
sky that was faint with the last sunset hues. The correspondent, plying the oars and dreaming of the slow and slower
movements of the lips of the soldier, was moved by a profound and perfectly impersonal comprehension. He was sorry
for the soldier of the Legion who lay dying in Algiers.

The thing which had followed the boat and waited had evidently grown bored at the delay. There was no longer to be
heard the slash of the cutwater, and there was no longer the
flame of the long trail. The light in the north still glimmered,
but it was apparently no nearer to the boat. Sometimes the
boom of the surf rang in the correspondent's ears, and he
turned the craft seaward then and rowed harder. Southward,
someone had evidently built a watch-fire on the beach. It was
too low and too far to be seen, but it made a shimmering,
roseate reflection upon the bluff in back of it, and this could be

[14]*"A soldier . . . land.":* from "Bingen on the Rhine," by Caroline Elizabeth
Sarah Norton

discerned from the boat. The wind came stronger, and some-times a wave suddenly raged out like a mountain cat, and there was to be seen the sheen and sparkle of a broken crest.

The captain, in the bow, moved on his water-jar and sat erect. "Pretty long night," he observed to the correspondent. He looked at the shore. "Those life-saving people take their time."

"Did you see that shark playing around?"

"Yes, I saw him. He was a big fellow, all right."

"Wish I had known you were awake."

Later the correspondent spoke into the bottom of the boat. "Billie!" There was a slow and gradual disentanglement. "Billie, will you spell me?"

"Sure," said the oiler.

As soon as the correspondent touched the cold, comfortable sea-water in the bottom of the boat and had huddled close to the cook's life-belt he was deep in sleep, despite the fact that his teeth played all the popular airs. This sleep was so good to him that it was but a moment before he heard a voice call his name in a tone that demonstrated the last stages of exhaustion. "Will you spell me?"

"Sure, Billie."

The light in the north had mysteriously vanished, but the correspondent took his course from the wide-awake captain.

Later in the night they took the boat farther out to sea, and the captain directed the cook to take one oar at the stern and keep the boat facing the seas. He was to call out if he should hear the thunder of the surf. This plan enabled the oiler and the correspondent to get respite together. "We'll give those boys a chance to get into shape again," said the captain. They curled down and, after a few preliminary chatterings and trembles, slept once more the dead sleep. Neither knew they had bequeathed to the cook the company of another shark, or perhaps the same shark.

As the boat caroused on the waves, spray occasionally bumped over the side and gave them a fresh soaking, but this had no power to break their repose. The ominous slash of the wind and the water affected them as it would have affected mummies.

"Boys," said the cook, with the notes of every reluctance in his voice, "she's drifted in pretty close. I guess one of you had better take her to sea again." The correspondent, aroused, heard the crash of the toppled crests.

As he was rowing, the captain gave him some whisky-and-water, and this steadied the chills out of him. "If I ever get ashore and anybody shows me even a photograph of an oar—"

At last there was a short conversation.

"Billie!—Billie, will you spell me?"

"Sure," said the oiler.

VII

When the correspondent again opened his eyes, the sea and the sky were each of the grey hue of the dawning. Later, carmine and gold was painted upon the waters. The morning appeared finally, in its splendor, with a sky of pure blue, and the sunlight flamed on the tips of the waves.

On the distant dunes were set many little black cottages, and a tall white windmill reared above them. No man, nor dog, nor bicycle appeared on the beach. The cottages might have formed a deserted village.

The voyagers scanned the shore. A conference was held in the boat. "Well," said the captain, "if no help is coming, we might better try a run through the surf right away. If we stay out here much longer we will be too weak to do anything for ourselves at all." The others silently acquiesced in this reasoning. The boat was headed for the beach. The correspondent wondered if none ever ascended the tall wind-tower, and if then they never looked seaward. This tower was a giant, standing with its back to the plight of the ants. It represented in a degree, to the correspondent, the serenity of nature amid the struggles of the individual—nature in the wind, and nature in the vision of men. She did not seem cruel to him then, nor beneficent, nor treacherous, nor wise. But she was indifferent, flatly indifferent. It is, perhaps, plausible that a man in this situation, impressed with the unconcern of the universe, should see the innumerable flaws of his life, and have them taste wickedly in his mind, and wish for another chance. A distinction between right and wrong seems absurdly clear to him, then, in this new ignorance of the grave-edge, and he understands that if he were given another opportunity he would mend his conduct and his words, and be better and brighter during an introduction or at a tea.

"Now, boys," said the captain, "she is going to swamp sure. All we can do is to work her in as far as possible, and then when she swamps, pile out and scramble for the beach. Keep cool now, and don't jump until she swamps sure."

The oiler took the oars. Over his shoulder he scanned the surf. "Captain," he said, "I think I'd better bring her about and keep her head-on to the seas and back her in."

"All right, Billie," said the captain. "Back her in." The oiler swung the boat then, and, seated in the stern, the cook and the correspondent were obliged to look over their shoulders to contemplate the lonely and indifferent shore.

The monstrous inshore rollers heaved the boat high until the men were again enabled to see the white sheets of water scudding up the slanted beach. "We won't get in very close," said the captain. Each time a man could wrest his attention from the rollers, he turned his glance toward the shore, and in the expression of the eyes during this contemplation there was a singular quality. The correspondent, observing the others, knew that they were not afraid, but the full meaning of their glances was shrouded.

As for himself, he was too tired to grapple fundamentally with the fact. He tried to coerce his mind into thinking of it, but the mind was dominated at this time by the muscles, and the muscles said they did not care. It merely occurred to him that if he should drown it would be a shame.

There were no hurried words, no pallor, no plain agitation. The men simply looked at the shore. "Now, remember to get well clear of the boat when you jump," said the captain.

Seaward the crest of a roller suddenly fell with a thunderous crash, and the long white comber came roaring down upon the boat.

"Steady now," said the captain. The men were silent. They turned their eyes from the shore to the comber and waited. The boat slid up the incline, leaped at the furious top, bounced over it, and swung down the long back of the wave. Some water had been shipped, and the cook bailed it out.

But the next crest crashed also. The tumbling, boiling flood of white water caught the boat and whirled it almost perpendicular. Water swarmed in from all sides. The correspondent had his hands on the gunwale at this time, and when the water entered at that place he swiftly withdrew his fingers, as if he objected to wetting them.

The little boat, drunken with this weight of water, reeled and snuggled deeper into the sea.

"Bail her out, cook! Bail her out!" said the captain.

"All right, Captain," said the cook.

"Now, boys, the next one will do for us sure," said the oiler. "Mind to jump clear of the boat."

The third wave moved forward, huge, furious, implacable. It fairly swallowed the dinghy, and almost simultaneously the men tumbled into the sea. A piece of life-belt had lain in the bottom of the boat, and as the correspondent went overboard he held this to his chest with his left hand.

The January water was icy, and he reflected immediately that it was colder than he had expected to find it off the coast of Florida. This appeared to his dazed mind as a fact important enough to be noted at the time. The coldness of the water was sad; it was tragic. This fact was somehow mixed and confused with his opinion of his own situation, so that it seemed almost a proper reason for tears. The water was cold.

When he came to the surface he was conscious of little but the noisy water. Afterward he saw his companions in the sea. The oiler was ahead in the race. He was swimming strongly and rapidly. Off to the correspondent's left, the cook's great white and corked back bulged out of the water; and in the rear the captain was hanging with his one good hand to the keel of the overturned dinghy.

There is a certain immovable quality to a shore, and the correspondent wondered at it amid the confusion of the sea.

It seemed also very attractive; but the correspondent knew that it was a long journey, and he paddled leisurely. The piece of life-preserver lay under him, and sometimes he whirled down the incline of a wave as if he were on a hand-sled.

But finally he arrived at a place in the sea where travel was beset with difficulty. He did not pause swimming to inquire what manner of current had caught him, but there his progress ceased. The shore was set before him like a bit of scenery on a stage, and he looked at it and understood with his eyes each detail of it.

As the cook passed, much farther to the left, the captain was calling to him, "Turn over on your back, cook! Turn over on your back and use the oar."

"All right, sir." The cook turned on his back, and, paddling with an oar, went ahead as if he were a canoe.

Presently the boat also passed to the left of the correspondent, with the captain clinging with one hand to the keel. He would have appeared like a man raising himself to look over a board fence if it were not for the extraordinary gymnastics of the boat. The correspondent marveled that the captain could still hold to it.

They passed on nearer to shore—the oiler, the cook, the captain—and following them went the water-jar, bouncing gaily over the seas.

The correspondent remained in the grip of this strange new enemy—a current. The shore, with its white slope of sand and its green bluff topped with little silent cottages, was spread like a picture before him. It was very near to him then, but he was impressed as one who, in a gallery, looks at a scene from Brittany or Algiers.

He thought: "I'm going to drown? Can it be possible? Can it be possible? Can it be possible?" Perhaps an individual must consider his own death to be the final phenomenon of nature.

But later a wave perhaps whirled him out of this small deadly current, for he found suddenly that he could again make progress toward the shore. Later still he was aware that the captain, clinging with one hand to the keel of the dinghy, had his face turned away from the shore and toward him, and was calling his name. "Come to the boat! Come to the boat!"

In his struggle to reach the captain and the boat, he reflected that when one gets properly wearied drowning must really be a comfortable arrangement—a cessation of hostilities accom-

panied by a large degree of relief; and he was glad of it, for
the main thing in his mind for some moments had been horror
of the temporary agony. He did not wish to be hurt.

Presently he saw a man running along the shore. He was
undressing with most remarkable speed. Coat, trousers,
shirt, everything flew magically off him.

"Come to the boat!" called the captain.

"All right, Captain." As the correspondent paddled, he saw
the captain let himself down to bottom and leave the boat.
Then the correspondent performed his one little marvel of
the voyage. A large wave caught him and flung him with ease
and supreme speed completely over the boat and far beyond
it. It struck him even then as an event in gymnastics and a true
miracle of the sea. An overturned boat in the surf is not a
plaything to a swimming man.

The correspondent arrived in water that reached only to
his waist, but his condition did not enable him to stand for
more than a moment. Each wave knocked him into a heap, and
the undertow pulled at him.

Then he saw the man who had been running and undressing, and undressing and running, come bounding into
the water. He dragged ashore the cook, and then waded toward the captain; but the captain waved him away and sent
him to the correspondent. He was naked—naked as a tree in
winter; but a halo was about his head, and he shone like a
saint. He gave a strong pull, and a long drag, and a bully heave
at the correspondent's hand. The correspondent, schooled
in the minor formulæ, said, "Thanks, old man." But suddenly
the man cried, "What's that?" He pointed a swift finger. The
correspondent said, "Go."

In the shallows, face downward, lay the oiler. His forehead
touched sand that was periodically, between each wave,
clear of the sea.

The correspondent did not know all that transpired afterward. When he achieved safe ground he fell, striking the sand
with each particular part of his body. It was as if he had
dropped from a roof, but the thud was grateful to him.

It seems that instantly the beach was populated with men
with blankets, clothes, and flasks, and women with coffee-

pots and all the remedies sacred to their minds. The welcome of the land to the men from the sea was warm and generous; but a still and dripping shape was carried slowly up the beach, and the land's welcome for it could only be the different and sinister hospitality of the grave.

When it came night, the white waves paced to and fro in the moonlight, and the wind brought the sound of the great sea's voice to the men on the shore, and they felt that they could then be interpreters.

FOR DISCUSSION

1. From beginning to end, this story is concerned entirely with the fate of four men in a tiny boat. What holds your interest, page after page? At what points do you expect some dramatic event that will change the course of this story, if not bring the situation to a climax? Does the story have a climax? Would you prefer a more dramatic ending? Would such an ending be consistent with the rest of the story?

2. The action of a story may be more psychological than physical. The way the characters think, feel, and react is of greater importance to the author and reader than the events in which the characters are involved or which affect their lives. Tell why you do, or do not, think the action of this story is primarily psychological. What would you say is Crane's purpose in writing this story? In your opinion, does he succeed in his purpose? Cite evidence from the story to support your answers to these questions.

3. What picture does Crane create in your mind of the behavior of the sea and the effect of this on the small boat and on the actions of the men? Which details of movement, sound, and color might the crew have noticed as the boat rose and fell? Why don't they notice them? What "sense of the situation" occupied the minds of all four men?

4. Why does Crane refer to the relationship of the men as a "subtle brotherhood"? How is it demonstrated in the way they speak, share duties, and sacrifice personal safety and comfort to the good of the group?

5. Twice the crew of the small boat have reason to believe they will be rescued. In each case, what arouses their hopes and then destroys them? How do the men react? Why is time such an

important element in their struggle for survival? Why are they not prepared for such a struggle?

6. Why do the men resent so bitterly the idea that, in attempting to save themselves, they might drown? Why is the last night on the open sea the most grueling experience of all? From such an experience, what would a man conclude about the attitude of nature toward him? How would he feel? Also, as in the case of the correspondent, how would this feeling affect his attitude toward other desolate souls?

7. Look again at Part VII, paragraph 3. Why does the correspondent see the windmill as "a giant, standing with its back to the plight of the ants"? What new conclusion does he draw about the attitude of nature toward man? Do you think that the events and experiences since the shipwreck prove or disprove this conclusion? From experience and reading, what conclusion can you draw?

8. As the men prepare to try a "run through the surf," they show no signs of fear. What reasons can you give for this? Have they shown fear on any other occasion? If so, point it out and tell the cause of this fear. What impresses you most about the actions of each of the four men as they try to reach the shore?

9. The ending of the story leaves much for the reader to think about and interpret. What significance do you find in the description of the rescuer as having a halo around his head and shining like a saint? Why should all the men survive except the oiler— the best swimmer and perhaps the man most familiar with the sea? Why, from the safety of the shore, do the men feel they can now be interpreters? What would they interpret—the sea, the experience they have shared, the relation between man and nature, the meaning of life when reduced to a struggle for survival?

10. If through this story Crane brings out a general truth or an observation about life, man, or nature, state the theme in your own words.

FOR COMPOSITION

1. Even when you finish "The Open Boat" you know practically nothing about the appearance of each man. Yet from what he says and does, thinks and feels, you know him as a person. Choose the man you find most interesting and gather from the story whatever details reveal his character and personality. From these details, describe the kind of person you think he is and what you do, or do not, admire in him.

2. As Crane pictures the sea, it is forever changing in color and movement. Each of these changes he captures in a striking sensory impression, image, or figure of speech; for example, "the foam was like tumbling snow" or "the waves continued their old impetuous swooping at the dinghy." In a short critical essay, tell why you think Crane's descriptions are effective. Include examples which impressed you particularly and tell why.

Jack London

London's best tales reflect his interest in the scientific method of observation. In some ways they resemble controlled experiments, as though the author had intentionally placed groups of characters in trying situations in order to observe their reactions. Many of his Yukon tales, like the one that follows, are studies of the way men react in their role as helpless pawns of the primitive forces of life. In the struggle for survival, to what extremes will a man go? To what instinctual behavior of his remote, primitive ancestors will he revert? If he is reduced to a state of bare subsistence, is he capable of acting in a civilized manner? These and similar questions interested London all his life, and he used fiction as a means to explore them.

Love of Life

This out of all will remain —
They have lived and have tossed:
So much of the game will be gain,
Though the gold of the dice has been lost.

They limped painfully down the bank, and once the foremost of the two men staggered among the rough-strewn rocks. They were tired and weak, and their faces had the drawn expression of patience which comes of hardship long endured. They were heavily burdened with blanket packs which were strapped to their shoulders. Headstraps, passing across the forehead, helped support these packs. Each man carried a rifle. They walked in a stooped posture, the shoulders well forward, the head still farther forward, the eyes bent upon the ground.

"I wish we had just about two of them cartridges that's layin' in that cache of ourn," said the second man.

His voice was utterly and drearily expressionless. He spoke without enthusiasm; and the first man, limping into the milky stream that foamed over the rocks, vouchsafed[1] no reply. The other man followed at his heels. They did not remove their footgear, though the water was icy cold—so cold that their ankles ached and their feet went numb. In places the water dashed against their knees, and both men staggered for footing.

The man who followed slipped on a smooth boulder, nearly fell, but recovered himself with a violent effort, at the same time uttering a sharp exclamation of pain. He seemed faint and dizzy and put out his free hand while he reeled, as though seeking support against the air. When he had steadied himself he stepped forward, but reeled again and nearly fell. Then he stood still and looked at the other man, who had never turned his head.

The man stood still for fully a minute, as though debating with himself. Then he called out:

"I say, Bill, I've sprained my ankle."

Bill staggered on through the milky water. He did not look around. The man watched him go, and though his face was expressionless as ever, his eyes were like the eyes of a wounded deer.

The other man limped up the farther bank and continued straight on without looking back. The man in the stream watched him. His lips trembled a little, so that the rough thatch of brown hair which covered them was visibly agitated. His tongue even strayed out to moisten them.

"Bill!" he cried out.

It was the pleading cry of a strong man in distress, but Bill's head did not turn. The man watched him go, limping grotesquely and lurching forward with stammering gait up the slow slope toward the soft sky line of the low-lying hill. He watched him go till he passed over the crest and disappeared. Then he turned his gaze and slowly took in the circle of the world that remained to him now that Bill was gone.

Near the horizon the sun was smoldering dimly, almost ob-

---

[1] *vouchsafed:* condescended to grant

scured by formless mists and vapors, which gave an impression of mass and density without outline or tangibility. The man pulled out his watch, the while resting his weight on one leg. It was four o'clock, and as the season was near the last of July or first of August—he did not know the precise date within a week or two—he knew that the sun roughly marked the northwest. He looked to the south and knew that somewhere beyond those bleak hills lay the Great Bear Lake; also, he knew that in that direction the Arctic Circle cuts its forbidding way across the Canadian Barrens. This stream in which he stood was a feeder to the Coppermine River, which in turn flowed north and emptied into Coronation Gulf and the Arctic Ocean. He had never been there, but he had seen it, once, on a Hudson Bay Company chart.

Again his gaze completed the circle of the world about him. It was not a heartening spectacle. Everywhere was soft sky line. The hills were all low lying. There were no trees, no shrubs, no grasses—naught but a tremendous and terrible desolation that sent fear swiftly dawning into his eyes.

"Bill!" he whispered, once and twice, "Bill!"

He cowered in the midst of the milky water, as though the vastness were pressing in upon him with overwhelming force, brutally crushing him with its complacent awfulness. He began to shake as with an ague fit, till the gun fell from his hand with a splash. This served to rouse him. He fought with his fear and pulled himself together, groping in the water and recovering the weapon. He hitched his pack farther over on his left shoulder, so as to take a portion of its weight from off the injured ankle. Then he proceeded, slowly and carefully, wincing with pain, to the bank.

He did not stop. With a desperation that was madness, unmindful of the pain, he hurried up the slope to the crest of the hill over which his comrade had disappeared—more grotesque and comical by far than that limping, jerking comrade. But at the crest he saw a shallow valley, empty of life. He fought with his fear again, overcame it, hitched the pack still farther over on his left shoulder, and lurched on down the slope.

The bottom of the valley was soggy with water, which the

thick moss held, spongelike, close to the surface. This water squirted out from under his feet at every step, and each time he lifted a foot the action culminated in a sucking sound as the wet moss reluctantly released its grip. He picked his way from muskeg[2] to muskeg, and followed the other man's footsteps along and across the rocky ledges which thrust like islets through the sea of moss.

Though alone, he was not lost. Farther on he knew he would come to where dead spruce and fir, very small and weazened,[3] bordered the shore of a little lake, the *titchin-nichilie*, in the tongue of the country, the "land of little sticks." And into that lake flowed a small stream, the water of which was not milky. There was rush grass on that stream—this he remembered well—but no timber, and he would follow it till its first trickle ceased at a divide. He would cross this divide to the first trickle of another stream, flowing to the west, which he would follow until it emptied into the river Dease, and here he would find a cache under an upturned canoe and piled over with many rocks. And in this cache would be ammunition for his empty gun, fishhooks and lines, a small net—all the utilities for the killing and snaring of food. Also, he would find flour—not much—a piece of bacon, and some beans.

Bill would be waiting for him there, and they would paddle away south down the Dease to the Great Bear Lake. And south across the lake they would go, ever south, till they gained the Mackenzie. And south, still south, they would go, while the winter raced vainly after them, and the ice formed in the eddies, and the days grew chill and crisp, south to some warm Hudson Bay Company post, where timber grew tall and generous and there was grub without end.

These were the thoughts of the man as he strove onward. But hard as he strove with his body, he strove equally hard with his mind, trying to think that Bill had not deserted him, that Bill would surely wait for him at the cache. He was compelled to think this thought, or else there would not be any use to strive, and he would have lain down and died. And as

---

[2] *muskeg:* a marsh filled with layers of moss and decaying vegetation
[3] *weazened:* (wizened) withered

the dim ball of the sun sank slowly into the northwest he covered every inch—and many times—of his and Bill's flight south before the down-coming winter. And he conned the grub of the cache and the grub of the Hudson Bay Company post over and over again. He had not eaten for two days; for a far longer time he had not had all he wanted to eat. Often he stooped and picked pale muskeg berries, put them into his mouth, and chewed and swallowed them. A muskeg berry is a bit of seed enclosed in a bit of water. In the mouth the water melts away and the seed chews sharp and bitter. The man knew there was no nourishment in the berries, but he chewed them patiently with a hope greater than knowledge and defying experience.

At nine o'clock he stubbed his toe on a rocky ledge, and from sheer weariness and weakness staggered and fell. He lay for some time, without movement, on his side. Then he slipped out of the pack straps and clumsily dragged himself into a sitting posture. It was not yet dark, and in the lingering twilight he groped about among the rocks for shreds of dry moss. When he had gathered a heap he built a fire—a smoldering, smudgy fire—and put a tin pot of water on to boil.

He unwrapped his pack and the first thing he did was to count his matches. There were sixty-seven. He counted them three times to make sure. He divided them into several portions, wrapping them in oil paper, disposing of one bunch in his empty tobacco pouch, of another bunch in the inside band of his battered hat, of a third bunch under his shirt on the chest. This accomplished, a panic came upon him, and he unwrapped them all and counted them again. There were still sixty-seven.

He dried his wet footgear by the fire. The moccasins were in soggy shreds. The blanket socks were worn through in places, and his feet were raw and bleeding. His ankle was throbbing, and he gave it an examination. It had swollen to the size of his knee. He tore a long strip from one of his two blankets and bound the ankle tightly. He tore other strips and bound them about his feet to serve for both moccasins and socks. Then he drank the pot of water, steaming hot, wound his watch, and crawled between his blankets.

He slept like a dead man. The brief darkness around midnight came and went. The sun arose in the northeast—at least the day dawned in that quarter, for the sun was hidden by gray clouds.

At six o'clock he awoke, quietly lying on his back. He gazed straight up into the gray sky and knew that he was hungry. As he rolled over on his elbow he was startled by a loud snort, and saw a bull caribou regarding him with alert curiosity. The animal was not more than fifty feet away, and instantly into the man's mind leaped the vision and the savor of a caribou steak sizzling and frying over a fire. Mechanically he reached for the empty gun, drew a bead, and pulled the trigger. The bull snorted and leaped away, his hoofs rattling and clattering as he fled across the ledges.

The man cursed and flung the empty gun from him. He groaned aloud as he started to drag himself to his feet. It was a slow and arduous task. His joints were like rusty hinges. They worked harshly in their sockets, with much friction, and each bending or unbending was accomplished only through a sheer exertion of will. When he finally gained his feet, another minute or so was consumed in straightening up, so that he could stand erect as a man should stand.

He crawled up a small knoll and surveyed the prospect. There were no trees, no bushes, nothing but a gray sea of moss scarcely diversified by gray rocks, gray lakelets, and gray streamlets. The sky was gray. There was no sun nor hint of sun. He had no idea of north, and he had forgotten the way he had come to this spot the night before. But he was not lost. He knew that. Soon he would come to the land of the little sticks. He felt that it lay off to the left somewhere, not far—possibly just over the next low hill.

He went back to put his pack into shape for traveling. He assured himself of the existence of his three separate parcels of matches, though he did not stop to count them. But he did linger, debating, over a squat moose-hide sack. It was not large. He could hide it under his two hands. He knew that it weighed fifteen pounds—as much as all the rest of the pack—and it worried him. He finally set it to one side and proceeded to roll the pack. He paused to gaze at the squat moose-hide sack. He picked it up hastily with a defiant glance about him, as though the desolation were trying to rob him of it; and when he rose to his feet to stagger on into the day, it was included in the pack on his back.

He bore away to the left, stopping now and again to eat muskeg berries. His ankle had stiffened, his limp was more pronounced, but the pain of it was as nothing compared with the pain of his stomach. The hunger pangs were sharp. They gnawed and gnawed until he could not keep his mind steady on the course he must pursue to gain the land of little sticks. The muskeg berries did not allay this gnawing, while they made his tongue and the roof of his mouth sore with their irritating bite.

He came upon a valley where rock ptarmigan[4] rose on whirring wings from the ledges and muskegs. Ker—ker—ker was the cry they made. He threw stones at them, but could not hit them. He placed his pack on the ground and stalked them as a cat stalks a sparrow. The sharp rocks cut through his pants legs till his knees left a trail of blood; but the hurt was lost in the hurt of his hunger. He squirmed over the wet moss, saturating his clothes and chilling his body; but he was not aware of it, so great was his fever for food. And always the ptarmigan rose, whirring, before him, till their ker—ker—ker became a mock to him, and he cursed them and cried aloud at them with their own cry.

Once he crawled upon one that must have been asleep. He did not see it till it shot up in his face from its rocky nook. He made a clutch as startled as was the rise of the ptarmigan, and there remained in his hand three tail feathers. As he watched its flight he hated it, as though it had done him some terrible wrong. Then he returned and shouldered his pack.

As the day wore along he came into valleys or swales[5] where game was more plentiful. A band of caribou passed by, twenty and odd animals, tantalizingly within rifle range. He felt a wild desire to run after them, a certitude that he could run them down. A black fox came toward him, carrying a

---

[4] *ptarmigan:* grouse
[5] *swales:* meadows, often marshy

ptarmigan in his mouth. The man shouted. It was a fearful
cry, but the fox, leaping away in fright, did not drop
the ptarmigan.

Late in the afternoon he followed a stream, milky with lime,
which ran through sparse patches of rush grass. Grasping
these rushes firmly near the root, he pulled up what resembled a young onion sprout no larger than a shingle nail.
It was tender, and his teeth sank into it with a crunch that
promised deliciously of food. But its fibers were tough.
It was composed of stringy filaments saturated with water,
like the berries, and devoid of nourishment. He threw off
his pack and went into the rush grass on hands and knees,
crunching and munching, like some bovine[6] creature.

He was very weary and often wished to rest, to lie down and
sleep; but he was continually driven on, not so much by his
desire to gain the land of little sticks as by his hunger. He
searched little ponds for frogs and dug up the earth with his
nails for worms, though he knew in spite that neither frogs
nor worms existed so far north.

He looked into every pool of water vainly until, as the long
twilight came on, he discovered a solitary fish, the size of a
minnow, in such a pool. He plunged his arm in up to the
shoulder, but it eluded him. He reached for it with both
hands and stirred up the milky mud at the bottom. In his
excitement he fell in, wetting himself to the waist. Then the
water was too muddy to admit of his seeing the fish, and
he was compelled to wait until the sediment had settled.

The pursuit was renewed, till the water was again muddied.
But he could not wait. He unstrapped the tin bucket and began to bail the pool. He bailed wildly at first, splashing himself and flinging the water so short a distance that it ran back
into the pool. He worked more carefully, striving to be cool,
though his heart was pounding against his chest and his hands
were trembling. At the end of half an hour the pool was nearly
dry. Not a cupful of water remained. And there was no fish.
He found a hidden crevice among the stones through which
it had escaped to the adjoining and larger pool—a pool which

[6]*bovine:* cowlike

he could not empty in a night and a day. Had he known of the crevice, he would have closed it with a rock at the beginning and the fish would have been his.

Thus he thought, and crumpled up and sank down upon the wet earth. At first he cried softly to himself, then he cried loudly to the pitiless desolation that ringed him around; and for a long time after he was shaken by great dry sobs.

He built a fire and warmed himself by drinking quarts of hot water, and made camp on a rocky ledge in the same fashion he had the night before. The last thing he did was to see that his matches were dry and to wind his watch. The blankets were wet and clammy. His ankle pulsed with pain. But he knew only that he was hungry, and through his restless sleep he dreamed of feasts and banquets and of food served and spread in all imaginable ways.

He awoke chilled and sick. There was no sun. The gray of earth and sky had become deeper, more profound. A raw wind was blowing, and the first flurries of snow were whitening the hilltops. The air about him thickened and grew white while he made a fire and boiled more water. It was wet snow, half rain, and the flakes were large and soggy. At first they melted as soon as they came in contact with the earth, but ever more fell, covering the ground, putting out the fire, spoiling his supply of moss fuel.

This was a signal for him to strap on his pack and stumble onward, he knew not where. He was not concerned with the land of little sticks, nor with Bill and the cache under the up-turned canoe by the river Dease. He was mastered by the verb "to eat." He was hunger-mad. He took no heed of the course he pursued, so long as that course led him through the swale bottoms. He felt his way through the wet snow to the watery muskeg berries, and went by feel as he pulled up the rush grass by the roots. But it was tasteless stuff and did not satisfy. He found a weed that tasted sour and he ate all he could find of it, which was not much, for it was a creeping growth, easily hidden under the several inches of snow.

He had no fire that night, nor hot water, and crawled under his blanket to sleep the broken hunger-sleep. The snow turned into a cold rain. He awakened many times to feel it falling on his upturned face. Day came—a gray day and no sun. It had ceased raining. The keenness of his hunger had departed. Sensibility, as far as concerned the yearning for food, had been exhausted. There was a dull, heavy ache in his stomach, but it did not bother him so much. He was more rational, and once more he was chiefly interested in the land of little sticks and the cache by the river Dease.

He ripped the remnant of one of his blankets into strips and bound his bleeding feet. Also, he recinched the injured ankle and prepared himself for a day of travel. When he came to his pack, he paused long over the squat moose-hide sack, but in the end it went with him.

The snow had melted under the rain, and only the hilltops showed white. The sun came out, and he succeeded in locating the points of the compass, though he knew now that he was lost. Perhaps, in his previous day's wanderings, he had edged away too far to the left. He now bore off to the right to counteract the possible deviation from his true course.

Though the hunger pangs were no longer so exquisite, he realized that he was weak. He was compelled to pause for frequent rests, when he attacked the muskeg berries and rush-grass patches. His tongue felt dry and large, as though covered with a fine hairy growth, and it tasted bitter in his mouth. His heart gave him a great deal of trouble. When he had traveled a few minutes it would begin a remorseless thump, thump, thump, and then leap up and away in a painful flutter of beats that choked him and made him go faint and dizzy.

In the middle of the day he found two minnows in a large pool. It was impossible to bail it, but he was calmer now and managed to catch them in his tin bucket. They were no longer than his little finger, but he was not particularly hungry. The dull ache in his stomach had been growing duller and fainter. It seemed almost that his stomach was dozing. He ate the fish raw, masticating with painstaking care, for the eating was an act of pure reason. While he had no desire to eat, he knew that he must eat to live.

In the evening he caught three more minnows, eating two and saving the third for breakfast. The sun had dried stray shreds of moss, and he was able to warm himself with hot water. He had not covered more than ten miles that day; and the next day, traveling whenever his heart permitted him, he covered no more than five miles. But his stomach did not give him the slightest uneasiness. It had gone to sleep. He was in a strange country, too, and the caribou were growing more plentiful, also the wolves. Often their yelps drifted across the desolation, and once he saw three of them slinking away before his path.

Another night; and in the morning, being more rational, he untied the leather string that fastened the squat moose-hide sack. From its open mouth poured a yellow stream of coarse gold dust and nuggets. He roughly divided the gold in halves, caching one half on a prominent ledge, wrapped in a piece of blanket, and returning the other half to the sack. He also began to use strips of the one remaining blanket for his feet. He still clung to his gun, for there were cartridges in that cache by the river Dease.

This was a day of fog, and this day hunger awoke in him again. He was very weak and was afflicted with a giddiness which at times blinded him. It was no uncommon thing now for him to stumble and fall; and stumbling once, he fell squarely into a ptarmigan nest. There were four newly hatched chicks, a day old—little specks of pulsating life no more than a mouthful; and he ate them ravenously, thrusting them alive into his mouth and crunching them like eggshells between his teeth. The mother ptarmigan beat about him with great outcry. He used his gun as a club with which to knock her over, but she dodged out of reach. He threw stones at her and with one chance shot broke a wing. Then she fluttered away, running, trailing the broken wing, with him in pursuit.

The little chicks had no more than whetted his appetite. He hopped and bobbed clumsily along on his injured ankle, throwing stones and screaming hoarsely at times; at other times hopping and bobbing silently along, picking himself up grimly and patiently when he fell, or rubbing his eyes with his hand when the giddiness threatened to overpower him.

The chase led him across swampy ground in the bottom of the valley, and he came upon footprints in the soggy moss.

They were not his own—he could see that. They must be Bill's. But he could not stop, for the mother ptarmigan was running on. He would catch her first, then he would return and investigate.

He exhausted the mother ptarmigan; but he exhausted himself. She lay panting on her side. He lay panting on his side, a dozen feet away, unable to crawl to her. And as he recovered she recovered, fluttering out of reach as his hungry hand went out to her. The chase was resumed. Night settled down and she escaped. He stumbled from weakness and pitched head foremost on his face, cutting his cheek, his pack upon his back. He did not move for a long while; then he rolled over on his side, wound his watch, and lay there until morning.

Another day of fog. Half of his last blanket had gone into foot wrappings. He failed to pick up Bill's trail. It did not matter. His hunger was driving him too compellingly—only —only he wondered if Bill, too, were lost. By midday the irk of his pack became too oppressive. Again he divided the gold, this time merely spilling half of it on the ground. In the afternoon he threw the rest of it away, there remaining to him only the half blanket, the tin bucket, and the rifle.

An hallucination began to trouble him. He felt confident that one cartridge remained to him. It was in the chamber of the rifle and he had overlooked it. On the other hand, he knew all the time that the chamber was empty. But the hallucination persisted. He fought it off for hours, then threw his rifle open and was confronted with emptiness. The disappointment was as bitter as though he had really expected to find the cartridge.

He plodded on for half an hour, when the hallucination arose again. Again he fought it, and still it persisted, till for very relief he opened his rifle to unconvince himself. At times his mind wandered farther afield, and he plodded on, a mere automaton,[7] strange conceits and whimsicalities gnawing at his brain like worms. But these excursions out of the real were of brief duration, for ever the pangs of the

---

[7] *automaton:* a person or animal acting in a mechanical manner

hunger-bite called him back. He was jerked back abruptly once from such an excursion by a sight that caused him nearly to faint. He reeled and swayed, doddering like a drunken man to keep from falling. Before him stood a horse. A horse! He could not believe his eyes. A thick mist was in them, intershot with sparkling points of light. He rubbed his eyes savagely to clear his vision, and beheld, not a horse, but a great brown bear. The animal was studying him with bellicose[8] curiosity.

The man had brought his gun halfway to his shoulder before he realized. He lowered it and drew his hunting knife from its beaded sheath at his hip. Before him was meat and life. He ran his thumb along the edge of his knife. It was sharp. The point was sharp. He would fling himself upon the bear and kill it. But his heart began its warning thump, thump, thump. Then followed the wild upward leap and tattoo of flutters, the pressing as of an iron band about his forehead, the creeping of the dizziness into his brain.

His desperate courage was evicted by a great surge of fear. In his weakness, what if the animal attacked him? He drew himself up to his most imposing stature, gripping the knife and staring hard at the bear. The bear advanced clumsily a couple of steps, reared up, and gave vent to a tentative growl. If the man ran, he would run after him; but the man did not run. He was animated now with the courage of fear. He, too, growled, savagely, terribly, voicing the fear that is to life germane[9] and that lies twisted about life's deepest roots.

The bear edged away to one side, growling menacingly, himself appalled by this mysterious creature that appeared upright and unafraid. But the man did not move. He stood like a statue till the danger was past, when he yielded to a fit of trembling and sank down into the wet moss.

He pulled himself together and went on, afraid now in a new way. It was not the fear that he should die passively from lack of food, but that he should be destroyed violently before starvation had exhausted the last particle of the endeavor in him that made toward surviving. There were the

[8] *bellicose:* hostile, warlike
[9] *germane:* closely related

wolves. Back and forth across the desolation drifted their howls, weaving the very air into a fabric of menace that was so tangible that he found himself, arms in the air, pressing it back from him as it might be the walls of a wind-blown tent.

Now and again the wolves, in packs of two and three, crossed his path. But they steered clear of him. They were not in sufficient numbers, and besides they were hunting the caribou, which did not battle, while this strange creature that walked erect might scratch and bite.

In the late afternoon he came upon scattered bones where the wolves had made a kill. The debris had been a caribou calf an hour before, squawking and running and very much alive. He contemplated the bones, clean-picked and polished, pink with the cell life in them which had not yet died. Could it possibly be that he might be that ere the day was done! Such was life, eh? A vain and fleeting thing. It was only life that pained. There was no hurt in death. To die was to sleep. It meant cessation, rest. Then why was he not content to die?

But he did not moralize long. He was squatting in the moss, a bone in his mouth, sucking at the shreds of life that still dyed it faintly pink. The sweet meaty taste, thin and elusive almost as a memory, maddened him. He closed his jaws on the bones and crunched. Sometimes it was the bone that broke, sometimes his teeth. Then he crushed the bones between the rocks, pounded them to a pulp, and swallowed them. He pounded his fingers, too, in his haste, and yet found a moment in which to feel surprise at the fact that his fingers did not hurt much when caught under the descending rock.

Came frightful days of snow and rain. He did not know when he made camp, when he broke camp. He traveled in the night as much as in the day. He rested wherever he fell, crawled on whenever the dying life in him flickered up and burned less dimly. He, as a man, no longer strove. It was the life in him, unwilling to die, that drove him on. He did not suffer. His nerves had become blunted, numb, while his mind was filled with weird visions and delicious dreams.

But ever he sucked and chewed on the crushed bones of the caribou calf, the least remnants of which he had gathered up and carried with him. He crossed no more hills or divides, but automatically followed a large stream which flowed through a wide and shallow valley. He did not see this stream nor this valley. He saw nothing save visions. Soul and body walked or crawled side by side, yet apart, so slender was the thread that bound them.

He awoke in his right mind, lying on his back on a rocky ledge. The sun was shining bright and warm. Afar off he heard the squawking of caribou calves. He was aware of vague memories of rain and wind and snow, but whether he had been beaten by the storm for two days or two weeks he did not know.

For some time he lay without movement, the genial sunshine pouring upon him and saturating his miserable body with its warmth. A fine day, he thought. Perhaps he could manage to locate himself. By a painful effort he rolled over on his side. Below him flowed a wide and sluggish river. Its unfamiliarity puzzled him. Slowly he followed it with his eyes, winding in wide sweeps among the bleak, bare hills, bleaker and barer and lower lying than any hills he had yet encountered. Slowly, deliberately, without excitement or more than the most casual interest, he followed the course of the strange stream toward the sky line and saw it emptying into a bright and shining sea. He was still unexcited. Most unusual, he thought, a vision or a mirage—more likely a vision, a trick of his disordered mind. He was confirmed in this by sight of a ship lying at anchor in the midst of the shining sea. He closed his eyes for a while, then opened them. Strange how the vision persisted! Yet not strange. He knew there were no seas or ships in the heart of the barren lands, just as he had known there was no cartridge in the empty rifle.

He heard a snuffle behind him—a half-choking gasp or cough. Very slowly, because of his exceeding weakness and stiffness, he rolled over on his other side. He could see nothing near at hand, but he waited patiently. Again came the snuffle and cough, and outlined between two jagged rocks not a score of feet away he made out the gray head of a wolf. The sharp ears were not pricked so sharply as he had seen them on other wolves; the eyes were bleared and bloodshot, the head seemed to droop limply and forlornly. The animal blinked continually in the sunshine. It seemed sick. As he looked it snuffled and coughed again.

This, at least, was real, he thought, and turned on the other side so that he might see the reality of the world which had been veiled from him before by the vision. But the sea still shone in the distance and the ship was plainly discernible. Was it reality, after all? He closed his eyes for a long while and thought, and then it came to him. He had been making north by east, away from the Dease Divide and into the Coppermine Valley. This wide and sluggish river was the Coppermine. That shining sea was the Arctic Ocean. That ship was a whaler, strayed east, far east, from the mouth of the Mackenzie, and it was lying at anchor in Coronation Gulf. He remembered the Hudson Bay Company chart he had seen long ago, and it was all clear and reasonable to him.

He sat up and turned his attention to immediate affairs. He had worn through the blanket wrappings, and his feet were shapeless lumps of raw meat. His last blanket was gone. Rifle and knife were both missing. He had lost his hat somewhere, with the bunch of matches in the band, but the matches against his chest were safe and dry inside the tobacco pouch and oil paper. He looked at his watch. It marked eleven o'clock and was still running. Evidently he had kept it wound.

He was calm and collected. Though extremely weak, he had no sensation of pain. He was not hungry. The thought of food was not even pleasant to him, and whatever he did was done by his reason alone. He ripped off his pants legs to the knees and bound them about his feet. Somehow he had succeeded in retaining the tin bucket. He would have some hot water before he began what he foresaw was to be a terrible journey to the ship.

His movements were slow. He shook as with a palsy. When he started to collect dry moss, he found he could not rise to his feet. He tried again and again, then contented himself with crawling about on hands and knees. Once he crawled near to the sick wolf. The animal dragged itself reluctantly out of his way, licking its chops with a tongue which seemed hardly to have the strength to curl. The man noticed that the tongue was not the customary healthy red. It was a yellowish brown and seemed coated with a rough and half-dry mucus.

After he had drunk a quart of hot water the man found he was able to stand, and even to walk as well as a dying man might be supposed to walk. Every minute or so he was compelled to rest. His steps were feeble and uncertain, just as the wolf's that trailed him were feeble and uncertain; and that night, when the shining sea was blotted out by blackness, he knew he was nearer to it by no more than four miles.

Throughout the night he heard the cough of the sick wolf, and now and then the squawking of the caribou calves. There was life all around him, but it was strong life, very much alive and well, and he knew the sick wolf clung to the sick man's trail in the hope that the man would die first. In the morning, on opening his eyes, he beheld it regarding him with a wistful and hungry stare. It stood crouched, with tail between its legs, like a miserable and woebegone dog. It shivered in the chill morning wind, and grinned dispiritedly when the man spoke to it in a voice that achieved no more than a hoarse whisper.

The sun rose brightly, and all morning the man tottered and fell toward the ship on the shining sea. The weather was perfect. It was the brief Indian Summer of the high latitudes. It might last a week. Tomorrow or next day it might be gone.

In the afternoon the man came upon a trail. It was of another man, who did not walk, but who dragged himself on all fours. The man thought it might be Bill, but he thought in a dull, uninterested way. He had no curiosity. In fact, sensation and emotion had left him. He was no longer susceptible to pain. Stomach and nerves had gone to sleep. Yet the life that was in him drove him on. He was very weary, but it refused to die. It was because it refused to die that he still ate muskeg berries and minnows, drank his hot water, and kept a wary eye on the sick wolf.

He followed the trail of the other man who dragged himself along, and soon came to the end of it—a few fresh-picked bones where the soggy moss was marked by the footpads of many wolves. He saw a squat moose-hide sack, mate to his own, which had been torn by sharp teeth. He picked it up, though its weight was almost too much for his feeble fingers. Bill had carried it to the last. Ha! Ha! He would have the laugh on Bill. He would survive and carry it to the ship in the shining sea. His mirth was hoarse and ghastly, like a raven's croak, and the sick wolf joined him, howling lugubriously.[10] The man ceased suddenly. How could he have the laugh on Bill if that were Bill; if those bones, so pinky-white and clean, were Bill?

He turned away. Well, Bill had deserted him; but he would not take the gold, nor would he suck Bill's bones. Bill would have, though, had it been the other way around, he mused as he staggered on.

He came to a pool of water. Stooping over in quest of minnows, he jerked his head back as though he had been stung. He had caught sight of his reflected face. So horrible was it that sensibility awoke long enough to be shocked. There were three minnows in the pool, which was too large to drain; and after several ineffectual attempts to catch them in the tin bucket he forbore. He was afraid, because of his great weakness, that he might fall in and drown. It was for this reason that he did not trust himself to the river astride one of the many drift logs which lined its sandpits.

That day he decreased the distance between him and the ship by three miles; the next day by two — for he was crawling now as Bill had crawled; and the end of the fifth day found the ship still seven miles away and him unable to make even a mile a day. Still the Indian Summer held on, and he continued to crawl and faint, turn and turn about; and ever the sick wolf coughed and wheezed at his heels. His knees had become raw meat like his feet, and though he padded them with the shirt from his back it was a red track he left behind him on the moss and stones. Once, glancing back, he saw the wolf licking hungrily his bleeding trail, and he saw sharply what his own end might be — unless — unless he could get the wolf. Then began as grim a tragedy of existence as was ever played — a sick man that crawled, a sick wolf that limped, two creatures dragging their dying carcasses across the desolation and hunting each other's lives.

[10] *lugubriously:* mournfully

Had it been a well wolf, it would not have mattered so much to the man; but the thought of going to feed the maw of that loathsome and all but dead thing was repugnant to him. He was finicky. His mind had begun to wander again, and to be perplexed by hallucinations, while his lucid intervals grew rarer and shorter.

He was awakened once from a faint by a wheeze close in his ear. The wolf leaped lamely back, losing its footing and falling in its weakness. It was ludicrous, but he was not amused. Nor was he even afraid. He was too far gone for that. But his mind was for the moment clear, and he lay and considered. The ship was no more than four miles away. He could see it quite distinctly when he rubbed the mists out of his eyes, and he could see the white sail of a small boat cutting the water of the shining sea. But he could never crawl those four miles. He knew that, and was very calm in the knowledge. He knew that he could not crawl half a mile. And yet he wanted to live. It was unreasonable that he should die after all he had undergone. Fate asked too much of him. And, dying, he declined to die. It was stark madness, perhaps, but in the very grip of Death he defied Death and refused to die.

He closed his eyes and composed himself with infinite precaution. He steeled himself to keep above the suffocating languor that lapped like a rising tide through all the wells of his being. It was very like a sea, this deadly languor, that rose and rose and drowned his consciousness bit by bit. Sometimes he was all but submerged, swimming through oblivion with a faltering stroke; and again, by some strange alchemy of soul, he would find another shred of will and strike out more strongly.

Without movement he lay on his back, and he could hear, slowly drawing nearer and nearer, the wheezing intake and output of the sick wolf's breath. It drew closer, ever closer, through an infinitude of time, and he did not move. It was at his ear. The harsh dry tongue grated like sandpaper against his cheek. His hands shot out—or at least he willed them to shoot out. The fingers were curved like talons, but they closed on empty air. Swiftness and certitude require strength, and the man had not this strength.

The patience of the wolf was terrible. The man's patience was no less terrible. For half a day he lay motionless, fighting off unconsciousness and waiting for the thing that was to feed upon him and upon which he wished to feed. Sometimes the languid sea rose over him and he dreamed long dreams; but ever through it all, waking and dreaming, he waited for the wheezing breath and the harsh caress of the tongue.

He did not hear the breath, and he slipped slowly from some dream to the feel of the tongue along his hand. He waited. The fangs pressed softly; the pressure increased; the wolf was exerting its last strength in an effort to sink teeth in the food for which it had waited so long. But the man had waited long, and the lacerated hand closed on the jaw. Slowly, while the wolf struggled feebly and the hand clutched feebly, the other hand crept across to a grip. Five minutes later the whole weight of the man's body was on top of the wolf. The hands had not sufficient strength to choke the wolf, but the face of the man was pressed close to the throat of the wolf and the mouth of the man was full of hair. At the end of half an hour the man was aware of a warm trickle in his throat. It was not pleasant. It was like molten lead being forced into his stomach, and it was forced by his will alone. Later the man rolled over on his back and slept.

There were some members of a scientific expedition on the whaleship *Bedford*. From the deck they remarked a strange object on the shore. It was moving down the beach toward the water. They were unable to classify it, and, being scientific men, they climbed into the whaleboat alongside and went ashore to see. And they saw something that was alive but which could hardly be called a man. It was blind, unconscious. It squirmed along the ground like some monstrous worm. Most of its efforts were ineffectual, but it was persistent, and it writhed and twisted and went ahead perhaps a score of feet an hour.

Three weeks afterward the man lay in a bunk on the whaleship *Bedford,* and with tears streaming down his wasted cheeks told who he was and what he had undergone. He also babbled incoherently of his mother, of sunny Southern California, and a home among the orange groves and flowers. The days were not many after that when he sat at table with the scientific men and ship's officers. He gloated over the spectacle of so much food, watching it anxiously as it went into the mouths of others. With the disappearance of each mouthful an expression of deep regret came into his eyes. He was quite sane, yet he hated those men at mealtime. He was haunted by a fear that the food would not last. He inquired of the cook, the cabin boy, the captain, concerning the food stores. They reassured him countless times; but he could not believe them, and pried cunningly about the lazaretto[11] to see with his own eyes.

It was noticed that the man was getting fat. He grew stouter with each day. The scientific men shook their heads and theorized. They limited the man at his meals, but still his girth increased and he swelled prodigiously under his shirt.

The sailors grinned. They knew. And when the scientific men set a watch on the man, they knew too. They saw him slouch for'ard after breakfast, and, like a mendicant,[12] with outstretched palm, accost a sailor. The sailor grinned and passed him a fragment of sea biscuit. He clutched it avariciously, looked at it as a miser looks at gold, and thrust it into his shirt bosom. Similar were the donations from other grinning sailors.

The scientific men were discreet. They let him alone. But they privily[13] examined his bunk. It was lined with hardtack;[14] the mattress was stuffed with hardtack; every nook and cranny was filled with hardtack. Yet he was sane. He was taking precautions against another possible famine — that was all. He would recover from it, the scientific men said; and he did, ere the *Bedford's* anchor rumbled down in San Francisco Bay.

---

[11] *lazaretto:* space between decks where provisions are stored
[12] *mendicant:* beggar
[13] *privily:* secretly
[14] *hardtack:* hard wafers of unleavened bread

FOR DISCUSSION

1. Why is it necessary for the man to kill the wolf? How does he do it? Do you think he is aware of what he is doing? In what ways is his "pursuit" of the wolf different from his earlier attempts to capture the fish and the mother ptarmigan? What has he learned from those attempts?

2. How do you interpret "love of life" as this phrase is used in the story? Is it "love of life" that (a) causes the man to discard his gold, (b) to hoard food on board the ship, and (c) to keep his watch wound? Explain. In your opinion is reason "on the same side" as the "love of life," or is it against it? Perhaps it is both for and against. Give evidence from the story to support your answer.

3. From what the author reveals about the two gold prospectors, try to reconstruct the events which took place prior to the time covered in the story. Do you think the relationship between these two was one of friendship or of dependence based on survival? What reason can you give for Bill's deserting his partner without even looking back?

4. The injured man is desperate at finding himself alone, but he is able to put down his fears. Why? To what thought does he have to cling? When he stops the first night, what do you learn about his condition and the terrible odds he faces if he continues his journey?

5. To what extremes is he driven by the hunger pains? What effect do they have on his mind and spirit? Why do they cease and then return again? Why is his chase of the mother ptarmigan so horrifying and so revealing? How does he react to the discovery that he is lost? How do you think he feels about throwing away the last of the gold?

6. Why are the periodic hallucinations so troubling? Discuss his encounter with the bear, his new fear, and the thoughts which pass through his mind as he chews the bones of the caribou calf. When he awakes on the rocky ledge, why are his memories of the past days or weeks so vague?

7. Note the ways in which London creates a contrast between the dying—wolf and man—and the world in which they both fight for survival. How does the man react to the discovery of the ship and, later, to the discovery of his dead partner's bones? What is ironic about this last experience? What forces the man to continue his struggle even though he is more dead than alive? When the men on the boat see him on the shore, of what does he remind them?

8. The climax of the story is clearly the rescue of the man. What reason can you see for the denouement? Without it would the story seem too grim? Would the reader feel uneasy about the fate of the man? What point does it reinforce about man's actions? State the theme of this story in your own words.

9. In your opinion could a man have endured the hardships London portrays in this story? Do you feel that the story would be equally effective and believable if London omitted some of the most brutal and shocking details? If so, point out which ones. Also point out several passages in which London's use of detail portrays an experience or reaction of the man which left a deep impression on you.

FOR COMPOSITION

1. Write a short essay on one of the following topics, expressing your own thoughts and feelings and citing as examples either an incident from the story or from your own experience:

   a. Human life is subject to the same laws that govern the rest of the natural world.

   b. Under trying conditions, man is guided principally by his instinct for self-preservation.

2. If you had been one of the "scientific men" who went ashore from the *Bedford*, what fact about the man and his condition would have made the deepest impression? Describe the man and your personal and scientific reactions to him in an imaginary letter to a fellow scientist.

AT HOME AND ABROAD

The closing years of the nineteenth century had seen the beginnings of the American industrial revolution. Across the country, science and industry were calling people from the farms and crowding them into the numerous factories of the cities. At the same time, immigrants from southern and eastern Europe began pouring into this country in a continuing stream that did not slacken until the beginning of World War I in 1914.

The immigrants who left Europe during this period entered an America that was still a land of opportunity but also a land of strange contrasts. While the annual income of most Americans was between $400 and $500, Andrew D. Carnegie enjoyed an average annual income of $10,000,000 with no income taxes to pay. Servants could be hired for $3.50 per week at a time when the Vanderbilts were spending $12,000,-000 on seven homes for various members of the family. While poor European families were struggling to reach America, wealthy American heiresses were traveling to Europe to exchange great fortunes for titles of nobility in fashionable international marriages.

If newcomers to America found life here somewhat less equitable than they had dreamed, they had reason to hope that any abuses would soon be corrected. For this prewar period was also an era of reform. President Theodore Roosevelt had already touched off the government's campaign against monopoly. Crusades were being waged for children's rights, temperance, conservation, civil service reform, women's suffrage, and a host of other worthy causes. The most zealous supporters of these reform movements were middle-class Americans who wanted this country to realize its historic ideals of equality and justice. These well-meaning reformers assumed, of course, that the "comfortable setting of the nineteenth century," based on family and church, would continue. They could not possibly foresee the transformation that technological changes and a great world war would soon bring about in American life.

In the final quarter of the nineteenth century, a trend in American literature toward "truthful representation" had found expression in the vigorous works of Stephen Crane, Frank Norris, and Jack London. All three had been influenced from abroad by the new naturalism of European writers with their concepts of man in relation to nature.

At the turn of the century, however, American writers went their separate ways, each picking up that strand of the past literary tradition most congenial to himself and modifying it to suit his own purposes and the changing times. O. Henry chose to concentrate on the short story form in the Poe tradition, concerning himself more with effect than with ideas, and experimenting with the ironic or surprise ending. Henry James, on the other hand, drew inspiration from Hawthorne's psychological stories and novels, but tempered Hawthorne's romanticism with the realism set forth by his friend William Dean Howells. Willa Cather adopted a realistic presentation of the rural life she considered "the good life." The stories of Sherwood Anderson and F. Scott Fitzgerald were written within a sociological context, exhibiting the naturalistic influence of Norris and Crane.

O. HENRY once told a friend, "I would like to live a lifetime on each street in New York. Every house has a drama in it."

He believed that even the most ordinary lives contain the seeds of romance and that the people one meets every day on the streets deserve the writer's attention as much as the eminent and glamorous. His major collection of short stories he entitled *The Four Million* to parody the remark by a noted socialite that there were only four hundred people worth knowing in New York.

O. Henry's best and most characteristic writing is found in his sentimental, often humorous short stories about everyday life in New York. His remarkable talent for capturing and conveying the sights and sounds of the city have led some critics to place him with such consciously regional writers as Bret Harte and Sarah Orne Jewett. O. Henry's truly democratic attitude and his compassionate nature enabled him to treat all his characters — even those on the fringes of society — with the warmth and understanding their humanity deserves.

He claimed that he wrote most of his stories at a single sitting and rarely revised them before publication. His less important stories reveal this haste, but his best have all the earmarks of painstaking craftsmanship. Like Poe, he had the ability to add twists to his plots which, though they surprise the reader, may, after careful consideration, prove quite consistent with what has taken place before.

HENRY JAMES is considered one of the finest novelists America has produced, yet he spent the greater part of his life abroad. At the age of twelve, he made a five year tour of Europe with his father and brother. At thirty-two, he moved to England, where he spent the rest of his life except for one brief visit to the United States. In 1915, one year before his death, he became a British subject.

James once said that his quarrel with America was a "lover's quarrel." Far from hating his country, he often affirmed his allegiance to it. He simply felt more comfortable in England with its European culture. It has been pointed out that in James's novels, his most admirable characters are almost always Americans, while his Europeans are seen as morally decayed.

The intricacy of James's prose style reflects the complexity and subtlety of the effects he wished to create and the ideas he wished to convey. He was careful to examine every possible facet of a given situation or human relationship before advancing the action to a new stage in its development. Consequently, his involved style is characterized by long sentences and, often, by an extraordinary number of qualifying modifiers and subordinate clauses. In fact, the richness of many of his more involved passages can be fully appreciated only on a second or third reading.

WILLA CATHER, in contrast to the sophisticated Henry James, spent her formative years among the European farmer-immigrants of Nebraska. The prairie life she loved was simple, but it was neither provincial nor uncultured. To illustrate the cosmopolitan character of her life, she was fond of recalling that on Sundays she frequently listened to sermons in three languages. What she admired most were the sturdy virtues of that agrarian society—hard work, kindness, and responsibility, together with a generosity of mind and spirit—all of which made for personal integrity. Her later experiences as a high school teacher and as a magazine editor in New York convinced her that urban living tended to destroy those virtues. In her novels and short stories, she drew first upon the memories of her girlhood to reconstruct realistically what had seemed to her to be the good life. Later, as America changed, she mourned the disappearance of the old virtues, and also sought those virtues in other regions, such as the Southwest and old Quebec, which were still unspoiled by the blight of industrial civilization.

Miss Cather took her responsibilities as a writer seriously. Faithful to the virtues she reverenced, she strove for honest interpretation as well as aesthetic effect. Her work showed craftsmanship rather than excitement, but she succeeded, as few writers have, in depicting, without sentimentality and without distortion, the goodness of life in an older, rural America

Although SHERWOOD ANDERSON was the same age as Willa Cather, he belonged to the next generation in spirit as well as in literary achievement. He did not become a writer until, at the age of thirty-six, he made a dramatic break with his family and business and went off to Chicago. Later, in Paris, he became one of the group headed by Gertrude Stein, a brilliant personality who influenced the literary style of several writers, including Sherwood Anderson and Ernest Hemingway. Anderson wanted to break away from the rigid plot structure of the short story and give it a "new looseness." He wanted to write, as he said, "by feel rather than by plan."

The results of Anderson's efforts to use "fiction as a substitute for poetry and religion" were uneven; his best work, however, was not only popular but also influential in the development of the modern short story. His subject matter was drawn from small-town life, with the central character of the story usually being either a victim of Puritanical repression or a rebel against it. He was "a writer whose sympathy went out most to the little frame house, on often mean enough streets in American towns, to defeated people, often with thwarted lives."

Along with Anderson, many writers of the 1920's made Puritanism a primary target of their writing because they held it responsible for much of the hypocrisy and unhappiness in modern life. Leading the crusade was the Baltimore journalist, H. L. Mencken, editor of *The American Mercury,* a magazine devoted to lampooning Puritanism in all its forms, religious and secular. Mencken held up the "boobus Americanus" for constant ridicule and encouraged able young writers to join him in his war against such "stupidities" as Prohibition, social and fraternal orders, and "sloppy stories in slick magazines."

A young writer, F. SCOTT FITZGERALD, took a somewhat different view of his country in the decade following World War I. "America was going on the greatest, gaudiest spree in history," he wrote, "and there was going to be plenty to tell about it." What he told turned out to be—like his life—amusing, exciting, and pathetic. When his first novel appeared in 1920, he was greeted as an important new writer with a "special grace" and a "pride in craft." By 1929 he was earning $27,000 a year from his short stories alone. He enjoyed repeating the familiar American success story and tried to keep

pace with the Jazz Age, which he had named. "Sometimes I
don't know whether Zelda [his wife] and I are real or whether
we are characters in one of my novels," he wrote.

After the heady experience of being famous came the
humiliation of being forgotten, and in 1936 Fitzgerald revealed the depths of his physical and mental breakdown in
a frank personal account, "The Crack-Up." Recently, as
part of the current revival of interest in the 1920's, a considerable number of readers have rediscovered his stories
and found in them an absorbing record of those days.

All of the writers in this section, coming through the turn
of the century, were soon faced with a period of international
struggle and conflict. Though O. Henry and Henry James
were dead before America entered World War I, the other
three writers became well acquainted with wartime America
and with the period of economic boom that followed in the
1920's. Then, with the stock market crash on Wall Street in
October of 1929, the painful meaning of economic disaster
and depression gradually became clear to these writers and
to people in all walks of life. They began to realize that
America had come to the end of an era, with a dark and uncertain future ahead.

Willa Cather, rooted in an older tradition, held to her ideals
of moral realism and literary craftsmanship. Sherwood Anderson's talents failed to mature in the decade following the
crash. F. Scott Fitzgerald, more than any of the other writers
a child of his time, revealed in his writing and in his personal
tragedy the disintegration of a world that he had helped to
create and that had, in turn, destroyed him.

O. Henry

O. Henry, though an urban Easterner in every sense, wrote with the comic flair of such Westerners as Bret Harte and Mark Twain. Reminiscent of traditional Western humor, his characters are usually caricatures, his plots are exaggerated, and his prose style is often disproportionately grand for the humble subjects he is treating. At times, as in the following story, he deliberately uses a pretentious vocabulary and inappropriate "learned" allusions in order to add to the humor.

The Cop and the Anthem

On his bench in Madison Square Soapy moved uneasily. When wild geese honk high of nights, and when women without sealskin coats grow kind to their husbands, and when Soapy moves uneasily on his bench in the park, you may know that winter is near at hand.

A dead leaf fell in Soapy's lap. That was Jack Frost's card. Jack is kind to the regular denizens of Madison Square, and gives fair warning of his annual call. At the corners of four streets he hands his pasteboard[1] to the North Wind, footman of the mansion of All Outdoors, so that the inhabitants thereof may make ready.

Soapy's mind became cognizant of the fact that the time had come for him to resolve himself into a singular Committee of Ways and Means to provide against the coming rigor. And therefore he moved uneasily on his bench.

The hibernatorial ambitions of Soapy were not of the highest. In them were no considerations of Mediterranean cruises, of soporific[2] Southern skies or drifting in the Vesuvian

---

[1] *pasteboard:* (slang) calling card
[2] *soporific:* sleep-inducing

Bay.[3] Three months on the Island was what his soul craved. Three months of assured board and bed and congenial company, safe from Boreas[4] and bluecoats, seemed to Soapy the essence of things desirable.

For years the hospitable Blackwell's[5] had been his winter quarters. Just as his more fortunate fellow New Yorkers had bought their tickets to Palm Beach and the Riviera each winter, so Soapy had made his humble arrangements for his annual hegira[6] to the Island. And now the time was come. On the previous night three Sabbath newspapers, distributed beneath his coat, about his ankles and over his lap, had failed to repulse the cold as he slept on his bench near the spurting fountain in the ancient square. So the Island loomed big and timely in Soapy's mind. He scorned the provisions made in the name of charity for the city's dependents. In Soapy's opinion the Law was more benign than Philanthropy. There was an endless round of institutions, municipal and eleemosynary,[7] on which he might set out and receive lodging and food accordant with the simple life. But to one of Soapy's proud spirit the gifts of charity are encumbered. If not in coin you must pay in humiliation of spirit for every benefit received at the hands of philanthropy. As Caesar had his Brutus, every bed of charity must have its toll of a bath, every loaf of bread its compensation of a private and personal inquisition. Wherefore it is better to be a guest of the law, which, though conducted by rules, does not meddle unduly with a gentleman's private affairs.

Soapy, having decided to go to the Island, at once set about accomplishing his desire. There were many easy ways of doing this. The pleasantest was to dine luxuriously at some expensive restaurant; and then, after declaring insolvency, be handed over quietly and without uproar to a policeman. An accommodating magistrate would do the rest.

---

[3] *Vesuvian Bay:* the bay of Naples, in Italy

[4] *Boreas:* god of the north wind, in Greek mythology

[5] *Blackwell's:* Blackwell's Island, once the site of the city prison of New York, now called Welfare Island

[6] *hegira:* flight

[7] *eleemosynary:* charitable

Soapy left his bench and strolled out of the square and across the level sea of asphalt, where Broadway and Fifth Avenue flow together. Up Broadway he turned, and halted at a glittering café, where are gathered together nightly the choicest products of the grape, the silkworm, and the protoplasm. Soapy had confidence in himself from the lowest button of his vest upward. He was shaven, and his coat was decent and his neat black, ready-tied four-in-hand had been presented to him by a lady missionary on Thanksgiving Day. If he could reach a table in the restaurant unsuspected, success would be his. The portion of him that would show above the table would raise no doubt in the waiter's mind. A roasted mallard duck, thought Soapy, would be about the thing—with a bottle of Chablis,[8] and then Camembert,[9] a demitasse, and a cigar. One dollar for the cigar would be enough. The total would not be so high as to call forth any supreme manifestation of revenge from the café management; and yet the meal would leave him filled and happy for the journey to his winter refuge.

But as Soapy set foot inside the restaurant door the head waiter's eye fell upon his frayed trousers and decadent shoes. Strong and ready hands turned him about and conveyed him in silence and haste to the sidewalk and averted the ignoble fate of the menaced mallard.

Soapy turned off Broadway. It seemed that his route to the coveted Island was not to be an epicurean one. Some other way of entering limbo[10] must be thought of.

At a corner of Sixth Avenue electric lights and cunningly displayed wares behind plate glass made a shop window conspicuous. Soapy took a cobblestone and dashed it through the glass. People came running around the corner, a policeman in the lead. Soapy stood still, with his hands in his pockets, and smiled at the sight of brass buttons.

"Where's the man that done that?" inquired the officer, excitedly.

---

[8] *Chablis:* a white Burgundy wine
[9] *Camembert:* a rich, soft cheese
[10] *limbo:* prison

"Don't you figure out that I might have had something to do with it?" said Soapy, not without sarcasm, but friendly, as one greets good fortune.

The policeman's mind refused to accept Soapy even as a clue. Men who smash windows do not remain to parley with the law's minions. They take to their heels. The policeman saw a man halfway down the block running to catch a car. With drawn club he joined in the pursuit. Soapy, with disgust in his heart, loafed along, twice unsuccessful.

On the opposite side of the street was a restaurant of no great pretensions. It catered to large appetites and modest purses. Its crockery and atmosphere were thick; its soup and napery[11] thin. Into this place Soapy took his accusive shoes and telltale trousers without challenge. At a table he sat and consumed beefsteak, flapjacks, doughnuts, and pie. And then to the waiter he betrayed the fact that the minutest coin and himself were strangers.

"Now, get busy and call a cop," said Soapy. "And don't keep a gentleman waiting."

"No cop for youse," said the waiter, with a voice like butter cakes and an eye like the cherry in a Manhattan cocktail. "Hey, Con!"

Neatly upon his left ear on the callous pavement two waiters pitched Soapy. He arose joint by joint, as a carpenter's rule opens, and beat the dust from his clothes. Arrest seemed but a rosy dream. The Island seemed very far away. A policeman who stood before a drugstore two doors away laughed and walked down the street.

Five blocks Soapy traveled before his courage permitted him to woo capture again. This time the opportunity presented what he fatuously[12] termed to himself a "cinch." A young woman of a modest and pleasing guise was standing before a show window gazing with sprightly interest at its display of shaving mugs and inkstands, and two yards from the window a large policeman of severe demeanor leaned against a water plug.

[11] *napery:* table linen
[12] *fatuously:* foolishly

It was Soapy's design to assume the role of the despicable and execrated "masher." The refined and elegant appearance of his victim and the contiguity[13] of the conscientious cop encouraged him to believe that he would soon feel the pleasant official clutch upon his arm that would insure his winter quarters on the right little, tight little isle.

Soapy straightened the lady missionary's ready-made tie, dragged his shrinking cuffs into the open, set his hat at a killing cant,[14] and sidled toward the young woman. He made eyes at her, was taken with sudden coughs and "hems," smiled, smirked, and went brazenly through the impudent and contemptible litany of the "masher." With half an eye Soapy saw that the policeman was watching him fixedly. The young woman moved away a few steps, and again bestowed her absorbed attention upon the shaving mugs. Soapy followed, boldly stepping to her side, raised his hat, and said:

"Ah there, Bedelia! don't you want to come and play in my yard?"

The policeman was still looking. The persecuted young woman had but to beckon a finger and Soapy would be practically en route for his insular haven. Already he imagined he could feel the cozy warmth of the station house. The young woman faced him and, stretching out a hand, caught Soapy's coat sleeve.

"Sure, Mike," she said, joyfully, "if you'll blow me to a pail of suds. I'd have spoke to you sooner, but the cop was watching."

With the young woman playing the clinging ivy to his oak Soapy walked past the policeman overcome with gloom. He seemed doomed to liberty.

At the next corner he shook off his companion and ran. He halted in the district where by night are found the lightest streets, hearts, vows, and librettos. Women in furs and men in greatcoats moved gaily in the wintry air. A sudden fear seized Soapy that some dreadful enchantment had rendered

---

[13]*contiguity:* nearness
[14]*cant:* slant

him immune to arrest. The thought brought a little of panic upon it, and when he came upon another policeman lounging grandly in front of a transplendent theater he caught at the immediate straw of "disorderly conduct."

On the sidewalk Soapy began to yell drunken gibberish at the top of his harsh voice. He danced, howled, raved, and otherwise disturbed the welkin.[15]

The policeman twirled his club, turned his back to Soapy, and remarked to a citizen.

"'Tis one of them Yale lads celebratin' the goose egg they give to the Hartford College. Noisy; but no harm. We've instructions to lave them be."

Disconsolate, Soapy ceased his unavailing racket. Would never a policeman lay hands on him? In his fancy the Island seemed an unattainable Arcadia.[16] He buttoned his thin coat against the chilling wind. In a cigar store he saw a well-dressed man lighting a cigar at a swinging light. His silk umbrella he had set by the door on entering. Soapy stepped inside, secured the umbrella, and sauntered off with it slowly. The man at the cigar light followed hastily.

"My umbrella," he said sternly.

"Oh, is it?" sneered Soapy, adding insult to petit larceny.[17] "Well, why don't you call a policeman? I took it. Your umbrella! Why don't you call a cop? There stands one on the corner."

The umbrella owner slowed his steps. Soapy did likewise, with a presentiment that luck would again run against him. The policeman looked at the two curiously.

"Of course," said the umbrella man — "that is — well, you know how these mistakes occur — I — if it's your umbrella I hope you'll excuse me — I picked it up this morning in a restaurant — if you recognize it as yours, why — I hope you'll — "

"Of course it's mine," said Soapy, viciously.

The ex-umbrella man retreated. The policeman hurried to assist a tall blonde in an opera cloak across the street in

---

[15] *welkin:* the sky
[16] *Arcadia:* a remote part of ancient Greece; thus, a peaceful, remote place
[17] *petit larceny:* minor theft

front of a street car that was approaching two blocks away. Soapy walked eastward through a street damaged by improvements. He hurled the umbrella wrathfully into an excavation. He muttered against the men who wear helmets and carry clubs. Because he wanted to fall into their clutches, they seemed to regard him as a king who could do no wrong.

At length Soapy reached one of the avenues to the east where the glitter and turmoil was but faint. He set his face down this toward Madison Square, for the homing instinct survives even when the home is a park bench.

But on an unusually quiet corner Soapy came to a standstill. Here was an old church, quaint and rambling and gabled. Through one violet-stained window a soft light glowed, where, no doubt, the organist loitered over the keys, making sure of his mastery of the coming Sabbath anthem. For there drifted out to Soapy's ears sweet music that caught and held him transfixed against the convolutions of the iron fence.

The moon was above, lustrous and serene; vehicles and pedestrians were few; sparrows twittered sleepily in the eaves—for a little while the scene might have been a country churchyard. And the anthem that the organist played cemented Soapy to the iron fence, for he had known it well in the days when his life contained such things as mothers and roses and ambitions and friends and immaculate thoughts and collars.

The conjunction of Soapy's receptive state of mind and the influences about the old church wrought a sudden and wonderful change in his soul. He viewed with swift horror the pit into which he had tumbled, the degraded days, unworthy desires, dead hopes, wrecked faculties, and base motives that made up his existence.

And also in a moment his heart responded thrillingly to this novel mood. An instantaneous and strong impulse moved him to battle with his desperate fate. He would pull himself out of the mire; he would make a man of himself again; he would conquer the evil that had taken possession of him. There was time; he was comparatively young yet; he would resurrect his old eager ambitions and pursue them without faltering. Those solemn but sweet organ notes had set up a revolution in him. Tomorrow he would go into the roaring downtown district and find work. A fur importer had once offered him a place as driver. He would find him tomorrow and ask for the position. He would be somebody in the world. He would—

Soapy felt a hand laid on his arm. He looked quickly around into the broad face of a policeman.

"What are you doin' here?" asked the officer.

"Nothin'," said Soapy.

"Then come along," said the policeman.

"Three months on the Island," said the Magistrate in the Police Court the next morning.

FOR DISCUSSION

1. Why does Soapy prefer to be a "guest of the law" rather than accept the benefits of charitable institutions? What problem does he have to solve in order to achieve what his soul craves?

2. In what way is the conclusion of this story ironical? (See *irony*, page 515) As you point out Soapy's earlier attempts to bring about his arrest, tell why each failed and the effect of each failure both on Soapy and on the story as a whole.

3. O. Henry, unlike Poe, does not make a point of achieving a totality of effect, and in many stories he does not achieve it. What reasons can you give to support the opinion that this story does have such an effect—that it does, in fact, depend on it for the over-all humor? Note, for example, the tone which is established in the *exposition*. (See page 295ff.) Note, also, how the language contributes to that tone: "arose joint by joint, as a carpenter's rule opens"; "his accusive shoes and telltale trousers"; "playing the clinging ivy to his oak." Point out other examples and devices—including the scene outside the church—by which O. Henry achieves a particular "totality of effect." What word, or words, best describe that effect?

FOR COMPOSITION

1. In a short composition state whether you think that O. Henry is or is not, passing judgment on people like Soapy, on policemen, or on institutions of charity. Cite evidence from the story.
2. At the beginning of the story, Soapy considers three months confinement on Blackwell's Island as "the essence of things desirable." In two or three paragraphs, explain why he has a change of heart as he listens to the organ music—or thinks he has. Was he a believable character, at least while you were reading the story? Explain.

Henry James

Henry James believed that conversation was one of the most exalted of human activities. As a rule, the motives and feelings of his characters are revealed through what they say rather than through what they do. The relationships between his characters are usually perceived and communicated to the reader by a first-person narrator, as in the following story, or by some other curious and highly sensitive character whom James called the "central intelligence." To know and to understand a Jamesian character, such as Brooksmith, the reader must look patiently for clues which are sometimes so slight that, in a superficial reading, they may be missed entirely.

Brooksmith

We are scattered now, the friends of the late Mr. Oliver Offord; but whenever we chance to meet I think we are conscious of a certain esoteric[1] respect for each other. "Yes, you too have been in Arcadia,"[2] we seem not too grumpily to allow. When I pass the house in Mansfield Street I remember that Arcadia was there. I don't know who has it now, and don't want to know; it's enough to be so sure that if I should ring the bell there would be no such luck for me as that Brooksmith should open the door. Mr. Offord, the most agreeable, the most attaching of bachelors, was a retired diplomatist, living on his pension and on something of his own over and above; a good deal confined, by his infirmities, to his fireside and delighted to be found there any afternoon in the year, from five o'clock on, by such visitors as Brook-

---

[1] *esoteric:* understood only by a chosen few
[2] *Arcadia:* a remote part of Greece; thus a peaceful, remote place

smith allowed to come up. Brooksmith was his butler and his most intimate friend, to whom we all stood, or I should say sat, in the same relation in which the subject of the sovereign finds himself to the prime minister. By having been for years, in foreign lands, the most delightful Englishman any one had ever known, Mr. Offord had in my opinion rendered signal service to his country. But I suppose he had been too much liked—liked even by those who didn't like it—so that as people of that sort never get titles or dotations³ for the horrid things they've *not* done, his principal reward was simply that we went to see him.

Oh we went perpetually, and it was not our fault if he was not overwhelmed with this particular honor. Any visitor who came once came again; to come merely once was a slight nobody, I'm sure, had ever put upon him. His circle there- fore was essentially composed of habitués,⁴ who were habitués for each other as well as for him, as those of a happy salon should be. I remember vividly every element of the place, down to the intensely Londonish look of the grey opposite houses, in the gap of the white curtains of the high windows, and the exact spot where, on a particular afternoon, I put down my tea-cup for Brooksmith, lingering an instant, to gather it up as if he were plucking a flower. Mr. Offord's drawing-room was indeed Brooksmith's garden, his pruned and tended human parterre,⁵ and if we all flourished there and grew well in our places it was largely owing to his supervision.

Many persons have heard much, though most have doubt- less seen little, of the famous institution of the salon, and many are born to the depression of knowing that this finest flower of social life refuses to bloom where the English tongue is spoken. The explanation is usually that our women have not the skill to cultivate it—the art to direct through a smiling land, between suggestive shores, a sinuous⁶ stream of talk. My affectionate, my pious memory of Mr. Offord contradicts

---

³*dotations:* endowments
⁴*habitués:* frequenters, regular visitors (French)
⁵*parterre:* patterned garden
⁶*sinuous:* winding

this induction[7] only, I fear more insidiously to confirm it
The shallow and slightly smoked drawing-room in which he
spent so large a portion of the last years of his life certainly
deserved the distinguished name; but on the other hand it
couldn't be said at all to owe its stamp to any intervention,
throwing into relief the fact that there was no Mrs. Offord.
The dear man had indeed, at the most, been capable of one
of those sacrifices to which women are deemed peculiarly
apt: he had recognized — under the influence, in some degree,
it is true, of physical infirmity — that if you wish people to
find you at home you must manage not to be out. He had in
short accepted the truth which many dabblers in the social
art are slow to learn, that you must really, as they say, take a
line, and that the only way as yet discovered of being at home
is to stay at home. Finally his own fireside had become a
summary of his habits. Why should he ever have left it? —
since this would have been leaving what was notoriously
pleasantest in London, the compact charmed cluster (thinning
away indeed into casual couples) round the fine old last-
century chimney-piece which, with the exception of the
remarkable collection of miniatures, was the best thing the
place contained. Mr. Offord wasn't rich; he had nothing but
his pension and the use for life of the somewhat superannuated[8] house.

When I'm reminded by some opposed discomfort of the
present hour how perfectly we were all handled there, I ask
myself once more what had been the secret of such perfection.
One had taken it for granted at the time, for anything that is
supremely good produces more acceptance than surprise. I
felt we were all happy, but I didn't consider how our happiness was managed. And yet there were questions to be asked,
questions that strike me as singularly obvious now that there's
nobody to answer them. Mr. Offord had solved the insoluble;
he had, without feminine help — save in the sense that ladies
were dying to come to him and that he saved the lives of
several — established a salon; but I might have guessed that

[7] *induction:* generalization
[8] *superannuated:* out of date

there was a method in his madness, a law in his success. He hadn't hit it off by a mere fluke. There was an art in it all, and how was the art so hidden? Who indeed if it came to that was the occult artist? Launching this enquiry the other day I had already got hold of the tail of my reply. I was helped by the very wonder of some of the conditions that came back to me — those that used to seem as natural as sunshine in a fine climate.

How was it for instance that we never were a crowd, never either too many or too few, always the right people *with* the right people — there must really have been no wrong people at all — always coming and going, never sticking fast nor overstaying, yet never popping in or out with an indecorous familiarity? How was it that we all sat where we wanted and moved when we wanted and met whom we wanted and escaped whom we wanted; joining, according to the accident of inclination, the general circle or falling in with a single talker on a convenient sofa? Why were all the sofas so convenient, the accidents so happy, the talkers so ready, the listeners so willing, and subjects presented to you in a rotation as quickly foreordained as the courses at dinner? A dearth of topics would have been as unheard of as a lapse in the service. These speculations couldn't fail to lead me to the fundamental truth that Brooksmith had been somehow at the bottom of the mystery. If he hadn't established the salon at least he had carried it on. Brooksmith in short was the artist!

We felt this covertly at the time, without formulating it, and were conscious, as an ordered and prosperous community, of his evenhanded justice, all untainted with flunkeyism.[9] He had none of that vulgarity — his touch was infinitely fine. The delicacy of it was clear to me on the first occasion my eyes rested, as they were so often to rest again, on the domestic revealed, in the turbid light of the street, by the opening of the housedoor. I saw on the spot that though he had plenty of school he carried it without arrogance — he had remained articulate and human. *L'Ecole Anglaise*[10] Mr. Offord used laughingly to call him when, later on, it happened more than

---

[9] *flunkeyism:* cringing, flattering behavior
[10] *L'Ecole Anglaise:* the English school (French)

once that we had some conversation about him. But I remember accusing Mr. Offord of not doing him quite ideal justice. That he wasn't one of the giants of the school, however, was admitted by my old friend, who really understood him perfectly and was devoted to him, as I shall show; which doubtless poor Brooksmith had himself felt, to his cost, when his value in the market was originally determined. The utility of his class in general is estimated by the foot and the inch, and poor Brooksmith had only about five feet three to put into circulation. He acknowledged the inadequacy of this provision, and I'm sure was penetrated with the everlasting fitness of the relation between service and stature. If *he* had been Mr. Offord he certainly would have found Brooksmith wanting, and indeed the laxity of his employer on this score was one of many things he had had to condone and to which he had at last indulgently adapted himself.

I remember the old man's saying to me: "Oh my servants, if they can live with me a fortnight they can live with me for ever. But it's the first fortnight that tries 'em." It was in the first fortnight for instance that Brooksmith had had to learn that he was exposed to being addressed as "my dear fellow" and "my poor child." Strange and deep must such a probation have been to him, and he doubtless emerged from it tempered and purified. This was written to a certain extent in his appearance; in his spare brisk little person, in his cloistered[11] white face and extraordinarily polished hair, which told of responsibility, looked as if it were kept up to the same high standard as the plate; in his small clear anxious eyes, even in the permitted, though not exactly encouraged, tuft on his chin. "He thinks me rather mad, but I've broken him in, and now he likes the place, he likes the company," said the old man. I embraced this fully after I had become aware that Brooksmith's main characteristic was a deep and shy refinement, though I remember I was rather puzzled when, on another occasion, Mr. Offord remarked: "What he likes is the talk—mingling in the conversation." I was conscious I had never seen Brooksmith permit himself this freedom, but I

[11] *cloistered:* withdrawn

guessed in a moment that what Mr. Offord alluded to was a participation more intense than any speech could have represented—that of being perpetually present on a hundred legitimate pretexts, errands, necessities, and breathing the very atmosphere of criticism, the famous criticism of life. "Quite an education, sir, isn't it, sir?" he said to me one day at the foot of the stairs when he was letting me out; and I've always remembered the words and the tone as the first sign of the quickening drama of poor Brooksmith's fate. It was indeed an education, but to what was this sensitive young man of thirty-five, of the servile class, being educated?

Practically and inevitably, for the time, to companionship, to the perpetual, the even exaggerated reference and appeal of a person brought to dependence by his time of life and his infirmities and always addicted moreover—this was the exaggeration—to the art of giving you pleasure by letting you do things for him. There were certain things Mr. Offord was capable of pretending he liked you to do even when he didn't—this, I mean, if he thought you liked them. If it happened that you didn't either—which was rare, yet might be —of course there were cross-purposes; but Brooksmith was there to prevent their going very far. This was precisely the way he acted as moderator; he averted misunderstandings or cleared them up. He had been capable, strange as it may appear, of acquiring for this purpose an insight into the French tongue, which was often used at Mr. Offord's; for besides being habitual to most of the foreigners, and they were many, who haunted the place or arrived with letters—letters often requiring a little worried consideration, of which Brooksmith always had cognizance[12]—it had really become the primary language of the master of the house. I don't know if all the *malentendus*[13] were in French, but almost all the explanations were, and this didn't a bit prevent Brooksmith's following them. I know Mr. Offord used to read passages to him from Montaigne[14] and Saint-Simon,[15] for he read per-

[12] *cognizance:* awareness
[13] *malentendus:* misunderstandings (French)
[14] *Montaigne:* French sixteenth-century essayist
[15] *Saint-Simon:* French social philosopher of the nineteenth century

petually when alone—when *they* were alone, that is—and Brooksmith was always about. Perhaps you'll say no wonder Mr. Offord's butler regarded him as "rather mad." However, if I'm not sure what he thought about Montaigne I'm convinced he admired Saint-Simon. A certain feeling for letters must have rubbed off on him from the mere handling of his master's books, which he was always carrying to and fro and putting back in their places.

I often noticed that if an anecdote or a quotation, much more a lively discussion, was going forward, he would, if busy with the fire or the curtains, the lamp or the tea, find a pretext for remaining in the room till the point should be reached. If his purpose was to catch it you weren't discreet, you were in fact scarce human, to call him off, and I shall never forget a look, a hard stony stare—I caught it in its passage—which, one day when there were a good many people in the room, he fastened upon the footman who was helping him in the service and who, in an undertone, had asked him some irrelevant question. It was the only manifestation of harshness I ever observed on Brooksmith's part, and I at first wondered what was the matter. Then I became conscious that Mr. Offord was relating a very curious anecdote, never before perhaps made so public, and imparted to the narrator by an eyewitness of the fact, bearing on Lord Byron's life in Italy. Nothing would induce me to reproduce it here, but Brooksmith had been in danger of losing it. If I ever should venture to reproduce it I shall feel how much I lose in not having my fellow auditor to refer to.

The first day Mr. Offord's door was closed was therefore a dark date in contemporary history. It was raining hard and my umbrella was wet, but Brooksmith received it from me exactly as if this were a preliminary for going upstairs. I observed however that instead of putting it away he held it poised and trickling over the rug, and I then became aware that he was looking at me with deep acknowledging eyes— his air of universal responsibility. I immediately understood— there was scarce need of question and answer as they passed between us. When I took in that our good friend had given up as never before, though only for the occasion, I exclaimed dolefully: "What a difference it will make – and to how many people!"

"I shall be one of them, sir!" said Brooksmith; and that was the beginning of the end.

Mr. Offord came down again, but the spell was broken, the great sign being that the conversation was for the first time not directed. It wandered and stumbled, a little frightened, like a lost child – it had let go the nurse's hand. "The worst of it is that now we shall talk about my health – *c'est la fin de tout*,"[16] Mr. Offord said when he reappeared; and then I recognized what a note of change that would be – for he had never tolerated anything so provincial. We "ran" to each other's health as little as to the daily weather. The talk became ours, in a word – not his; and as ours, even when *he* talked, it could only be inferior. In this form it was a distress to Brooksmith, whose attention now wandered from it altogether: he had so much closer a vision of his master's intimate conditions than our superficialities represented. There were better hours, and he was more in and out of the room, but I could see he was conscious of the decline, almost of the collapse, of our great institution. He seemed to wish to take counsel with me about it, to feel responsible for its going on in some form or other. When for the second period – the first had lasted several days – he had to tell me that his employer didn't receive, I half-expected to hear him say after a moment "Do you think I ought to, sir, in his place?" – as he might have asked me, with the return of autumn, if I thought he had better light the drawing-room fire.

He had a resigned philosophic sense of what his guests – our guests, as I came to regard them in our colloquies[17] – would expect. His feeling was that he wouldn't absolutely have approved of himself as a substitute for Mr. Offord; but he was so saturated with the religion of habit that he would have made, for our friends, the necessary sacrifice to the divinity. He would take them on a little further and till they could look about them. I think I saw him also mentally con-

---

[16] *c'est . . . tout:* it's the end of everything (French)
[17] *colloquies:* conversations

fronted with the opportunity to deal—for once in his life—
with some of his own dumb preferences, his limitations of
sympathy, *weeding* a little in prospect and returning to a
purer tradition. It was not unknown to me that he considered
that toward the end of our host's career a certain laxity of
selection had crept in.

At last it came to be the case that we all found the closed
door more often than the open one; but even when it was
closed Brooksmith managed a crack for me to squeeze through;
so that practically I never turned away without having paid
a visit. The difference simply came to be that the visit was
to Brooksmith. It took place in the hall, at the familiar foot
of the stairs, and we didn't sit down, at least Brooksmith
didn't; moreover it was devoted wholly to one topic and always had the air of being already over—beginning, so to say,
at the end. But it was always interesting—it always gave me
something to think about. It's true that the subject of my
meditation was ever the same—ever "It's all very well, but
what *will* become of Brooksmith?" Even my private answer
to this question left me still unsatisfied. No doubt Mr. Offord
would provide for him, but *what* would he provide?—that
was the great point. He couldn't provide society; and society
had become a necessity of Brooksmith's nature. I must add
that he never showed a symptom of what I may call sordid
solicitude—anxiety on his own account. He was rather livid
and intensely grave, as befitted a man before whose eyes
the "shade of that which once was great" was passing away.
He had the solemnity of a person winding up, under depressing circumstances, a long-established and celebrated business; he was a kind of social executor or liquidator. But his
manner seemed to testify exclusively to the uncertainty of
our future. I couldn't in those days have afforded it—I lived
in two rooms in Jermyn Street and didn't "keep a man";
but even if my income had permitted I shouldn't have ventured to say to Brooksmith (emulating Mr. Offord) "My dear
fellow, I'll take you on." The whole tone of our intercourse
was so much more an implication that it was *I* who should
now want a lift. Indeed there was a tacit assurance in Brooksmith's whole attitude that he should have me on his mind.

One of the most assiduous[18] members of our circle had been
Lady Kenyon, and I remember his telling me one day that
her ladyship had in spite of her own infirmities, lately much
aggravated, been in person to inquire. In answer to this I
remarked that she would feel it more than any one. Brooksmith had a pause before saying in a certain tone—there's
no reproducing some of his tones—"I'll go and see her." I
went to see her myself and learned he had waited on her;
but when I said to her, in the form of a joke but with a core
of earnest, that when all was over some of us ought to com-
bine, to club together, and set Brooksmith up on his own
account, she replied a trifle disappointingly: "Do you mean
in a public-house?" I looked at her in a way that I think
Brooksmith himself would have approved and then I answered: "Yes, the Offord Arms," What I had meant of course
was that for the love of art itself we ought to look to it that
such a peculiar faculty and so much acquired experience
shouldn't be wasted. I really think that if we had caused a
few black-edged cards to be struck off and circulated—"Mr.
Brooksmith will continue to receive on the old premises
from four to seven; business carried on as usual during the
alterations"—the greater number of us would have rallied.

Several times he took me upstairs—always by his own
proposal—and our dear old friend, in bed (in a curious
flowered and brocaded casaque[19] which made him, especially
as his head was tied up in a handkerchief to match, look, to
my imagination, like the dying Voltaire) held for ten minutes
a sadly shrunken little salon. I felt indeed each time as if I
were attending the last coucher[20] of some social sovereign.
He was royally whimsical about his sufferings and not at all
concerned—quite as if the Constitution provided for the case
—about his successor. He glided over *our* sufferings charm-
ingly, and none of his jokes—it was a gallant abstention, some
of them would have been so easy—were at our expense. Now
and again, I confess, there was one at Brooksmith's, but so

---

[18] *assiduous:* constant
[19] *casaque:* a kind of blouse
[20] *coucher:* going-to-bed ceremony (French)

pathetically sociable as to make the excellent man look at
me in a way that seemed to say: "Do exchange a glance with
me, or I shan't be able to stand it." What he wasn't able to
stand was not what Mr. Offord said about him, but what he
wasn't able to say in return. His idea of conversation for
himself was giving you the convenience of speaking to him;
and when he went to "see" Lady Kenyon for instance it was
to carry her the tribute of his receptive silence. Where would
the speech of his betters have been if proper service had
been a manifestation of sound? In that case the fundamental
difference would have had to be shown by *their* dumbness,
and many of them, poor things, were dumb enough without
that provision. Brooksmith took an unfailing interest in the
preservation of the fundamental difference; it was the thing
he had most on his conscience.

What had become of it however when Mr. Offord passed
away like any inferior person—was relegated to eternal
stillness after the manner of a butler above-stairs? His aspect
on the event—for the several successive days—may be
imagined, and the multiplication by funereal observance
of the things he didn't say. When everything was over—it
was late the same day—I knocked at the door of the house
of mourning as I so often had done before. I could never call
on Mr. Offord again, but I had come literally to call on Brooksmith. I wanted to ask him if there was anything I could do
for him, tainted with vagueness as this enquiry could only be.
My presumptuous dream of taking him into my own service
had died away: my service wasn't worth his being taken into.
My offer could only be to help him to find another place,
and yet there was an indelicacy, as it were, in taking for
granted that his thoughts would immediately be fixed on
another. I had a hope that he would be able to give his life
a different form—though certainly not the form, the frequent
result of such bereavements, of his setting up a little shop.
That would have been dreadful; for I should have wished to
forward any enterprise he might embark in, yet how could I
have brought myself to go and pay him shillings and take
back coppers over a counter? My visit then was simply an
intended compliment. He took it as such, gratefully and with

all the tact in the world. He knew I really couldn't help him
and that I knew he knew I couldn't; but we discussed the
situation—with a good deal of elegant generality—at the
foot of the stairs, in the hall already dismantled, where I had
so often discussed other situations with him. The executors
were in possession, as was still more apparent when he made
me pass for a few minutes into the dining-room, where
various objects were muffled up for removal.

Two definite facts, however, he had to communicate; one
being that he was to leave the house for ever that night (servants, for some mysterious reason, seem always to depart by
night), and the other—he mentioned it only at the last and
with hesitation—that he was already aware his late master
had left him a legacy of eighty pounds. "I'm very glad," I said,
and Brooksmith was of the same mind: "It was so like him to
think of me." This was all that passed between us on the
subject, and I know nothing of his judgment of Mr. Offord's
memento. Eighty pounds are always eighty pounds, and no
one has ever left me an equal sum; but, all the same, for
Brooksmith, I was disappointed. I don't know what I had
expected, but it was almost a shock. Eighty pounds might
stock a small shop—a *very* small shop; but, I repeat, I couldn't
bear to think of that. I asked my friend if he had been able to
save a little, and he replied: "No, sir; I've had to do things."
I didn't enquire what things they might have been; they were
his own affair, and I took his word for them as assentingly as if
he had had the greatness of an ancient house to keep up;
especially as there was something in his manner that seemed
to convey a prospect of further sacrifice.

"I shall have to turn round a bit, sir—I shall have to look
about me," he said; and then he added indulgently, mag-
nanimously: "If you should happen to hear of anything for
me—"

I couldn't let him finish; this was, in its essence, too much
in the really grand manner. It would be a help to my getting
him off my mind to be able to pretend I *could* find the right
place, and that help he wished to give me, for it was doubtless
painful to him to see me in so false a position. I interposed
with a few words to the effect of how well aware I was that

wherever he should go, whatever he should do, he would miss our old friend terribly—miss him even more than I should, having been with him so much more. This led him to make the speech that has remained with me as the very text of the whole episode.

"Oh sir, it's sad for you, very sad indeed, and for a great many gentlemen and ladies; that it is, sir. But for me, sir, it is, if I may say so, still graver even than that: it's just the loss of something that was everything. For me, sir," he went on with rising tears, "he was just *all*, if you know what I mean, sir. You have others, sir, I dare say—not that I would have you understand me to speak of them as in any way tantamount.[21] But you have the pleasures of society, sir; if it's only in talking about him, sir, as I dare say you do freely—for all his blest memory has to fear from it—with gentlemen and ladies who have had the same honor. That's not for me, sir, and I've to keep my associations to myself. Mr. Offord was *my* society, and now, you see, I just haven't any. You go back to conversation, sir, after all, and I go back to my place," Brooksmith stammered, without exaggerated irony or dramatic bitterness, but with a flat unstudied veracity[22] and his hand on the knob of the street-door. He turned it to let me out and then he added: "I just go downstairs, sir, again, and I stay there."

"My poor child," I replied in my emotion, quite as Mr. Offord used to speak, "my dear fellow, leave it to me: *we'll* look after you, we'll all do something for you."

"Ah if you could give me some one *like* him! But there ain't two such in the world," Brooksmith said as we parted.

He had given me his address—the place where he would be to be heard of. For a long time I had no occasion to make use of the information: he proved on trial so very difficult a case. The people who knew him and had known Mr. Offord didn't want to take him, and yet I couldn't bear to try to thrust him among strangers—strangers to his past when not to his present. I spoke to many of our old friends about him and found them all governed by the odd mixture of feelings of which I myself was conscious—as well as disposed, further,

[21] *tantamount:* equal, equivalent
[22] *veracity:* honesty

to entertain a suspicion that he was "spoiled," with which I
then would have nothing to do. In plain terms a certain embar
rassment, a sensible awkwardness when they thought of it,
attached to the idea of using him as a menial: they had met
him so often in society. Many of them would have asked him,
and did ask him, or rather did ask me to ask him, to come and
see them; but a mere visiting-list was not what I wanted for
him. He was too short for people who were very particular;
nevertheless I heard of an opening in a diplomatic household
which led me to write him a note, though I was looking much
less for something grand than for something human. Five days
later I heard from him. The secretary's wife had decided,
after keeping him waiting till then, that she couldn't take a
servant out of a house in which there hadn't been a lady. The
note had a P.S.: "It's a good job there wasn't, sir, such a lady
as some."

A week later he came to see me and told me he was "suited,"
committed to some highly respectable people—they were
something quite immense in the City—who lived on the Bayswater side of the Park. "I dare say it will be rather poor, sir,"
he admitted; "but I've seen the fireworks, haven't I, sir?—it
can't be fireworks every night. After Mansfield Street there
ain't much choice." There was a certain amount, however, it
seemed; for the following year, calling one day on a country
cousin, a lady of a certain age who was spending a fortnight in
town with some friends of her own, a family unknown to me
and resident in Chester Square, the door of the house was
opened, to my surprise and gratification, by Brooksmith in
person. When I came out I had some conversation with him
from which I gathered that he had found the large City people
too dull for endurance, and I guessed, though he didn't say
it, that he had found them vulgar as well. I don't know what
judgment he would have passed on his actual patrons if my
relative hadn't been their friend; but in view of that
connection he abstained from comment.

None was necessary, however, for before the lady in question brought her visit to a close they honored me with an
invitation to dinner, which I accepted. There was a largeish
party on the occasion, but I confess I thought of Brooksmith

rather more than of the seated company. They required no depth of attention — they were all referable to usual irredeemable inevitable types. It was the world of cheerful commonplace and conscious gentility and prosperous density, a full-fed material insular world, a world of hideous florid plate and ponderous order and thin conversation. There wasn't a word said about Byron, or even about a minor bard then much in view. Nothing would have induced me to look at Brooksmith in the course of the repast, and I felt sure that not even my overturning the wine would have induced him to meet my eye. We were in intellectual sympathy — we felt, as regards each other, a degree of social responsibility. In short we had been in Arcadia together, and we had both come to *this*! No wonder we were ashamed to be confronted. When he had helped on my overcoat, as I was going away, we parted, for the first time since the earliest days of Mansfield Street, in silence. I thought he looked lean and wasted, and I guessed that his new place wasn't more "human" than his previous one. There was plenty of beef and beer, but there was no reciprocity. The question for him to have asked before accepting the position wouldn't have been "How many footmen are kept?" but "How much imagination?"

The next time I went to the house — I confess it wasn't very soon — I encountered his successor, a personage who evidently enjoyed the good fortune of never having quitted his natural level. Could any be higher? he seemed to ask — over the heads of three footmen and even of some visitors. He made me feel as if Brooksmith were dead; but I didn't dare to enquire — I couldn't have borne his "I haven't the least idea, sir." I dispatched a note to the address that worthy had given me after Mr. Offord's death, but I received no answer. Six months later however I was favored with a visit from an elderly dreary dingy person who introduced herself to me as Mr. Brooksmith's aunt and from whom I learned that he was out of place and out of health and had allowed her to come and say to me that if I could spare half an hour to look in at him he would take it as a rare honor.

I went the next day — his messenger had given me a new address — and found my friend lodged in a short sordid street in Marylebone, one of those corners of London that wear the last expression of sickly meanness. The room into which I was shown was above the small establishment of a dyer and cleaner who had inflated kid gloves and discoloured shawls in his shopfront. There was a great deal of grimy infant life up and down the place, and there was a hot moist smell within, as of the "boiling" of dirty linen. Brooksmith sat with a blanket over his legs at a clean little window where, from behind stiff bluish-white curtains, he could look across at a huckster's and a tinsmith's and a small greasy public-house. He had passed through an illness and was convales-cent, and his mother, as well as his aunt, was in attendance on him. I liked the nearer relative, who was bland and in-tensely humble, but I had my doubts of the remoter, whom I connected perhaps unjustly with the opposite public-house—she seemed somehow greasy with the same grease—and whose furtive eye followed every movement of my hand as if to see if it weren't going into my pocket. It didn't take this direction—I couldn't, unsolicited, put myself at that sort of ease with Brooksmith. Several times the door of the room opened and mysterious old women peeped in and shuf-fled back again. I don't know who they were; poor Brooksmith seemed encompassed with vague prying beery females.

He was vague himself, and evidently weak, and much embarrassed, and not an allusion was made between us to Mansfield Street. The vision of the salon of which he had been an ornament hovered before me however, by contrast, sufficiently. He assured me he was really getting better, and his mother remarked that he would come round if he could only get his spirits up. The aunt echoed this opinion, and I became more sure that in her own case she knew where to go for such a purpose. I'm afraid I was rather weak with my old friend, for I neglected the opportunity, so exception-ally good, to rebuke the levity[23] which had led him to throw up honorable positions—fine stiff steady berths in Bayswater and Belgravia, with morning prayers, as I knew, attached to one of them. Very likely his reasons had been profane and sentimental; he didn't want morning prayers, he wanted

[23] *levity:* fickleness

to be somebody's dear fellow; but I couldn't be the person to rebuke him. He shuffled these episodes out of sight—I saw he had no wish to discuss them. I noted further, strangely enough, that it would probably be a questionable pleasure for him to see me again: he doubted now even of my power to condone his aberrations.[24] He didn't wish to have to explain; and his behavior was likely in future to need explanation. When I bade him farewell he looked at me a moment with eyes that said everything: "How can I talk about those exquisite years in this place, before these people, with the old women poking their heads in? It was very good of you to come to see me; it wasn't my idea—*she* brought you. We've said everything: it's over; you'll lose all patience with me, and I'd rather you shouldn't see the rest." I sent him some money in a letter the next day, but I saw the rest only in the light of a barren sequel.

A whole year after my visit to him I became aware once, in dining out, that Brooksmith was one of the several servants who hovered behind our chairs. He hadn't opened the door of the house to me, nor had I recognized him in the array of retainers in the hall. This time I tried to catch his eye, but he never gave me a chance, and when he handed me a dish I could only be careful to thank him audibly. Indeed I partook of two *entrees* of which I had my doubts, subsequently converted into certainties, in order not to snub him. He looked well enough in health, but much older, and wore in an exceptionally marked degree the glazed and expressionless mask of the British domestic *de race*;[25] I saw with dismay that if I hadn't known him I should have taken him, on the showing of his countenance, for an extravagant illustration of irresponsive servile gloom. I said to myself that he had become a reactionary, gone over to the Philistines,[26] thrown himself into religion, the religion of his "place," like a foreign lady *sur le retour*.[27] I divined moreover that he was

[24] *aberrations:* deviations from normal behavior
[25] *de race:* as a class (French)
[26] *Philistines:* persons regarded as lacking in, and indifferent to, culture; named after the ancient enemies of the Israelites
[27] *sur le retour:* in the decline of life (French)

only engaged for the evening—he had become a mere waiter, had joined the band of the white-waistcoated who "go out." There was something pathetic in this fact—it was a terrible vulgarization of Brooksmith. It was the mercenary prose of butlerhood; he had given up the struggle for the poetry. If reciprocity was what he had missed where was the reciprocity now? Only in the bottoms of the wine-glasses and the five shillings—or whatever they get—clapped into his hand by the permanent man. However, I supposed he had taken up a precarious branch of his profession because it after all sent him less downstairs. His relations with London society were more superficial, but they were of course more various. As I went away on this occasion I looked out for him eagerly among the four or five attendants whose perpendicular persons, fluting the walls of London passages, are supposed to lubricate the process of departure; but he was not on duty. I asked one of the others if he were not in the house, and received the prompt answer: "Just left, sir. Anything I can do for you, sir?" I wanted to say "Please give him my kind regards"; but I abstained—I didn't want to compromise him; and I never came across him again.

Often and often, in dining out, I looked for him, sometimes accepting invitations on purpose to multiply the chances of my meeting him. But always in vain; so that as I met many other members of the casual class over and over again I at last adopted the theory that he always procured a list of expected guests beforehand and kept away from the banquets which he thus learned I was to grace. At last I gave up hope, and one day at the end of three years I received another visit from his aunt. She was drearier and dingier, almost squalid, and she was in great tribulation and want. Her sister, Mrs. Brooksmith, had been dead a year, and three months later her nephew had disappeared. He had always looked after her a bit—since her troubles; I never knew what her troubles had been—and now she hadn't so much as a petticoat to pawn. She had also a niece, to whom she had been everything before her troubles, but the niece had treated her most shameful. These were details; the great and romantic fact was Brooksmith's final evasion of his fate. He had gone out to wait one evening as usual, in a white waistcoat she had done up for him with her own hands—being due at a large party up Kensington way. But he had never come home again and had never arrived at the large party, nor at any party that anyone could make out. No trace of him had come to light—no gleam of the white waistcoat had pierced the obscurity of his doom. This news was a sharp shock to me, for I had ideas about his real destination. His aged relative had promptly, as she said, guessed the worst. Somehow and somewhere he had got out of the way altogether, and now I trust that, with characteristic deliberation, he is changing the plates of the immortal gods. As my depressing visitant also said, he never *had* got his spirits up. I was fortunately able to dismiss her with her own somewhat improved. But the dim ghost of poor Brooksmith is one of those that I see. He had indeed been spoiled.

FOR DISCUSSION

1. The narrator remarks that "the first day Mr. Offord's door was closed was . . . a dark date in contemporary history." What was so unusual about Mr. Offord's afternoon gatherings? Why were they so successful? Who, in the opinion of the narrator, was the hidden artist largely responsible? What evidence does the narrator give to support his conclusion?
2. Brooksmith is indeed an unusual servant. How is this borne out (a) by his appearance and manners and (b) by his inability to adjust to life after Mr. Offord's death? Do you agree with the narrator that "He had indeed been spoiled"? If so, in what ways?
3. What is Brooksmith's attitude toward social-class distinctions? Cite specific instances to show how it is revealed by what he says and does and by what others say about him.
4. What was the nature of the relationship between Brooksmith and Mr. Offord? How did Mr. Offord's guests feel about Brooksmith? In what ways were their feelings revealed? How would you describe the relationship between Brooksmith and the narrator? Discuss what each thought and felt about this relationship.
5. This story is told from the first-person point of view. Why do you think James chose this particular character as the narrator? What kind of person is he? Do you think the story would have been as interesting if told from the omniscient point of view? Would

you have felt as deeply involved in Brooksmith's problems and as sympathetic toward him? Discuss.

6. As in most of James's stories, character supersedes plot in importance. In this story, at what point does the main character (Brooksmith) face a problem which he has to solve? What is this problem? What circumstances make it particularly hard for him to solve it and for the narrator to help him?

7. Brooksmith's first attempt to solve his problem involves him in a conflict. Is it between two opposing forces within himself? Is it between him and some outside force; for example, another person, environment, social-class restrictions? Discuss the nature of the conflict and his attempts to resolve it. In your opinion, does he succeed, fail, or give up trying? Cite evidence from the story to support your answers.

8. Like Hawthorne, James is principally concerned with portraying what is hidden from the casual observer: the reality of the inner life. This inner life he carefully reveals, making certain the reader knows exactly the meaning he intends to convey. As a result, some of his sentences are unusually long and somewhat involved, and his story unfolds with deliberate slowness. Find a passage in the story which you consider a good example of James's style and tell why you think it is different from the style of other stories you have read.

FOR COMPOSITION

1. Brooksmith is *not* the usual man servant in appearance, in what he considers a satisfactory job, or in his attitude toward his employer and the people he entertains. In two or three paragraphs, point out specific ways in which Brooksmith is different, citing examples from the story.

2. In a short composition, develop the narrator's statement, "Mr. Offord's drawingroom was indeed Brooksmith's garden." Use details provided in the story.

Willa Cather

Miss Cather's writing depicts the goodness of life in the older, rural America of her girlhood. The following story of a good man in a good land is one of her clearest expressions of faith in the homely frontier virtues of simplicity and kindness. Anton Rosicky was a European, but more important than that, he was a new American who found happiness in a life close to the soil of the Middle West. From the author's point of view, he not only drew strength from the country but also contributed a strength of character that made the country truly great.

Neighbor Rosicky

I

When Doctor Burleigh told Neighbor Rosicky he had a bad heart, Rosicky protested.

"So? No, I guess my heart was always pretty good. I got a little asthma, maybe. Just a awful short breath when I was pitchin' hay last summer, dat's all."

"Well now, Rosicky, if you know more about it than I do, what did you come to me for? It's your heart that makes you short of breath, I tell you. You're sixty-five years old, and you've always worked hard, and your heart's tired. You've got to be careful from now on, and you can't do heavy work any more. You've got five boys at home to do it for you."

The old farmer looked up at the doctor with a gleam of amusement in his queer triangular-shaped eyes. His eyes were large and lively, but the lids were caught up in the middle in a curious way, so that they formed a triangle. He did not look like a sick man. His brown face was creased but not wrinkled, he had a ruddy color in his smooth-shaven cheeks and in his lips, under his long brown mustache. His hair was thin and ragged around his ears, but very little gray. His forehead, naturally high and crossed by deep parallel lines, now ran all the way up to his pointed crown. Rosicky's face had the habit of looking interested — suggested a contented disposition and a reflective quality that was gay rather than grave. This gave him a certain detachment, the easy manner of an onlooker and observer.

"Well, I guess you ain't got no pills fur a bad heart, Doctor Ed. I guess the only thing is fur me to git me a new one."

Doctor Burleigh swung round in his desk chair and frowned at the old farmer. "I think if I were you I'd take a little care of the old one, Rosicky."

Rosicky shrugged. "Maybe I don't know how. I expect you mean fur me not to drink my coffee no more."

"I wouldn't, in your place. But you'll do as you choose about that. I've never yet been able to separate a Bohemian from his coffee or pipe. I've quit trying. But the sure thing is you've got to cut out farm work. You can feed the stock and do chores about the barn, but you can't do anything in the fields that makes you short of breath."

"How about shelling corn?"

"Of course not!"

Rosicky considered with puckered brows.

"I can't make my heart go no longer'n it wants to, can I, Doctor Ed?"

"I think it's good for five or six years yet, maybe more, if you'll take the strain off it. Sit around the house and help Mary. If I had a good wife like yours, I'd want to stay around the house."

His patient chuckled. "It ain't no place fur a man. I don't like no old man hanging round the kitchen too much. An' my wife, she's a awful hard worker her own self."

"That's it; you can help her a little. My Lord, Rosicky, you are one of the few men I know who has a family he can get some comfort out of; happy dispositions, never quarrel among themselves, and they treat you right. I want to see you live a few years and enjoy them."

"Oh, they're good kids, all right," Rosicky assented.

The doctor wrote him a prescription and asked him how his oldest son, Rudolph, who had married in the spring, was getting on. Rudolph had struck out for himself, on rented land. "And how's Polly? I was afraid Mary mightn't like an American daughter-in-law, but it seems to be working out all right."

"Yes, she's a fine girl. Dat widder woman bring her daughters up very nice. Polly got lots of spunk, an' she got some style, too. Da's nice, for young folks to have some style." Rosicky inclined his head gallantly. His voice and his twinkly smile were an affectionate compliment to his daughter-in-law.

"It looks like a storm, and you'd better be getting home before it comes. In town in the car?" Doctor Burleigh rose.

"No, I'm in de wagon. When you got five boys, you ain't got much chance to ride round in de Ford. I ain't much for cars, noway."

"Well, it's a good road out to your place; but I don't want you bumping around in a wagon much. And never again on a hay-rake, remember!"

Rosicky placed the doctor's fee delicately behind the desk telephone, looking the other way, as if this were an absent-minded gesture. He put on his plush cap and his corduroy jacket with a sheepskin collar, and went out.

The doctor picked up his stethoscope and frowned at it as if he were seriously annoyed with the instrument. He wished it had been telling tales about some other man's heart, some old man who didn't look the doctor in the eye so knowingly, or hold out such a warm brown hand when he said good-by. Doctor Burleigh had been a poor boy in the country before he went away to medical school; he had known Rosicky almost ever since he could remember, and he had a deep affection for Mrs. Rosicky.

Only last winter he had had such a good breakfast at Rosicky's, and that when he needed it. He had been out all night on a long, hard confinement case at Tom Marshall's — a big rich farm where there was plenty of stock and plenty of feed and a great deal of expensive farm machinery of the newest model, and no comfort whatever. The woman had too many children and too much work, and she was no manager. When the baby was born at last, and handed over to the assisting neighbor woman, and the mother was properly attended to, Burleigh refused any breakfast in that slovenly house, and drove his buggy—the snow was too deep for a car—eight miles to Anton Rosicky's place. He didn't know another farmhouse where a man could get such a warm welcome, and such good strong coffee with rich cream. No wonder the old chap didn't want to give up his coffee!

He had driven in just when the boys had come back from the barn and were washing up for breakfast. The long table, covered with a bright oilcloth, was set out with dishes waiting for them, and the warm kitchen was full of the smell of coffee and hot biscuit and sausage. Five big handsome boys, running from twenty to twelve, all with what Burleigh called natural good manners—they hadn't a bit of the painful self-consciousness he himself had to struggle with when he was a lad. One ran to put his horse away, another helped him off with his fur coat and hung it up, and Josephine, the youngest child and only daughter, quickly set another place under her mother's direction.

With Mary, to feed creatures was the natural expression of affection—her chickens, the calves, her big hungry boys. It was a rare pleasure to feed a young man whom she seldom saw and of whom she was as proud as if he belonged to her. Some country housekeepers would have stopped to spread a white cloth over the oilcloth, to change the thick cups and plates for their best china, and the wooden-handled knives for plated ones. But not Mary.

"You must take us as you find us, Doctor Ed. I'd be glad to put out my good things for you if you was expected, but I'm glad to get you any way at all."

He knew she was glad—she threw back her head and spoke out as if she were announcing him to the whole prairie. Rosicky hadn't said anything at all; he merely smiled his twinkling smile, put some more coal on the fire, and went into his own room to pour the doctor a little drink in a medicine glass. When they were all seated, he watched his wife's face from his end of the table and spoke to her in Czech. Then, with the instinct of politeness which seldom failed him, he turned to the doctor and said slyly, "I was just tellin' her not to ask you no questions about Mrs. Marshall till you eat some breakfast. My wife, she's terrible fur to ask questions."

The boys laughed, and so did Mary. She watched the Doctor devour her biscuit and sausage, too much excited to eat anything herself. She drank her coffee and sat taking in everything about her visitor. She had known him when he was a poor country boy, and was boastfully proud of his success, always saying, "What do people go to Omaha for, to see a doctor, when we got the best one in the state right here?" If Mary liked people at all, she felt physical pleasure in the sight of them, personal exultation in any good fortune that came to them. Burleigh didn't know many women like that, but he knew she was like that.

When his hunger was satisfied, he did, of course, have to tell them about Mrs. Marshall, and he noticed what a friendly interest the boys took in the matter.

Rudolph, the oldest one (he was still living at home then), said, "The last time I was over there, she was lifting them big heavy milk cans, and I knew she oughtn't to be doing it."

"Yes, Rudolph told me about that when he come home, and I said it wasn't right," Mary put in warmly. "It was all right for me to do them things up to the last, for I was terrible strong, but that woman's weakly. And do you think she'll be able to nurse it, Ed?" She sometimes forgot to give him the title she was so proud of. "And to think of your being up all night and then not able to get a decent breakfast! I don't know what's the matter with such people."

"Why, Mother," said one of the boys, "if Doctor Ed had got breakfast there, we wouldn't have him here. So you ought to be glad."

"He knows I'm glad to have him, John, any time. But I'm sorry for that poor woman, how bad she'll feel the doctor had to go away in the cold without his breakfast."

"I wish I'd been in practice when these were getting born." The doctor looked down the row of close-clipped heads. "I missed some good breakfasts by not being."

The boys began to laugh at their mother because she flushed

so red, but she stood her ground and threw up her head. "I don't care, you wouldn't have got away from this house without breakfast. No doctor ever did. I'd have had something ready fixed that Anton could warm up for you."

The boys laughed harder than ever, and exclaimed at her: "I'll bet you would!" "She would, that!"

"Father, did you get breakfast for the doctor when we were born?"

"Yes, and he used to bring me my breakfast, too, mighty nice. I was always awful hungry!" Mary admitted with a guilty laugh.

While the boys were getting the doctor's horse, he went to the window to examine the house plants. "What do you do to your geraniums to keep them blooming all winter, Mary? I never pass this house that from the road I don't see your windows full of flowers."

She snapped off a dark red one, and a ruffled new green leaf, and put them in his buttonhole. "There, that looks better. You look too solemn for a young man, Ed. Why don't you git married? I'm worried about you. Settin' at breakfast, I looked at you real hard, and I seen you've got some gray hairs already."

"Oh, yes! They're coming. Maybe they'd come faster if I married."

"Don't talk so. You'll ruin your health eating at the hotel. I could send your wife a nice loaf of nut bread, if you only had one. I don't like to see a young man getting gray. I'll tell you something, Ed; you make some strong black tea and keep it handy in a bowl, and every morning just brush it into your hair, an' it'll keep the gray from showin' much. That's the way I do!"

Sometimes the Doctor heard the gossipers in the drugstore wondering why Rosicky didn't get on faster. He was industrious, and so were his boys, but they were rather free and easy, weren't pushers, and they didn't always show good judgment. They were comfortable, they were out of debt, but they didn't get much ahead. Maybe, Doctor Burleigh reflected, people as generous and warmhearted and affectionate as the Rosickys never got ahead much; maybe you couldn't enjoy your life and put it into the bank, too.

II

When Rosicky left Doctor Burleigh's office he went into the farm-implement store to light his pipe and put on his glasses and read over the list Mary had given him. Then he went into the general-merchandise place next door and stood about until the pretty girl with the plucked eyebrows, who always waited on him, was free. Those eyebrows, two thin India-ink strokes, amused him, because he remembered how they used to be. Rosicky always prolonged his shopping by a little joking; the girl knew the old fellow admired her, and she liked to chaff with him.

"Seems to me about every other week you buy ticking, Mr. Rosicky, and always the best quality," she remarked as she measured off the heavy bolt with red stripes.

"You see, my wife is always makin' goose-fedder pillows, an' de thin stuff don't hold in dem little down fedders."

"You must have lots of pillows at your house."

"Sure. She makes quilts of dem, too. We sleeps easy. Now she's makin' a fedder quilt for my son's wife. You know Polly, that married my Rudolph. How much my bill, Miss Pearl?"

"Eight eighty-five."

"Chust make it nine, and put in some candy for de women."

"As usual. I never did see a man buy so much candy for his wife. First thing you know, she'll be getting too fat."

"I'd like dat. I ain't much fur all dem slim women like what de style is now."

"That's one for me, I suppose, Mr. Bohunk!"[1] Pearl sniffed and elevated her India-ink strokes.

When Rosicky went out to his wagon, it was beginning to snow—the first snow of the season, and he was glad to see it. He rattled out of town and along the highway through a wonderfully rich stretch of country, the finest farms in the country. He admired this High Prairie, as it was called, and always liked to drive through it. His own place lay in a rougher territory, where there was some clay in the soil and it was not so productive. When he bought his land, he hadn't the money

---

[1] *bohunk:* (slang) a person from eastern Europe, usually Bohemian, Hungarian, or Czechoslovakian

to buy on High Prairie; so he told his boys, when they grumbled, that if their land hadn't some clay in it, they wouldn't own it at all. All the same, he enjoyed looking at these fine farms, as he enjoyed looking at a prize bull.

After he had gone eight miles, he came to the graveyard, which lay just at the edge of his own hay land. There he stopped his horses and sat still on his wagon seat, looking about at the snowfall. Over yonder on the hill he could see his own house, crouching low, with the clump of orchard behind and the windmill before, and all down the gentle hill slope the rows of pale gold cornstalks stood out against the white field. The snow was falling over the cornfield and the pasture and the hay land, steadily, with very little wind — a nice dry snow. The graveyard had only a light wire fence about it and was all overgrown with long red grass. The fine snow, settling into this red grass and upon the few little evergreens and the headstones, looked very pretty.

It was a nice graveyard, Rosicky reflected, sort of snug and homelike, not cramped or mournful — a big sweep all round it. A man could lie down in the long grass and see the complete arch of the sky over him, hear the wagons go by; in summer the mowing machine rattled right up to the wire fence. And it was so near home. Over there across the cornstalks his own roof and windmill looked so good to him that he promised himself to mind the doctor and take care of himself. He was awful fond of his place, he admitted. He wasn't anxious to leave it. And it was a comfort to think that he would never have to go farther than the edge of his own hayfield. The snow, falling over his barnyard and the graveyard, seemed to draw things together like. And they were all old neighbors in the graveyard, most of them friends; there was nothing to feel awkward or embarrassed about. Embarrassment was the most disagreeable feeling Rosicky knew. He didn't often have it — only with certain people whom he didn't understand at all.

Well, it was a nice snowstorm; a fine sight to see the snow falling so quietly and graciously over so much open country. On his cap and shoulders, on the horses' backs and manes, light, delicate, mysterious it fell; and with it a dry cool fragrance was released into the air. It meant rest for vegetation and men and beasts, for the ground itself; a season of long nights for sleep, leisurely breakfasts, peace by the fire. This and much more went through Rosicky's mind, but he merely told himself that winter was coming, clucked to his horses, and drove on.

When he reached home, John, the youngest boy, ran out to put away his team for him, and he met Mary coming up from the outside cellar with her apron full of carrots. They went into the house together. On the table, covered with oilcloth figured with clusters of blue grapes, a place was set, and he smelled hot coffeecake of some kind. Anton never lunched in town; he thought that extravagant, and anyhow he didn't like the food. So Mary always had something ready for him when he got home.

After he was settled in his chair, stirring his coffee in a big cup, Mary took out of the oven a pan of kolache[2] stuffed with apricots, examined them anxiously to see whether they had got too dry, put them beside his plate, and then sat down opposite him.

Rosicky asked her in Czech if she wasn't going to have any coffee.

She replied in English, as being somehow the right language for transacting business, "Now what did Doctor Ed say, Anton? You tell me just what."

"He said I was to tell you some compliments, but I forgot 'em." Rosicky's eyes twinkled.

"About you, I mean. What did he say about your asthma?"

"He says I ain't got no asthma." Rosicky took one of the little rolls in his broad brown fingers. The thickened nail of his right thumb told the story of his past.

"Well, what is the matter? And don't try to put me off."

"He don't say nothing much, only I'm a little older, and my heart ain't so good like it used to be."

Mary started and brushed her hair back from her temples with both hands as if she were a little out of her mind. From the way she glared, she might have been in a rage with him.

"He says there's something the matter with your heart? Doctor Ed says so?"

[2]*kolache:* a filled bun

"Now don't yell at me like I was a hog in the garden, Mary. You know I always did like to hear a woman talk soft. He didn't say anything de matter wid my heart, only it ain't so young like it used to be, an' he tell me not to pitch hay or run de corn sheller."

Mary wanted to jump up, but she sat still. She admired the way he never under any circumstances raised his voice or spoke roughly. He was city-bred, and she was country-bred; she often said she wanted her boys to have their papa's nice ways.

"You never have no pain there, do you? It's your breathing and your stomach that's been wrong. I wouldn't believe nobody but Doctor Ed about it. I guess I'll go see him myself. Didn't he give you no advice?"

"Chust to take it easy like, an' stay round de house dis winter. I guess you got some carpenter work for me to do. I kin make some new shelves for you, and I want dis long time to build a closet in de boys' room and make dem two little fellers keep dere clo'es hung up."

Rosicky drank his coffee from time to time, while he considered. His mustache was of the soft long variety and came down over his mouth like the teeth of a buggy rake over a bundle of hay. Each time he put down his cup, he ran his blue handkerchief over his lips. When he took a drink of water, he managed very neatly with the back of his hand.

Mary sat watching him intently, trying to find any change in his face. It is hard to see anyone who has become like your own body to you. Yes, his hair had got thin, and his high forehead had deep lines running from left to right. But his neck, always clean shaved except in the busiest seasons, was not loose or baggy. It was burned a dark reddish-brown, and there were deep creases in it, but it looked firm and full of blood. His cheeks had a good color. On either side of his mouth there was a halfmoon down the length of his cheek, not wrinkles, but two lines that had come there from his habitual expression. He was shorter and broader than when she married him; his back had grown broad and curved, a good deal like the shell of an old turtle, and his arms and legs were short.

He was fifteen years older than Mary, but she had hardly

ever thought about it before. He was her man, and the kind of man she liked. She was rough, and he was gentle—city-bred, as she always said. They had been shipmates on a rough voyage, and had stood by each other in trying times. Life had gone well with them because, at bottom, they had the same ideas about life. They agreed, without discussion, as to what was most important and what was secondary. They didn't often exchange opinions, even in Czech—it was as if they had thought the same thought together. A good deal had to be sacrificed and thrown overboard in a hard life like theirs, and they had never disagreed as to the things that could go. It had been a hard life, and a soft life, too. There wasn't anything brutal in the short, broad-backed man with the three-cornered eyes and the forehead that went on to the top of his skull. He was a city man, a gentle man, and though he had married a rough farm girl, he had never touched her without gentleness.

They had been at one accord not to hurry through life, not to be always skimping and saving. They saw their neighbors buy more land and feed more stock than they did, without discontent. Once when the creamery agent came to the Rosickys to persuade them to sell him their cream, he told them how much money the Fasslers, their nearest neighbors, had made on their cream last year.

"Yes," said Mary, "and look at them Fassler children! Pale, pinched little things, they look like skimmed milk. I'd rather put some color into my children's faces than put money into the bank."

The agent shrugged and turned to Anton.

"I guess we'll do like she says," said Rosicky.

III

Mary very soon got into town to see Doctor Ed, and then she had a talk with her boys and set a guard over Rosicky. Even John, the youngest, had his father on his mind. If Rosicky went to throw hay down from the loft, one of the boys ran up the ladder and took the fork from him. He sometimes complained that though he was getting to be an old man, he wasn't an old woman yet.

That winter he stayed in the house in the afternoons and carpentered, or sat in the chair between the window full of plants and the wooden bench where the two pails of drinking water stood. This spot was called "Father's corner," though it was not a corner at all. He had a shelf there, where he kept his Bohemian papers and his pipes and tobacco, and his shears and needles and thread and tailor's thimble. Having been a tailor in his youth, he couldn't bear to see a woman patching at his clothes, or at the boys'. He liked tailoring, and always patched all the overalls and jackets and work shirts. Occasionally he made over a pair of pants one of the older boys had outgrown, for the little fellow.

While he sewed, he let his mind run back over his life. He had a good deal to remember, really; life in three countries. The only part of his youth he didn't like to remember was the two years he had spent in London, in Cheapside, working for a German tailor who was wretchedly poor. Those days, when he was nearly always hungry, when his clothes were dropping off him for dirt, and the sound of a strange language kept him in continual bewilderment, had left a sore spot in his mind that wouldn't bear touching.

He was twenty when he landed at Castle Garden in New York, and he had a protector who got him work in a tailor shop in Vesey Street, down near the Washington Market. He looked upon that part of his life as very happy. He became a good workman, he was industrious, and his wages were increased from time to time. He minded his own business and envied nobody's good fortune. He went to night school and learned to read English. He often did overtime work and was well paid for it, but somehow he never saved anything. He couldn't refuse a loan to a friend, and he was self-indulgent. He liked a good dinner, and a little went for beer, a little for tobacco; a good deal went to the girls. He often stood through an opera on Saturday nights; he could get standing room for a dollar. Those were the great days of opera in New York, and it gave a fellow something to think about for the rest of the week. Rosicky had a quick ear, and a childish love of all the stage splendor; the scenery, the costumes, the ballet. He usually went with a chum, and after the performance they had beer and maybe some oysters somewhere. It was a fine life; for the first five years or so it satisfied him completely. He was never hungry or cold or dirty, and everything amused him: a fire, a dogfight, a parade, a storm, a ferry ride. He thought New York the finest, richest, friendliest city in the world.

Moreover, he had what he called a happy home life. Very near the tailor shop was a small furniture factory, where an old Austrian, Loeffler, employed a few skilled men and made unusual furniture, most of it to order, for the rich German housewives uptown. The top floor of Loeffler's five-story factory was a loft, where he kept his choice lumber and stored the odd pieces of furniture left on his hands. One of the young workmen he employed was a Czech, and he and Rosicky became fast friends. They persuaded Loeffler to let them have a sleeping room in one corner of the loft. They bought good beds and bedding and had their pick of the furniture kept up there. The loft was low-pitched, but light and airy, full of windows, and good-smelling by reason of the fine lumber put up there to season. Old Loeffler used to go down to the docks and buy wood from South America and the East from the sea captains. The young men were as foolish about their house as a bridal pair. Zichec, the young cabinetmaker, devised every sort of convenience, and Rosicky kept their clothes in order. At night and on Sundays, when the quiver of machinery underneath was still, it was the quietest place in the world, and on summer nights all the sea winds blew in. Zichec often practiced on his flute in the evening. They were both fond of music and went to the opera together. Rosicky thought he wanted to live like that forever.

But as the years passed, all alike, he began to get a little restless. When spring came round, he would begin to feel fretted, and he got to drinking. He was likely to drink too much of a Saturday night. On Sunday he was languid and heavy, getting over his spree. On Monday he plunged into work again. So he never had time to figure out what ailed him, though he knew something did. When the grass turned green in Park Place, and the lilac hedge at the back of Trinity churchyard put out its blossoms, he was tormented by a longing to run away. That was why he drank too much; to get a temporary illusion of freedom and wide horizons.

Rosicky, the old Rosicky, could remember as if it were yesterday the day when the young Rosicky found out what was the matter with him. It was on a Fourth of July afternoon, and he was sitting in Park Place in the sun. The lower part of New York was empty. Wall Street, Liberty Street, Broadway, all empty. So much stone and asphalt with nothing going on, so many empty windows. The emptiness was intense, like the stillness in a great factory when the machinery stops and the belts and bands cease running. It was too great a change, it took all the strength out of one. Those blank buildings, without the stream of life pouring through them, were like empty jails. It struck young Rosicky that this was the trouble with big cities; they built you in from the earth itself, cemented you away from any contact with the ground. You lived in an unnatural world, like the fish in an aquarium, who were probably much more comfortable than they ever were in the sea.

On that very day he began to think seriously about the articles he had read in the Bohemian papers, describing prosperous Czech farming communities in the West. He believed he would like to go out there as a farm hand; it was hardly possible that he could ever have land of his own. His people had always been workmen; his father and grandfather had worked in shops. His mother's parents had lived in the country, but they rented their farm and had a hard time to get along. Nobody in his family had ever owned any land—that belonged to a different station of life altogether. Anton's mother died when he was little, and he was sent into the country to her parents. He stayed with them until he was twelve, and formed those ties with the earth and the farm animals and growing things which are never made at all unless they are made early. After his grandfather died, he went back to live with his father and stepmother, but she was very hard on him, and his father helped him to get passage to London.

After that Fourth of July day in Park Place, the desire to return to the country never left him. To work on another man's farm would be all he asked; to see the sun rise and set and to plant things and watch them grow. He was a very simple man. He was like a tree that has not many roots, but one taproot that goes down deep. He subscribed for a Bohemian paper printed in Chicago, then for one printed in Omaha. His mind got farther and farther west. He began to save a little money to buy his liberty. When he was thirty-five, there was a great meeting in New York of Bohemian athletic societies, and Rosicky left the tailor shop and went home with the Omaha delegates to try his fortune in another part of the world.

IV

Perhaps the fact that his own youth was well over before he began to have a family was one reason why Rosicky was so fond of his boys. He had almost a grandfather's indulgence for them. He had never had to worry about any of them— except, just now, a little about Rudolph.

On Saturday night the boys always piled into the Ford, took little Josephine, and went to town to the moving-picture show. One Saturday morning they were talking at the break-fast table about starting early that evening, so that they would have an hour or so to see the Christmas things in the stores before the show began. Rosicky looked down the table.

"I hope you boys ain't disappointed, but I want you to let me have de car tonight. Maybe some of you can go in with de neighbors."

Their faces fell. They worked hard all week, and they were still like children. A new jackknife or a box of candy pleased the older ones as much as the little fellow.

"If you and Mother are going to town," Frank said, "maybe you could take a couple of us along with you, anyway."

"No, I want to take de car down to Rudolph's, and let him an' Polly go in to de show. She don't git into town enough, an' I'm afraid she's gettin' lonesome, an' he can't afford no car yet."

That settled it. The boys were a good deal dashed. Their father took another piece of apple cake and went on: "Maybe next Saturday night de two little fellers can go along wid dem."

"Oh, is Rudolph going to have the car every Saturday night?"

Rosicky did not reply at once; then he began to speak seriously: "Listen, boys; Polly ain't lookin' so good. I don't like to see nobody lookin' sad. It comes hard fur a town girl to be a farmer's wife. I don't want no trouble to start in Rudolph's family. When it starts, it ain't so easy to stop. An American girl don't git used to our ways all at once. I like to tell Polly she and Rudolph can have the car every Saturday night till after New Year's, if it's all right with you boys."

"Sure it's all right, Papa," Mary cut in.

"And it's good you thought about that. Town girls is used to more than country girls. I lay awake nights, scared she'll make Rudolph discontented with the farm."

The boys put as good a face on it as they could. They surely looked forward to their Saturday nights in town. That evening Rosicky drove the car the half mile down to Rudolph's new, bare little house.

Polly was in a short sleeved gingham dress, clearing away the supper dishes. She was a trim, slim little thing, with blue eyes and shingled yellow hair, and her eyebrows were reduced to a mere brush stroke like Miss Pearl's.

"Good evening, Mr. Rosicky. Rudolph's at the barn, I guess." She never called him father, or Mary mother. She was sensitive about having married a foreigner. She never in the world would have done it if Rudolph hadn't been such a handsome, persuasive fellow and such a gallant lover. He had graduated in her class in the high school in town, and their friendship began in the ninth grade.

Rosicky went in, though he wasn't exactly asked. "My boys ain't goin' to town tonight, an' I brought de car over fur you two to go in to de picture show."

Polly, carrying dishes to the sink, looked over her shoulder at him. "Thank you. But I'm late with my work tonight, and pretty tired. Maybe Rudolph would like to go in with you."

"Oh, I don't go to de shows! I'm too old-fashioned. You won't feel so tired after you ride in de air a ways. It's a nice clear night, an' it ain't cold. You go an' fix yourself up, Polly, an' I'll wash de dishes an' leave everything nice fur you."

Polly blushed and tossed her bob. "I couldn't let you do that, Mr. Rosicky. I wouldn't think of it."

Rosicky said nothing. He found a bib apron on a nail behind
the kitchen door. He slipped it over his head and then took
Polly by her two elbows and pushed her gently toward the
door of her own room. "I washed up de kitchen many times
for my wife, when de babies was sick or somethin'. You go
an' make yourself look nice. I like you to look prettier'n any
of dem town girls when you go in. De young folks must have
some fun, an' I'm goin' to look out fur you, Polly."

That kind, reassuring grip on her elbows, the old man's
funny bright eyes, made Polly want to drop her head on his
shoulder for a second. She restrained herself, but she lingered
in his grasp at the door of her room, murmuring tearfully:
"You always lived in the city when you were young, didn't
you? Don't you ever get lonesome out here?"

As she turned round to him, her hand fell naturally into his,
and he stood holding it and smiling into her face with his
peculiar, knowing, indulgent smile without a shadow of
reproach in it. "Dem big cities is all right fur de rich but dey
is terrible hard fur de poor."

"I don't know. Sometimes I think I'd like to take a chance.
You lived in New York, didn't you?"

"An' London, Da's bigger still. I learned my trade dere.
Here's Rudolph comin', you better hurry."

"Will you tell me about London some time?"

"Maybe. Only I ain't no talker, Polly. Run an' dress yourself up."

The bedroom door closed behind her, and Rudolph came in
from the outside, looking anxious. He had seen the car and
was sorry any of his family should come just then. Supper
hadn't been a very pleasant occasion. Halting in the doorway,
he saw his father in a kitchen apron, carrying dishes to the
sink. He flushed crimson and something flashed in his eye.
Rosicky held up a warning finger.

"I brought de car over fur you an' Polly to go to de picture
show, an' I made her let me finish here so you won't be late.
You go put on a clean shirt, quick!"

"But don't the boys want the car, Father?"

"No, tonight dey don't." Rosicky fumbled under his apron
and found his pants pocket. He took out a silver dollar and

said in a hurried whisper: "You go an' buy dat girl some ice cream an' candy tonight, like you was courtin'. She's awful good friends wid me."

Rudolph was very short of cash, but he took the money as if it hurt him. There had been a crop failure all over the county. He had more than once been sorry he'd married this year.

In a few minutes the young people came out, looking clean and a little stiff. Rosicky hurried them off, and then he took his own time with the dishes. He scoured the pots and pans and put away the milk and swept the kitchen. He put some coal in the stove and shut off the draughts, so the place would be warm for them when they got home late at night. Then he sat down and had a pipe and listened to the clock tick.

Generally speaking, marrying an American girl was certainly a risk. A Czech should marry a Czech. It was lucky that Polly was the daughter of a poor widow woman; Rudolph was proud, and if she had a prosperous family to throw up at him, they could never make it go. Polly was one of four sisters, and they all worked; one was bookkeeper in the bank, one taught music, and Polly and her younger sister had been clerks, like Miss Pearl. All four of them were musical, had pretty voices, and sang in the Methodist choir, which the eldest sister directed.

Polly missed the sociability of a store position. She missed the choir, and the company of her sisters. She didn't dislike housework, but she disliked so much of it. Rosicky was a little anxious about this pair. He was afraid Polly would grow so discontented that Rudy would quit the farm and take a factory job in Omaha. He had worked for a winter up there, two years ago, to get money to marry on. He had done very well, and they would always take him back at the stockyards. But to Rosicky that meant the end of everything for his son. To be a landless man was to be a wage earner, a slave all your life; to have nothing; to be nothing.

Rosicky thought he would come over and do a little carpentering for Polly after the New Year. He guessed she needed jollying. Rudolph was a serious sort of chap, serious in love and serious about his work.

Rosicky shook out his pipe and walked home across the
fields. Ahead of him the lamplight shone from his kitchen windows. Suppose he were still in a tailor shop on Vesey Street,
with a bunch of pale, narrow-chested sons working on machines, all coming home tired and sullen to eat supper in a
kitchen that was a parlor also; with another crowded, angry
family quarreling just across the dumbwaiter[3] shaft, and
squeaking pulleys at the windows where dirty washings hung
on dirty lines above a court full of old brooms and mops and
ash cans . . . .

He stopped by the windmill to look up at the frosty winter
stars and drew a long breath before he went inside. That
kitchen with the shining windows was dear to him; but the
sleeping fields and bright stars and the noble darkness were
dearer still.

V

On the day before Christmas the weather set in very cold;
no snow, but a bitter, biting wind that whistled and sang over
the flat land and lashed one's face like fine wires. There was
baking going on in the Rosicky kitchen all day, and Rosicky
sat inside, making over a coat that Albert had outgrown into
an overcoat for John. Mary had a big red geranium in bloom
for Christmas, and a row of Jerusalem cherry trees, full of
berries. It was the first year she had ever grown these; Doctor
Ed brought her the seeds from Omaha when he went to some
medical convention. They reminded Rosicky of plants he had
seen in England; and all afternoon, as he stitched, he sat
thinking about those two years in London, which his mind
usually shrank from even after all this while.

He was a lad of eighteen when he dropped down into London, with no money and no connections except the address of
a cousin who was supposed to be working at a confectioner's.
When he went to the pastry shop, however, he found that the
cousin had gone to America. Anton tramped the streets for
several days, sleeping in doorways and on the Embankment,[4]
until he was in utter despair. He knew no English, and the

---

[3]*dumbwaiter:* a small elevator
[4]*Embankment:* bank of the Thames River in London

sound of the strange language all about him confused him. By chance he met a poor German tailor who had learned his trade in Vienna, and could speak a little Czech. This tailor, Lifschnitz, kept a repair shop in a Cheapside basement, underneath a cobbler. He didn't much need an apprentice, but he was sorry for the boy and took him in for no wages but his keep and what he could pick up. The pickings were supposed to be coppers given you when you took work home to a customer. But most of the customers called for their clothes themselves, and the coppers that came Anton's way were very few. He had, however, a place to sleep. The tailor's family lived upstairs in three rooms; a kitchen, a bedroom, where Lifshnitz and his wife and five children slept, and a living room. Two corners of this living room were curtained off for lodgers; in one Rosicky slept on an old horsehair sofa, with a feather quilt to wrap himself in. The other corner was rented to a wretched, dirty boy, who was studying the violin. He actually practiced there. Rosicky was dirty, too. There was no way to be anything else. Mrs. Lifshnitz got the water she cooked and washed with from a pump in a brick court, four flights down. There were bugs in the place, and multitudes of fleas, though the poor woman did the best she could. Rosicky knew she often went empty to give another potato or a spoonful of dripping to the two hungry, sad-eyed boys who lodged with her. He used to think he would never get out of there, never get a clean shirt to his back again. What would he do, he wondered, when his clothes actually dropped to pieces and the worn cloth wouldn't hold patches any longer?

It was still early when the old farmer put aside his sewing and his recollections. The sky had been a dark gray all day, with not a gleam of sun, and the light failed at four o'clock. He went to shave and change his shirt while the turkey was roasting. Rudolph and Polly were coming over for supper.

After supper they sat round in the kitchen, and the younger boys were saying how sorry they were it hadn't snowed. Everybody was sorry. They wanted a deep snow that would lie long and keep the wheat warm, and leave the ground soaked when it melted.

"Yes, sir!" Rudolph broke out fiercely; "if we have another dry year like last year, there's going to be hard times in this country."

Rosicky filled his pipe. "You boys don't know what hard times is. You don't owe nobody, you got plenty to eat an' keep warm, an' plenty water to keep clean. When you got them, you can't have it very hard."

Rudolph frowned, opened and shut his big right hand, and dropped it clenched upon his knee. "I've got to have a good deal more than that, Father, or I'll quit this farming gamble. I can always make good wages railroading, or at the packing house, and be sure of my money."

"Maybe so," his father answered dryly.

Mary, who had just come in from the pantry and was wiping her hands on the roller towel, thought Rudy and his father were getting too serious. She brought her darning basket and sat down in the middle of the group.

"I ain't much afraid of hard times, Rudy," she said heartily. "We've had a plenty, but we've always come through. Your father wouldn't never take nothing very hard, not even hard times. I got a mind to tell you a story on him. Maybe you boys can't hardly remember the year we had that terrible hot wind, that burned everything up on the Fourth of July? All the corn an' the gardens. An' that was in the days when we didn't have alfalfa yet—I guess it wasn't invented.

"Well, that very day your father was out cultivatin' corn, and I was here in the kitchen makin' plum preserves. We had bushels of plums that year. I noticed it was terrible hot, but it's always hot in the kitchen when you're preservin', an' I was too busy with my plums to mind. Anton come in from the field about three o'clock, an' I asked him what was the matter.

"'Nothin',' he says, 'but it's pretty hot, an' I think I won't work no more today.' He stood round for a few minutes, an' then he says: 'Ain't you near through? I want you should git up a nice supper for us tonight. It's Fourth of July.'

"I told him to git along, that I was right in the middle of preservin', but the plums would taste good on hot biscuit. 'I'm goin' to have fried chicken, too,' he says, and he went off an' killed a couple. You three oldest boys was little fellers, playin'

around outside, real hot an' sweaty, an' your father took you to
the horse tank down by the windmill an' took off your clothes
an' put you in. Them two box elder trees was little then, but
they made shade over the tank. Then he took off all his own
clothes, an' got in with you. While he was playin' in the water
with you, the Methodist preacher drove into our place to say
how all the neighbors was goin' to meet at the schoolhouse
that night, to pray for rain. He drove right to the windmill, of
course, and there was your father and you three with no
clothes on. I was in the kitchen door, an' I had to laugh, for
the preacher acted like he ain't never seen a naked man before. He surely was embarrassed, an' your father couldn't git
to his clothes; they was all hangin' up on the windmill to let
the sweat dry out of 'em. So he laid in the tank where he was,
an' put one of you boys on top of him to cover him up a little,
an' talked to the preacher.

"When you got through playin' in the water, he put clean
clothes on you and a clean shirt on himself, an' by that time
I'd begun to get supper. He says: 'It's too hot in here to eat
comfortable. Let's have a picnic in the orchard. We'll eat our
supper behind the mulberry hedge, under them linden trees.'

"So he carried our supper down, an' a bottle of my wild-
grape wine, an' everything tasted good, I can tell you. The
wind got cooler as the sun was goin' down, and it turned out
pleasant, only I noticed how the leaves was curled up on the
linden trees. That made me think, an' I asked your father if
that hot wind all day hadn't been terrible hard on the gardens
an' the corn.

"'Corn,' he says, 'there ain't no corn.'

"'What you talkin' about?' I said. 'Ain't we got forty acres?'

"'We ain't got an ear,' he says, 'nor nobody else ain't got
none. All the corn in this country was cooked by three o'clock
today, like you'd roasted it in an oven.'

"'You mean you won't get no crop at all?' I asked him. I
couldn't believe it, after he'd worked so hard.

"'No crop this year,' he says. 'That's why we're havin' a
picnic. We might as well enjoy what we got.'

"An' that's how your father behaved, when all the neighbors
was so discouraged they couldn't look you in the face. An' we

enjoyed ourselves that year, poor as we was, an' our neighbors wasn't a bit better off for bein' miserable. Some of 'em grieved till they got poor digestions and couldn't relish what they did have."

The younger boys said they thought their father had the best of it. But Rudolph was thinking that, all the same, the neighbors had managed to get ahead more, in the fifteen years since that time. There must be something wrong about his father's way of doing things. He wished he knew what was going on in the back of Polly's mind. He knew she liked his father, but he knew, too, that she was afraid of something. When his mother sent over coffee-cake or prune tarts or a loaf of fresh bread, Polly seemed to regard them with a certain suspicion. When she observed to him that his brothers had nice manners, her tone implied that it was remarkable they should have. With his mother she was stiff and on her guard. Mary's hearty frankness and gusts of good humor irritated her. Polly was afraid of being unusual or conspicuous in any way, of being "ordinary," as she said!

When Mary had finished her story, Rosicky laid aside his pipe.

"You boys like me to tell you about some of dem hard times I been through in London?" Warmly encouraged, he sat rubbing his forehead along the deep creases. It was bothersome to tell a long story in English (he nearly always talked to the boys in Czech), but he wanted Polly to hear this one.

"Well, you know about dat tailor shop I worked in in London? I had one Christmas dere I ain't never forgot. Times was awful bad before Christmas; de boss ain't got much work, an' have it awful hard to pay his rent. It ain't so much fun, bein' poor in a big city like London, I'll say! All de windows is full of good t'ings to eat an' all de pushcarts in de streets is full, an' you smell 'em all de time, an' you ain't got no money — not a darn bit. I didn't mind de cold so much, though I didn't have no overcoat, chust a short jacket I'd outgrowed so it wouldn't meet on me, an' my hands was chapped raw. But I always had a good appetite, like you all know, an' de sight of dem pork pies in the windows was awful fur me!

"Day before Christmas was terrible foggy dat year, an' dat

fog gits into your bones and makes you all damp like. Mrs. Lifschnitz didn't give us nothin' but a little bread an' drippin' for supper, because she was savin' to try for to give us a good dinner on Christmas Day. After supper de boss say I can go an' enjoy myself, so I went into de streets to listen to de Christmas singers. Dey sing old songs an' make very nice music, an' I run round after dem a good ways, till I got awful hungry. I t'ink maybe if I go home, I can sleep till morning an' forgit my belly.

"I went into my corner real quiet, and roll up in my fedder quilt. But I ain't got my head down till I smell somet'ing good. Seem like it git stronger an' stronger, an' I can't git to sleep noway. I can't understand dat smell. Dere was a gas light in a hall across de court, dat always shine in at my window a little. I got up and look around. I got a little wooden box in my corner fur a stool, 'cause I ain't got no chair. I picks up dat box, and under it dere is a roast goose on a platter! I can't believe my eyes. I carry it to de window where de light comes in, an' touch it and smell it to find out, an' den I taste it to be sure. I say, I will eat chust one little bite of dat goose, so I can go to sleep, and tomorrow I won't eat none at all. But I tell you, boys, when I stop, one half of dat goose was gone!"

The narrator bowed his head, and the boys shouted. But little Josephine slipped behind his chair and kissed him on the neck beneath his ear.

"Poor little Papa, I don't want him to be hungry!"

"Da's long ago, child. I ain't never been hungry since I had your mudder to cook fur me."

"Go on and tell us the rest, please," said Polly.

"Well, when I come to realize what I done, of course, I felt terrible. I felt better in de stomach, but very bad in de heart. I set on my bed wid dat platter on my knees, an' it all come to me; how hard dat poor woman save to buy dat goose, and how she get some neighbor to cook it dat got more fire, an' how she put it in my corner to keep it away from dem hungry children. Dey was a old carpet hung up to shut my corner off, an' de children wasn't allowed to go in dere. An' I know she put it in my corner because she trust me more'n she did de violin boy. I can't stand it to face her after I spoil de Christmas. So

I put on my shoes and go out into de city. I tell myself I better throw myself in de river; but I guess I ain't dat kind of a boy.

"It was after twelve o'clock, an' terrible cold, an' I start out to walk about London all night. I walked along de river awhile, but dey was lots of drunks all along; men, and women too. I chust move along to keep away from de police. I git onto de Strand, an' den over to New Oxford Street, where dere was a big German restaurant on de ground floor, wid big windows all fixed up fine, an' I could see de people havin' parties inside. While I was lookin' in, two men and two ladies come out, laughin' and talkin' and feelin' happy about all dey been eatin' an' drinkin', and dey was speakin' Czech — not like de Austrians, but like de homefolks talk it.

"I guess I went crazy, an' I done what I ain't never done before nor since. I went right up to dem gay people an' begun to beg dem: 'Fellow countrymen, for God's sake give me money enough to buy a goose!'

"Dye laugh, of course, but de ladies speak awful kind to me, an' dey take me back into de restaurant and give me hot coffee and cakes, an' make me tell all about how I happened to come to London, an' what I was doin' dere. Dey take my name and where I work down on paper, an' both of dem ladies give me ten shillings.

"De big market at Covent Garden ain't very far away, an' by dat time it was open. I go dere an' buy a big goose an' some pork pies, an' potatoes and onions, an' cakes an' oranges fur de children — all I could carry! When I git home, everybody is still asleep. I pile all I bought on de kitchen table, an' go in an' lay down on my bed, an' I ain't waken up till I hear dat woman scream when she come out into her kitchen. My goodness, but she was surprise! She laugh an' cry at de same time, an' hug me and waken all de children. She ain't stop fur no breakfast; she git de Christmas dinner ready dat morning, and we all sit down an' eat all we can hold. I ain't never seen dat violin boy have all he can hold before.

"Two three days after dat, de two men come to hunt me up, an' dey ask my boss, and he give me a good report an' tell dem I was a steady boy all right. One of dem Bohemians was very smart an' run a Bohemian newspaper in New York, an'

de odder was a rich man, in de importing business, an' dey
been traveling togedder. Dey told me how t'ings was easier
in New York, an' offered to pay my passage when dey was
goin' home soon on a boat. My boss say to me: 'You go. You
ain't got no chance here, an' I like to see you git ahead, fur
you always been a good boy to my woman, and fur dat fine
Christmas dinner you give us all.' An' da's how I got to
New York."

That night when Rudolph and Polly, arm in arm, were running home across the fields with the bitter wind at their
backs, his heart leaped for joy when she said she thought they
might have his family come over for supper on New Year's
Eve. "Let's get up a nice supper, and not let your mother
help at all; make her be company for once."

"That would be lovely of you, Polly," he said humbly.
He was a very simple, modest boy, and he, too, felt vaguely
that Polly and her sisters were more experienced and worldly
than his people.

VI

The winter turned out badly for farmers. It was bitterly
cold, and after the first light snows before Christmas there
was no snow at all—and no rain. March was as bitter as
February. On those days when the wind fairly punished the
country, Rosicky sat by his window. In the fall he and the boys
had put in a big wheat planting, and now the seed had frozen
in the ground. All that land would have to be plowed up and
planted over again, planted in corn. It had happened before,
but he was younger then, and he never worried about what
had to be. He was sure of himself and of Mary; he knew they
could bear what they had to bear, that they would always pull
through somehow. But he was not so sure of the young ones,
and he felt troubled because Rudolph and Polly were having
such a hard start.

Sitting beside his flowering window while the panes rattled
and the wind blew in under the door, Rosicky gave himself to
reflection as he had not done since those Sundays in the loft
of the furniture factory in New York, long ago. Then he was

trying to find what he wanted in life for himself; now he was trying to find what he wanted for his boys, and why it was he so hungered to feel sure they would be here, working this very land, after he was gone.

They would have to work hard on the farm, and probably they would never do much more than make a living. But if he could think of them as staying here on the land, he wouldn't have to fear any great unkindness for them. Hardships, certainly; it was a hardship to have the wheat freeze in the ground when seed was so high; and to have to sell your stock because you had no feed. But there would be other years when everything came along right, and you caught up. And what you had was your own. You didn't have to choose between bosses and strikers, and go wrong either way. You didn't have to do with dishonest and cruel people. They were the only things in his experience he had found terrifying and horrible; the look in the eyes of a dishonest and crafty man, of a scheming and rapacious[5] woman.

In the country, if you had a mean neighbor, you could keep off his land and make him keep off yours. But in the city, all the foulness and misery and brutality of your neighbors was part of your life. The worst things he had come upon in his journey through the world were human—depraved and poisonous specimens of man. To this day he could recall certain terrible faces in the London streets. There were mean people everywhere, to be sure, even in their own country town here. But they weren't tempered, hardened, sharpened, like the treacherous people in cities who live by grinding or cheating or poisoning their fellow men. He had helped to bury two of his fellow workmen in the tailoring trade, and he was distrustful of the organized industries that see one out of the world in big cities. Here, if you were sick, you had Doctor Ed to look after you; and if you died, fat Mr. Haycock, the kindest man in the world, buried you.

It seemed to Rosicky that for good, honest boys like his, the worst they could do on the farm was better than the best they would be likely to do in the city. If he'd had a mean boy, now,

[5] *rapacious:* greedy

one who was crooked and sharp and tried to put anything over on his brothers, then town would be the place for him. But he had no such boy. As for Rudolph, the discontented one, he would give the shirt off his back to anyone who touched his heart. What Rosicky really hoped for his boys was that they could get through the world without ever knowing much about the cruelty of human beings. "Their mother and me ain't prepared them for that," he sometimes said to himself.

These thoughts brought him back to a grateful consideration of his own case. What an escape he had had, to be sure! He, too, in his time, had had to take money for repair work from the hand of a hungry child who let it go so wistfully; because it was money due his boss. And now, in all these years, he had never had to take a cent from anyone in bitter need—never had to look at the face of the woman become like a wolf's from struggle and famine. When he thought of these things, Rosicky would put on his cap and jacket and slip down to the barn and give his work horses a little extra oats, letting them eat it out of his hand in their slobbery fashion. It was his way of expressing what he felt, and made him chuckle with pleasure.

The spring came warm, with blue skies—but dry, dry as a bone. They boys began plowing up the wheat fields to plant them over in corn. Rosicky would stand at the fence corner and watch them, and the earth was so dry it blew up on clouds of brown dust that hid the horses and the sulky plow and the driver. It was a bad outlook.

The big alfalfa field that lay between the home place and Rudolph's came up green, but Rosicky was worried because during that open windy winter a great many Russian thistle plants had blown in there and lodged. He kept asking the boys to rake them out; he was afraid their seed would root and "take the alfalfa." Rudolph said that was nonsense. The boys were working so hard planting corn, their father felt he couldn't insist about the thistles, but he set great store by that big alfalfa field. It was a feed you could depend on— and there was some deeper reason, vague, but strong. The peculiar green of the clover woke early memories in old

Rosicky, went back to something in his childhood in the old world. When he was a little boy, he had played in fields of that strong blue-green color.

One morning, when Rudolph had gone to town in the car, leaving a work team idle in his barn, Rosicky went over to his son's place, put the horses to the buggy rake, and set about quietly raking up those thistles. He behaved with guilty caution, and rather enjoyed stealing a march on Doctor Ed, who was just then taking his first vacation in seven years of practice and was attending a clinic in Chicago. Rosicky got the thistles raked up, but did not stop to burn them. That would take some time, and his breath was pretty short, so he thought he had better get the horses back to the barn.

He got them into the barn and to their stalls, but the pain had come on so sharp in his chest that he didn't try to take the harness off. He started for the house, bending lower with every step. The cramp in his chest was shutting him up like a jackknife. When he reached the windmill, he swayed and caught at the ladder. He saw Polly coming down the hill, running with the swiftness of a slim greyhound. In a flash she had her shoulder under his armpit.

"Lean on me, Father, hard! Don't be afraid. We can get to the house all right."

Somehow they did, though Rosicky became blind with pain; he could keep on his legs, but he couldn't steer his course. The next thing he was conscious of was lying on Polly's bed, and Polly bending over him wringing out bath towels in hot water and putting them on his chest. She stopped only to throw coal into the stove, and she kept the teakettle and the black pot going. She put these hot applications on him for nearly an hour, she told him afterward, and all that time he was drawn up stiff and blue, with the sweat pouring off him.

As the pain gradually loosed its grip, the stiffness went out of his jaws, the black circles around his eyes disappeared, and a little of his natural color came back. When his daughter-in-law buttoned his shirt over his chest at last, he sighed.

"Da's fine, de way I feel now, Polly. It was a awful bad spell, an' I was so sorry it all come on you like it did."

Polly was flushed and excited. "Is the pain really gone? Can I leave you long enough to telephone over to your place?" Rosicky's eyelids fluttered. "Don't telephone, Polly. It ain't no use to scare my wife. It's nice and quiet here, an' if I ain't too much trouble to you, just let me lay still till I feel like myself. I ain't got no pain now. It's nice here."

Polly bent over him and wiped the moisture from his face. "Oh, I'm so glad it's over!" she broke out impulsively. "It just broke my heart to see you suffer so, Father."

Rosicky motioned her to sit down on the chair where the teakettle had been, and looked up at her with that lively affectionate gleam in his eyes. "You was awful good to me, I won't never forgit dat. I hate it to be sick on you like dis. Down at de barn I say to myself, dat young girl ain't had much experience in sickness, I don't want to scare her, an' maybe she's got a baby comin' or somet'ing."

Polly took his hand. He was looking at her so intently and affectionately and confidingly; his eyes seemed to caress her face, to regard it with pleasure. She frowned with her funny streaks of eyebrows, and then smiled back at him.

"I guess maybe there is something of that kind going to happen. But I haven't told anyone yet, not my mother or Rudolph. You'll be the first to know."

His hand pressed hers. She noticed that it was warm again. The twinkle in his yellow-brown eyes seemed to come nearer.

"I like mighty well to see dat little child, Polly," was all he said. Then he closed his eyes and lay half smiling. But Polly sat still, thinking hard. She had a sudden feeling that nobody in the world, not her mother, not Rudolph, or anyone, really loved her as much as old Rosicky did. It perplexed her. She sat frowning and trying to puzzle it out. It was as if Rosicky had a special gift for loving people, something that was like an ear for music or an eye for color. It was quiet, unobtrusive; it was merely there. You saw it in his eyes — perhaps that was why they were merry. You felt it in his hands, too. After he dropped off to sleep, she sat holding his warm, broad, flexible brown hand. She had never seen another in the least like it. She wondered if it wasn't a kind of gypsy hand, it was so alive and quick and light in its communications — very strange in a farmer. Nearly all the farmers she knew had huge lumps of fists, like mauls,[6] or they were knotty and bony and uncomfortable looking, with stiff fingers. But Rosicky's was like quicksilver, flexible, muscular, about the color of a pale cigar, with deep, deep creases across the palm. It wasn't nervous, it wasn't a stupid lump; it was a warm, brown, human hand, with some cleverness in it, a great deal of generosity, and something else which Polly could only call "gypsylike" — something nimble and lively and sure, in the way that animals are.

Polly remembered that hour long afterward; it had been like an awakening to her. It seemed to her that she had never learned so much about life from anything as from old Rosicky's hand. It brought her to herself; it communicated some direct and untranslatable message.

When she heard Rudolph coming in the car, she ran out to meet him.

"Oh, Rudy, your father's been awful sick! He raked up those thistles he's been worrying about, and afterward he could hardly get to the house. He suffered so I was afraid he was going to die."

Rudolph jumped to the ground. "Where is he now?"

"On the bed. He's asleep. I was terribly scared, because, you know, I'm so fond of your father." She slipped her arm through his and they went into the house. That afternoon they took Rosicky home and put him to bed, though he protested that he was quite well again.

The next morning he got up and dressed and sat down to breakfast with his family. He told Mary that his coffee tasted better than usual to him, and he warned the boys not to bear any tales to Doctor Ed when he got home. After breakfast he sat down by his window to do some patching and asked Mary to thread several needles for him before she went to feed her chickens — her eyes were better than his, and her hands steadier. He lit his pipe and took up John's overalls. Mary had been watching him anxiously all morning, and as she went out of the door with her bucket of scraps, she saw that he was smiling. He was thinking, indeed, about Polly, and how he

---

[6] *mauls:* heavy mallets

might never have known what a tender heart she had if he hadn't got sick over there. Girls nowadays didn't wear their heart on their sleeve. But now he knew Polly would make a fine woman after the foolishness wore off. Either a woman had that sweetness at her heart or she hadn't. You couldn't always tell by the look of them; but if they had that, everything came out right in the end.

After he had taken a few stitches, the cramp began in his chest, like yesterday. He put his pipe cautiously down on the window sill and bent over to ease the pull. No use—he had better try to get to his bed if he could. He rose and groped his way across the familiar floor, which was rising and falling like the deck of a ship. At the door he fell. When Mary came in, she found him lying there, and the moment she touched him she knew that he was gone.

Doctor Ed was away when Rosicky died, and for the first few weeks after he got home he was hard-driven. Every day he said to himself that he must get out to see that family that had lost their father. One soft, warm moonlight night in early summer he started for the farm. His mind was on other things, and not until his road ran by the graveyard did he realize that Rosicky wasn't over there on the hill where the red lamplight shown, but here, in the moonlight. He stopped his car, shut off the engine, and sat there for awhile.

A sudden hush had fallen on his soul. Everything here seemed strangely moving and significant, though signifying what, he did not know. Close by the wire fence stood Rosicky's mowing machine, where one of the boys had been cutting hay that afternoon; his own work horses had been going up and down there. The new-cut hay perfumed all the night air. The moonlight silvered the long, billowy grass that grew over the graves and hid the fence; the few little evergreens stood out black in it, like shadows in a pool. The sky was very blue and soft, the stars rather faint because the moon was full.

For the first time it struck Doctor Ed that this was really a beautiful graveyard. He thought of city cemeteries; acres of shrubbery and heavy stone, so arranged and lonely and unlike anything in the living world. Cities of the dead, indeed; cities of the forgotten, of the "put away." But this was open and free, this little square of long grass which the wind forever stirred. Nothing but the sky overhead, and the many-colored fields running on until they met that sky. The horses worked here in summer; the neighbors passed on their way to town; and over yonder, in the cornfield, Rosicky's own cattle would be eating fodder as winter came on. Nothing could be more undeathlike than this place; nothing could be more right for a man who had helped to do the work of great cities and had always longed for the open country and had got to it at last. Rosicky's life seemed to him complete and beautiful.

FOR DISCUSSION

1. The entire story is focused on Anton Rosicky. What kind of person is he? What do you consider his most outstanding trait; for example, patience, courage, kindliness, honesty? Show how this trait is revealed through what he says and, more important, through what he does.

2. What advantages for presenting Anton Rosicky can you see in having Dr. Burleigh play an important part at the beginning of the story and at the end?

3. What reason can you see for Miss Cather's shifting the action of the story from one place to another and from the present to the past and back again?

4. What part of the story is told by means of a flashback? (See page 515.) Why is the use of this device more effective than a recounting by the author of what had occurred prior to the time covered in the story?

5. The latter half of the story is dominated by Rosicky's concern over Rudolph and Polly. What experiences of his own helped him to have a sympathetic understanding of their situation? What definite steps does he take to help them through a crisis in their marriage?

6. Willa Cather takes pains to show that the values which Anton Rosicky cherished—and represented—are developed best in a rural society. She wrote that "big cities . . . built you in from the earth itself, cemented you away from any contact with the ground." What evidence does she draw from Anton's experience to support her contention that city life is less desirable than rural life? Give reasons why you do, or do not, agree with her.

7. Near the end of the story Anton is worried that he and his wife might not have prepared their sons adequately for the "cruelty of human beings." Do you think it is wrong for parents to shield their children from the sordid and cruel realities of life? As you state your opinion, show how it is borne out by the Rosicky family.

8. Why is Rudolph and Polly's marriage considered risky? Do you think that young married couples today face a similar problem? Give reasons to support your opinion.

9. How would you describe the tempo or pace of Willa Cather's story? Why is it appropriate to the story she had to tell?

10. What, if anything, can be done to preserve the kind of America Willa Cather cherished? Has it completely disappeared? Was she idealizing a way of life that was destined to be lost in the urbanization and industrialization of America? Discuss.

FOR COMPOSITION

1. "To be a landless man was to be a wage earner, a slave all your life; to have nothing; to be nothing." Write a composition defending or refuting this idea expressed by Anton Rosicky.

2. "Neighbor Rosicky" tells much about one marriage that has succeeded (Anton and Mary's) and about another that has not yet been firmly established (Rudolph and Polly's). In a short composition present what you think are the necessary ingredients for a successful marriage.

Sherwood Anderson

Sherwood Anderson was no stranger to the kind of industrial tyranny which he describes in this unusual piece of naturalistic writing. A successful manufacturer and salesman of roof paint, he walked out of his business in 1912 to become, at the age of thirty-six, one of America's leading writers of fiction. His reaction to the soulless efficiency of mass production was typical of many artists and intellectuals of that time, and of the twentieth century in general.

Lift Up Thine Eyes

It is a big assembling plant in a city of the Northwest. They assemble there the Bogel car. It is a car that sells in large numbers and at a low price. The parts are made in one great central plant and shipped to the places where they are to be assembled. There is little or no manufacturing done in the assembling plant itself. The parts come in. These great companies have learned to use the railroad cars for storage.

At the central plant everything is done on schedule. As soon as the parts are made they go into railroad cars. They are on their way to the assembling plants scattered all over the United States and they arrive on schedule.

The assembling plant assembles cars for a certain territory. A careful survey has been made. This territory can afford to buy so and so many cars per day.

"But suppose the people do not want the cars?"

"What has that to do with it?"

People, American people, no longer buy cars. They do not buy newspapers, books, foods, pictures, clothes. Things are sold to people now. If a territory can take so and so many Bogel cars, find men who can make them take the cars. That is the way things are done now.

In the assembling plant everyone works "on the belt." This is a big steel conveyor, a kind of moving sidewalk, waist-high. It is a great river running down through the plant. Various tributary streams come into the main stream, the main belt. They bring tires, they bring headlights, horns, bumpers for cars. They flow into the main stream. The main stream has its source at the freight cars, where the parts are unloaded, and it flows out to the other end of the factory and into other freight cars.

The finished automobiles go into the freight cars at the delivery end of the belt. The assembly plant is a place of peculiar tension. You feel it when you go in. It never lets up. Men here work always on tension. There is no let-up to the tension. If you can't stand it, get out.

It is the belt. The belt is boss. It moves always forward. Now the chassis goes on the belt. A hoist lifts it up and places it just so. There is a man at each corner. The chassis is deposited on the belt and it begins to move. Not too rapidly. There are things to be done.

How nicely everything is calculated. Scientific men have done this. They have watched men work. They have stood looking, watch in hand. There is care taken about everything. Look up. Lift up thine eyes. Hoists are bringing engines, bodies, wheels, fenders. These come out of side streams flowing into the main stream. They move at a pace very nicely calculated. They will arrive at the main stream at just a certain place at just a certain time.

In this shop there is no question of wages to be wrangled about. The men work but eight hours a day and are well paid. They are, almost without exception, young, strong men. It is, however, possible that eight hours a day in this place may be much longer than twelve or even sixteen hours in the old carelessly run plants.

They can get better pay here than at any other shop in town. Although I am a man wanting a good many minor comforts in life, I could live well enough on the wages made by the workers in this place. Sixty cents an hour to begin and then, after a probation period of sixty, if I can stand the pace, seventy cents or more.

To stand the pace is the real test. Special skill is not required. It is all perfectly timed, perfectly calculated. If you are a body upholsterer, so many tacks driven per second. Not too many. If a man hurries too much too many tacks drop on the floor. If a man gets too hurried he is not efficient. Let an expert take a month, two months, to find out just how many tacks the average good man can drive per second.

There must be a certain standard maintained in the finished product. Remember that. It must pass inspection after inspection.

Do not crowd too hard.

Crowd all you can.

Keep crowding.

There are fifteen, twenty, thirty, perhaps fifty such assembling plants, all over the country, each serving its own section. Wires pass back and forth daily. The central office—from which all the parts come—at Jointville is the nerve center. Wires come in and go out of Jointville. In so and so many hours Williamsburg, with so and so many men, produced so and so many cars.

Now Burkesville is ahead. It stays ahead. What is up at Burkesville? An expert flies there.

The man at Burkesville was a major in the army. He is the manager there. He is a cold, rather severe, rather formal man. He has found out something. He is a real Bogel man, an ideal Bogel man. There is no foolishness about him. He watches the belt. He does not say foolishly to himself, "I am the boss here." He knows the belt is boss.

He says there is a lot of foolishness talked about the belt. The experts are too expert, he says. He has found out that the belt can be made to move just a little faster than the experts say. He has tried it. He knows. Go and look for yourself. There are the men out there on the belt, swarming along the belt, each in his place. They are all right, aren't they?

Can you see anything wrong?

Just a trifle more speed in every man. Shove the pace up

just a little, not much. With the same number of men, in the same number of hours, six more cars a day.

That's the way a major gets to be a colonel, a colonel a general. Watch that fellow at Burkesville, the man with the military stride, the cold steady voice. He'll go far.

Everything is nicely, perfectly calculated in all the Bogel assembling plants. There are white marks on the floor everywhere. Everything is immaculately clean. No one smokes, no one chews tobacco, no one spits. There are white bands on the cement floor along which the men walk. As they work, sweepers follow them. Tacks dropped on the floor are at once swept up. You can tell by the sweepings in a plant where there is too much waste, too much carelessness. Sweep everything carefully and frequently. Weigh the sweepings. Have an expert examine the sweepings. Report to Jointville.

Jointville says: "Too many upholsterers' tacks wasted in the plant at Port Smith. Belleville produced one hundred and eleven cars a day, with seven hundred and forty-nine men, wasting only nine hundred and six tacks."

It is a good thing to go through the plant now and then, select one man from all the others, give him a new and bigger job, just like that, offhand. If he doesn't make good, fire him.

It is a good thing to go through the plant occasionally, pick out some man, working apparently just as the others are, fire him.

If he asks why, just say to him, "You know."

He'll know why all right. He'll imagine why.

The thing is to build up Jointville. This country needs a religion. You have got to build up the sense of a mysterious central thing, a thing working outside your knowledge.

Let the notion grow and grow that there is something superhuman at the core of all this.

Lift up thine eyes, lift up thine eyes.

The central office reaches down into your secret thoughts. It knows, it knows.

Jointville knows.

Do not ask questions of Jointville. Keep up the pace.

Get the cars out.

Get the cars out.

Get the cars out.

The pace can be accelerated a little this year. The men have all got tuned into the old pace now.

Step it up a little, just a little.

They have got a special policeman in all the Bogel assembling plants. They have got a special doctor there. A man hurts his finger a little. It bleeds a little, a mere scratch. The doctor reaches down for him. The finger is fixed. Jointville wants no blood poisonings, no infections.

The doctor puts men who want jobs through a physical examination, as in the army. Try his nerve reactions. We want only the best men here, the youngest, the fastest.

Why not?

We pay the best wages, don't we?

The policeman in the plant has a special job. That's queer. It is like this. Now and then the big boss passes through. He selects a man off the belt.

"You're fired."

"Why?"

"You know."

Now and then a man goes off his nut. He goes fantoed. He howls and shouts. He grabs up a hammer.

A stream of crazy profanity comes from his lips.

There is Jointville. That is the central thing. That controls the belt.

The belt controls me.

It moves.

It moves.

It moves.

I've tried to keep up.

I tell you I have been keeping up.

Jointville is God.

Jointville controls the belt.

The belt is God.

God has rejected me.

You're fired.

Sometimes a man, fired like that, goes nutty. He gets dangerous. A strong policeman on hand knocks him down, takes him out.

You walk within certain definite white lines.

It is calculated that a man, rubbing automobile bodies with pumice, makes thirty thousand and twenty-one arm strokes per day. The difference between thirty thousand and twenty-one and twenty-eight thousand and four will tell a vital story of profits or loss at Jointville.

Do you think things are settled at Jointville, or at the assembling plants of the Bogel car scattered all over America? Do you think men know how fast the belt can be made to move, what the ultimate, the final pace will be, can be?

Certainly not.

There are experts studying the nerves of men, the movements of men. They are watching, watching. Calculations are always going on. The thing is to produce goods and more goods at less cost. Keep the standard up. Increase the pace a little.

Stop waste.

Calculate everything.

A man walking to and from his work between white lines saves steps. There is a tremendous science of lost motion not perfectly calculated yet.

More goods at less cost.

Increase the pace.

Keep up standards.

It is so you advance civilization.

In the Bogel assembling plants, as at Jointville itself, there isn't any laughter. No one stops work to play. No one fools around or throws things, as they used to do in the old factories. That is why Bogel is able to put the old-fashioned factories, one by one, out of business.

It is all a matter of calculation. You feel it when you go in. You feel rigid lines. You feel movement. You feel a strange tension in the air. There is a quiet terrible intensity.

The belt moves. It keeps moving. The day I was there a number of young boys had come in. They had been sent by a Bogel car dealer, away back somewhere in the country. They had driven in during the night and were to drive Bogel cars back over country roads to some dealer. A good many Bogel cars go out to dealers from the assembling plants, driven out by boys like that.

Such boys, driving all night, fooling along the road, getting no sleep.

They have a place for them to wait for the cars in the Bogel assembling plants. You have been at dog shows and have seen how prize dogs are exhibited, each in his nice clean cage. They have nice clean cages like that for country boys who drive in to Bogel assembling plants to get cars:

The boys come in. There is a place to lie down in there. It is clean. After the boy goes into his cage a gate is closed. He is fastened in.

If a country boy, sleepy like that, waiting for his car, wandered about in a plant he might get hurt.

There might be damage suits, all sorts of things.

Better to calculate everything. Be careful. Be exact.

Jointville thought of that. Jointville thinks of everything. It is the center of power, the new mystery.

Every year in America Jointville comes nearer and nearer being the new center. Men nowadays do not look to Washington. They look to Jointville.

Lift up thine eyes, lift up thine eyes.

FOR DISCUSSION

1. Which evils in modern industry is Anderson attacking?
2. What specific criticisms are implicit in his account of a "scientifically calculated" system of production? Can you defend this system? Has it been "humanized" in recent years?
3. What is unconventional about the form in which this work was written?
4. "Lift up thine eyes," which Anderson uses as a kind of refrain, is suggestive of the Old Testament. (See Psalms 121 and 123.) What effect does he achieve by this recurrent phrase?
5. Is it true that the mass production of material goods has become the religion of the American people, or has Anderson exaggerated? Defend your position with logical arguments.

FOR COMPOSITION

1. Write an essay on a recent example of automation in American life. What have been its effects on people? How do you feel about these effects? (Use *The Reader's Guide to Periodical Literature* to locate information on this subject in magazines.)
2. In a short composition, point out several ways in which mechanization has affected education and present what you consider to be the advantages and disadvantages. Among other things, you might consider objective testing, machine-scoring, televised lessons, and teaching-machines.

F. Scott Fitzgerald

F. Scott Fitzgerald's literary re-creations of the Jazz Age made him famous and wealthy at the age of twenty-five. His own life of glittering success disintegrating into later tragedy might easily have been the fate of one of his characters. The following story is one of several which he wrote about Josephine Perry, a typical flapper of the 1920's. After several flirtations in her native Chicago, Josephine has come East, where she is trying to find her place in a new collegiate setting at Yale.

A Woman with a Past

I

Driving slowly through New Haven, two of the young girls became alert. Josephine and Lillian darted soft frank glances into strolling groups of three or four undergraduates, into larger groups on corners, which swung about as one man to stare at their receding heads. Believing that they recognized an acquaintance in a solitary loiterer, they waved wildly, whereupon the youth's mouth fell open, and as they turned the next corner he made a dazed dilatory[1] gesture with his hand. They laughed. "We'll send him a post card when we get back to school tonight, to see if it really was him."

Adele Craw, sitting on one of the little seats, kept on talking to Miss Chambers, the chaperone. Glancing sideways at her, Lillian winked at Josephine without batting an eye, but Josephine had gone into a reverie.[2]

[1] *dilatory:* slow, late
[2] *reverie:* daydream

This was New Haven—city of her adolescent dreams, of glittering proms where she would move on air among men as intangible as the tunes they danced to. City sacred as Mecca, shining as Paris, hidden as Timbuktu. Twice a year the life-blood of Chicago, her home, flowed into it, and twice a year flowed back, bringing Christmas or bringing summer. Bingo, bingo, bingo, that's the lingo; love of mine, I pine for one of your glances; the darling boy on the left there; underneath the stars I wait.

Seeing it for the first time, she found herself surprisingly unmoved—the men they passed seemed young and rather bored with the possibilities of the day, glad of anything to stare at; seemed undynamic and purposeless against the background of bare elms, lakes of dirty snow and buildings crowded together under the February sky. A wisp of hope, a well-turned-out derby-crowned man, hurrying with stick and suitcase toward the station, caught her attention, but his reciprocal glance was too startled, too ingenuous.[3] Josephine wondered at the extent of her own disillusionment.

She was exactly seventeen and she was blasé.[4] Already she had been a sensation and a scandal; she had driven mature men to a state of disequilibrium; she had, it was said, killed her grandfather, but as he was over eighty at the time perhaps he just died. Here and there in the Middle West were discouraged little spots which upon inspection turned out to be the youths who had once looked full into her green and wistful eyes. But her love affair of last summer had ruined her faith in the all-sufficiency of men. She had grown bored with the waning September days—and it seemed as though it had happened once too often. Christmas with its provocative shortness, its traveling glee clubs, had brought no one new. There remained to her only a persistent, a physical hope—hope in her stomach that there was someone whom she would love more than he loved her.

They stopped at a sporting-goods store and Adele Craw, a pretty girl with clear honorable eyes and piano legs, purchased the sporting equipment which was the reason for their

[3] *ingenuous:* innocent
[4] *blasé:* satiated and bored

trip—they were the spring hockey committee for the school. Adele was in addition the president of the senior class and the school's ideal girl. She had lately seen a change for the better in Josephine Perry—rather as an honest citizen might guilelessly[5] approve a peculator[6] retired on his profits. On the other hand, Adele was simply incomprehensible to Josephine —admirable, without doubt, but a member of another species. Yet with the charming adaptability that she had hitherto reserved for men, Josephine was trying hard not to disillusion her, trying to be honestly interested in the small, neat, organized politics of the school.

Two men who had stood with their backs to them at another counter turned to leave the store, when they caught sight of Miss Chambers and Adele. Immediately they came forward. The one who spoke to Miss Chambers was thin and rigid of face. Josephine recognized him as Miss Brereton's nephew, a student at New Haven, who had spent several week-ends with his aunt at the school. The other man Josephine had never seen before. He was tall and broad, with blond curly hair and an open expression in which strength of purpose and a nice consideration were pleasantly mingled. It was not the sort of face that generally appealed to Josephine. The eyes were obviously without a secret, without a sidewise gambol,[7] without a desperate flicker to show that they had a life of their own apart from the mouth's speech. The mouth itself was large and masculine; its smile was an act of kindness and control. It was rather with curiosity as to the sort of man who would be attentive to Adele Craw that Josephine continued to look at him, for his voice that obviously couldn't lie greeted Adele as if this meeting was the pleasant surprise of his day.

In a moment Josephine and Lillian were called over and introduced.

"This is Mr. Waterbury"—that was Miss Brereton's nephew —"and Mr. Dudley Knowleton."

Glancing at Adele, Josephine saw on her face an expression

---

[5] *guilelessly:* innocently
[6] *peculator:* embezzler
[7] *gambol:* playful movement

of tranquil pride, even of possession. Mr. Knowleton spoke politely, but it was obvious that though he looked at the younger girls he did not quite see them. But since they were friends of Adele's he made suitable remarks, eliciting[8] the fact that they were both coming down to New Haven to their first prom the following week. Who were their hosts? Sophomores; he knew them slightly. Josephine thought that was unnecessarily superior. Why, they were charter members of the Loving Brothers' Association – Ridgeway Saunders and George Davey – and on the glee-club trip the girls they picked out to rush in each city considered themselves a sort of elite, second only to the girls they asked to New Haven.

"And oh, I've got some bad news for you," Knowleton said to Adele. "You may be leading the prom. Jack Coe went to the infirmary with appendicitis, and against my better judgment I'm the provisional chairman." He looked apologetic. "Being one of these stone-age dancers, the two-step king, I don't see how I ever got on the committee at all."

When the car was on its way back to Miss Brereton's school, Josephine and Lillian bombarded Adele with questions.

"He's an old friend from Cincinnati," she explained demurely.[9] "He's captain of the baseball team and he was last man for Skull and Bones."[10]

"You're going to the prom with him?"

"Yes. You see, I've known him all my life."

Was there a faint implication in this remark that only those who had known Adele all her life knew her at her true worth?

"Are you engaged?" Lillian demanded.

Adele laughed. "Mercy, I don't think of such matters. It doesn't seem to be time for that sort of thing yet, does it?" ("Yes," interpolated Josephine silently.) "We're just good friends. I think there can be a perfectly healthy friendship between a man and a girl without a lot of—"

"Mush," supplied Lillian helpfully.

---

[8] *eliciting:* drawing forth

[9] *demurely:* modestly, soberly

[10] *last man for Skull and Bones:* The last man tapped for membership in this society is considered the outstanding member of the Yale student body.

"Well, yes, but I don't like that word. I was going to say without a lot of sentimental romantic things that ought to come later."

"Bravo, Adele!" said Miss Chambers somewhat perfunctorily.[11]

But Josephine's curiosity was unappeased.

"Doesn't he say he's in love with you, and all that sort of thing?"

"Mercy, no! Dud doesn't believe in such stuff any more than I do. He's got enough to do at New Haven, serving on the committees and the team."

"Oh!" said Josephine.

She was oddly interested. That two people who were attracted to each other should never even say anything about it but be content to "not believe in such stuff," was something new in her experience. She had known girls who had no beaus, others who seemed to have no emotions, and still others who lied about what they thought and did; but here was a girl who spoke of the attentions of the last man tapped for Skull and Bones as if they were two of the limestone gargoyles that Miss Chambers had pointed out on the just completed Harkness Hall. Yet Adele seemed happy—happier than Josephine, who had always believed that boys and girls were made for nothing but each other, and as soon as possible.

In the light of his popularity and achievements, Knowleton seemed more attractive. Josephine wondered if he would remember her and dance with her at the prom, or if that depended on how well he knew her escort, Ridgeway Saunders. She tried to remember whether she had smiled at him when he was looking at her. If she had really smiled he would remember her and dance with her. She was still trying to be sure of that over her two French irregular verbs and her ten stanzas of the Ancient Mariner that night; but she was still uncertain when she fell asleep.

[11] *perfunctorily:* mechanically

II

Three gay young sophomores, the founders of the Loving Brothers' Association, took a house together for Josephine, Lillian and a girl from Farmington and their three mothers. For the girls it was a first prom, and they arrived at New Haven with all the nervousness of the condemned; but a Sheffield[12] fraternity tea in the afternoon yielded up such a plethora[13] of boys from home, and boys who had visited there and friends of those boys, and new boys with unknown possibilities but obvious eagerness, that they were glowing with self-confidence as they poured into the glittering crowd that thronged the armory at ten.

It was impressive; for the first time Josephine was at a function run by men upon men's standards — an outward projection of the New Haven world from which women were excluded and which went on mysteriously behind the scenes. She perceived that their three escorts, who had once seemed the very embodiments of worldliness, were modest fry in this relentless microcosm[14] of accomplishment and success. A man's world! Looking around her at the glee-club concert, Josephine had felt a grudging admiration for the good fellowship, the good feeling. She envied Adele Craw, barely glimpsed in the dressing-room, for the position she automatically occupied by being Dudley Knowleton's girl tonight. She envied her more stepping off under the draped bunting through a gateway of hydrangeas at the head of the grand march, very demure and faintly unpowdered in a plain white dress. She was temporarily the center of all attention, and at the sight something that had long lain dormant[15] in Josephine awakened — her sense of a problem, a scarcely defined possibility.

"Josephine," Ridgeway Saunders began, "you can't realize how happy I am now that it's come true. I've looked forward to this so long, and dreamed about it — "

12 *Sheffield:* school of science at Yale

13 *plethora:* overabundance

14 *microcosm:* the world on a small scale

15 *dormant:* inactive

She smiled up at him automatically, but her mind was elsewhere, and as the dance progressed the idea continued to obsess her. She was rushed from the beginning; to the men from the tea were added a dozen new faces, a dozen confident or timid voices, until, like all the more popular girls, she had her own queue[16] trailing her about the room. Yet all this had happened to her before, and there was something missing. One might have ten men to Adele's two, but Josephine was abruptly aware that here a girl took on the importance of the man who had brought her.

She was discomforted by the unfairness of it. A girl earned her popularity by being beautiful and charming. The more beautiful and charming she was, the more she could afford to disregard public opinion. It seemed absurd that simply because Adele had managed to attach a baseball captain, who mightn't know anything about girls at all, or be able to judge their attractions, she should be thus elevated in spite of her thick ankles, her rather too pinkish face.

Josephine was dancing with Ed Bement from Chicago. He was her earliest beau, a flame of pigtail days in dancing school when one wore white cotton stockings, lace drawers with a waist attached and ruffled dresses with the inevitable sash.

"What's the matter with me?" she asked Ed, thinking aloud. "For months I've felt as if I were a hundred years old, and I'm just seventeen and that party was only seven years ago."

"You've been in love a lot since then," Ed said.

"I haven't," she protested indignantly. "I've had a lot of silly stories started about me, without any foundation, usually by girls who were jealous."

"Jealous of what?"

"Don't get fresh," she said tartly. "Dance me near Lillian."

Dudley Knowleton had just cut in on Lillian. Josephine spoke to her friend; then waiting until their turns would bring them face to face over a space of seconds, she smiled at Knowleton. This time she made sure that smile intersected as well as met glance, that he passed beside the circumfer-

---

[16] *queue:* line

ence of her fragrant charm. If this had been named like French perfume of a later day it might have been called "Please." He bowed and smiled back; a minute later he cut in on her.

It was in an eddy in a corner of the room and she danced slower so that he adapted himself, and for a moment they went around in a slow circle.

"You looked so sweet leading the march with Adele," she told him. "You seemed so serious and kind, as if the others were a lot of children. Adele looked sweet, too." And she added on an inspiration, "At school I've taken her for a model."

"You have!" She saw him conceal his sharp surprise as he said, "I'll have to tell her that."

He was handsomer than she had thought, and behind his cordial good manners there was a sort of authority. Though he was correctly attentive to her, she saw his eyes search the room quickly to see if all went well; he spoke quietly, in passing, to the orchestra leader, who came down deferentially[17] to the edge of his dais.[18] Last man for Bones. Josephine knew what that meant—her father had been Bones. Ridgeway Saunders and the rest of the Loving Brothers' Association would certainly not be Bones. She wondered, if there had been a Bones for girls, whether she would be tapped—or Adele Craw with her ankles, symbol of solidity.

> Come on o-ver here,
> Want to have you near;
> Come on join the part-y,
> Get a wel-come heart-y.

"I wonder how many boys here have taken you for a model," she said. "If I were a boy you'd be exactly what I'd like to be. Except I'd be terribly bothered having girls falling in love with me all the time."

"They don't," he said simply. "They never have."

"Oh, yes—but they hide it because they're so impressed with you, and they're afraid of Adele."

[17] *deferentially:* respectfully
[18] *dais:* platform

"Adele wouldn't object." And he added hastily, "—if it ever happened. Adele doesn't believe in being serious about such things."

"Are you engaged to her?"

He stiffened a little. "I don't believe in being engaged till the right time comes."

"Neither do I," agreed Josephine readily. "I'd rather have one good friend than a hundred people hanging around being mushy all the time."

"Is that what that crowd does that keeps following you around tonight?"

"What crowd?" she asked innocently.

"The fifty percent of the sophomore class that's rushing you."

"A lot of parlor snakes," she said ungratefully.

Josephine was radiantly happy now as she turned beautifully through the newly enchanted hall in the arms of the chairman of the prom committee. Even this extra time with him she owed to the awe which he inspired in her entourage;[19] but a man cut in eventually and there was a sharp fall in her elation. The man was impressed that Dudley Knowleton had danced with her; he was more respectful, and his modulated admiration bored her. In a little while, she hoped, Dudley Knowleton would cut back, but as midnight passed, dragging on another hour with it, she wondered if after all it had only been a courtesy to a girl from Adele's school. Since then Adele had probably painted him a neat little landscape of Josephine's past. When finally he approached her she grew tense and watchful, a state which made her exteriorly pliant and tender and quiet. But instead of dancing he drew her into the edge of a row of boxes.

"Adele had an accident on the cloakroom steps. She turned her ankle a little and tore her stocking on a nail. She'd like to borrow a pair from you because you're staying near here and we're way out at the Lawn Club."

"Of course."

"I'll run over with you—I have a car outside."

---

[19] *entourage:* train of admirers

"But you're busy, you mustn't bother."

"Of course I'll go with you."

There was thaw in the air; a hint of thin and lucid[20] spring hovered delicately around the elms and cornices of buildings whose bareness and coldness had so depressed her the week before. The night had a quality of asceticism,[21] as if the essence of masculine struggle were seeping everywhere through the little city where men of three centuries had brought their energies and aspirations for winnowing.[22] And Dudley Knowleton sitting beside her, dynamic and capable, was symbolic of it all. It seemed that she had never met a man before.

"Come in, please," she said as he went up the steps of the house with her. "They've made it very comfortable."

There was an open fire burning in the dark parlor. When she came downstairs with the stockings she went in and stood beside him, very still for a moment, watching it with him. Then she looked up, still silent, looked down, looked at him again.

"Did you get the stockings?" he asked, moving a little.

"Yes," she said breathlessly. "Kiss me for being so quick."

He laughed as if she said something witty and moved toward the door. She was smiling and her disappointment was deeply hidden as they got into the car.

"It's been wonderful meeting you," she told him. "I can't tell you how many ideas I've gotten from what you said."

"But I haven't any ideas."

"You have. All that about not getting engaged till the proper time comes. I haven't had much opportunity to talk to a man like you. Otherwise my ideas would be different, I guess. I've just realized that I've been wrong about a lot of things. I used to want to be exciting. Now I want to help people."

"Yes," he agreed, "that's very nice."

He seemed about to say more when they arrived at the armory. In their absence supper had begun; and crossing the

---

[20] *lucid:* clear, bright
[21] *asceticism:* self-denial
[22] *winnowing:* separating out the worthless parts

great floor by his side, conscious of many eyes regarding them, Josephine wondered if people thought that they had been up to something.

"We're late," said Knowleton when Adele went off to put on the stockings. "The man you're with has probably given you up long ago. You'd better let me get you something here."

"That would be too divine."

Afterward, back on the floor again, she moved in a sweet aura of abstraction. The followers of several departed belles merged with hers until now no girl on the floor was cut in on with such frequency. Even Miss Brereton's nephew, Ernest Waterbury, danced with her in stiff approval. Danced? With a tentative change of pace she simply swung from man to man in a sort of hand-right-and-left around the floor. She felt a sudden need to relax, and as if in answer to her mood a new man was presented, a tall, sleek Southerner with a persuasive note:

"You lovely creacha. I been strainin my eyes watchin your cameo face floatin round. You stand out above all these othuz like an Amehken Beauty Rose over a lot of field daisies."

Dancing with him a second time, Josephine hearkened to his pleadings.

"All right. Let's go outside."

"It wasn't outdaws I was considerin," he explained as they left the floor. "I happen to have a mortgage on a nook right here in the building."

"All right."

Book Chaffee, of Alabama, led the way through the cloakroom, through a passage to an inconspicuous door.

"This is the private apartment of my friend Sergeant Boone, instructa of the battery. He wanted to be particularly sure it'd be used as a nook tonight and not a readin room or anything like that."

Opening the door he turned on a dim light; she came in and he shut it behind her, and they faced each other.

"Mighty sweet," he murmured. His tall face came down, his long arms wrapped around her tenderly, and very slowly so that their eyes met for quite a long time, he drew her up to

him. Josephine kept thinking that she had never kissed a
Southern boy before.

They started apart at the sudden sound of a key turning in
the lock outside. Then there was a muffled snicker followed
by retreating footsteps, and Book sprang for the door and
wrenched at the handle, just as Josephine noticed that this
was not only Sergeant Boone's parlor; it was his bedroom
as well.

"Who was it?" she demanded. "Why did they lock us in?"

"Some funny boy. I'd like to get my hands on him."

"Will he come back?"

Book sat down on the bed to think. "I couldn't say. Don't
even know who it was. But if somebody on the committee
came along it wouldn't look too good, would it?"

Seeing her expression change, he came over and put his
arm around her. "Don't you worry, honey. We'll fix it."

She returned his kiss, briefly but without distraction. Then
she broke away and went into the next apartment, which was
hung with boots, uniform coats and various military
equipment.

"There's a window up here," she said. It was high in the
wall and had not been opened for a long time. Book mounted
on a chair and forced it ajar.

"About ten feet down," he reported, after a moment, "but
there's a big pile of snow just underneath. You might get a
nasty fall and you'll sure soak your shoes and stockin's."

"We've got to get out," Josephine said sharply.

"We'd better wait and give this funny man a chance—"

"I won't wait. I want to get out. Look—throw out all the
blankets from the bed and I'll jump on that: or you jump first
and spread them over the pile of snow."

After that it was merely exciting. Carefully Book Chaffee
wiped the dust from the window to protect her dress; then
they were struck silent by a footstep that approached—and
passed the outer door. Book jumped, and she heard him kicking profanely as he waded out of the soft drift below. He
spread the blankets. At the moment when Josephine swung
her legs out the window, there was the sound of voices out-

side the door and the key turned again in the lock. She landed
softly, reaching for his hand, and convulsed with laughter
they ran and skidded down the half block toward the corner,
and reaching the entrance to the armory, they stood panting
for a moment, breathing in the fresh night. Book was reluctant
to go inside.

"Why don't you let me conduct you where you're stayin?
We can sit around and sort of recuperate."

She hesitated, drawn toward him by the community of
their late predicament; but something was calling her inside,
as if the fulfillment of her elation awaited her there.

"No," she decided.

As they went in she collided with a man in a great hurry,
and looked up to recognize Dudley Knowleton.

"So sorry," he said. "Oh hello—"

"Won't you dance me over to my box?" she begged him
impulsively. "I've torn my dress."

As they started off he said abstractedly: "The fact is, a little
mischief has come up and the buck has been passed to me. I
was going along to see about it."

Her heart raced wildly and she felt the need of being another sort of person immediately.

"I can't tell you how much it's meant meeting you. It
would be wonderful to have one friend I could be serious
with without being all mushy and sentimental. Would you
mind if I wrote you a letter—I mean, would Adele mind?"

"Lord, no." His smile had become utterly unfathomable to
her. As they reached the box she thought of one more thing:

"Is it true that the baseball team is training at Hot Springs
during Easter?"

"Yes. You going there?"

"Yes. Good night, Mr. Knowleton."

But she was destined to see him once more. It was outside
the men's coat room, where she waited among a crowd of
other pale survivors and their paler mothers, whose wrinkles
had doubled and tripled with the passing night. He was explaining something to Adele, and Josephine heard the phrase,
"The door was locked, and the window open—"

Suddenly it occurred to Josephine that, meeting her coming

in damp and breathless, he must have guessed at the truth—
and Adele would doubtless confirm his suspicion. Once
again the spectre of her old enemy, the plain and jealous
girl, arose before her. Shutting her mouth tight together she
turned away.

But they had seen her, and Adele called to her in her cheerful ringing voice:

"Come say good night. You were so sweet about the stockings. Here's a girl you won't find doing shoddy, silly things,
Dudley," Impulsively she leaned and kissed Josephine on
the cheek. "You'll see I'm right, Dudley—next year she'll be
the most respected girl in school."

III

As things go in the interminable days of early March, what
happened next happened quickly. The annual senior dance
at Miss Brereton's school came on a night soaked through with
spring, and all the junior girls lay awake listening to the sighing tunes from the gymnasium. Between the numbers, when
boys up from New Haven and Princeton wandered about the
grounds, cloistered glances looked down from dark open windows upon the vague figures.

Not Josephine, though she lay awake like the others. Such
vicarious[23] diversions had no place in the sober patterns she
was spinning now from day to day; yet she might as well have
been in the forefront of those who called down to the men and
threw notes and entered into conversations, for destiny had
suddenly turned against her and was spinning a dark web of
its own.

Lit-tle lady, don't be depressed and blue,
After all, we're both in the same can-noo—

Dudley Knowleton was over in the gymnasium fifty yards
away, but proximity[24] to a man did not thrill her as it would
have done a year ago—not, at least, in the same way. Life,

[23] *vicarious:* imagined participation in another's experience
[24] *proximity:* nearness

she saw now, was a serious matter, and in the modest darkness a line of a novel ceaselessly recurred to her: "He is a man fit to be the father of my children." What were the seductive graces, the fast lines of a hundred parlor snakes compared to such realities. One couldn't go on forever kissing comparative strangers behind half-closed doors.

Under her pillow now were two letters, answers to her letters. They spoke in a bold round hand of the beginning of baseball practice; they were glad Josephine felt as she did about things; and the writer certainly looked forward to seeing her at Easter. Of all the letters she had ever received they were the most difficult from which to squeeze a single drop of heart's blood—one couldn't even read the "Yours" of the subscription as "Your"—but Josephine knew them by heart. They were precious because he had taken the time to write them; they were eloquent in the very postage stamp because he used so few.

She was restless in her bed—the music had begun again in the gymnasium:

> Oh, my love, I've waited so long for you,
> Oh, my love, I'm singing this song for you—
> Oh-h-h—

From the next room there was light laughter, and then from below a male voice, and a long interchange of comic whispers. Josephine recognized Lillian's laugh and the voices of two other girls. She could imagine them as they lay across the window in their nightgowns, their heads just showing from the open window. "Come right down," one boy kept saying. "Don't be formal—come just as you are."

There was a sudden silence, then a quick crunching of footsteps on gravel, a suppressed snicker and a scurry, and the sharp, protesting groan of several beds in the next room and the banging of a door down the hall. Trouble for somebody, maybe. A few minutes later Josephine's door half opened, she caught a glimpse of Miss Kwain against the dim corridor light, and then the door closed.

The next afternoon Josephine and four other girls, all of

whom denied having breathed so much as a word into the night, were placed on probation. There was absolutely nothing to do about it. Miss Kwain had recognized their faces in the window and they were all from two rooms. It was an injustice, but it was nothing compared to what happened next. One week before Easter vacation the school motored off on a one-day trip to inspect a milk farm—all save the ones on probation. Miss Chambers, who sympathized with Josephine's misfortune, enlisted her services in entertaining Mr. Ernest Waterbury, who was spending a week-end with his aunt. This was only vaguely better than nothing, for Mr. Waterbury was a very dull, very priggish young man. He was so dull and so priggish that the following morning Josephine was expelled from school.

It had happened like this: They had strolled in the grounds, they had sat down at a garden table and had tea. Ernest Waterbury had expressed a desire to see something in the chapel, just a few minutes before his aunt's car rolled up the drive. The chapel was reached by descending winding mock-medieval stairs; and, her shoes still wet from the garden, Josephine had slipped on the top step and fallen five feet directly into Mr. Waterbury's unwilling arms, where she lay helpless, convulsed with irresistible laughter. It was in this position that Miss Brereton and the visiting trustee had found them.

"But I had nothing to do with it!" declared the ungallant Mr. Waterbury. Flustered and outraged, he was packed back to New Haven, and Miss Brereton, connecting this with last week's sin, proceeded to lose her head. Josephine, humiliated and furious, lost hers, and Mr. Perry, who happened to be in New York, arrived at the school the same night. At his passionate indignation, Miss Brereton collapsed and retracted, but the damage was done, and Josephine packed her trunk. Unexpectedly, monstrously, just as it had begun to mean something, her school life was over.

For the moment all her feelings were directed against Miss Brereton, and the only tears she shed at leaving were of anger and resentment. Riding with her father up to New York, she saw that while at first he had instinctively and wholeheartedly taken her part, he felt also a certain annoyance with her misfortune.

"We'll all survive, "he said. "Unfortunately, even that old idiot Miss Brereton will survive. She ought to be running a reform school." He brooded for a moment. "Anyhow, your mother arrives tomorrow and you and she can go down to Hot Springs as you planned."

"Hot Springs!" Josephine cried, in a choked voice. "Oh, no!"

"Why not?" he demanded in surprise. "It seems the best thing to do. Give it a chance to blow over before you go back to Chicago."

"I'd rather go to Chicago," said Josephine breathlessly. "Daddy, I'd much rather go to Chicago."

"That's absurd. Your mother's started East and the arrangements are all made. At Hot Springs you can get out and ride and play golf and forget that old she-devil—"

"Isn't there another place in the East we could go? There's people I know going to Hot Springs who'll know all about this, people that I don't want to meet—girls from school."

"Now, Jo, you keep your chin up—this is one of those times. Sorry I said that about letting it blow over in Chicago; if we hadn't made other plans we'd go back and face every old shrew and gossip in town right away. When anybody slinks off in a corner they think you've been up to something bad. If anybody says anything to you, you tell them the truth—what I said to Miss Brereton. You tell them she said you could come back and I damn well wouldn't let you go back."

"They won't believe it."

There would be, at all events, four days of respite[25] at Hot Springs before the vacations of the schools. Josephine passed this time taking golf lessons from a professional so newly arrived from Scotland that he surely knew nothing of her misadventure; she even went riding with a young man one afternoon, feeling almost at home with him after his admission that he had flunked out of Princeton in February—a confidence, however, which she did not reciprocate in kind. But

---

[25]*respite:* temporary rest or relief

in the evenings, despite the young man's importunity,[26] she stayed with her mother, feeling nearer to her than she ever had before.

But one afternoon in the lobby Josephine saw by the desk two dozen good-looking young men waiting by a stack of bat cases and bags, and knew that what she dreaded was at hand. She ran upstairs with an invented headache dined there that night, but after dinner she walked restlessly around their apartment. She was ashamed not only of her situation but of her reaction to it. She had never felt any pity for the unpopular girls who skulked in dressing-rooms because they could attract no partners on the floor, or for girls who were outsiders at Lake Forest,[27] and now she was like them—hiding miserably out of life. Alarmed lest already the change was written in her face, she paused in front of the mirror, fascinated as ever by what she found there.

"The darn fools," she said aloud. And as she said it her chin went up and the faint cloud about her eyes lifted. The phrases of the myriad[28] love letters she had received passed before her eyes; behind her, after all, was the reassurance of a hundred lost and pleading faces, of innumerable tender and pleading voices. Her pride flooded back into her till she could see the warm blood rushing up into her cheeks.

There was a knock at the door—it was the Princeton boy.

"How about slipping downstairs?" he proposed. "There's a dance. It's full of E-lies, the whole Yale baseball team. I'll pick up one of them and introduce you and you'll have a big time. How about it?"

"All right, but I don't want to meet anybody. You'll just have to dance with me all evening."

"You know that suits me."

She hurried into a new spring evening dress of the frailest fairy blue. In the excitement of seeing herself in it, it seemed as if she had shed the old skin of winter and emerged a shining chrysalis[29] with no stain; and going downstairs her feet fell

---

[26] *importunity:* insistence
[27] *Lake Forest:* wealthy suburb of Chicago
[28] *myriad:* countless
[29] *chrysalis:* the pupa (of a butterfly)

softly just off the beat of the music from below. It was a tune
from a play she had seen a week ago in New York, a tune with
a future—ready for gayeties as yet unthought of, lovers not
yet met. Dancing off, she was certain that life had innumerable
beginnings. She had hardly gone ten steps when she was cut
in upon by Dudley Knowleton.

"Why, Josephine!" He had never used her first name before
—he stood holding her hand. "Why, I'm so glad to see you.
I've been hoping and hoping you'd be here."

She soared skyward on a rocket of surprise and delight.
He was actually glad to see her—the expression on his face
was obviously sincere. Could it be possible that he hadn't
heard?

"Adele wrote me you might be here. She wasn't sure."

—Then he knew and didn't care; he liked her anyhow.

"I'm in sackcloth and ashes," she said.

"Well, they're very becoming to you."

"You know what happened—" she ventured.

"I do. I wasn't going to say anything, but it's generally
agreed that Waterbury behaved like a fool—and it's not going
to be much help to him in the elections next month. Look—I
want you to dance with some men who are just starving for a
touch of beauty."

Presently she was dancing with, it seemed to her, the entire
team at once. Intermittently Dudley Knowleton cut back in,
as well as the Princeton man, who was somewhat indignant
at this unexpected competition. There were many girls from
many schools in the room, but with an admirable team spirit
the Yale men displayed a sharp prejudice in Josephine's
favor; already she was pointed out from the chairs along the
wall.

But interiorly she was waiting for what was coming, for the
moment when she would walk with Dudley Knowleton into
the warm, Southern night. It came naturally, just at the end of
a number, and they strolled along an avenue of early-blooming
lilacs and turned a corner and another corner. . . .

"You were glad to see me, weren't you?" Josephine said.

"Of course."

"I was afraid at first. I was sorriest about what happened at

school because of you. I'd been trying so hard to be different—
because of you."

"You mustn't think of that school business any more. Everybody that matters knows you got a bad deal. Forget it and
start over."

"Yes," she agreed tranquilly. She was happy. The breeze
and the scent of lilacs—that was she, lovely and intangible;
the rustic bench where they sat and the trees—that was he,
rugged and strong beside her, protecting her.

"I'd thought so much of meeting you here," she said after
a minute. "You'd been so good for me, that I thought maybe in
a different way I could be good for you—I mean I know ways
of having a good time that you don't know. For instance, we've
certainly got to go horseback riding by moonlight some night.
That'll be fun."

He didn't answer.

"I can really be very nice when I like somebody—that's
really not often," she interpolated hastily, "not seriously. But
I mean when I do feel seriously that a boy and I are really
friends I don't believe in having a whole mob of other boys
hanging around taking up time. I like to be with him all the
time, all day and all evening, don't you?"

He stirred a little on the bench; he leaned forward with
his elbows on his knees, looking at his strong hands. Her
gently modulated voice sank a note lower.

"When I like anyone I don't even like dancing. It's sweeter
to be alone."

Silence for a moment.

"Well, you know"—he hesitated, frowning—"as a matter
of fact, I'm mixed up in a lot of engagements made some time
ago with some people." He floundered about unhappily. "In
fact, I won't even be at the hotel after tomorrow. I'll be at the
house of some people down the valley—a sort of house party.
As a matter of fact, Adele's getting here tomorrow."

Absorbed in her own thoughts, she hardly heard him at
first, but at the name she caught her breath sharply.

"We're both to be at this house party while we're here, and
I imagine it's more or less arranged what we're going to do. Of
course, in the daytime I'll be here for baseball practice.

"I see." Her lips were quivering. "You won't be—you'll be with Adele."

"I think that—more or less—I will. She'll—want to see you, of course."

Another silence while he twisted his big fingers and she helplessly imitated the gesture.

"You were just sorry for me," she said. "You like Adele—much better."

"Adele and I understand each other. She's been more or less my ideal since we were children together."

"And I'm not your kind of girl." Josephine's voice trembled with a sort of fright. "I suppose because I've kissed a lot of boys and got a reputation for a speed and raised the deuce."

"It isn't that."

"Yes, it is," she declared passionately. "I'm just paying for things." She stood up. "You'd better take me back inside so I can dance with the kind of boys that like me."

She walked quickly down the path, tears of misery streaming from her eyes. He overtook her by the steps, but she only shook her head and said, "Excuse me for being so fresh. I'll grow up—I got what was coming to me—it's all right."

A little later when she looked around the floor for him he had gone—and Josephine realized with a shock that for the first time in her life, she had tried for a man and failed. But, save in the very young, only love begets love, and from the moment Josephine had perceived that his interest in her was merely kindness she realized the wound was not in her heart but in her pride. She would forget him quickly, but she would never forget what she had learned from him. There were two kinds of men, those you played with and those you might marry. And as this passed through her mind, her restless eyes wandered casually over the group of stags, resting very lightly on Mr. Gordon Tinsley, the current catch of Chicago, reputedly the richest young man in the Middle West. He had never paid any attention to young Josephine until tonight. Ten minutes ago he had asked her to go driving with him tomorrow.

But he did not attract her—and she decided to refuse. One mustn't run through people, and, for the sake of a romantic half-hour, trade a possibility that might develop—quite seriously—later, at the proper time. She did not know that this was the first mature thought that she had ever had in her life, but it was.

The orchestra were packing their instruments and the Princeton man was still at her ear, still imploring her to walk out with him into the night. Josephine knew without cogitation[30] which sort of man he was—and the moon was bright on the windows. So with a certain sense of relaxation she took his arm and they strolled out to the pleasant bower she had so lately quitted, and their faces turned toward each other, like little moons under the great white one which hovered high over the Blue Ridge; his arm dropped softly about her yielding shoulder.

"Well?" he whispered.

"Well?"

[30] *cogitation:* thought

FOR DISCUSSION

1. Successful stories about teen-agers are rare. What is your opinion of this story? Are the characterizations of Josephine Perry and the other young people credible and honest? Defend your answers.

2. As a newcomer to the social set at Yale, Josephine is seeking to establish a place for herself. What role does she see herself playing in this new setting?

3. How had Josephine acquired her "past"? In what respects does it affect her efforts to be a social success? What injustices does she suffer because of her "past"? In what ways does she perhaps get her just deserts?

4. What tactics does she use to reach her goal, especially in her relations with Dudley Knowleton? Are these tactics the only ones she might have used? Are they the best ones? Give your opinion.

5. Cite examples of snobbery in the operation of the social set described in the story. In what way is Josephine a victim of this snobbery? How is she also guilty of practicing it?

6. At the end of the story, did you feel sorry for Josephine? Do you think this was, or was not, the author's intention? Perhaps you

have mixed feelings. Describe your various reactions to Josephine and the reasons for them.
7. Analyze the character of Dudley Knowleton. What kind of person is he? Judging by his behavior at the Yale Prom and later at Hot Springs, what would you say is his attitude toward Josephine?
8. Discuss the relationship between Josephine and Adele Craw. Do you think Adele has only Josephine's best interests at heart? Is Josephine envious of Adele? Be able to support your answers with evidence given in the story.
9. Re-read the conclusion that Josephine reaches near the end of the story as a result of her experience with Dudley Knowleton. Do you think that Fitzgerald intended to show that Josephine has changed, or was he being ironic? Give reasons for your answer.
10. Fitzgerald once wrote to his daughter as follows: "All I believe in in life is the rewards for virtue (according to your talents) and punishments for not fulfilling your duties, which are doubly costly." In the light of this statement, what opinion do you think Fitzgerald might have had of his own creation, Josephine Perry?

FOR COMPOSITION

1. Write a description of Josephine as she appears to one of these characters: Adele, Dudley, Book Chaffee, or Ernest Waterbury. Be sure to stick to the point of view of the character you choose.
2. In a short informal essay, express your thoughts and feelings about one of these topics:
Going Steady
The Attitudes and Behavior of Young People Today
Teen-Age Marriages

THE MODERN VIEWPOINT

The opening quarter of the twentieth century had proved a most difficult period for the American nation. War and economic disaster had fostered a generation of disillusioned artists and intellectuals, many of whom took up exile in Europe. Out of this self-exiled "lost generation" came Ernest Hemingway, destined to exert a deeper influence on modern American literature than perhaps any other writer.

William Faulkner deplored the mean-spirited vulgarity of the modern age in his fiction, though he maintained a belief in man's essential dignity and worth. John Steinbeck represented the angry social consciousness of the 1930's, showing the unhappy lives of the depression poor in some of his best fiction. These three writers were greatly influential in shaping the modern viewpoint of other American writers.

The authors in this section began writing during the trying years of the 1930's, when the country was struggling to its feet under President Franklin D. Roosevelt's New Deal and when the threat of a world war was making itself felt for the second time. They wrote during that Second World War and during the later Korean War and have continued to write up to the present time.

KATHERINE ANNE PORTER, a native of Texas, writes of self-betrayal in its various forms, giving a somewhat pessimistic view of human nature. However, her portrayal of human motivation shows subtlety and perception, as well as skillful mastery of the ironic word and deed. These qualities are particularly evident in her use of the complex interior monologue. Her style is economical and straightforward, yet is sparked with vivid detail; and her short novels and numerous stories are characterized by boldness and imagination, along with technical virtuosity. Her important collection of stories, *Flowering Judas*, appeared in 1930, and since then she has produced a small but significant body of fiction. She is regarded as one of the major writers of the short story today.

A highly gifted writer, EUDORA WELTY is a native of Mississippi, where she still resides. She has concerned herself with some of the same problems that interested William Faulkner, although her method of presenting Southern life is quite different. The obscure and helpless people about whom she writes seem unable—at least in their actions—to break out of certain traditional patterns that their Southern culture has imposed on them. As a consequence, they often seek in fantasy an escape from reality. Miss Welty is a master in her use of fantasy to give her readers new insights into her characters. In her exploration of human consciousness to discover the truth about people, she may reveal an apparently normal person as grotesque, or an apparently inconsequential person as truly admirable. She is typically modern in her experimental techniques and in her interest in the psychology of the individual, but her talent is unique.

TRUMAN CAPOTE, though born in New Orleans, prefers not to be labeled a "Southern writer" because he has lived in so many parts of the country besides the South. Many of his stories, however, have a Southern setting and are notable for their local color. His insecure childhood, resulting from the divorce of his parents, was perhaps partly responsible for the delicately grotesque characters he has created in some of his stories. These characters are often haunted personalities, victims of their own isolation from a world which they feel is inimical. All of his work shows subtle insight into human nature and remarkable powers of observation, as well as a sense of humor.

Whereas the stories of Miss Porter, Miss Welty, and Capote reveal their Southern background, the stories of J. F. POWERS show a concern with a different part of the country and a different way of life. A native of Illinois and a Catholic, Powers frequently uses his stories as a means of examining critically the role of the Church in modern life. Powers, however, is primarily interested in the drama of human conflict and human weaknesses, as such, which he frequently points to through an effective use of satire.

The writers in this section had all published stories by the end of World War II and had earned recognition as writers by 1950. Some of the factors that will be seen to shape the writing of the newer voices in the 1950's and 60's in American literature were already influencing the writers in this section, as well.

Katherine Anne Porter

Katherine Anne Porter has often been called a "master of irony." In a style that is both straightforward and subtle, she penetrates to the very depths of human nature. The following story, a kind of a dialogue between husband and wife, shows her keen perception of their marital situation.

Rope

On the third day after they moved to the country he came walking back from the village carrying a basket of groceries and a twenty-four-yard coil of rope. She came out to meet him, wiping her hands on her green smock. Her hair was tumbled, her nose was scarlet with sunburn; he told her that already she looked like a born country woman. His gray flannel shirt stuck to him, his heavy shoes were dusty. She assured him he looked like a rural character in a play.

Had he brought the coffee? She had been waiting all day long for coffee. They had forgot it when they ordered at the store the first day.

Gosh, no, he hadn't. Lord, now he'd have to go back. Yes, he would if it killed him. He thought, though, he had everything else. She reminded him it was only because he didn't drink coffee himself. If he did he would remember it quick enough. Suppose they ran out of cigarettes? Then she saw the rope. What was that for? Well, he thought it might do to hang clothes on, or something. Naturally she asked him if he thought they were going to run a laundry? They already had a fifty-foot line hanging right before his eyes. Why, hadn't he noticed it, really? It was a blot on the landscape to her.

He thought there were a lot of things a rope might come in

392

handy for. She wanted to know what, for instance. He thought
a few seconds, but nothing occurred. They could wait and
see, couldn't they? You need all sorts of strange odds and ends
around a place in the country. She said, yes, that was so; but
she thought just at that time when every penny counted, it
seemed funny to buy more rope. That was all. She hadn't
meant anything else. She hadn't just seen, not at first, why
he felt it was necessary.

Well, thunder, he had bought it because he wanted to, and
that was all there was to it. She thought that was reason
enough, and couldn't understand why he hadn't said so, at
first. Undoubtedly it would be useful, twenty-four yards of
rope, there were hundreds of things, she couldn't think of any
at the moment, but it would come in. Of course. As he had
said, things always did in the country.

But she was a little disappointed about the coffee, and oh,
look, look, look at the eggs! Oh, my, they're all running! What
had he put on top of them? Hadn't he known eggs mustn't
be squeezed? Squeezed, who had squeezed them, he wanted
to know. What a silly thing to say. He had simply brought them
along in the basket with the other things. If they got broke it
was the grocer's fault. He should know better than to put
heavy things on top of eggs.

She believed it was the rope. That was the heaviest thing
in the pack, she saw him plainly when he came in from the
road, the rope was a big package on top of everything. He
desired the whole wide world to witness that this was not a
fact. He had carried the rope in one hand and the basket in
the other, and what was the use of her having eyes if that was
the best they could do for her?

Well, anyhow, she could see one thing plain: no eggs for
breakfast. They'd have to scramble them now, for supper. It
was too damned bad. She had planned to have steak for
supper. No ice, meat wouldn't keep. He wanted to know why
she couldn't finish breaking the eggs in a bowl and set them
in a cool place.

Cool place! if he could find one for her, she'd be glad to
set them there. Well, then, it seemed to him they might very
well cook the meat at the same time they cooked the eggs and

then warm up the meat for tomorrow. The idea simply choked her. Warmed-over meat, when they might as well have had it fresh. Second best and scraps and makeshifts, even to the meat! He rubbed her shoulder a little. It doesn't really matter so much, does it darling? Sometimes when they were playful, he would rub her shoulder and she would arch and purr. This time she hissed and almost clawed. He was getting ready to say that they could surely manage somehow when she turned on him and said, if he told her they could manage somehow she would certainly slap his face.

He swallowed the words red hot, his face burned. He picked up the rope and started to put it on the top shelf. She would not have it on the top shelf, the jars and tins belonged there; positively she would not have the top shelf cluttered up with a lot of rope. She had borne all the clutter she meant to bear in the flat in town, there was space here at least and she meant to keep things in order.

Well, in that case, he wanted to know what the hammer and nails were doing up there? And why had she put them there when she knew very well he needed that hammer and those nails upstairs to fix the window sashes? She simply slowed down everything and made double work on the place with her insane habit of changing things around and hiding them.

She was sure she begged his pardon, and if she had had any reason to believe he was going to fix the sashes this summer she would have left the hammer and nails right where he put them; in the middle of the bedroom floor where they could step on them in the dark. And now if he didn't clear the whole mess out of there she would throw them down the well.

Oh, all right, all right—could he put them in the closet? Naturally not, there were brooms and mops and dustpans in the closet, and why couldn't he find a place for his rope outside her kitchen? Had he stopped to consider there were seven God-forsaken rooms in the house, and only one kitchen?

He wanted to know what of it? And did she realize she was making a complete fool of herself? And what did she take him for, a three-year-old idiot? The whole trouble with her was she needed something weaker than she was to heckle and tyrannize over. He wished to God now they had a couple of children she could take it out on. Maybe he'd get some rest.

Her face changed at this, she reminded him he had forgot
the coffee and had bought a worthless piece of rope. And when
she thought of all the things they actually needed to make the
place even decently fit to live in, well, she could cry, that was
all. She looked so forlorn, so lost and despairing he couldn't
believe it was only a piece of rope that was causing all the
racket. What *was* the matter, for God's sake?

Oh, would he please hush and go away, and *stay* away, if
he could, for five minutes? By all means, yes, he would. He'd
stay away indefinitely if she wished. Lord, yes, there was
nothing he'd like better than to clear out and never come
back. She couldn't for the life of her see what was holding
him, then. It was a swell time. Here she was, stuck, miles
from a railroad, with a half-empty house on her hands, and
not a penny in her pocket, and everything on earth to do; it
seemed the God-sent moment for him to get out from under.
She was surprised he hadn't stayed in town as it was until
she had come out and done the work and got things straightened out. It was his usual trick.

It appeared to him that this was going a little far. Just a
touch out of bounds, if she didn't mind his saying so. Why the
hell had he stayed in town the summer before? To do a half-
dozen extra jobs to get the money he had sent her. That was
it. She knew perfectly well they couldn't have done it otherwise. She had agreed with him at the time. And that was the
only time so help him he had ever left her to do anything
by herself.

Oh, he could tell that to his great-grandmother. She had her
notion of what had kept him in town. Considerably more than
a notion, if he wanted to know. So, she was going to bring all
that up again, was she? Well, she could just think what she
pleased. He was tired of explaining. It may have looked funny
but he had simply got hooked in, and what could he do? It
was impossible to believe that she was going to take it seriously. Yes, yes, she knew how it was with a man: if he was
left by himself a minute, some woman was certain to kidnap
him. And naturally he couldn't hurt her feelings by refusing!

Well, what was she raving about? Did she forget she had

told him those two weeks alone in the country were the happiest she had known for four years? And how long had they been married when she said that? All right, shut up! If she thought that hadn't stuck in his craw.

She hadn't meant she was happy because she was away from him. She meant she was happy getting the devilish house nice and ready for him. That was what she had meant, and now look! Bringing up something she had said a year ago simply to justify himself for forgetting her coffee and breaking the eggs and buying a wretched piece of rope they couldn't afford. She really thought it was time to drop the subject, and now she wanted only two things in the world. She wanted him to get that rope from underfoot, and go back to the village and get her coffee, and if he could remember it, he might bring a metal mitt for the skillets, and two more curtain rods, and if there were any rubber gloves in the village, her hands were simply raw, and a bottle of milk of magnesia from the drugstore.

He looked out at the dark blue afternoon sweltering on the slopes, and mopped his forehead and sighed heavily and said, if only she could wait a minute for *anything*, he was going back. He had said so, hadn't he, the very instant they found he had overlooked it?

Oh, yes, well . . . run along. She was going to wash windows. The country was so beautiful! She doubted they'd have a moment to enjoy it. He meant to go, but he could not until he had said that if she wasn't such a hopeless melancholiac[1] she might see that this was only for a few days. Couldn't she remember anything pleasant about the other summers? Hadn't they ever had any fun? She hadn't time to talk about it, and now would he please not leave that rope lying around for her to trip on? He picked it up, somehow it had toppled off the table, and walked out with it under his arm.

Was he going this minute? He certainly was. She thought so. Sometimes it seemed to her he had second sight about the precisely perfect moment to leave her ditched. She had meant to put the mattresses out to sun, if they put them out this

---

[1] *melancholiac:* one who has melancholia, a mental disorder characterized by brooding and gloominess

minute they would get at least three hours, he must have heard her say that morning she meant to put them out. So of course he would walk off and leave her to it. She supposed he thought the exercise would do her good.

Well, he was merely going to get her coffee. A four-mile walk for two pounds of coffee was ridiculous, but he was perfectly willing to do it. The habit was making a wreck of her, but if she wanted to wreck herself there was nothing he could do about it. If he thought it was coffee that was making a wreck of her, she congratulated him: he must have a damned easy conscience.

Conscience or no conscience, he didn't see why the mattresses couldn't very well wait until tomorrow. And anyhow, for God's sake, were they living *in* the house, or were they going to let the house ride them to death? She paled at this, her face grew livid[2] about the mouth, she looked quite dangerous, and reminded him that housekeeping was no more her work than it was his: she had other work to do as well, and when did he think she was going to find time to do it at this rate?

Was she going to start on that again? She knew as well as he did that his work brought in the regular money, hers was only occasional, if they depended on what *she* made—and she might as well get straight on this question once for all!

That was positively not the point. The question was, when both of them were working on their own time, was there going to be a division of the housework, or wasn't there? She merely wanted to know, she had to make her plans. Why, he thought that was all arranged. It was understood that he was to help. Hadn't he always, in summers?

Hadn't he, though? Oh, just hadn't he? And when, and where, and doing what? Lord, what an uproarious joke!

It was such a very uproarious joke that her face turned slightly purple, and she screamed with laughter. She laughed so hard she had to sit down, and finally a rush of tears spurted from her eyes and poured down into the lifted corners of her mouth. He dashed towards her and dragged her up to her feet

[2] *livid:* grayish-blue, lead-colored

and tried to pour water on her head. The dipper hung by a string on a nail and he broke it loose. Then he tried to pump water with one hand while she struggled in the other. So he gave it up and shook her instead.

She wrenched away, crying out for him to take his rope and go to hell, she had simply given him up: and ran. He heard her high-heeled bedroom slippers clattering and stumbling on the stairs.

He went out around the house and into the lane; he suddenly realized he had a blister on his heel and his shirt felt as if it were on fire. Things broke so suddenly you didn't know where you were. She could work herself into a fury about simply nothing. She was terrible, damn it: not an ounce of reason. You might as well talk to a sieve as that woman when she got going. Damned if he'd spend his life humoring her! Well, what to do now? He would take back the rope and exchange it for something else. Things accumulated, things were mountainous, you couldn't move them or sort them out or get rid of them. They just lay and rotted around. He'd take it back. Hell, why should he? He wanted it. What was it anyhow? A piece of rope. Imagine anybody caring more about a piece of rope than about a man's feelings. What earthly right had she to say a word about it? He remembered all the useless, meaningless things she bought for herself: Why? because I wanted it, that's why! He stopped and selected a large stone by the road. He would put the rope behind it. He would put it in the tool-box when he got back. He'd heard enough about it to last him a life-time.

When he came back she was leaning against the post box beside the road waiting. It was pretty late, the smell of broiled steak floated nose high in the cooling air. Her face was young and smooth and fresh-looking. Her unmanageable funny black hair was all on end. She waved to him from a distance, and he speeded up. She called out that supper was ready and waiting, was he starved?

You bet he was starved. Here was the coffee. He waved it at her. She looked at his other hand. What was that he had there?

Well, it was the rope again. He stopped short. He had meant to exchange it but forgot. She wanted to know why he should exchange it, if it was something he really wanted. Wasn't the air sweet now, and wasn't it fine to be here?

She walked beside him with one hand hooked into his leather belt. She pulled and jostled him a little as he walked, and leaned against him. He put his arm clear around her and patted her stomach. They exchanged wary smiles. Coffee, coffee for the Ootsum-Wootsums! He felt as if he were bringing her a beautiful present.

He was a love, she firmly believed, and if she had had her coffee in the morning, she wouldn't have behaved so funny ... There was a whippoorwill still coming back, imagine, clear out of season, sitting in the crab-apple tree calling all by himself. Maybe his girl stood him up. Maybe she did. She hoped to hear him once more, she loved whippoorwills ... He knew how she was, didn't he?

Sure, he knew how she was.

FOR DISCUSSION

1. You immediately become aware that there is something wrong between the two people in this story. How? What, on the surface, seems to be causing the trouble?
2. As you read further, what do these characters reveal to you about their own personalities? What do they reveal about the life they have led up to the time the story opens? What do you discover to be the real causes of their hostility toward each other?
3. What is unusual about the form of this story? Why is the form particularly suitable to the story?
4. Which details of the setting seem to contribute most to the oppressive atmosphere of the story?
5. Throughout the story your attention is focused on the coil of rope. Were you expecting a different sort of ending to the story? Explain. Why does the actual ending seem ironical? Find clues given by the author that might prepare you for an ending of this sort.
6. Do you consider the ending of the story happy? What does it tell you about this particular marriage?
7. What symbolic significance does the rope seem to acquire in the light of the couple's relationship?

FOR COMPOSITION

1. Do you consider the marriage in this story a typical one? Write a composition telling why you do or do not feel that it is. Be sure to include your ideas about the qualities a good marriage should have.
2. In a short composition, discuss Miss Porter's use of irony (see page 515) in the story. Show how she uses both irony of expression and irony of situation, using concrete examples from the story.

Eudora Welty

Eudora Welty's stories usually have a Mississippi setting and involve strange or eccentric people. In the following story, her psychological insight and gentle humor bring to life the character of old Phoenix Jackson. It is the mingling of humor and pathos together with a sharp eye for significant details that has given Miss Welty's stories wide appeal.

A Worn Path

It was December — a bright frozen day in the early morning. Far out in the country there was an old Negro woman with her head tied in a red rag, coming along a path through the pine woods. Her name was Phoenix Jackson. She was very old, and small, and she walked slowly in the dark pine shadows, moving a little from side to side in her steps, with the balanced heaviness and lightness of a pendulum in a grandfather clock. She carried a thin small cane made from an umbrella, and with this she kept tapping the frozen earth in front of her. This made a grave and persistent noise in the still air that seemed meditative, like the chirping of a solitary little bird.

She wore a dark striped dress reaching down to her shoe tops, and an equally long apron of bleached sugar sacks, with a full pocket: all neat and tidy, but every time she took a step she might have fallen over her shoelaces, which dragged from her unlaced shoes. She looked straight ahead. Her eyes were blue with age. Her skin had a pattern all its own of numberless branching wrinkles, and as though a whole little tree stood in the middle of her forehead, but a golden color ran underneath, and the two knobs of her cheeks were illumined by a yellow burning under the dark. Under the red rag her hair came down on her neck in the frailest of ringlets, still black, and with an odor like copper.

Now and then there was a quivering in the thicket. Old Phoenix said, "Out of my way, all you foxes, owls, beetles, jack rabbits, coons, and wild animals! Keep out from under these feet, little bobwhites. Keep the big wild hogs out of my path. Don't let none of those come running my direction. I got a long way." Under her small black-freckled hand her cane, limber as a buggy whip, would switch at the brush as if to rouse up any hiding things.

On she went. The woods were deep and still. The sun made the pine needles almost too bright to look at, up where the wind rocked. The cones dropped as light as feathers. Down in the hollow was the mourning dove — it was not too late for him.

The path ran up a hill. "Seem like there is chains about my feet, time I get this far," she said, in a voice of argument old people keep to use with themselves. "Something always take a hold of me on this hill — pleads I should stay."

After she got to the top, she turned and gave a full, severe look behind her where she had come. "Up through pines," she said at length. "Now down through oaks."

Her eyes opened their widest and she started down gently. But before she got to the bottom of the hill a bush caught her dress.

Her fingers were busy and intent, but her skirts were full and long, so that before she could pull them free in one place they were caught in another. It was not possible to allow the dress to tear. "I in the thorny bush," she said. "Thorns, you doing your appointed work. Never want to let folks pass — no, sir. Old eyes thought you was a pretty little *green* bush."

Finally, trembling all over, she stood free, and after a moment dared to stoop for her cane.

"Sun so high!" she cried, leaning back and looking, while the thick tears went over her eyes. "The time getting all gone here."

At the foot of this hill was a place where a log was laid across the creek.

"Now comes the trial," said Phoenix. Putting her right foot out, she mounted the log and shut her eyes. Lifting her skirt, leveling her cane fiercely before her like a festival figure in some parade, she began to march across. Then she opened her eyes, and she was safe on the other side.

"I wasn't as old as I thought." she said.

But she sat down to rest. She spread her skirts on the bank around her and folded her hands over her knees. Up above her was a tree in a pearly cloud of mistletoe. She did not dare to close her eyes, and when a little boy brought her a plate with a slice of marble cake on it she spoke to him. "That would be acceptable," she said. But when she went to take it there was just her own hand in the air.

So she left that tree, and had to go through a barbed-wire fence. There she had to creep and crawl, spreading her knees and stretching her fingers like a baby trying to climb the steps. But she talked loudly to herself: she could not let her dress be torn now, so late in the day, and she could not pay for having her arm or her leg sawed off if she got caught fast where she was.

At last she was safe through the fence and risen up out in the clearing. Big dead trees, like black men with one arm, were standing in the purple stalks of the withered cotton field. There sat a buzzard.

"Who you watching?"

In the furrow she made her way along.

"Glad this not the season for bulls," she said, looking sideways, "and the good Lord made his snakes to curl up and sleep in the winter. A pleasure I don't see no two-headed snake coming around that tree, where it come once. It took a while to get by him, back in the summer."

She passed through the old cotton, and went into a field of dead corn. It whispered and shook, and was taller than her head. "Through the maze now," she said, for there was no path.

Then there was something tall, black, and skinny there, moving before her.

At first she took it for a man. It could have been a man dancing in the field. But she stood still and listened, and it did not make a sound. It was as silent as a ghost.

"Ghost," she said sharply, "who be you the ghost of? For I have heard of nary death close by."

But there was no answer, only the ragged dancing in the wind.

She shut her eyes, reached out her hand, and touched a sleeve. She found a coat and inside that an emptiness, cold as ice.

"You scarecrow," she said. Her face lighted. "I ought to be shut up for good," she said with laughter. "My senses is gone. I too old. I the oldest people I ever know. Dance, old scarecrow," she said, "while I dancing with you."

She kicked her foot over the furrow, and with mouth drawn down shook her head once or twice in a little strutting way. Some husks blew down and whirled in streamers about her skirts.

Then she went on, parting her way from side to side with the cane, through the whispering field. At last she came to the end, to a wagon track, where the silver grass blew between the red ruts. The quail were walking around like pullets, seeming all dainty and unseen.

"Walk pretty," she said. "This the easy place. This the easy going." She followed the track, swaying through the quiet bare fields, through the little strings of trees silver in their dead leaves, past cabins silver from weather, with the doors and windows boarded shut, all like old women under a spell sitting there. "I walking in their sleep," she said, nodding her head vigorously.

In a ravine she went where a spring was, silently flowing through a hollowed log. Old Phoenix bent and drank. "Sweet gum makes the water sweet," she said, and drank more. "Nobody know who made this well, for it was here when I was born."

The track crossed a swampy part where the moss hung as white as lace from every limb. "Sleep on, alligators, and blow your bubbles." Then the cypress trees went into the road. Deep, deep it went down between the high, green-colored banks. Overhead the live oaks met, and it was as dark as a cave.

A big black dog with a lolling tongue came up out of the weeds by the ditch. She was meditating, and not ready, and when he came at her she only hit him a little with her cane. Over she went in the ditch, like a little puff of milkweed.

Down there, her senses drifted away. A dream visited her, and she reached her hand up, but nothing reached down and gave her a pull. So she lay there and presently went to talking. "Old woman," she said to herself, "that black dog came up out of the weeds to stall you off, and now there he sitting on his fine tail, smiling at you."

A white man finally came along and found her—a hunter, a young man, with his dog on a chain.

"Well, Granny!" he laughed. "What are you doing there?"

"Lying on my back like a June bug waiting to be turned over, mister," she said, reaching up her hand.

He lifted her up, gave her a swing in the air, and set her down. "Anything broken, Granny?"

"No, sir, them old dead weeds is springy enough," said Phoenix, when she had got her breath. "I thank you for your trouble."

"Where do you live, Granny?" he asked, while the two dogs were growling at each other.

"Away back younder, sir, behind the ridge. You can't even see it from here."

"On your way home?"

"No, sir, I going to town."

"Why, that's too far! That's as far as I walk when I come out myself, and I get something for my trouble." He patted the stuffed bag he carried, and there hung down a little closed claw. It was one of the bobwhites, with its beak hooked bitterly to show it was dead. "Now you go on home, Granny!"

"I bound to go to town, mister," said Phoenix. "The time come around."

He gave another laugh, filling the whole landscape. "I know you old colored people! Wouldn't miss going to town to see Santa Claus!"

But something held Old Phoenix very still. The deep lines

in her face went into a fierce and different radiation. Without warning, she had seen with her own eyes a flashing nickel fall out of the man's pocket on to the ground.

"How old are you, Granny?" he was saying.

"There is no telling, mister," she said, "no telling."

Then she gave a little cry and clapped her hands, and said, "Git on away from here, dog! Look! Look at that dog!" She laughed as if in admiration. "He ain't scared of nobody. He a big black dog." she whispered, "Sic him!"

"Watch me get rid of that cur," said the man. "Sic him, Pete! Sic him!"

Phoenix heard the dogs fighting, and heard the man running and throwing sticks. She even heard a gunshot. But she was slowly bending forward by that time, further and further forward, the lids stretched down over her eyes, as if she were doing this in her sleep. Her chin was lowered almost to her knees. The yellow palm of her hand came out from the fold of her apron. Her fingers slid down and along the ground under the piece of money with the grace and care they would have in lifting an egg from under a setting hen. Then she slowly straightened up; she stood erect, and the nickel was in her apron pocket. A bird flew by. Her lips moved. "God watching me the whole time. I come to stealing."

The man came back, and his own dog panted about them. "Well, I scared him off that time," he said, and then he laughed and lifted his gun and pointed it at Phoenix.

She stood straight and faced him.

"Doesn't the gun scare you?" he said, still pointing it.

"No, sir, I seen plenty go off closer by, in my day, and for less than what I done," she said, holding utterly still.

He smiled and shouldered the gun. "Well, Granny," he said, "you must be a hundred years old, and scared of nothing. I'd give you a dime if I had any money with me. But you take my advice and stay home, and nothing will happen to you."

"I bound to go on my way, mister," said Phoenix. She inclined her head in the red rag. Then they went in different directions, but she could hear the gun shooting again and again over the hill.

She walked on. The shadows hung from the oak trees to

the road like curtains. Then she smelled wood smoke, and smelled the river, and she saw a steeple and the cabins on their steep steps. Dozens of little black children whirled around her. There ahead was Natchez shining. Bells were ringing. She walked on.

In the paved city it was Christmas time. There were red and green electric lights strung and crisscrossed everywhere, and all turned on in the daytime. Old Phoenix would have been lost if she had not distrusted her eyesight and depended on her feet to know where to take her.

She paused quietly on the sidewalk, where people were passing by. A lady came along in the crowd, carrying an armful of red, green, and silver-wrapped presents; she gave off perfume like the red roses in hot summer, and Phoenix stopped her.

"Please, missy, will you lace up my shoe?" She held up her foot.

"What do you want, Grandma?"

"See my shoe," said Phoenix. "Do all right for out in the country, but wouldn't look right to go in a big building."

"Stand still then, Grandma," said the lady. She put her packages down on the sidewalk beside her and laced and tied both shoes tightly.

"Can't lace 'em with a cane," said Phoenix. "Thank you, missy. I doesn't mind asking a nice lady to tie up my shoe when I gets out on the street."

Moving slowly and from side to side, she went into the stone building and into a tower of steps, where she walked up and around and around until her feet knew to stop.

She entered a door, and there she saw nailed up on the wall the document that had been stamped with the gold seal and framed in the gold frame, which matched the dream that was hung up in her head.

"Here I be," she said. There was a fixed and ceremonial stiffness over her body.

"A charity case, I suppose," said an attendant who sat at the desk before her.

But Phoenix only looked above her head. There was sweat on her face; the wrinkles shone like a bright net.

"Speak up, Grandma," the woman said. "What's your name? We must have your history, you know. Have you been here before? What seems to be the trouble with you?"

Phoenix only gave a twitch to her face as if a fly were bothering her.

"Are you deaf?" cried the attendant.

But then the nurse came in.

"Oh, that's just old Aunt Phoenix," she said. "She doesn't come for herself; she has a little grandson. She makes these trips just as regular as clockwork — she lives away back off the Old Natchez Trace." She bent down. "Well, Aunt Phoenix, why don't you just take a seat? We won't keep you standing, after your long trip." She pointed.

The old woman sat down, bolt upright in the chair.

"Now, how is the boy?" asked the nurse.

Old Phoenix did not speak.

"I said, how is the boy?"

But Phoenix only waited and stared straight ahead, her face very solemn and withdrawn into rigidity.

"Is his throat any better?" asked the nurse. "Aunt Phoenix, don't you hear me? Is your grandson's throat any better since the last time you came for the medicine?"

With her hands on her knees, the old woman waited, silent erect, and motionless, just as if she were in armor.

"You mustn't take up our time this way, Aunt Phoenix," the nurse said. "Tell us quickly about your grandson, and get it over. He isn't dead, is he?"

At last there came a flicker and then a flame of comprehension across her face, and she spoke. "My grandson. It was my memory had left me. There I sat and forgot why I made my long trip."

"Forgot?" The nurse frowned. "After you came so far?"

Then Phoenix was like an old woman begging a dignified forgiveness for waking up frightened in the night. "I never did go to school — I was too old at the Surrender," she said in a soft voice. "I'm an old woman without an education. It was my memory fail me. My little grandson, he is just the same, and I forgot it in the coming."

"Throat never heals, does it?" said the nurse, speaking in a loud sure voice to Old Phoenix. By now she had a card with something written on it, a little list. "Yes. Swallowed lye. When was it — January — two — three years ago — "

Phoenix spoke unasked now. "No, missy, he not dead, he just the same. Every little while his throat begin to close up again, and he not able to swallow. He not get his breath. He not able to help himself. So the time come around, and I go on another trip for the soothing-medicine."

"All right. The doctor said as long as you came to get it, you could have it," said the nurse. "But it's an obstinate case."

"My little grandson, he sit up there in the house all wrapped up, waiting by himself," Phoenix went on. "We is the only two left in the world. He suffer and it don't seem to put him back at all. He got a sweet look. He going to last. He wear a little patch-quilt and peep out, holding his mouth open like a little bird. I remembers so plain now. I not going to forget him again, no, the whole enduring time. I could tell him from all the others in creation."

"All right." The nurse was trying to hush her now. She brought her a bottle of medicine. "Charity," she said, making a check mark in a book.

Old Phoenix held the bottle close to her eyes, and then carefully put it into her pocket.

"I thank you," she said.

"It's Christmas time, Grandma," said the attendant. "Could I give you a few pennies out of my purse?"

"Five pennies is a nickel," said Phoenix stiffly.

"Here's a nickel," said the attendant.

Phoenix rose carefully and held out her hand. She received the nickel and then fished the other nickel out of her pocket and laid it beside the new one. She stared at her palm closely, with her head on one side.

Then she gave a tap with her cane on the floor. "This is what come to me to do," she said. "I going to the store and buy my child a little windmill they sells, made out of paper. He going to find it hard to believe there such a thing in the world. I'll march myself back where he waiting, holding it straight up in this hand."

She lifted her free hand, gave a little nod, turned around,

and walked out of the doctor's office. Then her slow step
began on the stairs, going down.

FOR DISCUSSION

1. "A worn path" suggests that this way must have been traveled
   many times before; it was also a lonely way. Phoenix Jackson's
   journey to Natchez could be compared to a holy pilgrimage that
   many others like her have made through life. The Mississippi setting might have been different, but her experiences along the way
   are not unlike those of others who have gone on similar quests.
   Among these experiences, consider some of the hazards she en-
   counters. What does the thorny bush — doing its "appointed work"
   — represent to the old woman with her wry humor?
2. What allegorical meanings might be read into her crossing the log,
   thinking a little boy was offering her a slice of marble cake,
   coming upon the scarecrow?
3. The dog forces her into the ditch after she has come through a
   fairly easy stretch. She compensates for her over-confidence with
   an increased awareness of her extreme age and her limitations.
   How does she also show her keen sense of humor when the young
   hunter finds her?
4. The hunter obviously admires her, yet he attributes to her trip a
   motive that is childish compared with her real motive. What is the
   great difference between what the hunter *thought* she was going
   to Natchez for and what she was really going for?
5. When she retrieves the nickel he drops, is she stealing? Does
   this act debase her? Defend your answer.
6. In Natchez she does not hesitate to ask a lady to tie her shoelaces.
   What trait in her personality does this act reveal?
7. When Phoenix Jackson reaches her destination, she assumes a
   "ceremonial stiffness." There is a kind of dignified ritual in the
   way she conducts her business. What is psychologically right
   about her lapse of memory? Compare her condition with the state
   of religious ecstasy sometimes experienced by saints and
   prophets.
8. How does the behavior of the attendant and the nurse set off, by
   contrast, the greater charity of Phoenix Jackson's journey to
   Natchez?
9. Why is the little windmill which she plans to take back to her
   grandson truly a Christmas gift?

FOR COMPOSITION

The beauty of this fable is that it never loses touch with concrete reality. You could read it as a good story without regard to its deeper significance. You do the author and yourself greater credit, however, by. searching for those meanings that lie beneath the surface. This assignment is by no means easy, but try to write a short fable which will suggest some larger idea. You could base your story on some religious concept, a scientific principle, a social problem, or a personal experience. Make every effort to write a credible story, with the allegorical meaning not too obvious.

Truman Capote

Many of Truman Capote's stories reveal the Gothic influence in American fiction most notably present in Edgar Allan Poe's stories. Capote shows a penchant for fantasy and the grotesque, and for characters who are eccentric and strange. In the following story, a mysterious young visitor comes to haunt the life of a middle-aged widow living in New York City.

Miriam

For several years, Mrs. H. T. Miller had lived alone in a pleasant apartment (two rooms with kitchenette) in a remodeled brownstone near the East River. She was a widow: Mr. H. T. Miller had left a reasonable amount of insurance. Her interests were narrow, she had no friends to speak of, and she rarely journeyed farther than the corner grocery. The other people in the house never seemed to notice her: her clothes were matter-of-fact, her hair iron-gray, clipped and casually waved; she did not use cosmetics, her features were plain and inconspicuous, and on her last birthday she was sixty-one. Her activities were seldom spontaneous: she kept the two rooms immaculate, smoked an occasional cigarette, prepared her own meals and tended a canary.

Then she met Miriam. It was snowing that night. Mrs. Miller had finished drying the supper dishes and was thumbing through an afternoon paper when she saw an advertisement of a picture playing at a neighborhood theater. The title sounded good, so she struggled into her beaver coat, laced her galoshes and left the apartment, leaving one light burning in the foyer: she found nothing more disturbing than a sensation of darkness.

The snow was fine, falling gently, not yet making an impression on the pavement. The wind from the river cut only at street crossings. Mrs. Miller hurried, her head bowed, oblivious as a mole burrowing a blind path. She stopped at a drugstore and bought a package of peppermints.

A long line stretched in front of the box office; she took her place at the end. There would be (a tired voice groaned) a short wait for all seats. Mrs. Miller rummaged in her leather handbag till she collected exactly the correct change for admission. The line seemed to be taking its own time and, looking around for some distraction, she suddenly became conscious of a little girl standing under the edge of the marquee.

Her hair was the longest and strangest Mrs. Miller had ever seen: absolutely silver-white, like an albino's. It flowed waist-length in smooth, loose lines. She was thin and fragilely constructed. There was a simple, special elegance in the way she stood with her thumbs in the pockets of a tailored plum-velvet coat.

Mrs. Miller felt oddly excited, and when the little girl glanced toward her, she smiled warmly. The little girl walked over and said, "Would you care to do me a favor?"

"I'd be glad to, if I can," said Mrs. Miller.

"Oh, it's quite easy. I merely want you to buy a ticket for me; they won't let me in otherwise. Here, I have the money." And gracefully she handed Mrs. Miller two dimes and a nickel.

They went over to the theater together. An usherette directed them to a lounge; in twenty minutes the picture would be over.

"I feel just like a genuine criminal," said Mrs. Miller gaily, as she sat down. "I mean that sort of thing's against the law, isn't it? I do hope I haven't done the wrong thing. Your mother knows where you are, dear? I mean she does, doesn't she?"

The little girl said nothing. She unbuttoned her coat and folded it across her lap. Her dress underneath was prim and dark blue. A gold chain dangled about her neck, and her fingers, sensitive and musical-looking, toyed with it. Examining her more attentively, Mrs. Miller decided the truly distinctive feature was not her hair, but her eyes; they were hazel, steady, lacking any child-like quality whatsoever and, because of their size, seemed to consume her small face.

Mrs. Miller offered a peppermint. "What's your name, dear?"

"Miriam," she said, as though, in some curious way, it were information already familiar.

"Why, isn't that funny—my name's Miriam, too. And it's not a terribly common name either. Now, don't tell me your last name's Miller!"

"Just Miriam."

"But isn't that funny?"

"Moderately," said Miriam, and rolled the peppermint on her tongue.

Mrs. Miller flushed and shifted uncomfortably. "You have such a large vocabulary for such a little girl."

"Do I?"

"Well, yes," said Mrs. Miller, hastily changing the topic to: "Do you like the movies?"

"I really wouldn't know," said Miriam. "I've never been before."

Women began filling the lounge; the rumble of the newsreel bombs exploded in the distance. Mrs. Miller rose, tucking her purse under her arm. "I guess I'd better be running now if I want to get a seat," she said. "It was nice to have met you."

Miriam nodded ever so slightly.

It snowed all week. Wheels and footsteps moved soundlessly on the street, as if the business of living continued secretly behind a pale but impenetrable curtain. In the falling quiet there was no sky or earth, only snow lifting in the wind, frosting the window glass, chilling the rooms, deadening and hushing the city. At all hours it was necessary to keep a lamp lighted, and Mrs. Miller lost track of the days: Friday was no different from Saturday and on Sunday she went to the grocery: closed, of course.

That evening she scrambled eggs and fixed a bowl of tomato soup. Then, after putting on a flannel robe and cold-creaming her face, she propped herself up in bed with a hot-water bottle under her feet. She was reading the *Times* when the doorbell rang. At first she thought it must be a mistake and whoever it was would go away. But it rang and rang and settled to a persistent buzz. She looked at the clock: a little after eleven; it did not seem possible, she was always asleep by ten.

Climbing out of bed, she trotted barefoot across the living room. "I'm coming, please be patient." The latch was caught; she turned it this way and that way and the bell never paused an instant. "Stop it," she cried. The bolt gave way and she opened the door an inch. "What in heaven's name?"

"Hello," said Miriam.

"Oh . . . why, hello," said Mrs. Miller, stepping hesitantly into the hall. "You're that little girl."

"I thought you'd never answer, but I kept my finger on the button; I knew you were home. Aren't you glad to see me?"

Mrs. Miller did not know what to say. Miriam, she saw, wore the same plum-velvet coat and now she had also a beret to match; her white hair was braided in two shining plaits and looped at the ends with enormous white ribbons.

"Since I've waited so long, you could at least let me in," she said.

"It's awfully late. . . ."

Miriam regarded her blankly. "What difference does that make? Let me in. It's cold out here and I have on a silk dress." Then, with a gentle gesture, she urged Mrs. Miller aside and passed into the apartment.

She dropped her coat and beret on a chair. She was indeed wearing a silk dress. White silk. White silk in February. The skirt was beautifully pleated and the sleeves long; it made a faint rustle as she strolled about the room. "I like your place," she said. "I like the rug, blue's my favorite color." She touched a paper rose in a vase on the coffee table. "Imitation," she commented wanly. "How sad. Aren't imitations sad?" She seated herself on the sofa, daintily spreading her skirt.

"What do you want?" asked Mrs. Miller.

"Sit down," said Miriam. "It makes me nervous to see people stand."

Mrs. Miller sank to a hassock.[1] "What do you want?" she repeated.

"You know, I don't think you're glad I came."

For a second time Mrs. Miller was without an answer; her hand motioned vaguely. Miriam giggled and pressed back on a mound of chintz pillows. Mrs. Miller observed that the girl was less pale than she remembered; her cheeks were flushed.

"How did you know where I lived?"

Miriam frowned. "That's no question at all. What's your name? What's mine?"

"But I'm not listed in the phone book."

"Oh, let's talk about something else."

Mrs. Miller said. "Your mother must be insane to let a child like you wander around at all hours of the night—and in such ridiculous clothes. She must be out of her mind."

Miriam got up and moved to a corner where a covered bird cage hung from a ceiling chain. She peeked beneath the cover. "It's a canary," she said. "Would you mind if I woke him? I'd like to hear him sing."

"Leave Tommy alone," said Mrs. Miller, anxiously. "Don't you dare wake him."

"Certainly," said Miriam. "But I don't see why I can't hear him sing." And then, "Have you anything to eat? I'm starving! Even milk and a jam sandwich would be fine."

"Look," said Mrs. Miller, arising from the hassock, "look— if I make some nice sandwiches will you be a good child and run along home? It's past midnight, I'm sure."

"It's snowing," reproached Miriam. "And cold and dark."

"Well, you shouldn't have come here to begin with," said Mrs. Miller, struggling to control her voice. "I can't help the weather. If you want anything to eat you'll have to promise to leave."

Miriam brushed a braid against her cheek. Her eyes were thoughtful, as if weighing the proposition. She turned toward the bird cage. "Very well," she said, "I promise."

How old is she? Ten? Eleven? Mrs. Miller, in the kitchen, unsealed a jar of strawberry preserves and cut four slices of

---

[1] *hassock:* a firmly stuffed cushion used as a footstool or seat

bread. She poured a glass of milk and paused to light a cigarette. *And why has she come?* Her hand shook as she held
the match, fascinated, till it burned her finger. The canary
was singing; singing as he did in the morning and at no other
time. "Miriam," she called, "Miriam, I told you not to dis-
turb Tommy." There was no answer. She called again; all
she heard was the canary. She inhaled the cigarette and discovered she had lighted the cork-tip end and—oh, really,
she mustn't lose her temper.

She carried the food in on a tray and set it on the coffee
table. She saw first that the bird cage still wore its night cover.
And Tommy was singing. It gave her a queer sensation. And
no one was in the room. Mrs. Miller went through an alcove
leading to her bedroom; at the door she caught her breath.

"What are you doing?" she asked.

Miriam glanced up and in her eyes there was a look that was
not ordinary. She was standing by the bureau, a jewel case
opened before her. For a minute she studied Mrs. Miller,
forcing their eyes to meet, and she smiled. "There's nothing
good here," she said. "But I like this." Her hand held a cameo
brooch. "It's charming."

"Suppose—perhaps you'd better put it back," said Mrs.
Miller, feeling suddenly the need of some support. She leaned
against the door frame; her head was unbearably heavy; a
pressure weighted the rhythm of her heartbeat. The light
seemed to flutter defectively. "Please, child—a gift from
my husband . . ."

"But it's beautiful and I want it," said Miriam. *"Give it
to me."*

As she stood, striving to shape a sentence which would
somehow save the brooch, it came to Mrs. Miller there was no
one to whom she might turn; she was alone; a fact that had not
been among her thoughts for a long time. Its sheer emphasis
was stunning. But here in her own room in the hushed snow-
city were evidences she could not ignore or, she knew with
startling clarity, resist.

Miriam ate ravenously, and when the sandwiches and milk
were gone, her fingers made cobweb movements over the

plate, gathering crumbs. The cameo gleamed on her blouse, the blond profile like a trick reflection of its wearer. "That was very nice," she sighed, "though now an almond cake oɪ a cherry would be ideal. Sweets are lovely, don't you think?"

Mrs. Miller was perched precariously on the hassock, smoking a cigarette. Her hair net had slipped lopsided and loose strands straggled down her face. Her eyes were stupidly concentrated on nothing and her cheeks were mottled in red patches, as though a fierce slap had left permanent marks.

"Is there a candy—a cake?"

Mrs. Miller tapped ash on the rug. Her head swayed slightly as she tried to focus her eyes. "You promised to leave if I made the sandwiches," she said.

"Dear me, did I?"

"It was a promise and I'm tired and I don't feel well at all."

"Mustn't fret," said Miriam. "I'm only teasing."

She picked up her coat, slung it over her arm, and arranged her beret in front of a mirror. Presently she bent close to Mrs. Miller and whispered, "Kiss me good night."

"Please—I'd rather not," said Mrs. Miller.

Miriam lifted a shoulder, arched an eyebrow. "As you like," she said, and went directly to the coffee table, seized the vase containing the paper roses, carried it to where the hard surface of the floor lay bare, and hurled it downward. Glass sprayed in all directions and she stamped her foot on the bouquet.

Then slowly she walked to the door, but before closing it she looked back at Mrs. Miller with a slyly innocent curiosity.

Mrs. Miller spent the next day in bed, rising once to feed the canary and drink a cup of tea; she took her temperature and had none, yet her dreams were feverishly agitated; their unbalanced mood lingered even as she lay staring wide-eyed at the ceiling. One dream threaded through the others like an elusively mysterious theme in a complicated symphony, and the scenes it depicted were sharply outlined, as though sketched by a hand of gifted intensity: a small girl, wearing a bridal gown and a wreath of leaves, led a gray procession down a mountain path, and among them there was unusual silence till a woman at the rear asked, "Where is she taking us?" "No one knows," said an old man marching in front. "But isn't she pretty?" volunteered a third voice. "Isn't she like a frost flower . . . so shining and white?"

Tuesday morning she woke up feeling better; harsh slats of sunlight, slanting through Venetian blinds, shed a disrupting light on her unwholesome fancies. She opened the window to discover a thawed, mild-as-spring day; a sweep of clean new clouds crumpled against a vastly blue, out-of-season sky, and across the low line of rooftops she could see the river and smoke curving from tugboat stacks in a warm wind. A great silver truck plowed the snow-banked street, its machine sound humming on the air.

After straightening the apartment, she went to the grocer's, cashed a check and continued to Schrafft's where she ate breakfast and chatted happily with the waitress. Oh, it was a wonderful day — more like a holiday — and it would be so foolish to go home.

She boarded a Lexington Avenue bus and rode up to Eighty-sixth Street; it was here that she had decided to do a little shopping.

She had no idea what she wanted or needed, but she idled along, intent only upon the passers-by, brisk and preoccupied, who gave her a disturbing sense of separateness.

It was while waiting at the corner of Third Avenue that she saw the man: an old man, bowlegged and stooped under an armload of bulging packages; he wore a shabby brown coat and a checkered cap. Suddenly she realized they were exchanging a smile: there was nothing friendly about this smile, it was merely two cold flickers of recognition. But she was certain she had never seen him before.

He was standing next to an El pillar,[2] and as she crossed the street he turned and followed. He kept quite close; from the corner of her eye she watched his reflection wavering on the shopwindows.

Then in the middle of the block she stopped and faced him. He stopped also and cocked his head, grinning. But what

[2] *El pillar:* one of the posts that support the track for an elevated train

could she say? Do? Here, in broad daylight, on Eighty-sixth Street? It was useless and, despising her own helplessness, she quickened her steps.

Now Second Avenue is a dismal street, made from scraps and ends; part cobblestone, part asphalt, part cement; and its atmosphere of desertion is permanent. Mrs. Miller walked five blocks without meeting anyone, and all the while the steady crunch of his footfalls in the snow stayed near. And when she came to a florist's shop, the sound was still with her. She hurried inside and watched through the glass door as the old man passed; he kept his eyes straight ahead and didn't slow his pace, but he did one strange, telling thing: he tipped his cap.

"Six white ones, did you say?" asked the florist. "Yes," she told him, "white roses." From there she went to a glassware store and selected a vase, presumably a replacement for the one Miriam had broken, though the price was intolerable and the vase itself (she thought) grotesquely vulgar. But a series of unaccountable purchases had begun, as if by prearranged plan: a plan of which she had not the least knowledge or control.

She bought a bag of glazed cherries, and at a place called the Knickerbocker Bakery she paid forty cents for six almond cakes.

Within the last hour the weather had turned cold again; like blurred lenses, winter clouds cast a shade over the sun, and the skeleton of an early dusk colored the sky; a damp mist mixed with the wind and the voices of a few children who romped high on mountains of gutter snow seemed lonely and cheerless. Soon the first flake fell, and when Mrs. Miller reached the brownstone house, snow was falling in a swift screen and foot tracks vanished as they were printed.

The white roses were arranged decoratively in the vase. The glazed cherries shone on a ceramic plate. The almond cakes, dusted with sugar, awaited a hand. The canary fluttered on its swing and picked at a bar of seed.

At precisely five the doorbell rang. Mrs. Miller *knew* who it was. The hem of her housecoat trailed as she crossed the floor. "Is that you?" she called.

"Naturally," said Miriam, the word resounding shrilly from the hall. "Open this door."

"Go away," said Mrs. Miller.

"Please hurry . . . I have a heavy package."

"Go away," said Mrs. Miller. She returned to the living room, lighted a cigarette, sat down and calmly listened to the buzzer; on and on and on. "You might as well leave. I have no intention of letting you in."

Shortly the bell stopped. For possibly ten minutes Mrs. Miller did not move. Then, hearing no sound, she concluded Miriam had gone. She tiptoed to the door and opened it a sliver; Miriam was half-reclining atop a cardboard box with a beautiful French doll cradled in her arms.

"Really, I thought you were never coming," she said peevishly. "Here, help me get this in, it's awfully heavy."

It was not spell-like compulsion that Mrs. Miller felt, but rather a curious passivity; she brought in the box, Miriam the doll. Miriam curled up on the sofa, not troubling to remove her coat or beret, and watched disinterestedly as Mrs. Miller dropped the box and stood trembling, trying to catch her breath.

"Thank you," she said. In the daylight she looked pinched and drawn, her hair less luminous. The French doll she was loving wore an exquisite powdered wig and its idiot glass eyes sought solace in Miriam's. "I have a surprise," she continued. "Look into my box."

Kneeling, Mrs. Miller parted the flaps and lifted out another doll; then a blue dress which she recalled as the one Miriam had worn that first night at the theatre; and of the remainder she said, "It's all clothes. Why?"

"Because I've come to live with you," said Miriam, twisting a cherry stem. "Wasn't it nice of you to buy me the cherries . . .?"

"But you can't! For God's sake go away — go away and leave me alone!"

" . . . and the roses and the almond cakes? How really wonderfully generous. You know, these cherries are delicious. The last place I lived was with an old man; he was terribly poor and we never had good things to eat. But I think I'll be happy here." She paused to snuggle her doll closer. "Now, if you'll just show me where to put my things..."

Mrs. Miller's face dissolved into a mask of ugly red lines; she began to cry, and it was an unnatural, tearless sort of weeping, as though, not having wept for a long time, she had forgotten how. Carefully she edged backward till she touched the door.

She fumbled through the hall and down the stairs to a landing below. She pounded frantically on the door of the first apartment she came to; a short, redheaded man answered and she pushed past him. "Say, what the hell is this?" he said. "Anything wrong, lover?" asked a young woman who appeared from the kitchen, drying her hands. And it was to her that Mrs. Miller turned.

"Listen," she cried, "I'm ashamed behaving this way but— well, I'm Mrs. H. T. Miller and I live upstairs and . . ." She pressed her hands over her face. "It sounds so absurd . . . ."

The woman guided her to a chair, while the man excitedly rattled pocket change. "Yeah?"

"I live upstairs and there's a little girl visiting me, and I suppose that I'm afraid of her. She won't leave and I can't make her and—she's going to do something terrible. She's already stolen my cameo, but she's about to do something worse—something terrible!"

The man asked, "Is she a relative, huh?"

Mrs. Miller shook her head. "I don't know who she is. Her name's Miriam, but I don't know for certain who she is."

"You gotta calm down, honey," said the woman, stroking Mrs. Miller's arm. "Harry here'll tend to this kid. Go on, lover." And Mrs. Miller said, "The door's open—5A."

After the man left, the woman brought a towel and bathed Mrs. Miller's face. "You're very kind," Mrs. Miller said. "I'm sorry to act like such a fool, only this wicked child . . . ."

"Sure, honey," consoled the woman. "Now, you better take it easy."

Mrs. Miller rested her head in the crook of her arm; she was quiet enough to be asleep. The woman turned a radio dial; a piano and a husky voice filled the silence and the woman, tapping her foot, kept excellent time. "Maybe we oughta go up too," she said.

"I don't want to see her again. I don't want to be anywhere near her."

"Uh huh, but what you shoulda done, you shoulda called a cop."

Presently they heard the man on the stairs. He strode into the room frowning and scratching the back of his neck. "Nobody there," he said, honestly embarrassed. "She musta beat it."

"Harry, you're a jerk," announced the woman. "We been sitting here the whole time and we woulda seen . . ." she stopped abruptly, for the man's glance was sharp.

"I looked all over," he said, "and there just ain't nobody there. Nobody, understand?"

"Tell me," said Mrs. Miller, rising, "tell me, did you see a large box? Or a doll?"

"No ma'am, I didn't."

And the woman, as if delivering a verdict, said, "Well, for cryinoutloud. . . ."

Mrs. Miller entered her apartment softly; she walked to the center of the room and stood quite still. No, in a sense it had not changed: the roses, the cakes, and the cherries were in place. But this was an empty room, emptier than if the furnishings and familiars were not present, lifeless and petrified as a funeral parlor. The sofa loomed before her with a new strangeness: its vacancy had a meaning that would have been less penetrating and terrible had Miriam been curled on it. She gazed fixedly at the space where she remembered setting the box and, for a moment, the hassock spun desperately. And she looked through the window; surely the river was real, surely snow was falling—but then, one could not be certain witness to anything: Miriam, so vividly there—and yet, where was she? Where, where?

As though moving in a dream, she sank to a chair. The room was losing shape; it was dark and getting darker and there was nothing to be done about it; she could not lift her hand to light a lamp.

Suddenly, closing her eyes, she felt an upward surge, like a diver emerging from some deeper, greener depth. In times of terror or immense distress, there are moments when the mind waits, as though for a revelation, while a skein of calm is woven over thought; it is like a sleep, or a supernatural trance; and during this lull one is aware of a force of quiet reasoning: well, what if she had never really known a girl named Miriam? that she had been foolishly frightened on the street? In the end, like everything else, it was of no importance. For the only thing she had lost to Miriam was her identity, but now she knew she had found again the person who lived in this room, who cooked her own meals, who owned a canary, who was someone she could trust and believe in: Mrs. H. T. Miller.

Listening in contentment, she became aware of a double sound: a bureau drawer opening and closing; she seemed to hear it long after completion—opening and closing. Then gradually, the harshness of it was replaced by the murmur of a silk dress and this, delicately faint, was moving nearer and swelling in intensity till the walls trembled with the vibration and the room was caving under a wave of whispers. Mrs. Miller stiffened and opened her eyes to a dull, direct stare.

"Hello," said Miriam.

FOR DISCUSSION

1. How would you describe Mrs. Miller's life before Miriam enters the story? Although she is a widow, she doesn't consider herself lonely. What incident suddenly makes her aware that she *is* lonely? How is her isolation again brought home to her while she is shopping?

2. From the time Mrs. Miller meets Miriam, many things happen

that are out of the ordinary. Point these out. What things does Mrs. Miller do that are, for her, unusual?

3. Throughout the story, Capote uses realistic detail to build up an aura of the supernatural. How do his descriptions of the weather reinforce the overall mood? What bits of description seem to emphasize Miriam's unreal quality?

4. Describe Mrs. Miller's strange encounter with the old man while she is shopping. At what point in the story do you find an explanation for his uncanny recognition of her?

5. What sort of person is Miriam? What is Mrs. Miller's reaction to her as the story progresses?

6. What "verdict" do you think the man and woman downstairs are "delivering" upon Mrs. Miller? What is her state of mind when she returns upstairs? What is your "verdict"?

FOR COMPOSITION

1. Write a short composition giving your ideas about Mrs. Miller's condition and possible reasons for Miriam's appearance.

2. Descriptive details play a very important part in building the mood of stories like "Miriam," that are written in the Gothic tradition (see page 515). Compare the descriptive techniques of Poe, Faulkner, and Capote in the three stories you have read.

J. F. Powers

J. F. Powers' attitude toward people is both critical and compassionate, as this story reveals. It shows the human sorrow brought to a Negro family by circumstances they neither created nor encouraged. Powers presents the racial situation through the eyes of a small boy barely old enough to realize what is happening.

The Trouble

We watched at the window all that afternoon.

Old Gramma came out of her room and said, Now you kids get away from there this very minute, and we would until she went back to her room. We could hear her old rocking-chair creak when she got up or sat down and so we always ran away from the window before she came into the room to see if we were minding her good or looking out. Except once she went back to her room and didn't sit down, or maybe she did and got up easy so the chair didn't creak, or maybe we got our signals mixed, because she caught us all there and shooed us away and pulled down the green shade. The next time we were very sure she wasn't foxing us before we went to the window and lifted the shade just enough to peek out.

It was like waiting for rats as big as cats to run out from under a tenement so you could pick them off with a .22. Rats are about the biggest live game you can find in ordinary times and you see more of them than white folks in our neighborhood — in ordinary times. But the rats we waited for today were white ones and they were doing most of the shooting themselves. Sometimes some coloreds would come by with guns, but not often; they mostly had clubs. This morning we'd seen the whites catch up with a shot-in-the-leg colored and throw bricks and stones at his black head till it got all red and he was dead. I could still see the wet places in the alley. That's why we kept looking out the window. We wanted to see some whites get killed for a change, but we didn't much think we would, and I guess what we really expected to see was nothing, or maybe them killing another colored.

There was a rumpus downstairs in front and I could hear a mess of people tramping up the stairs. They kept on coming after the second floor and my sister Carrie, my twin, said maybe they were whites come to get *us* because we saw what they did to the shot-in-the-leg colored in the alley. I was scared for a minute, I admit, but when I heard their voices plainer I knew they were coloreds and it was all right, only I didn't see why there were so many of them.

Then I got scared again, only different now, empty scared all over, when they came down the hall on our floor, not stopping at anybody else's door. And then there they were, banging on our door, of all the doors in the building. They tried to come right on in, but the door was locked.

Old Gramma was the one locked it and she said she'd clean house if one of us kids so much as looked at the knob even. She threw the key down her neck somewhere and I went and told her that was our door the people were pounding on and where was the key. She reached down her neck and there was the key all right. But she didn't act much like she intended to open the door. She just stood there staring at it like it was somebody alive, saying the litany to the Blessed Virgin: *Mère du Christ, priez pour nous, Secours des chrétiens, priez.*[1] Then all the sudden she was crying, tears were blurry in her old yellow eyes, and she put the key in the lock, her veiny hands shaking, and unlocked the door.

They had Mama in their arms. I forgot all about Old Gramma but I guess she passed out. Anyway, she was on the floor and a couple of men were picking her up and a couple of

[1] *Mère du Christ, priez pour nous, Secours des chrétiens, priez:* Mother of Christ, pray for us; Help of Christians, pray. (French)

women were saying, Put her here, put her there. I wasn't
worried as much about Old Gramma as I was about Mama.

A bone, God it made me sick, had poked through the flesh
of Mama's arm, all bloody like a sharp stick, and something
terrible was wrong with her chest. I couldn't look any more
and Carrie was screaming. That started me crying. Tears got
in the way, but still I could see the baby, one-and-a-half, and
brother George, four-and-a-half, and they had their eyes wide
open at what they saw and weren't crying a bit, too young to
know what the hell.

They put Old Gramma in her room on the cot and closed the
door on her and some old woman friend of hers that kept
dipping a handkerchief in cold water and laying it on Old
Gramma's head. They put Mama on the bed in the room where
everybody was standing around and talking lower and lower
until pretty soon they were just whispering.

Somebody came in with a doctor, a colored one, and he had
a little black bag like they have in the movies. I don't think
our family ever had a doctor come to see us before. Maybe
before I was born Mama and Daddy did. I heard the doctor
tell Mr. Purvine, that works in the same mill Daddy does,
only the night shift, that he ought to set the bone, but honest
to God he thought he might as well wait as he didn't want to
hurt Mama if it wasn't going to make any difference.

He wasn't nearly as brisk now with his little black bag as
he had been when he came in. He touched Mama's forehead
a couple of times and it didn't feel good to him, I guess, because he looked tired after he did it. He held his hand on
her wrist of the good arm, but I couldn't tell what this meant
from his face. It mustn't have been any worse than the forehead, or maybe his face had nothing to do with what he
thought and I was imagining all this from seeing the shape
Mama was in. Finally he said, I'll try, and he began calling
for hot water and other things and pretty soon Mama was all
bandaged up white.

The doctor stepped away from Mama and over to some men
and women, six or seven of them now — a lot more had gone —
and asked them what had happened. He didn't ask all the
questions I wanted to ask — I guess he already knew some of

the answers — but I did find out Mama was on a streetcar coming home from the plant — Mama works now and we're saving for a cranberry farm — when the riot broke out in that section. Mr. Purvine said he called the mill and told Daddy to come home. But Mr. Purvine said he wasn't going to work tonight himself, the way the riot was spreading and the way the coloreds were getting the worst of it.

As usual, said a man with glasses on, the Negroes ought to organize and fight the thing to a finish. The doctor frowned at that. Mr. Purvine said he didn't know. But one woman and another man said that was the right idea.

If we must die, said the man with glasses on, let it not be like hogs hunted and penned in an inglorious spot! The doctor said, Yes, we all know that, but the man with glasses on went on, because the others were listening to him, and I was glad he did, because I was listening to him too: We must meet the common foe; though far outnumbered, let us still be brave, and for their thousand blows deal one death-blow! What though before us lies the open grave? Like men we'll face the murderous, cowardly pack, pressed to the wall, dying, but — fighting back!

They all thought it was fine and a woman said that was poetry and I thought if that is what it is I know what I want to be now, a poetryman. I asked the man with glasses on if that was his poetry, though I did not think it was, for some reason, and the men and women all looked at me like they were surprised to see me there and like I ought not hear such things, except the man with glasses on, and he said, No, son, it was not his poetry, he wished it was, but it was Claude McKay's, a Negro, and I could find it in the public library. I decided I would go to the public library when the riot was over and it was the first time in my life I ever thought of the public library the way I did then.

They all left about this time, except the doctor and the old woman friend of Old Gramma's. She came out of Old Gramma's room, and when the door opened I saw Old Gramma lying on the cot with her eyes closed. The old woman asked me if I could work a can opener and I said, Yes, I can, and she handed me a can of vegetable soup from the shelf. She got a meal together and us kids sat down to eat. Not Carrie, though. She sat in our good chair with her legs under her and her eyes closed. Mama was sleeping and the doctor rolled up the shade at the window and looked out while we ate. I mean brother George and the baby. I couldn't eat. I just drank my glass of water. The old woman said, Here, here, I hadn't ought to let good food go to waste and was that any way to act at the table and I wasn't the first boy in the world to lose his mother.

I wondered was she crazy and I yelled I wasn't going to lose my mother and I looked to see and I was right. Mama was just sleeping and the doctor was there in case she needed him and everything was taken care of and—everything. The doctor didn't even turn away from the window when I yelled at the old woman and I thought at least he'd say I'd wake my mother up shouting that way, or maybe that I was right and the old woman was wrong. I got up from the table and stood by the doctor at the window. He only stayed there a minute more then and went over to feel Mama's wrist again. He did not touch her forehead this time.

Old Gramma came out of her room and said to me, Was that you raising so much cain in here, boy? I said, Yes, it was, and just when I was going to tell her what the old woman said about losing Mama I couldn't. I didn't want to hear it out loud again. I didn't even want to think it in my mind. Old Gramma went over and gazed down at Mama. She turned away quickly and told the old woman, Please, I'll just have a cup of hot water, that's all, I'm so upset. Then she went over to the doctor by the window and whispered something to him and he whispered something back and it must've been only one or two words, because he was looking out the window the next moment.

Old Gramma said she'd be back in a minute and went out the door and slip-slapping down the hall. I went to the window; the evening sun was going down, and I saw Old Gramma come out the back entrance of our building. She crossed the alley and went in the back door of the grocerystore.

A lot of racket cut loose about a block up the alley. It was still empty, though. Old Gramma came out of the grocerystore with something in a brown bag. She stopped in the middle of the alley and seemed to be watching the orange evening sun going down behind the buildings. The sun got in her hair and somehow under her skin kind of and it did a wonderful thing to her. She looked so young for a moment that I saw Mama in her, both of them beautiful New Orleans ladies.

The racket cut loose again, nearer now, and a pack of men came running down the alley, about three dozen whites chasing two coloreds. One of the whites was blowing a bugle—*tan tivvy tan tivvy tan tivvy*—like the white folks do when they go fox-hunting in the movies or Virginia. I looked down, quick, to see if Old Gramma had enough sense to come inside and I guess she did because she wasn't there. The two coloreds ran between two buildings, the whites ran after them and then the alley was quiet again. Old Gramma stepped out and I watched her stoop and pick up the brown bag that she had dropped before.

Another big noise made her drop it again. A whole smear of men swarmed out of the used-car lot and came galloping down the alley like wild buffaloes. Old Gramma scooted inside our building and the brown bag stayed in the alley. This time I couldn't believe my eyes, I saw what I thought I'd never see, I saw what us kids had been waiting to see ever since the riot broke out—a white man fixing to get himself nice and killed. A white man running—running, God Almighty, from about a million coloreds. And he was the one with the tan-tivvy bugle too. I hoped the coloreds would do the job up right.

The closer the white man came the worse it got for him, because the alley comes to a dead end when it hits our building. All at once, I don't know why, I was praying for that fool white man with the bugle to get away. But I didn't think he had a Chinaman's chance, the way he was going now, and maybe that's what made me pray for him.

Then he did a smart thing. He whipped the bugle over his shoulder like you do with a horseshoe for good luck and it hit the first colored behind him smack in the head, knocking him out, and that slowed up the others. The white man turned into the junkyard behind the furniture warehouse and the Victory Ballroom. Another smart thing, if he used his head. The space between the warehouse and the Victory is just wide enough for a man to run through. It's a long piece to the street, but if he made it there he'd be safe probably.

The long passageway must've looked too narrow to him, though, because the fool came rushing around the garage next to our building. For a moment he was the only one in the alley. The coloreds had followed him through the junkyard and probably got themselves all tangled up in garbage cans and rusty bed springs and ashpiles. But the white man was a goner just the same. In a minute they'd be coming for him for real. He'd have to run the length of the alley again to get away and the coloreds have got the best legs.

Then Old Gramma opened our back door and saved him.

I was very glad for the white man until suddenly I remembered poor Mama all broken to pieces on the bed and then I was sorry Old Gramma did it. The next moment I was glad again that she did. I understood now I did not care one way or the other about the white man. Now I was thinking of Mama—not of myself. I did not see what difference it could make to Mama if the white man lived or died. It only had something to do with us and him.

Then I got hold of a very strange idea. I told myself the trouble is somebody gets cheated or insulted or killed and everybody else tries to make it come out even by cheating and insulting or killing the cheaters and insulters and killers. Only they never do. I did not think they ever would. I told myself that I had a very big idea there and when the riot was over I would go to the public library and sit in the reading room and think about it. Or I would speak to Old Gramma about it, because it seemed like she had the same big idea and like she had had it a long time too.

The doctor was standing by me at the window all the time. He said nothing about what Old Gramma did, and now he stepped away from the window and so did I. I guess he felt the same way I did about the white man and that's why he stepped away from the window. The big idea again. He was afraid the coloreds down below would yell up at us, did we see the white man pass by. The coloreds were crazy mad all right. One of them had the white man's bugle and he banged on our door with it. I was worried Old Gramma had forgot to lock it and they might walk right in and that would be the end of the white man and the big idea.

But Old Gramma pulled another fast one. She ran out into the alley and pointed her yellow finger in about three wrong directions. In a second the alley was quiet and empty, except for Old Gramma. She walked slowly over against our building, where somebody had kicked the brown bag, and picked it up.

Old Gramma brought the white man right into our room, told him to sit down and poured herself a cup of hot water. She sipped it and said the white man could leave whenever he wanted to, but it might be better to wait a bit. The white man said he was much obliged, he hated to give us any trouble, and Oh, oh, is somebody sick over there, when he saw Mama, and that he'd just been passing by when a hundred nig—when he was attacked.

Old Gramma sipped her hot water. The doctor turned away from the window and said, Here they come again, take another look, and said, No, they're going back. He went over to Mama and held her wrist. I couldn't tell anything about her from his face. She was sleeping just the same. The doctor asked the white man, still standing, to sit down. Carrie only opened her eyes once and closed them. She hadn't changed her position in the good chair. Brother George and the baby stood in a corner with their eyes on the white man. The baby's legs buckled then—she'd only been walking about a week—and she collapsed softly to the floor. She worked her way up again without taking her eyes off the white man. He even looked funny and out of place to me in our room. I guess the man for the rent and Father Egan were the only white people come to see us since I could remember and now it was only the man for the rent since Father Egan died.

The doctor asked the white man did he work or own a business in this neighborhood. The white man said, No, glancing down at his feet, no, he just happened to be passing by when he was suddenly attacked like he said before. The doctor told Old Gramma she might wash Mama's face and neck again with warm water.

There was noise again in the alley, windows breaking and fences being pushed over. The doctor said, You could leave now, to the white man, it's a white mob this time, you'd be safe.

No, the white man said, I should say not, I wouldn't be seen with them, they're as bad as the others almost.

It is quite possible, the doctor said.

Old Gramma asked the white man if he would like a cup of tea.

Tea? No, he said, I don't drink tea, I didn't know you drank it.

I didn't know you knew her, the doctor said, looking at Old Gramma and the white man.

You colored folks, I mean, the white man said, Americans, I mean. Me, I don't drink tea, always considered it an English drink and bad for the kidneys.

The doctor did not answer. Old Gramma brought him a cup of tea.

And then Daddy came in. He ran over to Mama and fell down on his knees like he was dead, like seeing Mama with her arm broke and her chest so pushed in killed him on the spot. He lifted his face from the bed and kissed Mama on the lips; and then, Daddy, I could see, was crying, the strongest man in the world was crying with tears in his dark eyes and coming down the side of his big hard face. Mama called him her John Henry sometimes and there he was, her John Henry, the strongest man, black or white, in the whole damn world, crying.

He put his head down on the bed again. Nobody in the room moved until the baby toddled over to Daddy and patted him on the ear like she wanted to play the games those two make up with her little hands and his big ears and eyes and nose. But Daddy didn't move or say anything, if he even knew she was there, and the baby got a blank look in her eyes and walked away from Daddy and sat down, *plump,* on the floor across the room, staring at Daddy and the white man, back and forth, Daddy and the white man.

Daddy got up after a while and walked very slowly across the room and got himself a drink of water at the sink. For the first time he noticed the white man in the room. Who's he, he said, who's he? None of us said anything. Who the hell's he? Daddy wanted to know, thunder in his throat like there always is when he's extra mad or happy.

The doctor said the white man was Mr. Gorman and went over to Daddy and told him something in a low voice.

Innocent! What's he doing in this neighborhood then? Daddy said, loud as before. What's an *innocent* white man doing in this neighborhood now, answer me that! He looked at all of us in the room and none of us that knew what the white man was doing in this neighborhood wanted to explain to Daddy. Old Gramma and the doctor and me, none of us that knew, would tell.

I was just passing by, the white man said, as they can tell you.

The scared way he said it almost made me laugh. Was this a white man, I asked myself. Alongside Daddy's voice the white man's sounded plain foolish and weak, a little old pink tug squeaking at a big brown ocean liner about the right of way. Daddy seemed to forget all about him and began asking the doctor a lot of questions about Mama in a hoarse whisper I couldn't hear very well. Daddy's face got harder and harder and it didn't look like he'd ever crack a smile or shed a tear or anything soft again. Just hard, it got, hard as four spikes.

Old Gramma came and stood by Daddy's side and said she had called the priest when she was downstairs a while ago getting some candles. She was worried that the candles weren't blessed ones. She opened the brown bag then and that's what was inside, two white candles. I didn't know grocerystores carried them.

Old Gramma went to her room and took down the picture of the Sacred Heart all bleeding and put it on the little table by Mama's bed and set the candles in sticks on each side of it. She lit the candles and it made the Sacred Heart, punctured by the wreath of thorns, look bloodier than ever and made me think of that song, To Jesus' Heart All Burning, the kids sing at Our Saviour's on Sundays.

The white man went up to the doctor and said, I'm a Catholic too. But the doctor didn't say anything back, only nodded. He probably wasn't one himself, I thought, not many of the race are. Our family wouldn't be if Old Gramma and Mama didn't come from New Orleans, where Catholics are thicker than flies or Baptists.

Daddy got up from the table and said to the white man, So help me God, mister, I'll kill you in this room if my wife dies! The baby started crying and the doctor went to Daddy's side and turned him away from the white man and it wasn't hard to do because now Daddy was kind of limp and didn't look like he remembered anything about the white man or what he said he'd do to him if Mama . . . or anything.

I'll bet the priest won't show up, Daddy said.

The priest will come, Old Gramma said, the priest will always come when you need him, just wait. Her old lips were praying in French.

I hoped he would come like Old Gramma said, but I wasn't so sure. Some of the priests weren't much different from anybody else. They knew how to keep their necks in. Daddy said to Mama once if you only wanted to hear about social justice you could turn on the radio or go to the nearest stadium on the Fourth of July and there'd be an old white man in a new black suit saying it was a good thing and everybody ought to get some and if they'd just kick in more they might and anyway they'd be saved. One came to Our Saviour's last year and Father Egan said this is our new assistant and the next Sunday our new assistant was gone — poor health. But Daddy said he was transferred to a church in a white neighborhood because he couldn't stand to save black souls. Father Egan would've come a-flying, riot or no riot, but he was dead now and we didn't know much about the one that took his place.

Then he came, by God, the priest from Our Saviour's came to our room while the riot was going on. Old Gramma got all excited and said over and over she knew the priest would come. He was kind of young and skinny and pale, even for a white man, and he said, I'm Father Crowe, to everybody in the room and looked around to see who was who.

The doctor introduced himself and said Old Gramma was Old Gramma, Daddy was Daddy, we were the children, that was Mr. Gorman, who was just passing by, and over there was poor Mama. He missed Old Gramma's old woman friend; I guess he didn't know what to call her. The priest went over and took a look at Mama and nodded to the doctor and they went into Old Gramma's room together. The priest had a little black bag too and he took it with him. I suppose he was getting ready to give Mama Extreme Unction.[2] I didn't think they would wake her up for Confession or Holy Communion, she was so weak and needed the rest.

Daddy got up mad as a bull from the table and said, Remember what I said, mister, to the white man.

But why me, the white man asked, just because I'm white?

Daddy looked over at Mama on the bed and said, Yeah, just because you're white, yeah, that's why . . . Old Gramma took Daddy by the arm and steered him over to the table again and he sat down.

The priest and the doctor came out of Old Gramma's room and right away the priest faced the white man, like they'd been talking about him in Old Gramma's room, and asked him why he didn't go home. The white man said he'd heard some shouting in the alley a while ago that didn't sound so good to him and he didn't think it was safe yet and that was why.

I see, the priest said.

I'm a Catholic too, Father, the white man said.

That's the trouble, the priest said.

The priest took some cotton from his little black bag, dipped his fingers in holy oil and made the sign of the cross on Mama's eyes, nose, ears, mouth, and hands, rubbing the oil off with the cotton, and said prayers in Latin all the time he was doing it.

I want you all to kneel down now, the priest said, and we'll say the rosary. But we mustn't say it too loud because she is sleeping.

We all knelt down except the baby and Carrie. Carrie said she'd never kneel down to God again. Now Carrie, Old Gramma said, almost crying. She told Carrie it was for poor Mama and wouldn't Carrie kneel down if it was for poor Mama?

---

[2]*Extreme Unction:* in the Roman Catholic Church, the sacrament administered by a priest or bishop to a dying person

No! Carrie said, it must be a white God too! Then she began crying and she did kneel down after all.

Even the white man knelt down and the doctor and the old woman friend of Old Gramma's, a solid Baptist if I ever saw one, and we all said the rosary of the five sorrowful mysteries.

Afterwards the white man said to the priest, Do you mind if I leave when you do, Father? The priest didn't answer and the white man said, I think I'll be leaving now, Father. I wonder if you'd be going my way?

The priest finally said, All right, all right, come along, you won't be the first one to hide behind a Roman collar.

The white man said, I'm sure I don't know what you mean by that, Father. The priest didn't hear him, I guess, or want to explain, because he went over to Mama's bed.

The priest knelt once more by Mama and said a prayer in Latin out loud and made the sign of the cross over Mama! *In nomine Patris et Filii et Spiritus Sancti.*[3] He looked closer at Mama and motioned to the doctor. The doctor stepped over to the bed, felt Mama's wrist, put his head to her chest, where it wasn't pushed in, and stood up slowly.

Daddy and all of us had been watching the doctor when the priest motioned him over and now Daddy got up from the table, kicking the chair over he got up so fast, and ran to the bed. He sank, shaking all over, to his knees, and I believe he must've been crying again, although I thought he never would again and his head was down and I couldn't see for sure.

I began to get an awful bulging pain in my stomach. The doctor left the bed and grabbed the white man by the arm and was taking him to the door when Daddy jumped up, like he knew where they were going, and said, Wait a minute, mister!

The doctor and the white man stopped at the door. Daddy walked draggily over to them and stood in front of the white man, took a deep breath, and said in the stillest kind of whisper, I wouldn't touch you. That was all. He moved slowly back to Mama's bed and his big shoulders were sagged down like I never saw them before.

[3] *In nomine Patris et Filii et Spiritus Sancti:* In the name of the Father, and of the Son, and of the Holy Spirit. (Latin)

Old Gramma said *Jesus!* and stumbled down on her knees by Mama. Then the awful bulging pain in my stomach exploded and I knew that Mama wasn't just sleeping now and I couldn't breathe for a long while and then when I finally could I was crying like the baby and Brother George and so was Carrie.

FOR DISCUSSION

1. This story focuses the reader's attention upon questions of social justice, yet it also stresses the universal human qualities and feelings shared by all men. In what ways is the life of the family in the story like the lives of families you know? In what ways is it different? Which seem more important, the likenesses or the differences?

2. What is the basic conflict (see page 514) in this story? Is the family or any individual actively struggling against anyone or anything? Is the conflict resolved during the course of the story?

3. The story is told from the point of view of a young boy who does not understand the meaning of all that is happening. How does this make the situation even more meaningful to you as the reader? Why would the story have been less effective if told by the boy's father?

4. Why does the narrator want to see the bugle player get caught by the Negroes? At what point does he change his mind about the man? What mixed feelings does he have when Gramma saves the man? What does he think is "the trouble"?

5. What sort of man is the white bugler? What does the priest mean when he tells the man, "That's the trouble"?

6. The white man is surprised to learn that Gramma and the others drink tea. How is this fact significant of the racial problem in general? Why is it also significant that the father tells the white man, "I'll kill you in this room if my wife dies!"?

7. Powers, a Catholic himself, presents two views of the clergy. How would you characterize Father Egan and Father Crowe? Why is the family surprised that Father Crowe comes when he is called? What do you think Powers is saying about the clergy in relation to racial injustice?

8. Having read the story, what do *you* think "the trouble" is?

FOR COMPOSITION

1. What are your thoughts and feelings about the problems of racial injustice? Write a composition describing "the trouble" as you see it.
2. To get into the mind of another person and to understand how he or she thinks and feels is not easy. It is easier to sum up a person quickly and get to answers that make us comfortable, though the answers may be inadequate and even inaccurate. Choose one character from "The Trouble" and write a monologue in which that person expresses what he or she is truly thinking and feeling. Try to put yourself in the character's place and to see things through his or her eyes. Keep in mind that the person may have had a life very different from your own.

NEW VOICES

At no time have so many talented authors written so much for such a large reading audience as today. To trace a literary pattern in this welter of fiction is not easy, but many of the problems besetting writers are common to all mid-century Americans.

World War II provided a ready-made subject for a burst of competent stories, but none of them assumed the importance of Hemingway's World War I novel, *A Farewell to Arms.* Neither did the writers of these stories develop new forms or a new style of writing. Except for changes in time and place, the fiction of World War II differed very little from that of World War I.

The failure to create a fresh and original war literature has been attributed to the climate of opinion that prevailed after the war. This climate was principally of conformity and orthodoxy rather than of protest and individuality. Writing had become a profession at which many people could make a living. Writers, like most Americans at the time, seemed unwilling to risk the security of financial success by departing from accepted patterns and techniques.

Underlying the drive toward conformity were many very real anxieties. One was the fear of economic recession that, for a variety of reasons, did not develop. Another was the threat, growing out of the hysteria over the communist menace, of being accused of disloyalty or of a lack of integrity by public and government committees. Still another was a deep sense of guilt, shared by many people, over this country's use of atomic weapons. To cover up their fears and guilt, Americans worked harder than ever to improve their standard of living with all kinds of gadgets. Farm mechanization, air-conditioning, prefabricated homes and, especially, TV became part of an automated and electronic way of life. Many people could now point with pride to two cars in the garage and could look forward to more years in which to pay for them. At the turn of the century, life expectancy had been estimated at forty-nine years; by 1950 the figure had risen to sixty-seven. Given a longer life, many Americans sought—sometimes desperately—ways of spending their later years that were both pleasant and secure.

One anxiety overshadowed all others: the fear that peace was impossible. Scarcely five years after the close of World War II (1945), American soldiers were taking part in the Korean War. Its inconclusive ending was indicative of continued strife throughout the world. The ordeal of living in an unsettled world was almost as nerve-wracking as war.

Rather than protest against social and political restrictions, the writers of the 1950's turned for their subject matter to the inner forces that motivate human action and to the psychologically grotesque and the abnormal in society and the individual. In place of the so-called Silent Generation, there appeared a Beat Generation, which rejected the conventional comforts of modern civilization and sought pure sensory experience, sometimes of an unorthodox nature.

This trend continued into the 1960's with the "hippies," who made popular a colorful new style in clothing, originating from Carnaby Street in London. The effect of Op art and Pop art was also reflected in fashion designs, as well as in advertising, and in a generally freer atmosphere throughout the country.

With the 1960's, much of the numbness and fear of the previous decade had worn off, though war in various parts of the world that involved America gave rise to grave concern and criticism. In the meantime, artists in every field were searching the human heart to discover truths by which people could prevail and for positive values on which to base their work. The stories selected for this section are a sampling of the kind of work which the present generation of writers has done and is doing in the short story form.

KURT VONNEGUT, JR., a great favorite of young people, has stressed in his fiction the "tragic and comic possibilities of machines" and their impact on humanity. Early in his career, there was a tendency to dismiss him as a "science fiction writer," but it was soon recognized that he could not be fitted into any such facile category. He is a serious and discerning interpreter of the vagaries of human existence in the second half of the 20th century and in the 21st century as well. Being "serious" in this case does not imply being solemn, and his free-wheeling, imaginative humor is much admired.

The high reputation of RALPH ELLISON rests largely on his novel *Invisible Man,* published in 1952. This original and energetic novel received the National Book Award that year. Ellison's black hero faces the crucial problem of identity, and yet his situation transcends concerns of race and reflects the universal human condition. For this reason, the book is not only one of the best novels by an American black, but one of the best novels of our time. Ellison's skillful fusion of realism and surrealism, grim comedy and slapstick, is also present in "Flying Home," the short story included here.

One of the most promising modern writers is BERNARD MALAMUD, a New Yorker of thoroughly metropolitan background. Like many of his contemporaries seeking an audience, he first published his stories in the "little magazines" such as *American Mercury, Commentary,* and *Partisan Review.* "A Summer's Reading" appeared originally in *The New Yorker* and was later included in Malamud's collection of stories, *The Magic Barrel,* in 1958. Some of his best stories deal with Jewish experience in everyday life.

Malamud's practice of combining teaching with writing has become common among writers today. Thus at many colleges throughout the country, students have the opportunity of studying with first-rate authors of high professional repute.

The youngest author in this section, JOHN UPDIKE, is a prolific, versatile, and dedicated craftsman. He writes of everyday events with subtlety and wit, exhibiting a controlled, highly polished style. He already has four novels, two collections of poems, and two collections of short stories to his credit.

Kurt Vonnegut, Jr.

In this story, Kurt Vonnegut, Jr. takes a look at the world of 2158 A.D. when there are twelve billion people inhabiting the planet Earth. Like most statistics, this one probably has little meaning for most of us until a creative writer explores its impact in terms of everyday living. The consequences, as Vonnegut presents them, are fully believable, terribly funny, and altogether nightmarish.

Tomorrow and Tomorrow and Tomorrow

The year was 2158 A.D., and Lou and Emerald Schwartz were whispering on the balcony outside Lou's family's apartment on the seventy-sixth floor of Building 257 in Alden Village, a New York housing development that covered what had once been known as Southern Connecticut. When Lou and Emerald had married, Em's parents had tearfully described the marriage as being between May and December; but now, with Lou one hundred and twelve and Em ninety-three, Em's parents had to admit that the match had worked out well.

But Em and Lou weren't without their troubles, and they were out in the nippy air of the balcony because of them.

"Sometimes I get so mad, I feel like just up and diluting his anti-gerasone," said Em.

"That'd be against Nature, Em," said Lou, "it'd be murder. Besides, if he caught us tinkering with his anti-gerasone, not only would he disinherit us, he'd bust my neck. Just because he's one hundred and seventy-two doesn't mean Gramps isn't strong as a bull."

"Against Nature," said Em. "Who knows what Nature's like anymore? Ohhhhh—I don't guess I could ever bring myself to dilute his anti-gerasone or anything like that, but, gosh, Lou, a body can't help thinking Gramps is never going to leave if somebody doesn't help him along a little. Golly—we're so crowded a person can hardly turn around, and Verna's dying for a baby, and, Melissa's gone thirty years without one." She stamped her feet. "I get so sick of seeing his wrinkled old face, watching him take the only private room and the best chair and the best food, and getting to pick out what to watch on TV, and running everybody's life by changing his will all the time."

"Well, after all," said Lou bleakly, "Gramps *is* head of the family. And he can't help being wrinkled like he is. He was seventy before anti-gerasone was invented. He's going to leave, Em. Just give him time. It's his business. I know he's tough to live with, but be patient. It wouldn't do to do anything that'd rile him. After all, we've got it better'n anybody else, there on the daybed."

"How much longer do you think we'll get to sleep on the daybed before he picks another pet? The world's record's two months, isn't it?"

"Mom and Pop had it that long once, I guess."

"When *is* he going to leave, Lou?" said Emerald.

"Well, he's talking about giving up anti-gerasone right after the five-hundred-mile Speedway Race."

"Yes—and before that it was the Olympics, and before that the World's Series, and before that the Presidential Elections, and before that I-don't-know-what. It's been just one excuse after another for fifty years now. I don't think we're ever going to get a room to ourselves or an egg or anything."

"All right—call me a failure!" said Lou. "What can I do? I work hard and make good money, but the whole thing, practically, is taxed away for defense and old age pensions. And if it wasn't taxed away, where you think we'd find a vacant room to rent? Iowa, maybe? Well, who wants to live on the outskirts of Chicago?"

Em put her arms around his neck. "Lou, hon, I'm not calling you a failure. The Lord knows you're not. You just haven't had a chance to be anything or have anything because Gramps and the rest of his generation won't leave and let somebody else take over."

"Yeah, yeah," said Lou gloomily. "You can't exactly blame 'em, though, can you? I mean, I wonder how quick we'll knock off the anti-gerasone when we get Gramps' age."

"Sometimes I wish there wasn't any such thing as anti-gerasone!" said Emerald passionately. "Or I wish it was made out of something real expensive and hard-to-get instead of mud and dandelions. Sometimes I wish folks just up and died regular as clockwork, without anything to say about it, instead of deciding themselves how long they're going to stay around. There ought to be a law against selling the stuff to anybody over one hundred and fifty."

"Fat chance of that," said Lou, "with all the money and votes the old people've got." He looked at her closely. "You ready to up and die, Em?"

"Well, for heaven's sakes, what a thing to say to your wife. Hon! I'm not even one hundred yet." She ran her hands lightly over her firm, youthful figure, as though for confirmation. "The best years of my life are still ahead of me. But you can bet that when one hundred and fifty rolls around, old Em's going to pour her anti-gerasone down the sink, and quit taking up room, and she'll do it smiling."

"Sure, sure," said Lou, "you bet. That's what they all say. How many you heard of doing it?"

"There was that man in Delaware."

"Aren't you getting kind of tired of talking about him, Em? That was five months ago."

"All right, then—Gramma Winkler, right here in the same building."

"She got smeared by a subway."

"That's just the way she picked to go," said Em.

"Then what was she doing carrying a six-pack of anti-gerasone when she got it?"

Emerald shook her head wearily and covered her eyes. "I dunno, I dunno, I dunno. All I know is, something's just got to be done." She sighed. "Sometimes I wish they'd left a couple of diseases kicking around somewhere, so I could get one and go to bed for a little while. Too many people!" she cried, and her words cackled and gabbled and died in a thousand asphalt-paved, skyscraper-walled courtyards.

Lou laid his hand on her shoulder tenderly. "Aw, hon, I hate to see you down in the dumps like this."

"If we just had a car, like the folks used to in the old days," said Em, "we could go for a drive, and get away from people for a little while. Gee—if *those* weren't the days!"

"Yeah," said Lou, "before they'd used up all the metal."

"We'd hop in, and Pop'd drive up to a filling station and say, 'Fillerup!' "

"That *was* the nuts, wasn't it—before they'd used up all the gasoline."

"And we'd go for a carefree ride in the country."

"Yeah—all seems like a fairyland now, doesn't it, Em? Hard to believe there really used to be all that space between cities."

"And when we got hungry," said Em, "we'd find ourselves a restaurant, and walk in, big as you please and say, 'I'll have a steak and French-fries, I believe,' or, 'How are the pork chops today?' " She licked her lips, and her eyes glistened.

"Yeah man!" growled Lou. "How'd you like a hamburger with the works, Em?"

"Mmmmmmmmm."

"If anybody'd offered us processed seaweed in those days, we would have spit right in his eye, huh, Em?"

"Or processed sawdust," said Em.

Doggedly, Lou tried to find the cheery side of the situation. "Well, anyway, they've got the stuff so it tastes a lot less like seaweed and sawdust than it did at first; and they say it's actually better for us than what we used to eat."

"I felt fine!" said Em fiercely.

Lou shrugged. "Well, you've got to realize, the world wouldn't be able to support twelve billion people if it wasn't for processed seaweed and sawdust. I mean, it's a wonderful thing, really. I guess. That's what they say."

"They say the first thing that pops into their heads," said Em. She closed her eyes. "Golly—remember shopping, Lou? Remember how the stores used to fight to get our folks to buy

something? You didn't have to wait for somebody to die to get
a bed or chairs or a stove or anything like that. Just went in—
bing!—and bought whatever you wanted. Gee whiz that was
nice, before they used up all the raw materials. I was just a
little kid then, but I can remember so plain."

Depressed, Lou walked listlessly to the balcony's edge, and
looked up at the clean, cold, bright stars against the black
velvet of infinity. "Remember when we used to be bugs on
science fiction, Em? Flight seventeen, leaving for Mars,
launching ramp twelve. 'Board! All non-technical personnel
kindly remain in bunkers. Ten seconds . . . nine . . . eight . . .
seven . . . six . . . five . . . four . . . three . . . two . . . *one! Main
Stage! Barrrrrroooom!*"

"Why worry about what was going on on Earth?" said Em,
looking up at the stars with him. "In another few years, we'd
all be shooting through space to start life all over again on a
new planet."

Lou sighed. "Only it turns out you need something about
twice the size of the Empire State Building to get one lousy
colonist to Mars. And for another couple of trillion bucks he
could take his wife and dog. *That's* the way to lick overpopula-
tion—*emigrate!*"

"Lou—?"

"Hmmmm?"

"When's the Five-Hundred-Mile Speedway Race?"

"Uh—Memorial Day, May thirtieth."

She bit her lip. "Was that awful of me to ask?"

"Not very, I guess. Everybody in the apartment's looked it
up to make sure."

"I dont want to be awful," said Em, "but you've just got to
talk over these things now and then, and get them out of your
system."

"Sure you do. Feel better?"

"Yes—and I'm not going to lose my temper anymore, and
I'm going to be just as nice to him as I know how."

"That's my Em."

They squared their shoulders, smiled bravely, and went
back inside.

Gramps Schwartz, his chin resting on his hands, his hands on the crook of his cane, was staring irascibly at the five-foot television screen that dominated the room. On the screen, a news commentator was summarizing the day's happenings. Every thirty seconds or so, Gramps would jab the floor with his cane-tip and shout, "Hell! We did that a hundred years ago!"

Emerald and Lou, coming in from the balcony, were obliged to take seats in the back row, behind Lou's father and mother, brother and sister-in-law, son and daughter-in-law, grandson and wife, granddaughter and husband, great-grandson and wife, nephew and wife, grandnephew and wife, great-grand-niece and husband, great-grandnephew and wife, and, of course, Gramps, who was in front of everybody. All, save Gramps, who was somewhat withered and bent, seemed, by pre-anti-gerasone standards, to be about the same age—to be somewhere in their late twenties or early thirties.

"*Meanwhile,*" the commentator was saying, "*Council Bluffs, Iowa, was still threatened by stark tragedy. But two hundred weary rescue workers have refused to give up hope, and continue to dig in an effort to save Elbert Haggedorn, one hundred and eighty-three, who has been wedged for two days in a*
."

"I wish he'd get something more cheerful," Emerald whispered to Lou.

"Silence!" cried Gramps. "Next one shoots off his big bazoo while the TV's on is gonna find hisself cut off without a dollar—" and here his voice suddenly softened and sweetened— "when they wave that checkered flag at the Indianapolis Speedway, and old Gramps gets ready for the Big Trip Up Yonder." He sniffed sentimentally, while his heirs concentrated desperately on not making the slightest sound. For them, the poignancy of the prospective Big Trip had been dulled somewhat by its having been mentioned by Gramps about once a day for fifty years.

"*Dr. Brainard Keyes Bullard,*" said the commentator, "*President of Wyandotte College, said in an address tonight that most of the world's ills can be traced to the fact that Man's knowledge of himself has not kept pace with his knowledge of the physical world."*

"Hell!" said Gramps. "We said that a hundred years ago!"

"In Chicago tonight," said the commentator, *"a special celebration is taking place in the Chicago Lying-in Hospital. The guest of honor is Lowell W. Hitz, age zero. Hitz, born this morning, is the twenty-five-millionth child to be born in the hospital."* The commentator faded, and was replaced on the screen by young Hitz, who squalled furiously.

"Hell," whispered Lou to Emerald, "we said that a hundred years ago."

"I heard that!" shouted Gramps. He snapped off the television set, and his petrified descendants stared silently at the screen. "You, there, boy—"

"I didn't mean anything by it, sir," said Lou.

"Get me my will. You know where it is. You kids *all* know where it is. Fetch, boy!"

Lou nodded dully, and found himself going down the hall, picking his way over bedding to Gramps' room, the only private room in the Schwartz apartment. The other rooms were the bathroom, the living room, and the wide, windowless hallway, which was originally intended to serve as a dining area, and which had a kitchenette in one end. Six mattresses and four sleeping bags were dispersed in the hallway and living room, and the daybed, in the living room, accommodated the eleventh couple, the favorites of the moment.

On Gramps' bureau was his will, smeared, dog-eared, perforated, and blotched with hundreds of additions, deletions, accusations, conditions, warnings, advice, and homely philosophy. The document was, Lou reflected, a fifty-year diary, all jammed onto two sheets—a garbled, illegible log of day after day of strife. This day, Lou would be disinherited for the eleventh time, and it would take him perhaps six months of impeccable behavior to regain the promise of a share in the estate.

"Boy!" called Gramps.

"Coming, sir." Lou hurried back into the living room, and handed Gramps the will.

"Pen!" said Gramps.

He was instantly offered eleven pens, one from each couple.

"Not *that* leaky thing," he said, brushing Lou's pen aside. "Ah, there's a nice one. Good boy, Willy." He accepted Willy's pen. That was the tip they'd all been waiting for. Willy, then, Lou's father, was the new favorite.

Willy, who looked almost as young as Lou, though one hundred and forty-two, did a poor job of concealing his pleasure. He glanced shyly at the daybed, which would become his, and from which Lou and Emerald would have to move back into the hall, back to the worst spot of all by the bathroom door.

Gramps missed none of the high drama he's authored, and he gave his own familiar role everything he had. Frowning and running his finger along each line, as though he were seeing the will for the first time, he read aloud in a deep, portentous monotone, like a bass tone on a cathedral organ:

"I, Harold D. Schwartz, residing in Building 257 of Alden Village, New York City, do hereby make, publish, and declare this to be my last Will and Testament, hereby revoking any and all former wills and codicils by me at any time heretofore made." He blew his nose importantly, and went on, not missing a word, and repeating many for emphasis—repeating in particular his ever-more-elaborate specifications for a funeral.

At the end of these specifications, Gramps was so choked with emotion that Lou thought he might forget why he'd gotten out the will in the first place. But Gramps heroically brought his powerful emotions under control, and, after erasing for a full minute, he began to write and speak at the same time. Lou could have spoken his lines for him, he'd heard them so often.

"I have had many heartbreaks ere leaving this vale of tears for a better land," Gramps said and wrote. "But the deepest hurt of all has been dealt me by—" He looked around the group, trying to remember who the malefactor was.

Everyone looked helpfully at Lou, who held up his hand resignedly.

Gramps nodded, remembering, and completed the sentence: "my great-grandson, Louis J. Schwartz."

"Grandson, sir," said Lou.

"Don't quibble. You're in deep enough now, young man," said Gramps, but he changed the trifle. And from there he went without a misstep through the phrasing of the disinheritance, causes for which were disrespectfulness and quibbling.

In the paragraph following, the paragraph that had belonged to everyone in the room at one time or another, Lou's name was scratched out and Willy's substituted as heir to the apartment and, the biggest plum of all, the double bed in the private bedroom. "So!" said Gramps, beaming. He erased the date at the foot of the will, and substituted a new one, including the time of day. "Well—time to watch the McGarvey Family." The McGarvey Family was a television serial that Gramps had been following since he was sixty, or for one hundred and twelve years. "I can't wait to see what's going to happen next," he said.

Lou detached himself from the group and lay down on his bed of pain by the bathroom door. He wished Em would join him, and he wondered where she was.

He dozed for a few moments, until he was disturbed by someone's stepping over him to get into the bathroom. A moment later, he heard a faint gurgling sound, as though something were being poured down the washbasin drain. Suddenly, it entered his mind that Em had cracked up, and that she was in there doing something drastic about Gramps.

"Em—?" he whispered through the panel. There was no reply, and Lou pressed against the door. The worn lock, whose bolt barely engaged its socket, held for a second, then let the door swing inward.

"Morty!" gasped Lou.

Lou's great-grandnephew, Mortimer, who had just married and brought his wife home to the Schwartz menage, looked at Lou with consternation and surprise. Morty kicked the door shut, but not before Lou had glimpsed what was in his hand— Gramps' enormous economy-size bottle of anti-gerasone, which had been half-emptied, and which Morty was refilling to the top with tap water.

A moment later, Morty came out, glared defiantly at Lou, and brushed past him wordlessly to rejoin his pretty bride.

Shocked, Lou didn't know what on earth to do. He couldn't let Gramps take the mousetrapped anti-gerasone; but if he warned Gramps about it, Gramps would certainly make life in the apartment, which was merely insufferable now, harrowing.

Lou glanced into the living room, and saw that the Schwartzes, Emerald among them, were momentarily at rest, relishing the botches that McGarveys had made of *their* lives. Stealthily, he went into the bathroom, locked the door as well as he could, and began to pour the contents of Gramps' bottle down the drain. He was going to refill it with full-strength anti-gerasone from the twenty-two smaller bottles on the shelf. The bottle contained a half-gallon, and its neck was small, so it seemed to Lou that the emptying would take forever. And the almost imperceptible smell of anti-gerasone, like Worcestershire sauce, now seemed to Lou, in his nervousness, to be pouring out into the rest of the apartment through the keyhole and under the door.

"*Gloog-gloog-gloog-gloog-*," went the bottle monotonously. Suddenly, up came the sound of music from the living room, and there were murmurs and the scraping of chair legs on the floor. "*Thus ends,*" said the television announcer, "*the 29,121st chapter in the life of your neighbors and mine, the Mc-Garveys.*" Footsteps were coming down the hall. There was a knock on the bathroom door.

"Just a sec," called Lou cheerily. Desperately, he shook the big bottle, trying to speed up the flow. His palms slipped on the wet glass, and the heavy bottle smashed to splinters on the tile floor.

The door sprung open, and Gramps, dumfounded, stared at the mess.

Lou grinned engagingly through his nausea, and, for want of anything remotely resembling a thought, he waited for Gramps to speak.

"Well, boy," said Gramps at last, "looks like you've got a little tidying up to do."

And that was all he said. He turned around, elbowed his way through the crowd, and locked himself in his bedroom.

The Schwartzes contemplated Lou in incredulous silence for a moment longer, and then hurried back to the living room, as though some of his horrible guilt would taint them, too, if they looked too long. Morty stayed behind long enough to give Lou a quizzical, annoyed glance. Then he, too, went into the living room, leaving only Emerald standing in the doorway.

Tears streamed over her cheeks. "Oh, you poor lamb—please don't look so awful. It was my fault. I put you up to this."

"No," said Lou, finding his voice, "really you didn't. Honest, Em, I was just—"

"You don't have to explain anything to me, hon. I'm on your side no matter what." She kissed him on his cheek, and whispered in his ear. "It wouldn't have been murder, hon. It wouldn't have killed him. It wasn't such a terrible thing to do. It just would have fixed him up so he'd be able to go any time God decided He wanted him."

"What's gonna happen next, Em?" said Lou hollowly. "What's he gonna do?"

Lou and Emerald stayed fearfully awake almost all night, waiting to see what Gramps was going to do. But not a sound came from the sacred bedroom. At two hours before dawn, the pair dropped off to sleep.

At six o'clock they arose again, for it was time for their generation to eat breakfast in the kitchenette. No one spoke to them. They had twenty minutes in which to eat, but their reflexes were so dulled by the bad night that they had hardly swallowed two mouthfuls of egg-type processed seaweed before it was time to surrender their places to their son's generation.

Then, as was the custom for whomever had been most recently disinherited, they began preparing Gramps' breakfast, which would presently be served to him in bed, on a tray. They tried to be cheerful about it. The toughest part of the job was having to handle the honest-to-God eggs and bacon and oleomargarine on which Gramps spent almost all of the income from his fortune.

"Well," said Emerald, "I'm not going to get all panicky until I'm sure there's something to be panicky about."

"Maybe he doesn't know what it was I busted," said Lou hopefully.

"Probably thinks it was your watch crystal," said Eddie, their son, who was toying apathetically with his buckwheat-type processed sawdust cakes.

"Don't get sarcastic with your father," said Em, "and don't talk with your mouth full, either."

"I'd like to see anybody take a mouthful of this stuff and *not* say something," said Eddie, who was seventy-three. He glanced at the clock. "It's time to take Gramps his breakfast, you know."

"Yeah, it is, isn't it," said Lou weakly. He shrugged. "Let's have the tray, Em."

"We'll both go."

Walking slowly, smiling bravely, they found a large semi-circle of long-faced Schwartzes standing around the bedroom door.

Em knocked. "Gramps," she said brightly, "break-fast is rea-dy."

There was no reply, and she knocked again, harder.

The door swung open before her fist. In the middle of the room, the soft, deep, wide, canopied bed, the symbol of the sweet by-and-by to every Schwartz, was empty.

A sense of death, as unfamiliar to the Schwartzes as Zoroastrianism or the causes of the Sepoy Mutiny, stilled every voice and slowed every heart. Awed, the heirs began to search gingerly under the furniture and behind the drapes for all that was mortal of Gramps, father of the race.

But Gramps had left not his earthly husk but a note, which Lou finally found on the dresser, under a paperweight which was a treasured souvenir from the 2000 World's Fair. Unsteadily, Lou read it aloud:

" 'Somebody who I have sheltered and protected and taught the best I know how all these years last night turned on me like a mad dog and diluted my anti-gerasone, or tried to. I am no longer a young man. I can no longer bear the crushing burden of life as I once could. So, after last night's bitter experience, I say goodbye. The cares of this world will soon drop away like a cloak of thorns, and I shall know peace. By the time you find this, I will be gone.' "

"Gosh," said Willy brokenly, "he didn't even get to see how the Five-Hundred-Mile Speedway Race was going to come out."

"Or the World's Series," said Eddie.

"Or whether Mrs. McGarvey got her eyesight back," said Morty.

"There's more," said Lou, and he began reading aloud again: " 'I, Harold D. Schwartz . . . do hereby make, publish and declare this to be my last Will and Testament, hereby revoking any and all former will and codicils by me at any time heretofore made.' "

"No!" cried Willy. "Not another one!"

" 'I do stipulate,' " read Lou, " 'that all of my property, of whatsoever kind and nature, not be divided, but do devise and bequeath it to be held in common by my issue, without regard for generation, equally, share and share alike.' "

"Issue?" said Emerald.

Lou included the multitude in a sweep of his hand. "It means we all own the whole damn shootin' match."

All eyes turned instantly to the bed.

"Share and share alike?" said Morty.

"Actually," said Willy, who was the oldest person present, "it's just like the old system, where the oldest people head up things with their headquarters in here, and—"

"I like *that!*" said Em. "Lou owns as much of it as you do, and I say it ought to be for the oldest one who's still working. You can snooze around here all day, waiting for your pension check, and poor Lou stumbles in here after work, all tuckered out, and—"

"How about letting somebody who's never had any privacy get a little crack at it?" said Eddie hotly. "Hell, you old people had plenty of privacy back when you were kids. I was born and raised in the middle of the goddam barracks in the hall! How about—"

"Yeah?" said Morty. "Sure, you've all had it pretty tough, and my heart bleeds for you. But try honeymooning in the hall for a real kick."

"Silence!" shouted Willy imperiously. "The next person who opens his mouth spends the next six months by the bathroom. Now clear out of my room. I want to think."

A vase shattered against the wall, inches above his head. In the next moment, a free-for-all was underway, with each couple battling to eject every other couple from the room. Fighting coalitions formed and dissolved with the lightning changes of the tactical situation. Em and Lou were thrown into the hall, where they organized others in the same situation, and stormed back into the room.

After two hours of struggle, with nothing like a decision in sight, the cops broke in.

For the next half-hour, patrol wagons and ambulances hauled away Schwartzes, and then the apartment was still and spacious.

An hour later, films of the last stages of the riot were being televised to 500,000,000 delighted viewers on the Eastern Seaboard.

In the stillness of the three-room Schwartz apartment on the 76th floor of Building 257, the television set had been left on. Once more the air was filled with the cries and grunts and crashes of the fray, coming harmlessly now from the loudspeaker.

The battle also appeared on the screen of the television set in the police station, where the Schwartzes and their captors watched with professional interest.

Em and Lou were in adjacent four-by-eight cells, and were stretched out peacefully on their cots.

"Em—" called Lou through the partition, "you got a washbasin all your own too?"

"Sure. Washbasin, bed, light—the works. Ha! And we thought Gramps' room was something. How long's this been going on?" She held out her hand. "For the first time in forty years, hon, I haven't got the shakes."

"Cross your fingers," said Lou, "the lawyer's going to try to get us a year."

"Gee," said Em dreamily, "I wonder what kind of wires you'd have to pull to get solitary?"

"All right, pipe down," said the turnkey, "or I'll toss the whole kit and caboodle of you right out. And first one who lets on to anybody outside how good jail is ain't never getting back in!"

The prisoners instantly fell silent.

The living room of the Schwartz apartment darkened for a moment, as the riot scenes faded, and then the face of the announcer appeared, like the sun coming from behind a cloud. "*And now, friends,*" he said, "*I have a special message from the makers of anti-gerasone, a message for all you folks over one hundred and fifty. Are you hampered socially by wrinkles, by stiffness of joints and discoloration or loss of hair, all because these things came upon you before anti-gerasone was developed? Well, if you are, you need no longer suffer, need no longer feel different and out of things.*

"*After years of research, medical science has now developed* super-anti-gerasone! *In weeks, yes weeks, you can look, feel, and act as young as your great-great-grandchildren! Wouldn't you pay $5,000 to be indistinguishable from everybody else? Well, you don't have to. Safe, tested super-anti-gerasone costs you only dollars a day. The average cost of regaining all the sparkle and attractiveness of youth is less than fifty dollars.*

"*Write now for your free trial carton. Just put your name and address on a dollar postcard, and mail it to 'Super' Box 500,000, Schenectady, N. Y. Have you got that? I'll repeat it. 'Super.' Box . . .*" Underlining the announcer's words was the scratching of Gramps' fountain-pen, the one Willy had given him the night before. He had come in a few minutes previous from the Idle Hour Tavern, which commanded a view of Building 257 across the square of asphalt known as the Alden Village Green. He had called a cleaning woman to come straighten the place up, and had hired the best lawyer in town to get his descendants a conviction. Gramps had then moved the daybed before the television screen so that he could watch from a reclining position. It was something he'd dreamed of doing for years.

"Schen-*ec*-ta-dy," mouthed Gramps. "Got it." His face had changed remarkably. His facial muscles seemed to have relaxed, revealing kindness and equanimity under what had been taut, bad-tempered lines. It was almost as though his trial package of *Super*-anti-gerasone had already arrived. When something amused him on television, he smiled easily, rather than barely managing to lengthen the thin line of his mouth a millimeter. Life was good. He could hardly wait to see what was going to happen next.

FOR DISCUSSION

1. This is a story about the future, but the basic theme is something that is happening right now. What is that "something"?
2. Some things in the world of 2158 are apparently pretty much the same as they are today. Name a few of them. What is the author trying to tell us by these references to continuity in the context of vast social changes?
3. Vonnegut has been called a "black humorist." What does this term mean? Do you think it is properly applicable to Vonnegut, as judged by this story?
4. If you are interested in the technique of fiction, explain how the author manages to give us all this information without stopping the story to engage in dull "exposition."
5. How would you describe the personality of Gramps Schwartz? Do you think he really *is* going to take that "Big Trip Up Yonder" after the Indianapolis 500-Mile Speedway Race?

FOR COMPOSITION

1. Write an essay on "The Population Explosion." Don't get bogged down in statistics. Try to indicate the general dimensions of the problem, and suggest some of the options that may be open to mankind in seeking to solve it.
2. Vonnegut's fiction, as represented by this story, has often been characterized as "Orwellian." Write an essay comparing George Orwell's picture of *1984* with Vonnegut's picture of 2158. What do they have in common? How do they differ? Vonnegut has a decidedly lighter touch than Orwell; is he less serious?

Ralph Ellison

Ralph Ellison's story treats a major problem facing the Negro today—the problem of identity. In a flight both real and symbolic, his main character, a Negro pilot, tries to steer a course into uncharted regions between a Black world and a White world, and finds himself cut off from both.

Flying Home

When Todd came to, he saw two faces suspended above him in a sun so hot and blinding that he could not tell if they were black or white. He stirred, feeling a pain that burned as though his whole body had been laid open to the sun which glared into his eyes. For a moment an old fear of being touched by white hands seized him. Then the very sharpness of the pain began slowly to clear his head. Sounds came to him dimly. He done come to. Who are they? he thought. Naw he ain't, I coulda sworn he was white. Then he heard clearly:
"You hurt bad?"
Something within him uncoiled. It was a Negro sound.
"He's still out," he heard.
"Give 'im time ... Say, son, you hurt bad?"
Was he? There was that awful pain. He lay rigid, hearing their breathing and trying to weave a meaning between them and his being stretched painfully upon the ground. He watched them warily, his mind traveling back over a painful distance. Jagged scenes, swiftly unfolding as in a movie trailer,[1] reeled through his mind, and he saw himself piloting a tailspinning plane and landing and landing and falling from

[1] *movie trailer:* scenes from a forthcoming motion picture

the cockpit and trying to stand. Then, as in a great silence, he remembered the sound of crunching bone, and now, looking up into the anxious faces of an old Negro man and a boy from where he lay in the same field, the memory sickened him and he wanted to remember no more.

"How you feel, son?"

Todd hesitated, as though to answer would be to admit an inacceptable weakness. Then, "It's my ankle," he said.

"Which one?"

"The left."

With a sense of remoteness he watched the old man bend and remove his boot, feeling the pressure ease.

"That any better?"

"A lot. Thank you."

He had the sensation of discussing someone else, that his concern was with some far more important thing, which for some reason escaped him.

"You done broke it bad," the old man said. "We have to get you to a doctor."

He felt that he had been thrown into a tailspin. He looked at his watch; how long had he been here? He knew there was but one important thing in the world, to get the plane back to the field before his officers were displeased.

"Help me up," he said. "Into the ship."

"But it's broke too bad . . ."

"Give me your arm!"

"But, son . . ."

Clutching the old man's arm he pulled himself up, keeping his left leg clear, thinking, "I'd never make him understand," as the leather-smooth face came parallel with his own.

"Now, let's see."

He pushed the old man back, hearing a bird's insistent shrill. He swayed giddily. Blackness washed over him, like infinity.

"You best sit down."

"No, I'm O.K."

"But, son. You jus' gonna make it worse. . . ."

It was a fact that everything in him cried out to deny, even against the flaming pain in his ankle. He would have to try again.

"You mess with that ankle they have to cut your foot off," he heard.

Holding his breath, he started up again. It pained so badly that he had to bite his lips to keep from crying out and he allowed them to help him down with a pang of despair.

"It's best you take it easy. We gon' git you a doctor."

Of all the luck, he thought. Of all the rotten luck, now I have done it. The fumes of high-octane gasoline clung in the heat, taunting him.

"We kin ride him into town on old Ned," the boy said.

Ned? He turned, seeing the boy point toward an ox team browsing where the buried blade of a plow marked the end of a furrow. Thoughts of himself riding an ox through the town, past streets full of white faces, down the concrete runways of the airfield made swift images of humiliation in his mind. With a pang he remembered his girl's last letter. "Todd," she had written, "I don't need the papers to tell me you had the intelligence to fly. And I have always known you to be as brave as anyone else. The papers annoy me. Don't you be contented to prove over and over again that you're brave or skillful just because you're black, Todd. I think they keep beating that dead horse because they don't want to say why you boys are not yet fighting. I'm really disappointed, Todd. Anyone with brains can learn to fly, but then what? What about using it, and who will you use it for? I wish, dear, you'd write about this. I sometimes think they're playing a trick on us. It's very humiliating. . . ." He wiped cold sweat from his face, thinking, What does she know of humiliation? She's never been down South. Now the humiliation would come. When you must have them judge you, knowing that they never accept your mistakes as your own, but hold it against your whole race — that was humiliation. Yes, and humiliation was when you could never be simply yourself, when you were always a part of this old black ignorant man. Sure, he's all right. Nice and kind and helpful. But he's not you. Well, there's one humiliation I can spare myself.

"No," he said, "I have orders not to leave the ship. . . ."

"Aw," the old man said. Then turning to the boy, "Teddy, then you better hustle down to Mister Graves and get him to come. . . ."

"No, wait!" he protested before he was fully aware. Graves might be white. "Just have him get word to the field, please. They'll take care of the rest."

He saw the boy leave, running.

"How far does he have to go?"

"Might' nigh a mile."

He rested back, looking at the dusty face of his watch. But now they know something has happened, he thought. In the ship there was a perfectly good radio, but it was useless. The old fellow would never operate it. That buzzard knocked me back a hundred years, he thought. Irony danced within him like the gnats circling the old man's head. With all I've learned I'm dependent upon this "peasant's" sense of time and space. His leg throbbed. In the plane, instead of time being measured by the rhythms of pain and a kid's legs, the instruments would have told him at a glance. Twisting upon his elbows he saw where dust had powdered the plane's fuselage, feeling the lump form in his throat that was always there when he thought of flight. It's crouched there, he thought, like the abandoned shell of a locust. I'm naked without it. Not a machine, a suit of clothes you wear. And with a sudden embarrassment and wonder he whispered, "It's the only dignity I have. . . ."

He saw the old man watching, his torn overalls clinging limply to him in the heat. He felt a sharp need to tell the old man what he felt. But that would be meaningless. If I tried to explain why I need to fly back, he'd think I was simply afraid of white officers. But it's more than fear . . . a sense of anguish clung to him like the veil of sweat that hugged his face. He watched the old man, hearing him humming snatches of a tune as he admired the plane. He felt a furtive sense of resentment. Such old men often came to the field to watch the pilots with childish eyes. At first it had made him proud; they had been a meaningful part of a new experience. But soon he realized they did not understand his accomplishments and they came to shame and embarrass him, like the distasteful praise of an idiot. A part of the meaning of flying had gone then, and he had not been able to regain it. If I were a prizefighter I would be more human, he thought. Not a monkey doing tricks, but a man. They were pleased simply that he was a Negro who could fly, and that was not enough. He felt cut off from them by age, by understanding, by sensibility, by technology and by his need to measure himself against the mirror of other men's appreciation. Somehow he felt betrayed, as he had when as a child he grew to discover that his father was dead. Now for him any real appreciation lay with his white officers; and with them he could never be sure. Between ignorant black men and condescending whites, his course of flight seemed mapped by the nature of things away from all needed and natural landmarks. Under some sealed orders, couched in ever more technical and mysterious terms, his path curved swiftly away from both the shame the old man symbolized and the cloudy terrain of white men's regard. Flying blind, he knew but one point of landing and there he would receive his wings. After that the enemy would appreciate his skill and he would assume his deepest meaning, he thought sadly, neither from those who condescended nor from those who praised without understanding, but from the enemy who would recognize his manhood and skill in terms of hate. . . .

He sighed, seeing the oxen making queer, prehistoric shadows against the dry brown earth.

"You just take it easy, son," the old man soothed. "That boy won't take long. Crazy as he is about airplanes."

"I can wait," he said.

"What kinda airplane you call this here'n?"

"An Advanced Trainer," he said, seeing the old man smile. His fingers were like gnarled dark wood against the metal as he touched the low-slung wing.

"'Bout how fast can she fly?"

"Over two hundred an hour."

"Lawd! That's so fast I bet it don't seem like you moving!"

Holding himself rigid, Todd opened his flying suit. The shade had gone and he lay in a ball of fire.

"You mind if I take a look inside? I was always curious to see...."

"Help yourself. Just don't touch anything."

He heard him climb upon the metal wing, grunting. Now the questions would start. Well, so you don't have to think to answer....

He saw the old man looking over into the cockpit, his eyes bright as a child's.

"You must have to know a lot to work all these here things."

He was silent, seeing him step down and kneel beside him.

"Son, how come you want to fly way up there in the air?"

Because it's the most meaningful act in the world ... because it makes me less like you, he thought.

But he said: "Because I like it, I guess. It's as good a way to fight and die as I know."

"Yeah? I guess you right," the old man said. "But how long you think before they gonna let you all fight?"

He tensed. This was the question all Negroes asked, put with the same timid hopefulness and longing that always opened a greater void within him than that he had felt beneath the plane the first time he had flown. He felt light-headed. It came to him suddenly that there was something sinister about the conversation, that he was flying unwillingly into unsafe and uncharted regions. If he could only be insulting and tell this old man who was trying to help him to shut up!

"I bet you one thing ..."

"Yes?"

"That you was plenty scared coming down."

He did not answer. Like a dog on a trail the old man seemed to smell out his fears and he felt anger bubble within him.

"You sho' scared me. When I seen you coming down in that thing with it a-rollin' and a-jumpin' like a pitchin' hoss, I thought sho' you was a goner. I almost had me a stroke!"

He saw the old man grinning, "Ever'thin's been happening round here this morning, come to think of it."

"Like what?" he asked.

"Well, first thing I know, here come two white fellers

looking for Mister Rudolph, that's Mister Graves's cousin. That got me worked up right away. . . ."

"Why?"

"Why?" 'Cause he done broke outta the crazy house, that's why. He liable to kill somebody," he said. "They oughta have him by now though. Then here you come. First I think it's one of them white boys. Then doggone if you don't fall outta there. Lawd, I'd done heard about you boys but I haven't never seen one o' you-all. Cain't tell you how it felt to see somebody what look like me in a airplane!"

The old man talked on, the sound streaming around Todd's thoughts like air flowing over the fuselage of a flying plane. You were a fool, he thought, remembering how before the spin the sun had blazed bright against the billboard signs beyond the town, and how a boy's blue kite had bloomed beneath him, tugging gently in the wind like a strange, odd-shaped flower. He had once flown such kites himself and tried to find the boy at the end of the invisible cord. But he had been flying too high and too fast. He had climbed steeply away in exultation. Too steeply, he thought. And one of the first rules you learn is that if the angle of thrust is too steep the plane goes into a spin. And then, instead of pulling out of it and going into a dive you let a buzzard panic you. A lousy buzzard!

"Son, what made all that blood on the glass?"

"A buzzard," he said, remembering how the blood and feathers had sprayed back against the hatch. It had been as though he had flown into a storm of blood and blackness.

"Well, I declare! They's lots of 'em around here. They after dead things. Don't eat nothing what's alive."

"A little bit more and he would have made a meal out of me," Todd said grimly.

"They bad luck all right. Teddy's got a name foi 'em, calls 'em jimcrows," the old man laughed.

"It's a damned good name."

"They the damnedest birds. Once I seen a hoss all stretched out like he was sick, you know. So I hollers, 'Gid up from there, suh!' Just to make sho! An' doggone, son, if I don't see two ole jimcrows come flying right up outa that hoss's insides! Yessuh! The sun was shinin' on 'em and they couldn't a been no greasier if they'd been eating barbecue."

Todd thought he would vomit, his stomach quivered.

"You made that up," he said.

"Nawsuh! Saw him just like I see you."

"Well, I'm glad it was you."

"You see lots a funny things down here, son."

"No, I'll let you see them," he said.

"By the way, the white folks round here don't like to see you boys up there in the sky. They ever bother you?"

"No."

"Well, they'd like to."

"Someone always wants to bother someone else," Todd said. "How do you know?"

"I just know."

"Well," he said defensively, "no one has bothered us."

Blood pounded in his ears as he looked away into space. He tensed, seeing a black spot in the sky, and strained to confirm what he could not clearly see.

"What does that look like to you?" he asked excitedly.

"Just another bad luck, son."

Then he saw the movement of wings with disappointment. It was gliding smoothly down, wings outspread, tail feathers gripping the air, down swiftly—gone behind the green screen of trees. It was like a bird he had imagined there, only the sloping branches of the pines remained, sharp against the pale stretch of sky. He lay barely breathing and stared at the point where it had disappeared, caught in a spell of loathing and admiration. Why did they make them so disgusting and yet teach them to fly so well? It's like when I was up in heaven, he heard, starting.

The old man was chuckling, rubbing his stubbled chin.

"What did you say?"

"Sho', I died and went to heaven . . . maybe by time I tell you about it they be done come after you."

"I hope so," he said wearily.

"You boys ever sit around and swap lies?"

"Not often. Is this going to be one?"

"Well, I ain't so sho', on account of it took place when I was dead."

The old man paused, "That wasn't no lie 'bout the buzzards, though."

"All right," he said.

"Sho' you want to hear 'bout heaven?"

"Please," he answered, resting his head upon his arm.

"Well, I went to heaven and right away started to sproutin' me some wings. Six good ones, they was. Just like them the white angels had. I couldn't hardly believe it. I was so glad that I went off on some clouds by myself and tried 'em out. You know, 'cause I didn't want to make a fool outta myself the first thing. . . ."

It's an old tale, Todd thought. Told me years ago. Had forgotten. But at least it will keep him from talking about buzzards.

He closed his eyes, listening.

". . . First thing I done was to git up on a low cloud and jump off. And doggone, boy, if them wings didn't work! First I tried the right; then I tried the left; then I tried 'em both together. Then Lawd, I started to move on out among the folks. I let 'em see me. . . ."

He saw the old man gesturing flight with his arms, his face full of mock pride as he indicated an imaginary crowd, thinking, It'll be in the newspapers, as he heard, ". . . so I went and found me some colored angels—somehow I didn't believe I was an angel till I seen a real black one, ha, yes! Then I was sho'—but they tole me I better come down 'cause us colored folks had to wear a special kin' a harness when we flew. That was how come they wasn't flyin'. Oh yes, an' you had to be extra strong for a black man even, to fly with one of them harnesses. . . ."

This is a new turn, Todd thought, what's he driving at?

"So I said to myself, I ain't gonna be bothered with no harness! Oh naw! 'Cause if God let you sprout wings you oughta have sense enough not to let nobody make you wear something what gits in the way of flyin'. So I starts to flyin'. Heck, son," he chuckled, his eyes twinkling, "you know I had to let eve'ybody know that old Jefferson could fly good as anybody else. And I could too, fly smooth as a bird! I could even loop-the-loop—only I had to make sho' to keep my long white robe down roun' my ankles. . . ."

Todd felt uneasy. He wanted to laugh at the joke, but his body refused, as of an independent will. He felt as he had as a child when after he had chewed a sugar-coated pill which his mother had given him, she had laughed at his efforts to remove the terrible taste.

". . . Well," he heard, "I was doing all right 'til I got to speeding. Found out I could fan up a right strong breeze, I could fly so fast. I could do all kin'sa stunts too. I started flying up to the stars and divin' down and zooming roun' the moon. Man, I like to scare the devil outa some ole white angels. I was raisin' hell. Not that I meant any harm, son. But I was just feeling good. It was so good to know I was free at last. I accidentally knocked the tips offa some stars and they tell me I caused a storm and a coupla lynchings down here in Macon County—though I swear I believe them boys what said that was making up lies on me. . . ."

He's mocking me, Todd thought angrily. He thinks it's a joke. Grinning down at me . . . His throat was dry. He looked at his watch; why the hell didn't they come? Since they had to, why? One day I was flying down one of them heavenly streets. You got yourself into it, Todd thought. Like Jonah in the whale.

"Justa throwin' feathers in everybody's face. An' ole Saint Peter called me in. Said, 'Jefferson, tell me two things, what you doin' flyin' without a harness; an' how come you flyin' so fast?' So I tole him I was flyin' without a harness 'cause it got in my way, but I couldn'ta been flyin' so fast, 'cause I wasn't usin' but one wing. Saint Peter said, 'You wasn't flyin' with but one wing?' 'Yessuh,' I says, scared-like. So he says, 'Well, since you got sucha extra fine pair of wings you can leave off yo' harness awhile. But from now on none of that there one-wing flyin', 'cause you gittin' up too damn much speed!'"

And with one mouth full of bad teeth you're making too damned much talk, thought Todd. Why don't I send him after the boy? His body ached from the hard ground and seeking to shift his position he twisted his ankle and hated himself for crying out.

"It gittin' worse?"

"I . . . I twisted it," he groaned.

"Try not to think about it, son. That's what I do."

He bit his lip, fighting pain with counter-pain as the voice resumed its rhythmical droning. Jefferson seemed caught in his own creation.

". . . After all that trouble I just floated roun' heaven in slow motion. But I forgot, like colored folks will do, and got to flyin' with one wing again. This time I was restin' my old broken arm and got to flyin' fast enough to shame the devil. I was comin' so fast, Lawd, I got myself called befo' ole Saint Peter again. He said, 'Jeff, didn't I warn you 'bout that speedin'?' 'Yessuh,' I says, 'but it was an accident.' He looked at me sad-like and shook his head and I knowed I was gone. He said, 'Jeff, you and that speedin' is a danger to the heavenly community. If I was to let you keep on flyin', heaven wouldn't be nothin' but uproar. Jeff, you got to go!' Son, I argued and pleaded with that old white man, but it didn't do a bit of good. They rushed me straight to them pearly gates and gimme a parachute and a map of the state of Alabama . . ."

Todd heard him laughing so that he could hardly speak, making a screen between them upon which his humiliation glowed like fire.

"Maybe you'd better stop awhile," he said, his voice unreal.

"Ain't much more," Jefferson laughed. "When they gimme the parachute ole Saint Peter ask me if I wanted to say a few words before I went. I felt so bad I couldn't hardly look at him, specially with all them white angels standin' around. Then somebody laughed and made me mad. So I tole him, 'Well, you done took my wings. And you puttin' me out. You got charge of things so's I can't do nothin' about it. But you got to admit just this: While I was up here I was the flyinest sonofagun what ever hit heaven!'"

At the burst of laughter Todd felt such an intense humiliation that only great violence would wash it away. The laughter which shook the old man like a boiling purge set up vibrations of guilt within him which not even the intricate machinery of the plane would have been adequate to transform and he heard himself screaming, "Why do you laugh at me this way?"

He hated himself at that moment, but he had lost control. He saw Jefferson's mouth fall open, "What—?"

"Answer me!"

His blood pounded as though it would surely burst his temples and he tried to reach the old man and fell, screaming, "Can I help it because they won't let us actually fly? Maybe we are a bunch of buzzards feeding on a dead horse, but we can hope to be eagles, can't we? Can't we?"

He fell back, exhausted, his ankle pounding. The saliva was like straw in his mouth. If he had the strength he would strangle this old man. This grinning, gray-headed clown who made him feel as he felt when watched by the white officers at the field. And yet this old man had neither power, prestige, rank nor technique. Nothing that could rid him of this terrible feeling. He watched him, seeing his face struggle to express a turmoil of feeling.

"What you mean, son? What you talking 'bout . . .?"

"Go away. Go tell your tales to the white folks."

"But I didn't mean nothing like that. . . . I . . . I wasn't tryin' to hurt your feelings. . . ."

"Please. Get the hell away from me!"

"But I didn't, son. I didn't mean all them things a-tall."

Todd shook as with a chill, searching Jefferson's face for a trace of the mockery he had seen there. But now the face was somber and tired and old. He was confused. He could not be sure that there had ever been laughter there, that Jefferson had ever really laughed in his whole life. He saw Jefferson reach out to touch him and shrank away, wondering if anything except the pain, now causing his vision to waver, was real. Perhaps he had imagined it all.

"Don't let it get you down, son," the voice said pensively.

He heard Jefferson sigh wearily, as though he felt more than he could say. His anger ebbed, leaving only the pain.

"I'm sorry," he mumbled.

"You just wore out with pain, was all. . . ."

He saw him through a blur, smiling. And for a second he felt the embarrassed silence of understanding flutter between them.

"What you was doin' flying over this section, son? Wasn't you scared they might shoot you for a cow?"

Todd tensed. Was he being laughed at again? But before he could decide, the pain shook him and a part of him was lying calmly behind the screen of pain that had fallen between them, recalling the first time he had ever seen a plane. It was as though an endless series of hangars had been shaken ajar in the air base of his memory and from each, like a young wasp emerging from its cell, arose the memory of a plane.

The first time I ever saw a plane I was very small and planes were new in the world. I was four-and-a-half and the only plane that I had ever seen was a model suspended from the ceiling of the automobile exhibit at the State Fair. But I did not know that it was only a model. I did not know how large a real plane was, nor how expensive. To me it was a fascinating toy, complete in itself, which my mother said could only be owned by rich little white boys. I stood rigid with admiration, my head straining backwards as I watched the gray little plane describing arcs above the gleaming tops of the automobiles. And I vowed that, rich or poor, someday I would own such a toy. My mother had to drag me out of the exhibit and not even the merry-go-round, the Ferris wheel, or the racing horses could hold my attention for the rest of the Fair. I was too busy imitating the tiny drone of the plane with my lips, and imitating with my hands the motion, swift and circling, that it made in flight.

After that I no longer used the pieces of lumber that lay about our back yard to construct wagons and autos . . . now it was used for airplanes. I built biplanes, using pieces of board for wings, a small box for the fuselage, another piece of wood for the rudder. The trip to the Fair had brought something new into my small world. I asked my mother repeatedly when the Fair would come back again. I'd lie in the grass and watch the sky, and each fighting bird became a soaring plane. I would have been good a year just to have seen a plane again. I became a nuisance to everyone with my questions about airplanes. But planes were new to the old folks, too, and there was little that they could tell me. Only my uncle knew some of the answers. And better still, he could carve propellers from pieces of wood that would whirl rapidly in the wind, wobbling noisily upon oiled nails.

I wanted a plane more than I'd wanted anything; more than I wanted the red wagon with rubber tires, more than the train that ran on a track with its train of cars. I asked my mother over and over again:

"Mamma?"

"What do you want, boy?" she'd say.

"Mamma, will you get mad if I ask you?" I'd say.

"What do you want now? I ain't got time to be answering a lot of fool questions. What you want?"

"Mamma, when you gonna get me one . . . ?" I'd ask.

"Get you one what?" she'd say.

"You know, Mamma; what I been asking you. . . ."

"Boy," she'd say, "if you don't want a spanking you better come on an' tell me what you talking about so I can get on with my work."

"Aw, Mamma, you know. . . ."

"What I just tell you?" she'd say.

"I mean when you gonna buy me a airplane."

"AIRPLANE! Boy, is you crazy? How many times I have to tell you to stop that foolishness. I done told you them things cost too much. I bet I'm gon' wham the living daylight out of you if you don't quit worrying me 'bout them things!"

But this did not stop me, and a few days later I'd try all over again.

Then one day a strange thing happened. It was spring and for some reason I had been hot and irritable all morning. It was a beautiful spring. I could feel it as I played barefoot in the backyard. Blossoms hung from the thorny black locust trees like clusters of fragrant white grapes. Butterflies flickered in the sunlight above the short new dew-wet grass. I had gone in the house for bread and butter and coming out I heard a steady unfamiliar drone. It was unlike anything I had ever heard before. I tried to place the sound. It was no use. It was a sensation like that I had when searching for my father's

watch, heard ticking unseen in a room. It made me feel as
though I had forgotten to perform some task that my mother
had ordered . . . then I located it, overhead. In the sky, flying
quite low and about a hundred yards off was a plane! It came
so slowly that it seemed barely to move. My mouth hung wide;
my bread and butter fell into the dirt. I wanted to jump up and
down and cheer. And when the idea struck I trembled with
excitement: "Some little white boy's plane's done flew away
and all I got to do is stretch out my hands and it'll be mine!"
It was a little plane like that at the Fair, flying no higher
than the eaves of our roof. Seeing it come steadily forward I
felt the world grow warm with promise. I opened the screen
and climbed over it and clung there, waiting. I would catch
the plane as it came over and swing down fast and run into
the house before anyone could see me. Then no one could
come to claim the plane. It droned nearer. Then when it hung
like a silver cross in the blue directly above me I stretched out
my hand and grabbed. It was like sticking my finger through a
soap bubble. The plane flew on, as though I had simply
blown my breath after it. I grabbed again, frantically, trying to
catch the tail. My fingers clutched the air and disappointment
surged tight and hard in my throat. Giving one last desperate
grasp, I strained forward. My fingers ripped from the screen.
I was falling. The ground burst hard against me. I drummed
the earth with my heels and when my breath returned, I lay
there bawling.

My mother rushed through the door.

"What's the matter, chile! What on earth is wrong
with you?"

"It's gone! It's gone!"

"What gone?"

"The airplane . . ."

"Airplane?"

"Yessum, jus' like the one at the Fair. . . . I . . . I tried to
stop it an' it kep' right on going. . . ."

"When, boy?"

"Just now," I cried, through my tears.

"Where it go, boy, what way?"

"Yonder, there . . ."

She scanned the sky, her arms akimbo[2] and her checkered apron flapping in the wind as I pointed to the fading plane Finally she looked down at me, slowly shaking her head.

"It's gone! It's gone!" I cried.

"Boy, is you a fool?" she said. "Don't you see that there's a real airplane 'stead of one of them toy ones?"

"Real . . . ?" I forgot to cry. "Real?"

"Yass, real. Don't you know that thing you reaching for is bigger'n a auto? You here trying to reach for it and I bet it's flying 'bout two hundred miles higher'n this roof." She was disgusted with me. "You come on in this house before somebody else sees what a fool you done turned out to be. You must think these here lil ole arms of you'n is mighty long. . . ."

I was carried into the house and undressed for bed and the doctor was called. I cried bitterly, as much from the disappointment of finding the plane so far beyond my reach as from the pain.

When the doctor came I heard my mother telling him about the plane and asking if anything was wrong with my mind. He explained that I had had a fever for several hours. But I was kept in bed for a week and I constantly saw the plane in my sleep, flying just beyond my fingertips, sailing so slowly that it seemed barely to move. And each time I'd reach out to grab it I'd miss and through each dream I'd hear my grandma warning:

> Young man, young man,
> Yo' arms too short
> To box with God. . . .

"Hey, son!"

At first he did not know where he was and looked at the old man pointing, with blurred eyes.

"Ain't that one of you-all's airplanes coming after you?"

As his vision cleared he saw a small black shape above a distant field, soaring through waves of heat. But he could not be sure and with the pain he feared that somehow a horrible recurring fantasy of being split in twain by the whirling blades of a propeller had come true.

---

[2] *akimbo:* hands on hips with elbows bent outward

"You think he sees us?" he heard.

"See? I hope so."

"He's coming like a bat outa hell!"

Straining, he heard the faint sound of a motor and hoped it would soon be over.

"How you feeling?"

"Like a nightmare," he said.

"Hey, he's done curved back the other way!"

"Maybe he saw us," he said. "Maybe he's gone to send out the ambulance and ground crew." And, he thought with despair, maybe he didn't even see us.

"Where did you send the boy?"

"Down to Mister Graves," Jefferson said. "Man what owns this land."

"Do you think he phoned?"

Jefferson looked at him quickly.

"Aw sho'. Dabney Graves is got a bad name on accounta them killings but he'll call though. . . ."

"What killings?"

"Them five fellers . . . ain't you heard?" he asked with surprise.

"No."

"Everybody knows 'bout Dabney Graves, especially the colored. He done killed enough of us."

Todd had the sensation of being caught in a white neighborhood after dark.

"What did they do?" he asked.

"Thought they was men," Jefferson said. 'An' some he owed money, like he do me. . . ."

"But why do you stay here?"

"You black, son."

"I know, but . . ."

"You have to come by the white folks, too."

He turned away from Jefferson's eyes, at once consoled and accused. And I'll have to come by them soon, he thought with despair. Closing his eyes, he heard Jefferson's voice as the sun burned blood-red upon his lips.

"I got nowhere to go," Jefferson said, "an' they'd come after me if I did. But Dabney Graves is a funny fellow. He's all the time making jokes. He can be mean as hell, then he's liable to turn right around and back the colored against the white folks. I seen him do it. But me, I hates him for that more'n anything else. 'Cause just as soon as he gits tired helping a man he don't care what happens to him. He just leaves him stone cold. And then the other white folks is double hard on anybody he done helped. For him it's just a joke. He don't give a hilla beans for nobody—but hisself. . . ."

Todd listened to the thread of detachment in the old man's voice. It was as though he held his words arm's length before him to avoid their destructive meaning.

"He'd just as soon do you a favor and then turn right around and have you strung up. Me, I stays outa his way 'cause down here that's what you gotta do."

If my ankle would only ease for a while, he thought. The closer I spin toward the earth the blacker I become, flashed through his mind. Sweat ran into his eyes and he was sure that he would never see the plane if his head continued whirling. He tried to see Jefferson, what it was that Jefferson held in his hand? It was a little black man, another Jefferson! A little black Jefferson that shook with fits of belly-laughter while the other Jefferson looked on with detachment. Then Jefferson looked up from the thing in his hand and turned to speak, but Todd was far away, searching the sky for a plane in a hot dry land on a day and age he had long forgotten. He was going mysteriously with his mother through empty streets where black faces peered from behind drawn shades and someone was rapping at a window and he was looking back to see a hand and a frightened face frantically beckoning from a cracked door and his mother was looking down the empty perspective of the street and shaking her head and hurrying him along and at first it was only a flash he saw and a motor was droning as through the sun-glare he saw it gleaming silver as it circled and he was seeing a burst like a puff of white smoke and hearing his mother yell, Come along, boy, I got no time for them fool airplanes, I got no time, and he saw it a second time, the plane flying high, and the burst appeared suddenly and fell slowly, billowing out and sparkling like fireworks and he was watching and being hurried along as the air filled with a flurry of white pinwheeling cards that caught in the wind and scattered over the rooftops and into the gutters and a woman was running and snatching a card and reading it and screaming and he darted into the shower, grabbing as in winter he grabbed for snowflakes and bounding away at his mother's, Come on here, boy! Come on, I say! and he was watching as she took the card away, seeing her face grow puzzled and turning taut as her voice quavered, "Niggers Stay From The Polls," and died to a moan of terror as he saw the eyeless sockets of a white hood staring at him from the card and above he saw the plane spiraling gracefully, agleam in the sun like a fiery sword. And seeing it soar he was caught, transfixed between a terrible horror and a horrible fascination.

The sun was not so high now, and Jefferson was calling and gradually he saw three figures moving across the curving roll of the field.

"Look like some doctors, all dressed in white," said Jefferson.

They're coming at last, Todd thought. And he felt such a release of tension within him that he thought he would faint. But no sooner did he close his eyes than he was seized and he was struggling with three white men who were forcing his arms into some kind of coat. It was too much for him, his arms were pinned to his sides and as the pain blazed in his eyes, he realized that it was a straitjacket. What filthy joke was this?

"That oughta hold him, Mister Graves," he heard.

His total energies seemed focused in his eyes as he searched their faces. That was Graves; the other two wore hospital uniforms. He was poised between two poles of fear and hate as he heard the one called Graves saying, "He looks kinda purty in that there suit, boys. I'm glad you dropped by."

"This boy ain't crazy, Mister Graves," one of the others said. "He needs a doctor, not us. Don't see how you led us way out here anyway. It might be a joke to you, but your cousin Rudolph liable to kill somebody. White folks oı niggers, don't make no difference. . . ."

Todd saw the man turn red with anger. Graves looked down upon him, chuckling.

"This nigguh belongs in a straitjacket, too, boys. I knowed that the minit Jeff's kid said something 'bout a nigguh flyer. You all know you cain't let the nigguh git up that high without his going crazy. The nigguh brain ain't built right for high altitudes. . . ."

Todd watched the drawling red face, feeling that all the unnamed horror and obscenities that he had ever imagined stood materialized before him.

"Let's git outta here," one of the attendants said.

Todd saw the other reach toward him, realizing for the first time that he lay upon a stretcher as he yelled.

"Don't put your hands on me!"

They drew back, surprised.

"What's that you say, nigguh?" asked Graves.

He did not answer and thought that Graves's foot was aimed at his head. It landed on his chest and he could hardly breathe. He coughed helplessly, seeing Graves's lips stretch taut over his yellow teeth, and tried to shift his head. It was as though a half-dead fly was dragging slowly across his face and a bomb seemed to burst within him. Blasts of hot, hysterical laughter tore from his chest, causing his eyes to pop and he felt that the veins in his neck would surely burst. And then a part of him stood behind it all, watching the surprise in Graves's red face and his own hysteria. He thought he would never stop, he would laugh himself to death. It rang in his ears like Jefferson's laughter and he looked for him, centering his eyes desperately upon his face, as though somehow he had become his sole salvation in an insane world of outrage and humiliation. It brought a certain relief. He was suddenly aware that although his body was still contorted it was an echo that no longer rang in his ears. He heard Jefferson's voice with gratitude.

"Mister Graves, the Army done tole him not to leave his airplane."

"Nigguh, Army or no, you gittin' off my land! That airplane can stay 'cause it was paid for by taxpayers' money. But you gittin' off. An' dead or alive, it don't make no difference to me."

Todd was beyond it now, lost in a world of anguish.

"Jeff," Graves said, "you and Teddy come and grab holt. I want you to take this here black eagle over to that nigguh airfield and leave him."

Jefferson and the boy approached him silently. He looked away, realizing and doubting at once that only they could release him from his overpowering sense of isolation.

They bent for the stretcher. One of the attendants moved toward Teddy.

"Think you can manage it, boy?"

"I think I can, suh," Teddy said.

"Well, you better go behind then, and let yo' pa go ahead so's to keep that leg elevated."

He saw the white men walking ahead as Jefferson and the boy carried him along in silence. Then they were pausing and he felt a hand wiping his face; then he was moving again. And it was as though he had been lifted out of his isolation, back into the world of men. A new current of communication flowed between the man and boy and himself. They moved him gently. Far away he heard a mockingbird liquidly calling. He raised his eyes, seeing a buzzard poised unmoving in space. For a moment the whole afternoon seemed suspended and he waited for the horror to seize him again. Then like a song within his head he heard the boy's soft humming and saw the dark bird glide into the sun and glow like a bird of flaming gold.

FOR DISCUSSION

1. Why does Todd, as a flyer, feel himself isolated from the world of men—both black and white? How is his plane his "dignity?" In what sense is it also an instrument of snobbery?

2. Todd's girl, in his opinion, doesn't understand what humiliation really is. What is his idea of the ultimate humiliation?

3. In Todd's mind, what does old Jefferson represent? Trace the change in his attitude toward Jefferson from contempt, anger, and humiliation to a feeling of communication. In what sense has he returned "home"?

4. What accident from Todd's childhood parallels his plane crash? How are the causes of the two accidents similar in his own mind?

5. Why does Todd call "jimcrow" a "damned good name" for the buzzard? What is the significance of the bird's temporary change of color at the end of the story?
6. Ellison has painted his story in bold strokes of black, white, and red, with a highlighting splash of gold. What do the colors symbolize from Todd's point of view?

FOR COMPOSITION

1. Write a composition discussing, from your own viewpoint, the problem that Ellison is presenting. What are your feelings about the possibility of a solution? What steps do you think should be taken?
2. In a short composition, discuss Ellison's characterization in the story you have just read. Do all the characters seem equally lifelike? Do any of them seem stereotyped in any way? How does his characterization increase the effectiveness of his presentation of this particular problem?

Bernard Malamud

Bernard Malamud's stories show great insight into the problems of everyday life, at the same time revealing a basic faith in mankind. In the following story, George, a high school dropout, wants people to like and respect him. He builds an elaborate pretense of "picking up his education" on his own, but he soon finds that pretense is not enough.

A Summer's Reading

George Stoyonovich was a neighborhood boy who had quit high school on an impulse when he was sixteen, run out of patience, and though he was ashamed everytime he went looking for a job, when people asked him if he had finished and he had to say no, he never went back to school. This summer was a hard time for jobs and he had none. Having so much time on his hands, George thought of going to summer school, but the kids in his classes would be too young. He also considered registering in a night high school, only he didn't like the idea of the teachers always telling him what to do. He felt they had not respected him. The result was he stayed off the streets and in his room most of the day. He was close to twenty and had needs with the neighborhood girls, but no money to spend, and he couldn't get more than an occasional few cents because his father was poor, and his sister Sophie, who resembled George, a tall bony girl of twenty-three, earned very little and what she had she kept for herself. Their mother was dead, and Sophie had to take care of the house.

Very early in the morning George's father got up to go to

work in a fish market. Sophie left at about eight for her long
ride in the subway to a cafeteria in the Bronx. George had his
coffee by himself, then hung around in the house. When the
house, a five-room railroad flat[1] above a butcher store, got on
his nerves he cleaned it up—mopped the floors with a wet
mop and put things away. But most of the time he sat in his
room. In the afternoons he listened to the ball game. Otherwise he had a couple of old copies of the *World Almanac* he
had bought long ago, and he liked to read in them and also
the magazines and newspapers that Sophie brought home,
that had been left on the tables in the cafeteria. They were
mostly picture magazines about movie stars and sports
figures, also usually the *News* and *Mirror*. Sophie herself
read whatever fell into her hands, although she sometimes
read good books.

She once asked George what he did in his room all day and
he said he read a lot too.

"Of what besides what I bring home? Do you ever read any
worthwhile books?"

"Some," George answered, although he really didn't. He
had tried to read a book or two that Sophie had in the house
but found he was in no mood for them. Lately he couldn't
stand made-up stories, they got on his nerves. He wished he
had some hobby to work at—as a kid he was good in carpentry,
but where could he work at it? Sometimes during the day he
went for walks, but mostly he did his walking after the hot
sun had gone down and it was cooler in the streets.

In the evening after supper George left the house and wandered in the neighborhood. During the sultry days some of
the storekeepers and their wives sat in chairs on the thick,
broken sidewalks in front of their shops, fanning themselves,
and George walked past them and the guys hanging out on
the candy store corner. A couple of them he had known his
whole life, but nobody recognized each other. He had no
place special to go, but generally, saving it till the last, he
left the neighborhood and walked for blocks till he came to a
darkly lit little park with benches and trees and an iron

[1] *railroad flat:* an apartment having narrow rooms arranged in a line

railing, giving it a feeling of privacy. He sat on a bench here, watching the leafy trees and the flowers blooming on the inside of the railing, thinking of a better life for himself. He thought of the jobs he had had since he had quit school — delivery boy, stock clerk, runner, lately working in a factory — and he was dissatisfied with all of them. He felt he would someday like to have a good job and live in a private house with a porch, on a street with trees. He wanted to have some dough in his pocket to buy things with, and a girl to go with, so as not to be so lonely, especially on Saturday nights. He wanted people to like and respect him. He thought about these things often but mostly when he was alone at night. Around midnight he got up and drifted back to his hot and stony neighborhood.

One time while on his walk George met Mr. Cattanzara coming home very late from work. He wondered if he was drunk but then could tell he wasn't. Mr. Cattanzara, a stocky, bald-headed man who worked in a change booth on an IRT[2] station, lived on the next block after George's, above a shoe repair store. Nights, during the hot weather, he sat on his stoop in an undershirt, reading the *New York Times* in the light of the shoemaker's window. He read it from the first page to the last, then went up to sleep. And all the time he was reading the paper, his wife, a fat woman with a white face, leaned out of the window, gazing into the street, her thick white arms folded under her loose breast, on the window ledge.

Once in a while Mr. Cattanzara came home drunk, but it was a quiet drunk. He never made any trouble, only walked stiffly up the street and slowly climbed the stairs into the hall. Though drunk, he looked the same as always, except for his tight walk, the quietness, and that his eyes were wet. George liked Mr. Cattanzara because he remembered him giving him nickels to buy lemon ice with when he was a squirt. Mr. Cattanzara was a different type than those in the neighborhood. He asked different questions than the others when he met you, and he seemed to know what went on in all the news-

[2] *IRT:* New York City subway line

papers. He read them, as his fat sick wife watched from the window.

"What are you doing with yourself this summer, George?" Mr. Cattanzara asked. "I see you walkin' around at nights."

George felt embarrassed. "I like to walk."

"What are you doin' in the day now?"

"Nothing much just right now. I'm waiting for a job." Since it shamed him to admit he wasn't working, George said, "I'm staying home — but I'm reading a lot to pick up my education."

Mr. Cattanzara looked interested. He mopped his hot face with a red handkerchief.

"What are you readin'?"

George hesitated, then said, "I got a list of books in the library once, and now I'm gonna read them this summer." He felt strange and a little unhappy saying this, but he wanted Mr. Cattanzara to respect him.

"How many books are there on it?"

"I never counted them. Maybe around a hundred."

Mr. Cattanzara whistled through his teeth.

"I figure if I did that," George went on earnestly, "it would help me in my education. I don't mean the kind they give you in high school. I want to know different things than they learn there, if you know what I mean."

The change maker nodded. "Still and all, one hundred books is a pretty big load for one summer."

"It might take longer."

"After you're finished with some, maybe you and I can shoot the breeze about them?" said Mr. Cattanzara.

"When I'm finished," George answered.

Mr. Cattanzara went home and George continued on his walk. After that, though he had the urge to, George did nothing different from usual. He still took his walks at night, ending up in the little park. But one evening the shoemaker on the next block stopped George to say he was a good boy, and George figured that Mr. Cattanzara had told him all about the books he was reading. From the shoemaker it must have gone down the street, because George saw a couple of people smiling kindly at him, though nobody spoke to him personally.

He felt a little better around the neighborhood and liked it more, though not so much he would want to live in it forever. He had never exactly disliked the people in it, yet he had never liked them very much either. It was the fault of the neighborhood. To his surprise, George found out that his father and Sophie knew about his reading too. His father was too shy to say anything about it—he was never much of a talker in his whole life—but Sophie was softer to George, and she showed him in other ways she was proud of him.

As the summer went on George felt in a good mood about things. He cleaned the house every day, as a favor to Sophie, and he enjoyed the ball games more. Sophie gave him a buck a week allowance, and though it still wasn't enough and he had to use it carefully, it was a helluva lot better than just having two bits now and then. What he bought with the money —cigarettes mostly, an occasional beer or movie ticket—he got a big kick out of. Life wasn't so bad if you knew how to appreciate it. Occasionally he bought a paperback book from the newsstand, but he never got around to reading it, though he was glad to have a couple of books in his room. But he read thoroughly Sophie's magazines and newspapers. And at night was the most enjoyable time, because when he passed the storekeepers sitting outside their stores, he could tell they regarded him highly. He walked erect, and though he did not say much to them, or they to him, he could feel approval on all sides. A couple of nights he felt so good that he skipped the park at the end of the evening. He just wandered in the neighborhood, where people had known him from the time he was a kid playing punchball whenever there was a game of it going; he wandered there, then came home and got undressed for bed, feeling fine.

For a few weeks, he had talked only once with Mr. Cattanzara, and though the change maker had said nothing more about the books, asked no questions, his silence made George a little uneasy. For a while George didn't pass in front of Mr. Cattanzara's house anymore, until one night, forgetting himself, he approached it from a different direction than he usually did when he did. It was already past midnight. The street, except for one or two people, was deserted, and

George was surprised when he saw Mr. Cattanzara still reading his newspaper by the light of the street lamp overhead.
His impulse was to stop at the stoop and talk to him. He
wasn't sure what he wanted to say, though he felt the words
would come when he began to talk; but the more he thought
about it, the more the idea scared him, and he decided he'd
better not. He even considered beating it home by another
street, but he was too near Mr. Cattanzara, and the change
maker might see him as he ran, and get annoyed. So George
unobtrusively crossed the street, trying to make it seem as if
he had to look in a store window on the other side, which he
did, and then went on, uncomfortable at what he was doing.
He feared Mr. Cattanzara would glance up from his paper
and call him a dirty rat for walking on the other side of the
street, but all he did was sit there, sweating through his
undershirt, his bald head shining in the dim light as he read
his *Times*, and upstairs his fat wife leaned out of the window,
seeming to read the paper along with him. George thought she
would spy him and yell out to Mr. Cattanzara, but she never
moved her eyes off her husband.

George made up his mind to stay away from the change
maker until he had got some of his softback books read, but
when he started them and saw they were mostly story books,
he lost his interest and didn't bother to finish them. He lost
his interest in reading other things too. Sophie's magazines
and newspapers went unread. She saw them piling up on a
chair in his room and asked why he was no longer looking at
them, and George told her it was because of all the other
reading he had to do. Sophie said she had guessed that was
it. So for most of the day, George had the radio on, turning
to music when he was sick of the human voice. He kept the
house fairly neat, and Sophie said nothing on the days when
he neglected it. She was still kind and gave him his extra
buck, though things weren't so good for him as they had been
before.

But they were good enough, considering. Also his night
walks invariably picked him up, no matter how bad the day
was. Then one night George saw Mr. Cattanzara coming down
the street toward him. George was about to turn and run but

he recognized from Mr. Cattanzara's walk that he was drunk, and if so, probably he would not even bother to notice him. So George kept on walking straight ahead until he came abreast of Mr. Cattanzara and though he felt wound up enough to pop into the sky, he was not surprised when Mr. Cattanzara passed him without a word, walking slowly, his face and body stiff. George drew a breath in relief at his narrow escape, when he heard his name called, and there stood Mr. Cattanzara at his elbow, smelling like the inside of a beer barrel. His eyes were sad as he gazed at George, and George felt so intensely uncomfortable he was tempted to shove the drunk aside and continue on his walk.

But he couldn't act that way to him, and, besides, Mr. Cattanzara took a nickel out of his pants pocket and handed it to him.

"Go buy yourself a lemon ice, Georgie."

"It's not that time anymore, Mr. Cattanzara," George said, "I'm a big guy now."

"No, you ain't," said Mr. Cattanzara, to which George made no reply he could think of.

"How are all your books comin' along now?" Mr. Cattanzara asked. Though he tried to stand steady, he swayed a little.

"Fine, I guess," said George, feeling the red crawling up his face.

"You ain't sure?" The change maker smiled slyly, a way George had never seen him smile.

"Sure I'm sure. They're fine."

Though his head swayed in little arcs, Mr. Cattanzara's eyes were steady. He had small blue eyes which could hurt if you looked at them too long.

"George," he said, "name me one book on that list that you read this summer, and I will drink to your health."

"I don't want anybody drinking to me."

"Name me one so I can ask you a question on it. Who can tell, if it's a good book maybe I might wanna read it myself."

George knew he looked passable on the outside, but inside he was crumbling apart.

Unable to reply, he shut his eyes, but when—years later— he opened them, he saw that Mr. Cattanzara had, out of pity, gone away, but in his ears he still heard the words he had said when he left: "George, don't do what I did."

The next night he was afraid to leave his room, and though Sophie argued with him he wouldn't open the door.

"What are you doing in there?" she asked.

"Nothing."

"Aren't you reading?"

"No."

She was silent a minute, then asked, "Where do you keep the books you read? I never see any in your room outside of a few cheap trashy ones."

He wouldn't tell her.

"In that case you're not worth a buck of my hard-earned money. Why should I break my back for you? Go on out, you bum, and get a job."

He stayed in his room for almost a week, except to sneak into the kitchen when nobody was home. Sophie railed at him, then begged him to come out, and his old father wept, but George wouldn't budge, though the weather was terrible and his small room stifling. He found it very hard to breathe, each breath was like drawing a flame into his lungs.

One night, unable to stand the heat anymore, he burst into the street at one A.M., a shadow of himself. He hoped to sneak to the park without being seen, but there were people all over the block, wilted and listless, waiting for a breeze. George lowered his eyes and walked, in disgrace, away from them, but before long he discovered they were still friendly to him. He figured Mr. Cattanzara hadn't told on him. Maybe when he woke up out of his drunk the next morning, he had forgotten all about meeting George. George felt his confidence slowly come back to him.

That same night a man on a street corner asked him if it was true that he had finished reading so many books, and George admitted he had. The man said it was a wonderful thing for a boy his age to read so much.

"Yeah," George said, but he felt relieved. He hoped nobody would mention the books anymore, and when, after a couple of days, he accidentally met Mr. Cattanzara again, *he* didn't, though George had the idea he was the one who nad started the rumor that he had finished all the books.

One evening in the fall, George ran out of his house to the library, where he hadn't been in years. There were books all over the place, wherever he looked, and though he was struggling to control an inward trembling, he easily counted off a hundred, then sat down at a table to read.

FOR DISCUSSION

1. This story appears to be a simple, direct, and unadorned narration of events. Why is this style appropriate to the story and especially to its main character? What reasons can you give to prove that the story is, or is not, as simple as its style would seem to suggest?
2. Considering that the author provides little or no physical description of George, how does he make George "come to life" as a person? In examining the problem of characterization, consider from whose point of view the story is told.
3. Describe the kind of life George wants in contrast with what he has. What do the bursts of housekeeping activity reveal about him?
4. Why is he prompted to tell Mr. Cattanzara that he is "reading a lot"? What makes Mr. Cattanzara different from George's other acquaintances in the neighborhood?
5. What pleasures and problems does George's new status as a "reader" create for him? Why do "story books" fail to interest him?
6. What do you think Mr. Cattanzara means when he says, "George, don't do what I did"? What would lead you to think George does, or does not, understand what Mr. Cattanzara means?
7. Analyze the way in which George is finally influenced by Mr. Cattanzara's attitude toward him to go to the library and begin reading.

FOR COMPOSITION

1. Despite a remote connection or an indirect manner, someone may have influenced you in a certain way, just as Mr. Cattanzara influenced George. Describe your experience.
2. Do you think George's problem is common among young people today? Write a short composition presenting your views on this problem and include evidence to support your opinions.

John Updike

John Updike has a flair for writing about everyday occurrences with wit and technical skill. The following story shows a father telling his daughter a routine bedtime story. In the process, Updike provides subtle insight into their family life as well.

Should Wizard Hit Mommy?

In the evenings and for Saturday naps like today's, Jack told his daughter Jo a story out of his head. This custom, begun when she was two, was itself now nearly two years old, and his head felt empty. Each new story was a slight variation of a basic tale: a small creature, usually named Roger (Roger Fish, Roger Squirrel, Roger Chipmunk), had some problem and went with it to the wise old owl. The owl told him to go to the wizard, and the wizard performed a magic spell that solved the problem, demanding in payment a number of pennies greater than the number Roger Creature had but in the same breath directing the animal to a place where the extra pennies could be found. Then Roger was so happy he played many games with other creatures, and went home to his mother just in time to hear the train whistle that brought his daddy home from Boston. Jack described their supper, and the story was over. Working his way through this scheme was especially fatiguing on Saturday, because Jo never fell asleep in naps any more, and knowing this made the rite seem futile.

The little girl (not so little any more; the bumps her feet made under the covers were halfway down the bed, their big double bed that they let her be in for naps and when she was sick) had at last arranged herself, and from the way her fat face deep in the pillow shone in the sunlight sifting through the drawn shades, it did not seem fantastic that something magic would occur, and she would take her nap like an infant of two. Her brother, Bobby, was two, and already asleep with his bottle. Jack asked, "Who shall the story be about today?"

"Roger . . ." Jo squeezed her eyes shut and smiled to be thinking she was thinking. Her eyes opened, her mother's blue. "Skunk," she said firmly.

A new animal; they must talk about skunks at nursery school. Having a fresh hero momentarily stirred Jack to creative enthusiasm. "All right," he said. "Once upon a time, in the deep dark woods, there was a tiny little creature name of Roger Skunk. And he smelled very bad—"

"Yes," Jo said.

"He smelled so bad none of the other little woodland creatures would play with him." Jo looked at him solemnly; she hadn't foreseen this. "Whenever he would go out to play," Jack continued with zest, remembering certain humiliations of his own childhood, "all of the other tiny animals would cry, 'Uh-oh, here comes Roger Stinky Skunk,' and they would run away, and Roger Skunk would stand there all alone, and two little round tears would fall from his eyes." The corners of Jo's mouth drooped down and her lower lip bent forward as he traced with a forefinger along the side of her nose the course of one of Roger Skunk's tears.

"Won't he see the owl?" she asked in a high and faintly roughened voice.

Sitting on the bed beside her, Jack felt the covers tug as her legs switched tensely. He was pleased with this moment —he was telling her something true, something she must know—and had no wish to hurry on. But downstairs a chair scraped, and he realized he must get down to help Clare paint the living-room woodwork.

"Well, he walked along very sadly and came to a very big tree, and in the tiptop of the tree was an enormous wise old owl."

"Good."

"'Mr. Owl,' Roger Skunk said, 'all the other little animals run away from me because I smell so bad.' 'So you do,' the owl said. 'Very, very bad.' 'What can I do?' Roger Skunk said, and he cried very hard."

"The wizard, the wizard," Jo shouted, and sat right up, and a Little Golden Book spilled from the bed.

"Now, Jo. Daddy's telling the story. Do you want to tell Daddy the story?"

"No. You tell me."

"Then lie down and be sleepy."

Her head relapsed onto the pillow and she said, "Out of your head."

"Well." The owl thought and thought. At last he said, "Why don't you go see the wizard?"

"Daddy?"

"What?"

"Are magic spells *real?*" This was a new phase, just this last month, a reality phase. When he told her spiders eat bugs, she turned to her mother and asked, "Do they *really?*" and when Clare told her God was in the sky and all around them, she turned to her father and insisted, with a sly yet eager smile, "Is He *really?*"

"They're real in stories," Jack answered curtly. She had made him miss a beat in the narrative. "The owl said, 'Go through the dark woods, under the apple trees, into the swamp, over the crick—'"

"What's a crick?"

"A little river. 'Over the crick, and there will be the wizard's house.' And that's the way Roger Skunk went, and pretty soon he came to a little white house, and he rapped on the door." Jack rapped on the window sill, and under the covers Jo's tall figure clenched in an infantile thrill. "And then a tiny little old man came out, with a long white beard and a pointed blue hat, and said, 'Eh? Whatzis? Whatcher want? You smell awful.'" The wizard's voice was one of Jack's own favorite effects; he did it by scrunching up his face and somehow whining through his eyes, which felt for the interval rheumy. He felt being an old man suited him.

"'I know it,' Roger Skunk said, 'and all the little animals run away from me. The enormous wise owl said you could help me.'

"'Eh? Well, maybe. Come on in. Don't git too close.' Now, inside, Jo, there were all these magic things, all jumbled together in a big dusty heap, because the wizard did not have any cleaning lady."

"Why?"

"Why? Because he was a wizard, and a very old man."

"Will he die?"

"No. Wizards don't die. Well, he rummaged around and found an old stick called a magic wand and asked Roger Skunk what he wanted to smell like. Roger thought and thought and said, 'Roses.'"

"Yes. Good," Jo said smugly.

Jack fixed her with a trancelike gaze and chanted in the wizard's elderly irritable voice:

> "'Abracadabry, hocus-poo,
> Roger Skunk, how do you do,
> Roses, boses, pull an ear,
> Roger Skunk, you never fear:
> *Bingo!'*"

He paused as a rapt expression widened out from his daughter's nostrils, forcing her eyebrows up and her lower lip down in a wide noiseless grin, an expression in which Jack was startled to recognize his wife feigning pleasure at cocktail parties. "And all of a sudden," he whispered, "the whole inside of the wizard's house was full of the smell of— *roses!* 'Roses!' Roger Fish cried. And the wizard said, very cranky, 'That'll be seven pennies.'"

"Daddy."

"What?"

"Roger *Skunk*. You said Roger Fish."

"Yes. Skunk."

"You said Roger *Fish*. Wasn't that silly?"

"Very silly of your stupid old daddy. Where was I? Well, you know about the pennies."

"Say it."

"O.K. Roger Skunk said, 'But all I have is four pennies,' and he began to cry." Jo made the crying face again, but this time without a trace of sincerity. This annoyed Jack. Downstairs some more furniture rumbled. Clare shouldn't move heavy things; she was six months pregnant. It would be their third.

"So the wizard said, 'Oh, very well. Go to the end of the lane and turn around three times and look down the magic well and there you will find three pennies. Hurry up.' So Roger Skunk went to the end of the lane and turned around three times and there in the magic well were *three pennies!* So he took them back to the wizard and was very happy and ran out into the woods and all the other little animals gathered around him because he smelled so good. And they played tag, baseball, football, basketball, lacrosse, hockey, soccer, and pick-up-sticks."

"What's pick-up-sticks?"

"It's a game you play with sticks."

"Like the wizard's magic wand?"

"Kind of. And they played games and laughed all afternoon and then it began to get dark and they all ran home to their mommies."

Jo was starting to fuss with her hands and look out of the window, at the crack of day that showed under the shade. She thought the story was all over. Jack didn't like women when they took anything for granted; he liked them apprehensive, hanging on his words. "Now, Jo, are you listening?"

"Yes."

"Because this is very interesting. Roger Skunk's mommy said, 'What's that awful smell?'"

"Wha-at?"

"And Roger Skunk said, 'It's me, Mommy. I smell like roses.' And she said, 'Who made you smell like that?' And he said, 'The wizard,' and she said, 'Well, of all the nerve. You come with me and we're going right back to that very awful wizard.'"

Jo sat up, her hands dabbling in the air with genuine fright. "But Daddy, then he said about the other little animals run *away!*" Her hands skittered off into the underbrush.

"All right. He said, 'But Mommy, all the other little animals run away,' and she said, 'I don't care. You smelled the way a little skunk should have and I'm going to take you right back to that wizard,' and she took an umbrella and went back with Roger Skunk and hit that wizard right over the head."

"No," Jo said, and put her hand out to touch his lips, yet even in her agitation did not quite dare to stop the source of truth. Inspiration came to her. "Then the wizard hit *her* on the head and did not change that little skunk back."

"No," he said. "The wizard said 'O.K.' and Roger Skunk did not smell of roses any more. He smelled very bad again."

"But the other little amum — *oh!* — amum — "

"Joanne. It's Daddy's story. Shall Daddy not tell you any more stories?" Her broad face looked at him through sifted light, astounded. "This is what happened, then. Roger Skunk and his mommy went home and they heard Woo-oo, wooooo-oo and it was the choo-choo train bringing Daddy Skunk home from Boston. And they had lima beans, pork chops, celery, liver, mashed potatoes, and Pie-Oh-My for dessert. And when Roger Skunk was in bed Mommy Skunk came up and hugged him and said he smelled like her little baby skunk again and she loved him very much. And that's the end of the story."

"But Daddy."

"What?"

"Then did the other little ani-mals run away?"

"No, because eventually they got used to the way he was and did not mind it at all."

"What's evenshiladee?"

"In a little while."

"That was a stupid mommy."

"It was *not*," he said with rare emphasis, and believed, from her expression, that she realized he was defending his own mother to her, or something as odd. "Now I want you to put your big heavy head in the pillow and have a good long nap." He adjusted the shade so not even a crack of day showed, and tiptoed to the door, in the pretense that she was already asleep. But when he turned, she was crouching on top of the covers and staring at him. "Hey. Get under the covers and fall faaast asleep. Bobby's asleep."

She stood up and bounced gingerly on the springs. "Daddy."

"What?"

"Tomorrow, I want you to tell me the story that that wizard took that magic wand and hit that mommy"—her plump arms chopped fiercely—"right over the head."

"No. That's not the story. The point is that the little skunk loved his mommy more than he loved aaalll the other animals and she knew what was right."

"No. Tomorrow you say he hit that mommy. Do it." She kicked her legs up and sat down on the bed with a great heave and complaint of springs, as she had done hundreds of times before, except that this time she did not laugh. "Say it, Daddy."

"Well, we'll see. Now at least have a rest. Stay on the bed. You're a good girl."

He closed the door and went downstairs. Clare had spread the newspapers and opened the paint can and, wearing an old shirt of his on top of her maternity smock, was stroking the chair rail with a dipped brush. Above him footsteps vibrated and he called, *"Joanne.* Shall I come up there and spank you?" The footsteps hesitated.

"That was a long story," Clare said.

"The poor kid," he answered, and with utter weariness watched his wife labor. The woodwork, a cage of moldings and rails and baseboards all around them, was half old tan and half new ivory and he felt caught in an ugly middle position, and though he as well felt his wife's presence in the cage with him, he did not want to speak with her, work with her, touch her, anything.

FOR DISCUSSION

1. Telling his daughter a bedtime or naptime story seems essentially a fatiguing routine for Jack. Why?
2. How does his story differ this time from the ones he usually tells? What associations is he apparently making that he does not normally make?
3. Although little is said about Clare, you learn that Jo reminds Jack of his wife in several ways. What are they? Does Jack seem pleased with Jo's behavior? In particular, what occurrence causes him to call the little skunk "Roger Fish" by mistake?

4. Jack decides to change the customary ending to the story. Do you think he would have done so if he had been telling the story to his son? What, in his daughter's behavior, prompts him to make the change?
5. What is Jo's reaction to the change in the ending? Be sure to point out the difference between her attitude toward "the mommy" and Jack's.
6. Does this story present a picture of a happy, affectionate family? What do you think constitutes the "cage" in which Jack sees himself at the end of the story?
7. Comment upon Updike's use of dialogue in this story. Does it sound natural? Are Jo's comments what you would expect of a four-year-old? Choose specific passages to support your opinions.

FOR COMPOSITION

1. Using the information given to you in the story, along with your own imagination, write a short composition giving the thoughts you think might be running through Jack's mind during the last paragraph of the story.
2. Marriages are as different as the people involved. Write a composition comparing the marriage shown in this story with the one in Miss Porter's "Rope." Then contrast these two marriages with the one in Miss Cather's "Neighbor Rosicky."

About the Authors

Sherwood Anderson   (1876-1941) was born in Camden, Ohio, and left school to begin work at the age of fourteen. By 1906 he had become president of a mail-order firm for farm equipment, a position which led to his establishing his own mail-order business in Elyria, Ohio. During this time he began devoting more and more time to writing stories; and in 1912, he abandoned his business for a full-time writing career.

Of all Anderson's work, nothing attracted such serious attention as *Winesburg, Ohio* (1919), his collection of twenty-three stories of small-town life. Still recognized as his best, these stories are most typical of his honest search "for the truths that made people grotesque." Similar stories of frustration appeared later in *The Triumph of the Egg* (1921). Among his novels, *Poor White* (1920), with its Midwestern setting, has been generally regarded as his best. *The Portable Sherwood Anderson* (1949) has brought together in one volume his most memorable work.

George Washington Cable   (1844-1925) was born in New Orleans, and became the chief support of his mother and sisters at the age of fourteen, when his father died. He soon entered the Civil War as a Confederate soldier. During this time, he began the habit of rising very early in the morning in order to read books and teach himself French before the day began. After the war, he became proficient enough in the French language to delve into the old Creole archives of New Orleans. These records furnished the subject matter for his finest stories and novels.

He joined the New Orleans *Picayune* staff in 1869 as a reporter and was married the same year. His stories began appearing in *Scribner's Monthly* with some regularity, and six years later, in 1875, he published many of these stories in a collection titled *Old Creole Days*. Five years later he published his first novel, *The Grandissimes*. Though an ex-Confederate soldier and a former slaveholder, Cable became an earnest abolitionist. He moved to Northampton, Massachusetts, in 1885, where he published six more novels during his long life. All of his later writing reflected the spirit of social reform but failed to match the charm of his earlier stories of New Orleans.

Truman Capote (1924-   ) was born in New Orleans. His childhood was extremely insecure, and after his parents' divorce when he was four years old, he spent the next seven years living with various aunts. He was a poor student in school until one of his English teachers took an interest in him and began organizing special work for him. Soon he was writing stories and poems under her tutelage.

Capote's story "Miriam," which appeared in the magazine *Mademoiselle* when he was nineteen, brought him a contract with Random House; soon afterwards, he published his first novel, *Other Voices, Other Rooms* (1948), a delicate study of loneliness, which achieved considerable literary success. The novel was followed by a collection of his short stories, *A Tree of Night and Other Stories* (1949), and a collection of travel essays, *Local Color* (1950). His second novel, *The Grass Harp* (1951), was adapted for the stage the following year; and his third novel, *Breakfast at Tiffany's* (1958), became a movie. His most recent work has been a best seller, *In Cold Blood* (1966), which represents his effort to establish a serious new literary form, the nonfiction novel.

Willa Cather (1876-1947) was born in Virginia, but moved to Nebraska at the age of eight. After graduating from the University of Nebraska in 1895, she became a teacher of high school English. She left teaching for a position as managing editor of *McClure's Magazine*, where she remained from 1906 to 1912.

After 1912, Miss Cather devoted her full time to creative writing. In her first important novel, *O Pioneers!* (1913), she told the story of a Swedish family on the Nebraska prairie. In *My Antonia* (1918), a novel especially popular with high school students, she created an impressive and attractive character in the Bohemian girl, Antonia Shimerda, who survived hardships without losing her pioneer strength and humor. In 1922 her novel, *One of Ours*, won the Pulitzer Prize.

Later novels, *Death Comes for the Archbishop* (1927) and *Shadows on the Rock* (1931), are beautifully written stories of "spiritual pioneers" in New Mexico and old Quebec, respectively. Her short stories have appeared in three collections: *Youth and the Bright Medusa* (1920), *Obscure Destinies* (1932), and *The Old Beauty and Others* (1948), published posthumously.

James Fenimore Cooper   (1789-1851) spent his boyhood in Cooperstown, on Otsego Lake in upper New York State. He attended Yale for three years but failed to graduate because he was expelled for a student prank. During the next few years he was a midshipman in the United States Navy, an experience that provided him with much of the material for his novels of the sea. Cooper began to write when he became annoyed by an English novel he was reading aloud to his wife; he said that he could write a better one. His first novel was unsuccessful, but his second, *The Spy*, quickly established his reputation. He became so popular that his third novel, *The Pioneers*, sold 3,400 copies on its day of publication.

Of Cooper's many novels, the five written in his later years around the central figure of Natty Bumppo have remained the most popular. These five romances, known as "The Leatherstocking Tales," include *The Deerslayer* (1841), *The Last of the Mohicans* (1826), *The Pathfinder* (1840), *The Pioneers* (1823), and *The Prairie* (1827), in that order.

Cooper was already a leading literary figure in this country when he traveled abroad for seven years and met such prominent Europeans as Sir Walter Scott and the Marquis de Lafayette. His later life was marred by a series of legal battles, primarily libel suits that he brought against those who criticized his comments on American society.

Stephen Crane   (1871-1900) was the fourteenth child of a Newark, New Jersey, minister. While attending college, where he was an outstanding baseball player if a somewhat erratic student, he decided to become a writer. Orphaned by the death of his mother, he left college and lived a precarious existence in a New York slum.

Crane borrowed money to have his first novel, *Maggie: A Girl of the Streets* (1893), printed. It remained largely unsold and unnoticed, however, until it came to the attention of Hamlin Garland and William Dean Howells, who encouraged the young author.

His second novel, *The Red Badge of Courage* (1895), is his masterpiece. Its immediate success enabled Crane to obtain work as a journalist and war correspondent. Traveling widely, he wrote of his experiences and observations in sketches, stories, and poems. The total output of his short life included five finished novels, several collections of short stories, and two slender collections of free verse.

Crane was married and living in England when tuberculosis cut short his life at the age of twenty-eight.

Ralph Ellison (1914-   ) was born in Oklahoma City. He was given a scholarship from the state of Oklahoma to study music at Tuskegee Institute. In 1936 he came to New York City to study music composition and sculpture. At this time he became interested in writing and began contributing stories and articles to some of the better literary magazines. His first novel, and the only one to date, *Invisible Man* (1952), was hailed as one of the best novels of our time and won the National Book Award. More recently, he has published a volume of essays, *Shadow and Act* (1964). Ellison was a fellow at the American Academy in Rome from 1955 to 1957, and he has been a visiting professor at universities across the country.

William Faulkner (1897-1962) was born near Oxford, Mississippi, where he lived during most of his life. He never graduated from high school, but he did take a few courses at the University of Mississippi. He began his writing during that time.

Faulkner is regarded as one of the major American writers of the twentieth century. For his novels and short stories he was awarded the Nobel Prize for Literature in 1949 and the Howells Medal of the American Academy of Arts and Letters in 1950.

Although most of Faulkner's novels are more or less related, they were not written in chronological sequence. Therefore, the reader who is new to Faulkner's fictional Yoknapatawpha County, Mississippi, must find his own way. A possible introduction is *Go Down, Moses* (1942), which contains several loosely joined stories, including one of Faulkner's greatest, "The Bear." This story of a hunt is also the story of Ike McCaslin's initiation into manhood. Another means of entry into Faulkner's complicated fictional world might be through *Intruder in the Dust* (1948), one of his most popular novels, which recounts the suspenseful solution of a murder case in which the accused man, though innocent, is too proud to deny his guilt.

Among his most significant novels are *The Sound and the Fury* (1929), *As I Lay Dying* (1930), *Sanctuary* (1931), *Light in August* (1932), *Absalom, Absalom!* (1936), and *A Fable* (1954), which was awarded both the Pulitzer Prize and the National Book Award in 1954. He also wrote a number of brilliant short stories, which appear in his *Collected Stories*. This collection won the National Book Award in 1951.

F. Scott Fitzgerald (1896-1940) was born in St. Paul, Minnesota. He attended Princeton University, but left just before graduation in 1917 to serve as an officer in the Army. He began writing during this time. Three years later the publication of his successful first novel, *This Side of Paradise*, made him famous as "the spokesman of the Jazz Age."

Almost forgotten at the time of his death, Fitzgerald has become extremely popular since the 1920's have been "rediscovered." Among his novels, *The Great Gatsby* (1925) is most highly regarded. Jay Gatsby had the illusion that the fortune he had acquired in bootlegging and other criminal activities could buy him happiness. The story of Gatsby's tragedy has been told with such finesse that the reader feels sympathy for a character who might otherwise have been offensive. *Tender Is the Night* (1934) has its setting in Europe, and *The Last Tycoon* (1941), an unfinished novel, in Hollywood.

Fitzgerald's best short stories have been reprinted in *The Stories of F. Scott Fitzgerald* (1951), *Six Tales of the Jazz Age and Other Stories* (1960), and *Taps at Reveille* (1960).

Hamlin Garland (1860-1940), wishing to escape from pioneer farming in the Middle West, attended an Iowa academy, tried teaching school, and, at twenty-four, sold a land claim to finance a trip to Boston. There he began his career as a writer.

During a return visit to the farmland of South Dakota, Garland's eyes were opened to the loneliness and drudgery experienced by prairie farmers. He began writing about farm life in short stories which were later collected in *Main-Travelled Roads*. After producing many stories and novels, he turned to autobiography. *A Son of the Middle Border* and *A Daughter of the Middle Border* are his best-known works in this genre.

Bret Harte (1836-1902), more than any other writer, established the gold rush and the frontier days of the Far West as popular themes in American literature. Yet he lived in California for only seventeen years. During those years of his young manhood he led a varied life, working as a teacher, miner, printer, magazine editor, and writer.

"The Luck of Roaring Camp" and his other stories about California became enormously popular with Eastern readers, and in 1871 he returned to the East, where he had lived as a boy. In 1878 he received a consular appointment to Germany and lived abroad until his death.

Nathaniel Hawthorne (1804-1864) was born in Salem, Massachusetts, and like his friend Henry Wadsworth Longfellow, was educated at Bowdoin College. His first book, *Fanshawe*, printed anonymously and at his own expense, attracted so little attention that Hawthorne burned the unsold copies in anger and for twenty-two years refused to write another novel. His continuing lack of success in the years that followed brought him loneliness and despair. In 1837, however, he enjoyed a moderate success with his *Twice-Told Tales* and also met Sophia Peabody, whom he later married. He worked for two years at the Boston Customs House, leaving there in 1841 to take up residence at the Brook Farm community. While there, he met many of the prominent literary figures of his time. However, his dislike for manual labor and communal living caused him to leave.

While working periodically at odd jobs, Hawthorne was able to complete the novels and tales that won him a towering literary reputation. Three of his novels, *The Scarlet Letter* (1850), *The House of the Seven Gables* (1851), and *The Blithedale Romance* (1852), are considered American classics.

In 1853, his old school chum, President Franklin Pierce, appointed Hawthorne consul at Liverpool, England, where he served for four years, leaving there to tour Italy. Hawthorne died in Plymouth, New Hampshire, while vacationing with President Pierce.

Ernest Hemingway (1898-1961) was born and grew up in Oak Park, Illinois. He began writing in high school and after graduation became a reporter for the Kansas City *Star*. He left to serve in World War I as an ambulance driver on the Italian front. He was seriously wounded and was sent home, but he returned to Europe as foreign correspondent for the Toronto *Star*. It was during this period that he decided to become a creative writer. Serving as a war correspondent during the Spanish Civil War and World War II, he continued writing short stories and novels.

Two of his most famous works are about man's encounter with danger in warfare. His best novel, *A Farewell to Arms* (1929), is a love story as well as a picture of men at war during World War I in Italy. *For Whom the Bell Tolls* (1940) tells the story of Robert Jordan, an American volunteer in the Spanish Civil War.

The Old Man and the Sea, winner of the Pulitzer Prize in 1952 and the most popular of Hemingway's later novels, was awarded the Nobel Prize for Literature in 1954. The book celebrates the courage of a poor old fisherman in his struggle to bring in a great fish. In much of his early writing, particularly in his short stories, Hemingway had revealed a preoccupation with the duel between man and nature *The Short Stories of Ernest Hemingway* (1956) includes some of his best work in a form in which he excelled.

O. Henry (1862-1910), whose real name was William Sidney Porter, left his home state of North Carolina for Texas, where he engaged in a variety of occupations, including bookkeeping. He was convicted of embezzlement (a crime he always denied having committed) and practiced writing short stories while serving a prison sentence. When his sentence was shortened for good behavior, he moved to New York City to make a fresh start. He was hired by the New York *Sunday World* to write one story a week, and this period proved the most productive of his life. Perhaps his most characteristic work can be found in the collection entitled *The Four Million* (1909).

Washington Irving (1783-1859), the son of a wealthy merchant, was born and reared in New York City. Because of his poor health he did not follow his older brothers to college, but read for the law in several New York firms. Although he was admitted to the bar in 1806, Irving rarely practiced law, preferring to write and travel. He spent many years in Europe and, from 1842 to 1845, was the American minister to Spain. He spent his last thirteen years at Sunnyside, his country estate in Tarrytown, New York.

Irving is probably best remembered for his collection of essays and tales, *The Sketch Book* (1819-1820). This volume contains two of his best pieces, "Rip Van Winkle" and "The Legend of Sleepy Hollow."

Henry James (1843-1916) has been called by some critics "the master of the art of fiction." The son of a theologian and the younger brother of the eminent philosopher William James, Henry grew up in an atmosphere of culture and learning. Though he was born in New York City, a good part of his early education took place in France, Switzerland, and Germany. He attended Harvard Law School but could not muster enough interest in his studies to complete the course. William Dean Howells, the editor and writer, encouraged him to contribute reviews and stories to American periodicals.

James's love of travel and his fascination with European civilization caused him to spend much of his life on the Continent. During the course of his wide travels he came into contact with such towering literary figures as Turgenev, Maupassant, Zola, and Flaubert. Many of James's essays and works of fiction examine European culture and contrast it with that of America. He finally settled in London to devote himself entirely to writing.

James's works include travel essays, plays, short stories, and what have been described as some of the most important novels in the English language. Among his major novels are *The Portrait of a Lady* (1881), *The Wings of the Dove* (1902), *The Ambassadors* (1903), which he regarded as his best novel, and *The Golden Bowl* (1904). Two of his best short novels are *Daisy Miller* (1879) and *The Turn of the Screw* (1898).

Sarah Orne Jewett (1849-1909) was the daughter of a doctor in South Berwick, Maine, a village ten miles from the seacoast. Most of her education came from reading in the family library and from conversations with her father as he made his rounds of farms and fishing villages.

Although Ms. Jewett traveled in Europe and spent considerable time with literary friends in Boston, she always returned to South Berwick to write about its people and its surrounding countryside. Many of her sketches and stories were first published in *The Atlantic Monthly* and later collected in book form. *The Country of the Pointed Firs* is her best-known work.

Jack London (1876-1916) grew up in the San Francisco Bay area. Although he attended a few courses at the University of California, he was largely self-educated. During his adventurous life he roamed the United States as a hobo, joined the Klondike gold rush, and scouted thousands of miles over Alaska and Canada.

The Call of the Wild, London's first successful novel, gave him a reputation as a North Country writer. He also wrote numerous sea stories, among them the novel *The Sea Wolf.*

As the highest paid writer in the United States, London wrote many stories for the popular market that had little permanent value. However, his best works are still read throughout the world.

Bernard Malamud (1914-   ) was born in Brooklyn, New York. He graduated from the College of the City of New York in 1936 and did graduate work in English at Columbia University in 1942. He has drawn largely upon his childhood experiences in Brooklyn for his stories of Jewish life. His first book, *The Natural* (1952), has been described as a "surrealistic baseball novel." His second novel, *The Assistant* (1957), was followed by his best-known work, *The Magic*

Barrel (1958), a collection of thirteen short stories. His more recent works are *A New Life* (1961), *Idiots First* (1963), and the best-selling novel *The Fixer* (1966). One critic has compared Malamud to Dostoevsky, "tempered by Chagall's lyric nostalgia for a lost Jewish past." Malamud received the Rosenthal Award of the National Institute of Arts and Letters in 1958, and the National Book Award for Fiction in 1959.

Herman Melville   (1819-1891) was born and educated in New York and claimed that whaling ships were his "Yale and Harvard." After the failure of his father's importing business, Melville groped about on land and sea for a vocation. He worked as a clerk, a farmhand, and shipped before the mast, all before he was twenty. On his first return from sea, he taught school but soon left this position to join the crew of the *Acushnet* on a long whaling voyage to the South Seas. His experiences in that part of the world were as exciting and colorful as those he later wrote about. With a friend, he deserted ship in the Marquesas Islands, lived among cannibals, escaped on an Australian whaler, mutinied, was set ashore at Tahiti, and wondered about in the South Seas. In 1843, he enlisted on an American frigate at Honolulu and returned to the United States, where he was honorably discharged.

Shortly after his return home, Melville wrote *Typee* (1846) and *Omoo* (1847), two popular and successful novels about his adventures in the South Seas. His later book, *Moby Dick* (1851), failed to achieve the popular success of these two adventure novels, though it met with some critical success. Nevertheless, it was with *Moby Dick* that Melville reached his highest point of literary achievement and established himself as one of the major figures in American literature.

Frank Norris   (1870-1902), the son of well-to-do parents, grew up in Chicago and San Francisco. He spent a few years studying art in Paris and then attended the University of California and Harvard. While still a student, Norris wrote two novels that showed how strongly he was influenced by the French naturalist writer Emile Zola. The more important of these two novels, *McTeague*, was not published, however, until 1899, after he had become a war correspondent and had traveled to South Africa and Cuba. *McTeague*, with its Zolaesque realism, shocked readers, but established Norris as a novelist of note. In 1901 and 1903, he published his best known works, *The Octopus* and *The Pit*, the first two novels in his trilogy dealing with the story of American wheat. He was planning the third novel when he died suddenly at the age of thirty-two from appendicitis.

Edgar Allan Poe   (1809-1849) lived a life of hardship, frustration, and success marred by dissipation. He was born in Boston, the son of actor parents. When his mother died in 1811, he was taken into the home of Mr. and Mrs. John Allan who gave him an excellent education in both Richmond, Virginia, and Stoke Newington, England. His relationship with the Allans started to deteriorate when Poe left the University of Virginia because of gambling debts. Eventually he broke with the Allans, fled to Boston, and started to write poetry. Aided once again by John Allan, Poe was admitted to West Point but he provoked his own discharge by neglecting his duties. His story, "MS Found in a Bottle" won him a writing prize and also a position as editor of the *Southern Literary Messenger.* Elated by his success, he married his young cousin and brought her and her mother to Richmond. His articles were soon commanding attention, but within a year he left this position and went North. While working for various magazines in New York and Philadelphia, he was able to complete his *Tales of the Grotesque and Arabesque.* His detective story, "Murders in the Rue Morgue," and his volume of poems, *The Raven and Other Poems,* published in 1845, brought him wide critical acclaim. With the death of his wife, Poe collapsed. Gradually recovering his health, he wrote two of his best works, the poem, "Ulalume," and the essay, "The Poetic Principle." He was described by Lowell as "the most discriminating critic in America." He died in a Baltimore hospital in 1849 after being found unconscious in the gutter.

Katherine Anne Porter   (1894-   ) was born in Indian Creek, Texas and was educated in convent schools in Texas and Louisiana. She was a sensitive child and began experimenting with writing at a very early age.

Ms. Porter is best known for her short stories and short novels and one full-length novel, *Ship of Fools,* published in 1962 and subsequently made into a motion picture. She has published two collections of stories, *Flowering Judas and Other Stories* (1930) and *The Leaning Tower and Other Stories* (1944), and a collection of essays and criticism, *The Days Before* (1952). Her volume, *Pale Horse, Pale Rider* (1939), contains her well-known short novels, *Noon Wine, Old Mortality,* and the title story.

James Farl Powers   (1917-   ) was born in Jacksonville, Illinois. He attended parochial schools at Rockford and Quincy, Illinois, and the Quincy College Academy. He also studied at the evening school of Northwestern University in Chicago. His stories have appeared in many magazines, among which are *The New Yorker, Accent, Commonweal,* and *Opportunity: A Journal of Negro Life.* Two of his stories were selected for *O. Henry Memorial Award* volumes: "Lions, Harts, and Leaping Does" in 1944, and "The Trouble" in 1945. His first collection of stories, *Prince of Darkness and Other Stories* (1947), gained him a high place among short story writers. *Presence of Grace,* a second volume of stories, followed in 1962. In the same year, Powers published his first novel, *Morte d' Urban,* the story of a "live wire" Catholic priest, Father Urban. Chapters of this book had appeared previously as short stories in *The New Yorker* and in other magazines.

John Steinbeck (1902-1969) was born in Salinas County, California, and attended Stanford University. Later, he worked at various odd jobs while trying to publish some of his short stories. He finally settled in Monterey, California in 1930 to devote his full time to writing.

Although Steinbeck is invariably identified with his Pulitzer Prize winning novel, *The Grapes of Wrath,* he wrote several other works of particular appeal to high school students. One of his best is *The Red Pony* (1937), a short novel about a boy's experiences while growing up on a California ranch. Another successful book, *The Pearl* (1947), tells the tragic tale of what happened to a poor Mexican Indian, his family, and his community when he found a pearl of great value.

In *Tortilla Flat* (1935) and *Cannery Row* (1945), Steinbeck created a crew of raffish characters who enjoyed living more than they enjoyed working for a living. Between these humorous works he wrote *The Moon Is Down* (1942), a serious account of the Nazi invasion of Norway. Among his later novels were *The Wayward Bus* (1947), *East of Eden* (1952), and *The Winter of Our Discontent* (1961).

In awarding him the Nobel Prize for Literature in 1962, the Swedish Academy noted, in particular, that "his sympathies always go out to the oppressed, the misfits, and the distressed."

Mark Twain (1835-1910), who was born Samuel Langhorne Clemens in the frontier village of Florida, Missouri, grew up in the little town of Hannibal on the banks of the Mississippi River. When his father died, Twain, a boy of twelve, left school to work as a printer's apprentice on his brother's newspaper. In two of his most famous novels, *The Adventures of Tom Sawyer* and *The Adventures of Huckleberry Finn,* he described the life and people he remembered so well from his boyhood in Hannibal.

In 1853 Twain left Hannibal. He worked as a printer in different cities until, on a Mississippi River trip, he decided to become a steamboat pilot. The Civil War put an end to his piloting career, but his years on the river provided him with rich source material for the stories published first as *Old Times on the Mississippi,* and later as *Life on the Mississippi.*

After spending a few weeks as a Confederate soldier, Twain made the journey by stagecoach to Nevada. *Roughing It* describes the years he spent there as a journalist, prospector, and speculator. At the same time he was establishing his reputation as a humorous lecturer and writer.

By 1870 Twain had made several trips abroad, had married Olivia Langdon, and had settled in Hartford, Connecticut. *Innocents Abroad,* a humorous account of his travels, was tremendously successful, and the author was soon lionized wherever he went, in this country and abroad.

Financial troubles and family tragedies darkened Twain's later years. Though not legally responsible for debts he had incurred in a business failure, Twain determined to pay them off. He succeeded by means of an exhausting world lecture tour. The death of two daughters, his wife, and his brother made his private life bitter and lonely. In public life, however, he remained a popular idol until his death.

John Updike (1932-   ) was born in Chillington, Pennsylvania. He graduated from Harvard University in 1954 and received a fellowship to Oxford University, England the following year

Updike is one of the most prolific American writers today. His first collection of stories, *The Same Door,* and his first novel, *The Poorhouse Fair,* both appeared in the same year (1959), the latter winning the Rosenthal Award of the National Institute of Arts and Letters. A second novel was published the following year, *Rabbit, Run* (1960), and a second collection of stories, *Pigeon Feathers,* in 1962. His novel *The Centaur* (1963) won the National Book Award for Fiction, and was followed by a fourth novel, *Of the Farm* (1965).

Kurt Vonnegut, Jr. (1922-   ) was born in Indianapolis. After graduating from Cornell, he worked for a time for the General Electric Company at their headquarters in Schenectady, New York, and this experience as a very small cog in a giant technological organization has been projected repeatedly in his fiction (where Schenectady is given the name of "Illium")

Beginning with his first book *Player Piano* in 1952, Vonnegut has made a strong appeal to many young readers. In fact, his popularity began with an "underground" vogue on college campuses. His books are now widely read in college classes, and he is in much demand as a campus speaker.

Vonnegut has equal standing as a novelist and short story writer, and has also written for the stage. His novels include *The Sirens of Titan, Cats' Cradle, God Bless You, Mr. Rosewater, Slaughter-house Five*, and most recently, *Breakfast of Champions*. *Slaughter-house Five*, published in 1970 and made into a successful movie, is based in part on the author's experience as a prisoner of war in World War II.

Eudora Welty (1909-   ) was born in Jackson, Mississippi. She attended both Mississippi State College and Columbia University, and graduated from the University of Wisconsin in 1929. She worked as an advertising copywriter in New York and as a writer of government publicity in Jackson.

Ms. Welty received the O. Henry Memorial Award in 1941 and 1942 for two short stories, and in 1955 she was presented the Howells Medal of the American Academy of Arts and Letters.

Ms. Welty's stories appear in such magazines as *The Atlantic Monthly, Harper's,* and *The New Yorker*. Many of them are available also in book form under the following titles: *A Curtain of Green* (1941), *The Wide Net and Other Stories* (1943), and *The Bride of Inisfallen* (1955). Katherine Anne Porter has written of Ms. Welty's work: "These stories offer an extraordinary range of mood, pace, tone, and variety of material."

Like her stories, Ms. Welty's novels—*The Robber Bridegroom* (1942), *Delta Wedding* (1946), and *The Ponder Heart* (1954)—have a Mississippi setting and recount unusual incidents involving eccentric people.

Glossary of Literary Terms

action: what takes place during the course of a story.

> *action, rising:* the series of incidents that grow out of the problem to be solved and that build up to the climax.
>
> *action, falling:* See *denouement.*

alliteration: the repetition of a consonant sound, usually at the beginning of two or more words in a sentence; for example, "The gray goose gabbled in the farmyard."

allusion: a reference to some person, place, or event with literary, historical, or geographical significance.

analogy: a comparison of ideas or objects which are essentially different but which are alike in one significant way; for example, the analogy between the grasshopper and the man who lives only for the moment.

antagonist: the force (usually a person) that opposes the main character (the protagonist) in his attempt to solve a problem and thus resolve the conflict in which he is involved.

anticlimax: an outcome of a situation or series of events that, by contrast with what was anticipated, is ludicrous or disappointing. The anticlimax can often create a humorous effect.

atmosphere: the general over-all feeling of a literary work conveyed in large part by the setting and the mood.

character: a person in a work of fiction; sometimes an animal or object.

> *character, consistent:* a character whose actions, decisions, attitudes, etc., are in keeping with what the author has led the reader to expect.
>
> *character, dynamic:* a character who changes or develops during the course of a work of fiction.
>
> *character, static:* a character who does not change or develop during the course of a work of fiction.

characterization: the portrayal in a literary work of an imaginary person by what he says or does, by what others say about him or how they react to him, and by what the author reveals directly or through a narrator.

cliché: an expression used so often that it has lost its freshness and effectiveness.

climax: the point of highest interest or dramatic intensity. Usually it marks a turning point in the action, since the reader is no longer in doubt about the outcome.

coincidence: the chance occurrence of two events which take place at the same time.

conflict: the struggle between two opposing forces, ideas, or beliefs, which form the basis of the plot. The conflict is resolved when one force — usually the protagonist — succeeds or fails in overcoming the opposing force or gives up trying.

> *conflict, inner:* a struggle between conflicting forces within the heart and mind of the protagonist.

> *conflict, external:* a struggle between the protagonist and some outside force.

connotation: the implied or suggested meaning of a word or expression.

contrast: the bringing together of ideas, images, or characters to show how they differ.

denotation: the precise, literal meaning of a word or expression.

denouement: the unraveling of the plot, following the climax, in which the writer explains how and why everything turned out as it did.

dialect: the speech that is characteristic of a particular region or of a class or group of people.

dialogue: the printed conversation between two or more characters in a work of fiction.

didactic: morally instructive or intended to be so.

episode: a related group of incidents, or a major event, that comprises all or part of the main plot or, in a long work, is related to the main plot.

exposition: the background information that reveals what occurred prior to the time covered in a story; who the main characters are (sometimes before they appear); and what situation has arisen that will lead to a problem requiring a solution.

fable: a short tale that teaches a moral, often with animals or inanimate objects as characters.

fantasy: a tale involving such unreal characters and improbable events that the reader is not expected to believe it. Some fantasies are intended merely to entertain; others have a serious purpose as well; namely, to poke fun at outmoded customs or at the stupidity of certain people or groups of people.

figure of speech: the general term for a number of literary and poetic devices in which words or groups of words are used to create images in the mind or to make a comparison. See *hyperbole, metaphor, personification, simile.*

flashback: a device by which a writer interrupts the main action of a story to recreate a situation or incident of an earlier time as though it were occurring in the present.

foreshadowing: the dropping of important hints by the author to prepare the reader for what is to come and to help him to anticipate the outcome.

Gothic style: a late eighteenth and nineteenth century style of fiction characterized by the use of medieval settings, a murky atmosphere of horror and gloom, and macabre, mysterious, and violent incidents. Refers, also, to any style characterized by grotesque, macabre, or fantastic incidents or by an atmosphere of irrational violence, desolation, and decay.

historic present: the use of the present tense to relate incidents that occurred in the past.

hyperbole: a figure of speech employing obvious exaggeration; for example, "His mind was a million miles away."

idiom: the language or manner of speaking that is typical of a particular region or group of people.

incident: one of the events (usually minor) that make up the total action or plot of a work of fiction.

initial incident: the event in a story that introduces the conflict.

irony: a mode of expression in which the author says one thing and means the opposite. The term also applies to a situation, or the outcome of an event (or series of events), that is contrary to what is naturally hoped for or expected.

legend: a story that has come down from the past and that may have some basis in history

local color: literature in which the author stresses geographical setting, as well as the speech, dress, and mannerisms peculiar to a certain region.

locale: the particular place in which the action in a work of fiction occurs.

metaphor: a figure of speech in which two things are compared without the use of *like* or *as*; for example, "The fog is a gray veil over the city."

monologue: a passage in which a single character speaks alone and, usually, at some length.

mood: the frame of mind or state of feeling created by a piece of writing; for example, a skeptical mood or a sentimental mood.

moral: the lesson taught by a literary work.

motivation: the cause or reason that compels a character to act as he does.

myth: an imaginary tale, usually concerned with superhuman beings or gods, that attempts to account for some natural phenomenon.

narration: an account or story of an event, or series of events, true or imaginary. Also the act of narrating such an account or story.

naturalism: a literary theory which emphasizes the role of heredity and environment in human life and character development. Naturalistic writers thus tend to describe, in minute detail, the surroundings in which their characters live or have been reared. They observe man with scientific objectivity, avoiding any tendency to idealize or to omit details considered "repulsive."

paradox: a statement which, on the surface, seems contradictory, yet if interpreted figuratively, it involves an element of truth:

"The child is father of the man."
—William Wordsworth

parody: a humorous imitation or burlesque of a serious piece of literature or writing.

pathetic fallacy: the ascribing of human traits to nature or to inanimate objects; for example, "a stubborn door."

pathos: that quality that evokes in the reader a feeling of pity and compassion.

personal reminiscence: a recollection of a past experience or impression narrated by the author, usually in an informal style.

personification: a figure of speech in which human form or characteristics are given to animals, objects, or ideas; for example, "Liberty was a prisoner of Tyranny."

plot: the series of events or episodes that make up the action of a work of fiction.

point of view: the method used by the short-story writer or novelist to tell his story; the position, psychological as well as physical, from which he presents what happens and the characters involved in it.

> *point of view, first person:* the narration of a story by the main character or, possibly, a minor character. As the narrator, he uses the pronoun *I* in referring to himself.

> *point of view, omniscient:* the narration of a story as though by an all-knowing observer, who can be in several places at the same time and can see into the hearts and minds of all the characters.

> *point of view, omniscient third person:* the narration of a story by an all-knowing observer but limited primarily to what one of the characters (usually the main character) could know, see, hear, or experience.

protagonist: usually the main character, who faces a problem and, in his attempt to solve it, becomes involved in a conflict with an opposing force.

realistic: the faithful portrayal of people, scenes, and events as they are, not as the writer or artist would like them to be.

romantic: the portrayal of people, scenes, and events as they impress the writer or artist or as he imagines them to be. A romantic work has one or more of the following characteristics: an emphasis on feeling and imagination; a love of nature; a belief in the individual and the common man; an interest in the past, the unusual, the unfamiliar, the bizarre or picturesque; a revolt against authority or tradition.

satire: any piece of writing which criticizes manners, individuals, or political and social institutions by holding them up to ridicule.

setting: the time and place in which the events in a narrative take place.

simile: a figure of speech in which a comparison is made between two objects essentially unlike but resembling each other in one or more respects. The comparison is indicated by *like* or *as*; for example, "He fought like a lion."

stereotype: a character who conforms to certain widely accepted ideas of how such a person should look, think, or act; for example, the stereotypical "good student" wears glasses and does badly in athletics.

style: the distinctive manner in which the writer uses language: his choice and arrangement of words.

suspense: a feeling of excitement, curiosity, or expectation about the outcome of a narrative.

symbol: an object that stands for an idea, belief, superstition, social or political institution, etc. A pair of scales, for example, is often a symbol for justice.

tale: a simple story that recounts a real or imaginary event.

theme: the idea, general truth, or commentary on life or people brought out through a literary work.

tone: the feeling conveyed by the author's attitude toward his subject and the particular way in which he writes about it.

tragedy: a story in which the protagonist undergoes a morally significant struggle and is defeated, sometimes because of a flaw in his own character, more often because he is unable to overcome the force or forces opposing him.

unity: an arrangement of parts or material that will produce a single harmonious design or effect in a literary work.